Lies and Deception

BOOK ONE OF THE ROSE IN THE FIRE

MEGHAN E MCCOMB

Lies and Deception

Book One of *The Rose In The Fire*

ISBN 979-8-9907475-0-0

ASIN B0DJPWDBRL (Paperback)

ASIN B0DJKCZQC8 (Ebook)

Updated 2025 cover art and design by 100Covers

To Richard
who has affirmed to me over and over again
that I am not unloved or unwanted.
This book would not exist if you hadn't believed in me.
I love you with all my life and breath.

And to every deeply hurting person
who reads *The Rose In The Fire:*
May you be set free from Lies and Deception
and fully know The Hope That Never Dies
as you embrace with all your heart
The One Who Will Love You Forever.

Preface

AND CONTENT RATING

A naive young girl opens the door of her heart to sinister beings and invites them into her life, only to find herself helpless to escape from their deceitful tyranny without someone to save her.

My book series *The Rose in the Fire* uses a fantasy/fairy tale setting to paint an allegorical picture of spiritual warfare in the life of one young girl. It is complete fiction. However, the brief synopsis above could also describe what actually happened to me when I became involved in witchcraft and the occult as a young teen – which was the inspiration that led me to write this story.

Lies and Deception is the darkest book in the series and contains some intense themes and scenes that may be triggering. As a service to my readers, I offer here a content rating similar to what you would find for a movie. In particular, sections of Chapters 5, 8, 27-29, and 38-39 may be most concerning, so please read those with care.

Explicit Sexual Content: 0/5

Language/Profanity: 0/5

Violence: 3/5 (such as nightmares, bullying, assault, and attempted murder)

Intense themes: 3/5 (such as rage, horror, child abuse, alcoholism, depression, and thoughts of wanting to die)

Equivalent Movie Rating/Appropriate Age Suggestion: PG-13, perhaps later high school age and up.

You can learn more about my experiences and the interesting story of how this book series came to be by visiting my blog at www.theroseinthefire.com.

Contents

Chapter One

The Funeral

So here I am in mourning clothes, Aidan mused. *Finally alone.*

She stood before the large oval mirror admiring her outfit that had been ready for this day for months: long black wool skirt, starched black muslin blouse with no ruffles, and black shoes and stockings. Taking a hairbrush from the bureau, she began untangling the long soft waves of her auburn hair. She twisted it into a thick smooth rope and coiled it up at the back of her neck, securing it in place with hairpins. It was not a style she often wore and she worked at it for a long time. Once she had it pinned up, she fastened a black lace scarf to the bun with more hairpins and draped it forward over her face.

When she finally stood back to look at herself in the mirror again, the matronly woman in black who gazed at her from behind the veil was a total stranger. Was it the mourning clothes or her hairstyle, she wondered, that made her seem so much older than her seventeen years?

Arranging the scarf so that it hung behind her head like a wedding veil, Aidan bent closer to the mirror to study her face, which was plain and thin. Her fair skin was accented by the faintest sprinkling of freckles across her delicate nose and high cheekbones. She never would have thought of herself as a beautiful girl, but she did feel she had some lovely features, especially her deep-set eyes. Large and round, they were framed by thick black lashes that seemed to accentuate their dark blue-green color, and when she smiled, which was almost never, they sparkled like sunlight dappled on a rippling mountain stream.

She stepped back again and twirled around to admire the way the skirt swept against her legs and slender body. Satisfied, she decided that black was a good color for her complexion. Flashing a smile at herself in the mirror, she turned and hurried out of the room, rushing through the hallway and down the front staircase.

At the bottom was the large main room of the cottage Aidan had lived in all her life. It was a comfortable room with a hardwood floor, whitewashed walls and heavy dark beams crossing the ceiling. The wooden furniture was plain and worn, but the room was bright with touches of color – patchwork cushions, framed embroidered pictures, and oval rugs made from braided strips of cloth.

One wall was taken up by a huge grey stone fireplace next to the archway by the stairs that led into the dining room. Opposite the fireplace, a row of leaded glass windows filled most of the front wall of the room. Under them was a long built-in window seat piled with colorful handmade pillows. This was Aidan's favorite place to sit, for the windows offered a complete view of the front yard where she had carefully nurtured her beloved rose garden for as long as she could remember. In the summer when the bushes were in full bloom, she liked to open the windows wide to bring their sweet scent into the house.

But it was only the middle of April now and summer seemed a long way off.

Stepping around Aunt Mara's old rocking chair and sewing cabinet, which had been prominently placed by the hearth for as long as she could remember, Aidan bent down to stack wood pieces in the fireplace. Before long a pleasant blaze was crackling noisily. As she stood back to watch the fire grow larger, a shudder coursed down her spine and she shivered from a sudden chill that had nothing to do with the cold air in the room.

Aidan quickly turned away from the fireplace and surveyed the room to make sure it was tidy. She had no reason to worry about this, since she always kept the house spotlessly clean, but she knew people would start arriving at any moment.

Her gaze lingered briefly on the far end of the room where several embroidered linen samplers were scattered in proud display across the whitewashed wall. Beneath them furniture had been moved aside the night before when it seemed the best place for the undertaker to lay out the coffin. She glanced quickly at the plain pine box, shivered again, then turned back to poke at the fire one last time.

The clock on the mantel above her began chiming nine o'clock. Aidan rushed through the archway into the dining room and headed for the door to the kitchen, hoping to have time for a bite of breakfast. But just then there was a knock at the front door. She turned around reluctantly and went back to answer it.

Her first caller was the undertaker's wife, who was dressed in black taffeta and carried a basket over one arm.

"Hello, Mrs. Spencer," Aidan said. "Please come in."

Mrs. Spencer spoke in a mournful contralto as she swept into the house. "Aidan, my dear, I came as soon as I could because I knew you would be in need of help today. I've brought fresh biscuits for you."

"Thank you," Aidan said gratefully, taking the basket from her guest's hands. "Let me put this in the kitchen. Please make yourself comfortable."

When Aidan returned to the front room Mrs. Spencer was standing in front of the coffin, her bony hand pressing a lacy black handkerchief to her thin lips as she gazed at Aunt Mara's body lying so silent and still.

"After all this time," she whispered, her eyes never leaving the coffin. "Yet I still can't believe she's really gone. She was such a good person – my dear friend."

Aidan said nothing.

"My husband told me a bit of what happened," Mrs. Spencer said. "I do hope she passed peacefully?"

Aidan took a deep breath.

"Yes – she began to slip away late yesterday evening. I went at once for Dr. Caine, but there was nothing he could do. Her time had finally come."

She took another deep breath, feeling as though she were suffocating. The air in the room suddenly seemed musty, heavy with the odors of dried lavender and sweet woodruff that she had long ago sewn into tiny lace sachets which were now arranged around Aunt Mara's body. Tucking these sachets into a coffin to mask the odor of death was an old custom in the little mountain town of Hidden where she lived.

Mrs. Spencer seemed to mistake Aidan's sudden lack of air for tears, for she reached over and gently grasped her upper arm. Embarrassed at this gesture, Aidan quickly managed to catch her breath.

"It was about nine o'clock when she breathed her last. Dr. Caine and I were both with her at the end. He was kind enough to – to go and fetch your husband."

"Dreadful," Mrs. Spencer said mournfully, shuddering as she patted Aidan's arm. "How very dreadful all this has been for you, Aidan. Nursing her through all these months and then watching her die. I'm so sorry for you."

"Thank you, Mrs. Spencer," Aidan replied politely. "That's so kind of you."

Mrs. Spencer twisted her black lace handkerchief in her hands as she turned back to the coffin. Tears began to fill her eyes.

"Poor dear, she was so terribly ill at the last. She suffered more than any good woman should have to. No, life was not kind to Mara."

Aidan was quiet.

The undertaker's wife dabbed at her red-rimmed eyes with her handkerchief. There was something very well-rehearsed about her patronizing phrases and gestures.

"I remember when Samuel passed away – and then when her son died. Such a dreadful thing. It was just too much for her to bear. I shall never forget those funerals. All of Hidden grieved with her."

Abruptly she reached out again and clutched Aidan's hand, squeezing it firmly as she smiled tearfully.

"But then her whole life was changed when you came to her that night. Oh, my dear Aidan, I do hope you know that you brought so much joy into Mara's lonely life."

Embarrassed and uncomfortable, Aidan gently eased her fingers out of Mrs. Spencer's grasp. She turned and gazed into the coffin at the face of the woman who had raised her, sighing deeply – and feeling nothing.

Mara Maxwell Teague had been a handsome woman with a square jaw and strong features that seemed in death to be carved in stone. Her salt-and-pepper hair was pinned into two braids that crisscrossed over the top of her head in the style she had worn every day for as long as Aidan could remember. Her dark brown eyes were closed now, but Aidan would never forget the bright snapping fires that had flared up in them whenever she went into one of her drunken rages. Even now in the stillness standing before the coffin, she could hear the old woman's shrill voice that would leap without warning from a sharp rebuke to a strident screaming that would pierce the air like a dagger opening flesh.

Yes, Aidan supposed Aunt Mara's difficult life had been filled with sorrows, but she could feel neither sympathy for her life nor grief for her death. The only thing she could honestly say she felt now was – relief.

It was finally over. She was free.

But of course, she couldn't tell Mrs. Spencer or anyone else about that.

Just then there was another knock at the door. Mrs. Spencer patted Aidan's arm and hurried to answer it for her.

The next few hours were a dark blur as people dressed in black poured in to honor the departed. The women carried dishes of fragrant hot food and many brought brightly colored bouquets of spring flowers freshly picked from their gardens. Every vase and jar that Aidan could find was quickly put to use, but still the people and the flowers kept coming. Bouquets were heaped upon the coffin and gently arranged around Aunt Mara's body as the perfume of tulips, daffodils and hyacinths became almost overwhelming.

Somehow Aidan managed to endure the morning's flood of people. Mrs. Spencer stayed by her side for a long time, repeating the same well-rehearsed litany of comfort in her permanently mournful voice to everyone who came over to offer sympathy. When the undertaker's wife finally excused herself to check on the food preparation, Aidan was greatly relieved.

Dr. Caine came over then and sat with her for awhile. Although he looked haggard from lack of sleep the night before, he kindly took over answering people's questions, and for that she was most grateful.

Asa Maxwell, Aunt Mara's pompous older brother, found his way through the crush of people and briefly greeted her. As the owner of the only bank in Hidden, Uncle Asa had been the one who had taken care of all of Aunt Mara's financial matters. Aidan knew him fairly well, for he had been a regular visitor to the cottage. She barely had a chance to return his greeting before he was pulled away by others who wanted to offer their condolences to him.

Someone graciously filled a plate of food and brought it to her. She was very hungry but barely tasted the biscuits, sliced meat and baked beans as she listened to her neighbors relate their memories of Aunt Mara. From the way they praised the poor widow lying in the coffin, Aidan wondered if any of them had really known Aunt Mara at all.

She was relieved when Mr. Spencer approached her and told her the hearse was ready to take the coffin to the graveyard.

As the mourners walked quietly behind the horse-drawn wagon, the bell in the Town Hall clock tower tolled for Aunt Mara's death. The sound echoed across the valley as the funeral procession made its way through Hidden.

Aidan's black lace veil shielded her eyes from the cool April sunlight. Joyful spring brilliance mocked the solemnity of the occasion but only added to her growing sense of celebration. At last the funeral would soon be over and this tedious day, these long weeks and years, this unhappy first chapter of her life, would finally come to an end.

All along the way to the graveyard she listened to the townspeople whispering behind her, thinking she wasn't able to hear them.

"She certainly seems brave. Look, she isn't even crying."

"You know, I don't believe I've seen her shed one tear all day. She must be in shock over Mara's passing."

"Nonsense, she knew it would happen soon. Mara's health was failing all winter."

"I wonder what she'll do now. She's an odd one, for sure."

Trying to ignore them, Aidan squared her shoulders, held her back very straight, and walked on in silence.

The procession left the south end of town and proceeded along the winding dirt road that led toward the surrounding mountains. Not far along the road, it turned off onto a dirt path at the bottom of a grassy hill. Behind Aidan a sea of rustling black cloth billowed in the wind. In front of her the hearse creaked and the hitches rattled as Mr. Spencer's tired old black mare strained at the bit.

After what seemed like an eternal climb, the group crested the hill. Strong mountain wind pulled at veils, hats, and skirts as the weary mourners clustered together in the graveyard. The hearse stopped and Mr. Spencer beckoned to the pallbearers, who hoisted the coffin onto their shoulders and set it down in front of the freshly dug grave. Mara Teague would be laid to rest beside the husband of her youth and their infant son.

Uncle Asa stepped up next to the coffin to give the eulogy. He cleared his throat and spoke loudly in his reedy tenor voice.

"As most of you know, my sister Mara did not have an easy life. When she and I were young, our father died, leaving our mother to raise us by herself with no help and very few financial resources. Mara married Samuel Teague, but their happy life together ended in tragedy just seven years later when Samuel died suddenly following an illness. My sister had been told she could not have children, but soon after Samuel's death she discovered to her surprise that she was expecting a baby. Her joy was again turned to grief months later when her son died just days after his birth."

He cleared his throat again, then went on.

"But my sister was a remarkable woman. She was strong and capable and managed to bear her sorrows gracefully. Mara refused to let tragedy keep her from serving others. She took up her sewing, something she had always enjoyed, and made a nice little business for herself. Her beautiful quilts and embroidery will always be well remembered here in Hidden."

At his words the ladies in the crowd nodded and murmured approval. Uncle Asa again cleared his throat, impatiently waiting until he had everyone's attention once more.

"About fifteen years after the tragic birth and death of Mara's baby, as all of us will remember, someone left a large basket on her doorstep one night. In the basket was a little baby girl, perhaps three months old, with a note pinned to her blanket that said, 'Her name is Aidan. Please take good care of her.' We have never found out where the basket came from or why it was left at my sister's door, and I expect we never will. But Mara welcomed Aidan into her home and cared for her as though she were her own flesh and blood. It was a sacrifice for her to do this, but as we all know, she was a very kind and caring woman, and having a little girl helped to ease the pain of losing her husband and her own baby years before."

Uncle Asa turned his face and looked directly at Aidan. From behind her veil she returned his gaze. His eyes were the same dark color as Aunt Mara's and another shudder coursed down her spine. As he spoke to her she looked down at the dry yellow grass blowing across the toes of her black shoes in the mountain wind.

"Aidan, I hope it comforts you to know that you were Mara's greatest joy. And we are most grateful to you for caring for her so unselfishly through her illness in these last months of her life."

The others at the graveside nodded and murmured among themselves. Someone reached out to pat Aidan's shoulder. Her face flamed with embarrassment behind her veil as she stared down at her feet.

Uncle Asa turned back to the crowd and finished his eulogy.

"While we are sorry to see our friend and sister go now to the grave, we must be grateful that she is no longer suffering, not from pain or sorrow, not from sickness or infirmity. Let us remember Mara Maxwell Teague, then, with joy." He beckoned to the undertaker. "Mr. Spencer?"

The crowd responded with a short round of light applause. Mr. Spencer walked over to Aidan and said quietly, "It's customary for the family to be first to pay their respects."

Aidan was surprised. Her first reaction was to refuse, but she was suddenly afraid of what the others would think.

"Yes," she whispered back, reluctantly nodding.

Mr. Spencer led her to the coffin and opened the lid. The crowd stood back and watched as Aidan looked at Aunt Mara for the last time.

She lay there in her coffin, so small and still, the wind blowing stray wisps of pepper-and-salt hair across her pale lined face, looking as wilted as the limp purple tulips and pink hyacinths that surrounded her. Her thick fingers, in life so creative and always busy with needle and thread, were in death entwined around fading yellow daffodils. Her voice, often so shrill and raging, was blissfully silent, never to be heard again, lost now to the moaning of the mountain wind that would sweep forever across her grave.

All at once Aidan's heart began to race with the eerie feeling that all of this was too wonderful to be true. She had waited long months for this day, but now she found herself fully expecting that at any moment Aunt Mara would open her eyes, jump up, and lash out at her, shouting that she was a wicked and evil child who needed to be taught a lesson.

This horrifying premonition caused her to tremble violently, for she suddenly knew with absolute certainty that even if Aunt Mara did open her eyes, she would not hesitate to shut the coffin on the old woman and force her into the grave whether she were dead or alive.

Shaken by the power of this revelation, Aidan began tracing the lines of Aunt Mara's face with her eyes, as though by doing so she could etch the reality of this long-awaited moment upon her memory forever. Suddenly her heart was overcome by an explosive rush of such intense rage that she had to tear her gaze from the dead woman's face and raise her eyes to the glorious blue sky. At that moment a gust of wind whipped her veil across her face, momentarily sweeping her breath away. Lightheaded, she breathed deeply until the wind subsided.

As she lowered her eyes, looking again at the woman who had raised her, a cold smile spread across her lips beneath her veil. All her panic and rage were now gone.

In a voice filled with triumph, she whispered, "Now it is you who will be shut up inside a tiny little space. It will be black inside there forever. You will have no air to breathe and you won't be able to get out ever again, no matter how cold or hungry or thirsty or frightened you may be. Now *you* will know how it feels to be locked away in terrible darkness. You will be imprisoned there forever. And *I* – I am free of you at last!"

As Aidan gazed one last time at the crisscrossed braids and square jaw of the woman who had abused her, her contempt melted into such exultation that it was all she could do to keep from shouting out loud. Grateful for the black lace veil that hid her joy, she turned and nodded to Mr. Spencer as she stepped away from the grave.

Uncle Asa was next, followed by the other mourners who lined up and began filing silently along before the coffin to pay their brief last respects.

At long last, the funeral was over.

Mr. Spencer closed the lid of the coffin and his assistants began nailing it shut. As the first hammer stroke fell, the sound seemed to reverberate across the valley and echo back from the mountains.

The coffin was then carefully lowered into the grave. Men took up shovels and dug into the soft damp earth. For a long moment Aidan watched them filling in the grave. She could hear clods of soil thudding against wood.

Uncle Asa walked briskly up to her. To her surprise, instead of expressing any sorrow at the death of his only sister, he briefly shook Aidan's hand and spoke in a most businesslike way.

"Aidan, I have a meeting with Mara's lawyer later this afternoon. We shall review her will and go over all her debts and assets. Come to the bank at ten o'clock tomorrow morning and I will discuss our findings with you."

Shocked at his brusque manner, she stammered, "Yes, Uncle Asa."

"My condolences to you then. Good day."

He turned and quickly walked away.

"Good day, Uncle," she whispered in stunned reply. But he was already too far away to hear her.

Dr. Caine came up beside Aidan. Taking her arm, he spoke gently to her.

"Aidan, I know how hard this has been for you, but you know she felt nothing when she died. She was sleeping and felt no pain. Try to take comfort in knowing she did not suffer in death. You know she will never suffer again."

"Oh, Dr. Caine, thank you so much for everything," Aidan replied gratefully. She smiled at the doctor, who was a very kind man. "I do feel comforted. Really I do."

"You take care now, and let me know if there is anything more I can do," Dr. Caine said. He squeezed her arm gently and walked away.

The crowd was quickly breaking up and leaving the graveyard. A few people nodded goodbye to Aidan, but no one stopped to speak to her as they passed. Her shy smile was frozen onto her face beneath her veil as she nodded back. She watched them walk away from her, a stream of black flowing down the hill into Hidden.

As she turned back to look at the grave, Aidan caught sight of a tall slender woman standing some distance away from her. She was elegantly dressed all in black in a suit of fine wool trimmed with fur. Her hands were tucked into a matching fur muff and perched atop her silvery hair was a tiny satin hat with a net veil just covering her eyes. Her shadowed face was beautiful but not familiar. Aidan couldn't recall seeing her before during the day and wondered who in Hidden would be attending Aunt Mara's funeral wearing such fashionable clothing.

Just at that moment Mrs. Spencer bustled up to her. "My dear, if you should need anything, please don't hesitate to come and see us," she said in her patronizing voice. Squeezing Aidan's hand in parting, she added, "And you know I'm so sorry for her passing."

"Thank you, Mrs. Spencer," Aidan replied politely.

The undertaker's wife smiled sadly at her one last time and then rushed off to join the end of the crowd walking down the hill into Hidden.

Relieved to be alone, Aidan gratefully watched them go. The rustling of black fabric quickly faded away and all she could hear were the sweet sounds of men digging and the soft thudding of dirt falling into the grave, covering the coffin forever.

The wind caught her veil again and she reached up to toss it behind her head and out of her eyes. Suddenly she felt as though the graveside wind had blown away a black fog that had been surrounding her for a long time, as though she were seeing for the very first time the bright sunlight illuminating the cluster of quaint houses in the town below and the snow on the rocky peaks all around her. The mountain valley had never looked so beautiful.

What a glorious spring day! she thought. *The most glorious day of my life!*

Aidan turned to begin her walk down the hill and suddenly came face to face with the elegantly dressed woman she had seen a moment ago, who had come much closer to her. She froze and gasped as she realized with complete shock that she was staring at Lady Eleanora Fairhaven.

"Excuse me, Aidan, I didn't mean to startle you," the noblewoman said apologetically, stepping up to her and smiling.

The most influential and wealthy people in Hidden, Lord and Lady Fairhaven lived in a huge mansion on a hill outside town. Everything Aidan knew about them was based on gossip, for she had only ever seen them from a distance. Now here was Lady Fairhaven herself standing right in front of her and speaking to her! Small as the town was, she was certain that Aunt Mara couldn't have known her. Why on earth had this regal woman come to her funeral?

"Lady Fairhaven," she whispered reverently, and quickly dropped down into a deep curtsy.

"Oh my goodness, that isn't necessary – you don't need to do that!"

The noblewoman's voice was kind and gentle. Smiling, she quickly slipped her hand out of her fur muff and reached out to help Aidan up.

Trembling, Aidan looked at her outstretched hand, which was covered by a black lace glove. Beneath the lace on one of her long slender fingers she could see heavy gold wedding rings embellished with large diamonds that flashed in the sunlight. She stared at the rings in awe and then timidly reached up. The elegant hand closed firmly around hers.

As she stood up, she studied Lady Fairhaven's lovely countenance. Something in her smile almost convinced Aidan that underneath her fashionable ensemble and regal bearing the noblewoman was feeling just as shy as she was herself. She gently squeezed Aidan's hand before releasing it.

"I want to tell you how sorry I am about Mrs. Teague's death," she said sincerely. "Please accept my deepest condolences."

"Thank you."

There was a brief awkward silence between them.

"I – I don't know what to say," Aidan confessed. "I'm very honored that you came today."

"That's so kind of you," Lady Fairhaven said graciously. "I must make apologies for Lord Fairhaven, who could not attend. We've heard so much about you over the years that when the news of Mrs. Teague's death reached us this morning, I felt I simply must come to pay our respects to you. I do apologize that I arrived rather late. It was a wonderful thing you did, taking care of her when she was so ill."

Aidan smiled in embarrassment.

"Thank you, Lady Fairhaven. Did you know her very well?"

"No, I must confess that I hardly knew her at all. She sewed several comforters for me over the years. Usually I would have a servant pick them up, but once I came myself – but I'm sure you don't remember. It was several years ago. You were perhaps eight or nine."

Aidan was stunned to learn that Lady Fairhaven had actually been in her house.

"No, I'm sorry," she replied, "I don't remember that at all."

"I loved the comforters, and we still use them. Mrs. Teague was an excellent seamstress."

She hesitated, then went on.

"I remember the time I came to your house. She went upstairs for a moment and I saw you were busy scrubbing the dining room floor on your hands and knees. I watched you at your work. You were being so careful that you never noticed I was there at all."

Aidan felt her face redden with shame to learn that Lady Fairhaven had seen this. From the time she was small, Aunt Mara had forced her to scrub and clean the house so she could devote all her time to sewing. She had quickly learned to be industrious at it, for if Aunt Mara had been drinking and saw that something wasn't just right, she would almost always fly into a rage. Whenever that happened, Aidan would be whipped with Samuel's old leather belt and then locked into the tiny broom closet beneath the stairs.

"I was wondering what you will do now that Mrs. Teague is gone," Lady Fairhaven continued.

Astounded that the most prominent woman in Hidden should care about her welfare, Aidan stared into her face for a long moment, trying to discern if she were serious. But all she could see was warm sincerity in her lovely smile and a questioning look in her dark blue eyes behind the veil.

"Why – I don't know," she stammered. "I must meet with Uncle Asa tomorrow – he's the man who gave the eulogy."

Lady Fairhaven smiled in gentle amusement at Aidan's flustered words. "Yes, I know Asa," she said. "We've done business with him for many years. I know him well."

"He's taking care of Aunt Mara's will. I – I hadn't thought of all this before. I don't really know what I shall do now."

Lady Fairhaven reached out to pat her arm.

"Oh, but of course you don't. You must forgive me, Aidan, it's so unkind of me to ask you now. But I – well, what I wanted to say to you was – if you should need employment, please come and see me."

Aidan's mouth almost dropped open at her words.

"I have many servants," Lady Fairhaven went on, "but with summer coming on I can always use more help with cleaning and gardening. And when the summer is over, we shall see about the fall. Of course, I shall pay you well."

Shocked, Aidan blurted, "Oh – I love gardening – especially roses!"

Lady Fairhaven smiled again.

"Well, you needn't decide now, there's no hurry – I know this has been a very stressful day for you. Meet with Asa tomorrow and hear what he has to say. But you will give me an answer within the next few days, won't you?"

"Of course," Aidan said, completely in awe at the noblewoman's kindness. "Thank you, Lady Fairhaven. Thank you so much."

There was another moment of awkward silence between them. Then Lady Fairhaven said, "Well, I should be going now. Good day to you, Aidan."

"Good day," Aidan replied, dipping again into a quick nervous curtsy.

She watched the elegant lady walk gracefully away from her partway down the hill to a waiting carriage. A finely dressed footman helped her climb inside. Twin dapple grey horses nickered as the driver shook the reins and drove the carriage away.

Aidan watched it go, feeling as if she had just awakened from a dream.

Behind her she could still hear the sounds of digging. The chilly wind continued to whip at her skirt and veil, but now she sighed contentedly, her heart warm with fresh hope.

Slowly she took a step forward and began the long walk down the hill into Hidden.

Chapter Two

The Business Arrangement

The next morning, precisely at ten, Aidan settled herself into a leather-upholstered chair in Uncle Asa's large office at the bank. Not a man given to formalities, he got right down to business.

"Well, Aidan, I can't give you much encouragement where Mara's financial matters are concerned," he told her crisply. "You know she didn't have a great deal of money. When Samuel died he didn't leave her much, but the house was paid for and she managed a frugal budget. Once she found she could use her sewing as a means of support, she established a very nice little business for herself that was enough to feed you both and pay the bills."

He drummed his fingers lightly on the papers before him on his desk. There was not a trace of grief in his voice as he added, "Yes, I always admired my sister for her diligence and her good business sense. She was not a person to run from hard work."

"Yes, Uncle," Aidan said.

"Her will was quite simple," he continued. "Although Mara never went through the formality or expense of legally adopting you, for all intents and purposes she considered you her daughter. Accordingly, she left the cottage and all she had in it to you. What little money she had managed to save will have to go for taxes, and of course payment must be made for the lawyer and for the services of Dr. Caine and Mr. Spencer." He paused and then added sympathetically, "You will be fortunate if there is much of anything left over, I'm afraid."

Aidan was quiet. It frightened her to realize she had no money. She sat with her hands in her lap and her head down as the hopelessness of her situation began to sink in.

Then she remembered Lady Fairhaven's kind offer of the day before and looked back up at Uncle Asa.

To her surprise, his voice suddenly became gentle.

"What will you do now, Aidan? You will be able to live in the house, but how will you afford to take care of the place? How will you buy food for yourself?"

"I'll plant a huge garden for the summer," she told him. "And I'll go to work for Lady Fairhaven."

"Lady Fairhaven!" Uncle Asa's eyes opened wide in surprise. "And how will you manage to do that? What makes you think she will hire you?"

"She has already asked me. After the funeral yesterday."

Now Uncle Asa was quiet. He tapped his fingers silently on the papers before him and seemed to be dumbfounded by her words.

Aidan took a deep breath. "She came to pay her respects and offered me a job cleaning and gardening. I know there are many things I can't do, but cleaning and gardening are certainly two things I can do very well."

"I am very impressed, Aidan," Uncle Asa said. "I've known the Fairhavens for a very long time. I personally maintain their accounts, and I happen to know they are most particular about the people they hire. For Lady Fairhaven to come and seek you out and offer you employment – why, you should be very proud of this. But of course, everyone in Hidden knows of you. You have always been – well, let us be frank, shall we? – quite the curiosity to us here."

Aidan sighed resolutely and replied, "Yes, well, I suppose that's one way of putting it, Uncle."

As far back as Aidan could remember she had never set foot outside the valley where Hidden was located, yet she had always felt alone and out of place in the little town. She had lived all her life beneath the curious scrutiny of the townspeople, painfully aware that she was different from them.

Hidden was an ancient isolated town where everyone knew everyone else and where, indeed, everyone seemed to be somehow related to everyone else. It was nestled near the center of a wide picturesque valley high up in a vast range of great snow-covered mountains. This alpine area formed the borderland of the Kingdom of Davarius. Its Sovereign, who had never been to Hidden that anyone knew of, was Prince Bal'Davarius, a man said to have such black hair and eyes that he was often referred to as the Dark Prince.

The only road going into Hidden was a dirt path that ran through the mountains and down from the foothills, passing along the length of the valley and through the center of town as its main street before continuing back up over the foothills into the mountains on the other end. Paved centuries before with cobblestones, the main street was lined by several shops, an inn, Uncle Asa's bank, the Town Hall, the courthouse, and a few other buildings. Narrow side streets sprawled out on each side and formed a maze of rustic houses and cottages. The wide grassy valley and its foothills beyond made good grazing land for horses, sheep, cows and goats. Most of the townspeople, including Aidan, grew large gardens during the short mountain summers.

It had always seemed to Aidan that the people of Hidden were as cold and forbidding as the dark mountain shadows that fell over the town each day at dawn and dusk. Most of the time they were outwardly friendly enough and quite loyal to their neighbors and relatives, but to those from outside the town, although no one was ever openly hostile, they were generally very reserved and suspicious. Other than merchants who came to sell their wares, it was rare indeed that a sojourner would brave the rocky mountain road to visit the isolated valley, and then only in fair seasons, for the unpredictable winter weather made travel quite treacherous. Outsiders were such an uncommon sight in Hidden that Aidan in fact had never personally seen one.

Even though she had lived all of her seventeen years in the cottage where she had been left as an infant, Aidan knew she was still thought of as an outsider and was fully aware that this would never change. Her real mother and father, the place of her birth, how she had come to Hidden – all of these things were totally unknown. Her name written on a brief note pinned to a baby blanket had offered all the information as to who she was.

The only thing that was certain to all was that she was not from any family in Hidden. If that were so, the whole town would have known in an instant who her parents were.

So her presence in Hidden remained a complete mystery, both to the others in the town and to Aidan herself. Even now, although her neighbors usually seemed friendly enough to her, she often caught them giving her wary looks as she went about her way. No one had ever tried to be a real friend to her. She had always felt that they were still suspicious of her, still trying to decide whether or not she belonged with them, still not quite sure if they should welcome her into their circle.

Indeed, just the day before, Aidan had been bitterly amused to note that despite their display of sympathy and support at the funeral, not one of them had offered to help her or even to keep her company afterward. It had not surprised her in the least to find herself cleaning up all alone after the many guests who had filled her house and eaten a meal there that morning.

And Uncle Asa had been the first to leave the graveside.

Aidan watched him as he leaned back in his padded leather chair, which seemed huge around his small slender frame, and stroked thoughtfully at his neatly trimmed goatee as he considered what to say next.

"Well! I am quite sure you will do just fine working for Lady Fairhaven," he said at last. "You are honest and hardworking. She is kind and generous and will pay you very well for your service to her. But – of course –"

He stopped, pausing to choose his words carefully before going on.

"Yes, Uncle?"

He cleared his throat. "There is a better way for you to earn a living."

She shook her head, puzzled. "A better way?"

Uncle Asa took a deep breath.

"Aidan, you are not my flesh and blood, as you well know. My sister was most generous to take you in, given her unfortunate circumstances."

There was something serious in his tone and Aidan suddenly felt her stomach tighten. What was he about to say?

"Yes, Uncle," she replied, hoping her shaking voice did not betray her nervousness. "I do know this."

"As you know, I am – shall we say – a man of means."

He cleared his throat again softly, looking out the window as he spoke. His hands always seemed to be moving in nervous gestures. Now he continued stroking his goatee with his left hand while the fingers of his right hand drummed silently on the arm of his chair.

"But I have never married. When I came of age, there was simply no woman in Hidden suitable for me – that is, none who pleased me enough that I should consider matrimony."

Aidan felt her face blush crimson as her heart began to pound with dread. Was he about to propose?

"As I grew older," he continued, "I became quite set in my ways and decided I liked living alone. But I'm not a young man anymore and I have a great deal of money to pass on when I die. I would most prefer to have it go to you, for even though you are not my flesh and blood or even my legally adopted niece, I feel a certain sense of – family loyalty toward you."

Aidan was dumbfounded at what he was telling her, but something in his tone told her clearly that Uncle Asa's words had nothing to do with family loyalty.

"That is very kind of you, Uncle," she said carefully. "Please go on."

Uncle Asa turned his face to look into hers. His dark eyes were just like Aunt Mara's and his goatee and mustache were silvery in the sunlight from the window.

"Aidan, you always were a very bright girl," he said. "Very well then, I shall get right to the point. I should like to establish a business arrangement with you."

A surge of relief went through her as she realized that he was not going to propose, but her relief was immediately followed by deep suspicion.

"A – a business arrangement. What kind of business arrangement?"

Uncle Asa sat up and leaned forward, resting his elbows on the desk again and tapping his fingertips together, his eyes fixed upon her face.

"On my part, once a month I shall withdraw a large sum of money directly from one of my personal accounts here at the bank. The money will be your – shall we say – allowance. You will be free to spend it any way you like – for food, clothes, jewelry, however you wish to spend it, the choice will be completely yours. In addition, I shall arrange to take care of all the taxes and repairs on the cottage. Also, I shall change my will to designate that all of my earthly goods and money – which I can assure you are considerable – will go to you upon my death."

Aidan could hardly believe what she was hearing. Other than perhaps the Fairhavens, Uncle Asa was without doubt the wealthiest man in town, but she had always known him to be extremely stingy. She had often wondered why she and Aunt Mara had been forced to make do with so little when Uncle Asa, who certainly had the means to help them – and who had often been a guest at their table – had never even so much as invited them to his home for tea. It amazed her now to hear him making such a grand gesture to her and suddenly treating her as a close member of the family.

But it was perfectly clear that he was not just being generous. He wanted something from her in return, and she knew it.

"Well, this is most kind of you, Uncle," she replied carefully, her voice edged with skepticism. "But you did say that this was a business arrangement. What are you asking me to do as my part of this agreement?"

Uncle Asa's dark eyes glittered with tiny fires as he stared hard into hers.

"You shall become my mistress."

For the briefest of moments Aidan failed to grasp the meaning of his words and she waited for him to continue and explain. Then the full impact of what he was suggesting came to her. As her stomach lurched in shock, she drew in a sharp breath and gasped loudly.

"Your – your *mistress?!*"

He smiled patiently at her, a condescending smile she would remember forever after as a leer. He leaned back again, crossed one leg over the other, and rested his elbows on the arms of his chair, twining the fingers of his hands together on his thigh and tapping the ends of his thumbs against each other.

"Oh, come now, Aidan, my dear. Don't be so naive. You are a poor lovely young girl in need of money. I am a rich lonely old man in need of companionship. We would both benefit greatly from such an alliance."

He shrugged as though what he was suggesting were nothing more decadent than a casual invitation to lunch.

"If you please me, I shall make sure your every desire is met, and when I die I assure you that you will want for nothing for the rest of your life. This is a most generous offer. You have no idea how much you stand to gain."

Aidan's hands trembled and her face grew pale. She sat frozen before him in flustered panic, heart pounding, barely able to breathe, wondering what she should do.

Her impulse was to rise indignantly and tell Uncle Asa he could keep his money, but she hesitated as she considered the gravity of her situation. She was well aware that he had a great deal of power over her, and because of this she was very afraid of him. He was in complete control of Aunt Mara's estate, including her cottage, and she was not ignorant of the fact that if he so chose, there were measures he could take to force her into his "business arrangement." If he failed to pay the taxes she could lose her home, and if that happened she knew she would be quite helpless before him, for she had no money, no friends or family, and nowhere else to live.

But – his *mistress!*

It horrified Aidan to think he might actually have *that* much power over her.

Once again Uncle Asa's voice became gentle and patronizing.

"I can see that I have upset you," he said. "Would you like some time to consider my offer? There is no hurry, my dear. I can wait a day or two while you decide."

Finding her voice at last, Aidan stammered, "I – I don't know what to say."

Then she quickly gathered all her courage to do what her heart was telling her was right.

"No," she declared firmly. "No, Uncle Asa, I won't need any time to consider your offer. I shall refuse your 'business arrangement' right away. How dare you suggest that I become – become a prostitute for your private use!"

She jumped to her feet. Her whole body began to shake as a violent rush of hatred rose in her, the same rage she had felt for his sister at the graveside the day before. Sweeping her shawl around herself, she stood behind the chair and glared at him as she prepared to leave.

Scowling, Uncle Asa abruptly stood up behind the desk. His features were sharp and his eyes suddenly burned with anger. For a horrifying moment he looked so much like Aunt Mara going into one of her drunken tantrums that Aidan gasped in terror, fully expecting him to pursue her and beat her. But to her surprise, he stood still behind the desk and made no attempt to follow her.

"Very well then," he snapped, his voice derisive. "Go on and be a washerwoman for Lady Fairhaven. Go and fill your days with endless drudgery! But don't ever forget that – had you agreed to my most generous arrangement – you could have had a life of great luxury and pleasure. It would have been very wise for you to take my offer – and not to have insulted me."

Impatiently he began to shuffle piles of papers on his desk.

"I shall contact you when Mara's estate has been settled."

"Good day to you, Uncle," Aidan said icily, whirling around and reaching for the door.

"Aidan –"

She stopped, her back to him, her hand on the latch, heart pounding, waiting.

"Remember, my offer still stands whenever you decide to accept it." His voice was smooth and threatening. "And I have no doubt, my dear, that one day you shall discover you do want to change your mind."

Trembling with fury and indignation, Aidan yanked open the door and slammed it behind herself as she fled from his office.

Chapter Three

The Oath And The Stone Tower

As Aidan rushed out of the bank and into the brilliant sunlight, startled passers-by on the street turned to stare at her. She could sense her face flaming bright scarlet as she felt the eyes of the whole town upon her, certain they all somehow knew what had just taken place. Uncontrollable tears of deep humiliation and shame began to well in her eyes at the thought that Uncle Asa should imagine she was so desperate for money that she would actually consider becoming his kept woman.

Hoisting up her long black skirt, Aidan raced as fast as she could for the north end of town. She passed the end of the cobblestones and the last of the buildings on the main street and continued running along the dirt road that led into the mountains. Not far along she turned to the right onto a narrow side road and stopped, out of breath, staring far ahead at the tall grassy hill where the Fairhavens' huge mansion rose majestically above the valley.

Originally built as a fortified castle and greatly modified over several centuries, the palatial structure stood as a constant reminder of Hidden's ancient feudal heritage. Lord Fairhaven's powerful ancestors had founded the town long before and had once ruled the valley as well as a great deal of the surrounding alpine area. Hidden was presently governed by a mayor and a town council acting under the authority of Prince Bal'Davarius, but the wealthy

Fairhavens were well respected and greatly influential in the region, and in fact still owned most of the land in the valley.

Aidan had never come this way before and the sight of the formidable mansion made her feel as though she were trespassing. Lady Fairhaven had offered her employment and was expecting her reply, but now the mere thought of going up the hill and approaching the mansion was making her panic. She stood staring at it for a long time, gathering her courage. Then she began walking very slowly, her heart pounding with determination and dread, and came to the base of the hill.

As she climbed the winding path toward the mansion, her lungs burned within her and her legs felt like lead weights. At last she stumbled from the path, waded into the tall dry grass that covered the hillside, and stretched out to rest.

The ground was cold and damp beneath her back and the clean mountain wind soothing as it blew across her burning face. Thick yellow grass rustled in the wind and rose all around her like the walls of a tiny room. Far above wispy clouds ebbed and flowed in a graceful white dance against deep blue.

Pushing from her mind what had just happened in town, Aidan breathed slowly and deeply for a long time. Lying there on the hillside she drew strength and comfort from her mountain solitude as she lost all sense of time and space. She began to feel safe again as her heart embraced the whispering rhythms of the wind in the grass and the elegant waltz in the silent sky.

After awhile she became aware of the sound of rushing water somewhere nearby. She pulled herself to her feet and followed the sound until she came upon a mountain stream flowing springtime hard and fast through the thick grass. Crystal clear water tumbled over a wide bed of rocks on its way toward the valley.

Aidan gazed for a long time at the sunlight sparkling on the beautiful rippling water before bending down and putting her hand into its flow. The shock of icy cold that met her fingers caused them to tingle as she cupped her hand and took several long drinks. A chill spread through her body as clean icy water went down her throat. She plunged both hands into the stream and splashed some of the invigorating water onto her hot face. At that moment the wind came up strong and she shivered.

Fully refreshed, feeling somehow cleansed within, she shook drops of water from her hands and smoothed wrinkles from her clothes, brushing away grass and dirt. As she pulled her shawl tightly around her shoulders, she gazed at the impressive view of the valley and the mountains, which she had never seen from this hill. Thankfully, Hidden seemed very far away.

Above her the Fairhaven mansion rose up like an impenetrable fortress. She was quite close to it now and it seemed both elegant and threatening. The path immediately in front of it passed beneath three immense pairs of ancient oak trees that seemed dwarfed by the height of the mansion. It was terrifying to think of walking under those trees and actually going up to the door and knocking.

Irrational fears flooded her mind. What if meeting Lady Fairhaven had been a dream that had never really happened? Or what if it had happened, but the noblewoman had forgotten all about it? Or worse, what if her offer of employment had been nothing more than an insincere gesture of pity? What if she scolded Aidan for her boldness in coming to ask about the position, or laughed at her and sent her on her way?

What would she do then?

A piercing chill much colder than the water in the mountain stream froze her heart as the answer taunted her, whispering in the wind and the rustling grass.

She would have no choice but to go back to Uncle Asa and enter into his "business arrangement," for there would really be no other way for her to survive.

This realization hit Aidan with such force that she felt physical pain, as though Aunt Mara had just beaten her all over again with Samuel Teague's old leather belt.

"No," she moaned as she fully understood the severity of her situation. Then she cried out in anguish, her voice fighting against the mountain wind.

"No! I will never do it! I will find another way!"

Tears began to stream down her face. She was grateful now to be free of Aunt Mara's cruelty, but for the first time she realized that the old woman's death had left her truly alone. Alone in a town cut off from the rest of the world by the imposing mountains all around it. Alone and helpless in the midst of uncaring people who were as suspicious of her as she was of them.

Alone without hope – or love.

Yesterday she had celebrated her newfound freedom. Today she was forced to face the stark reality that she was not free at all. Yesterday she had rejoiced to be alone. Today she knew beyond all uncertainty that she was trapped in a prison of complete isolation.

Defiantly Aidan cried out to the mountains all around her.

"I swear by all that is good and kind and true and beautiful in this world that I will not be alone forever!"

The gusting wind abruptly ceased as though to listen to her. Suddenly her voice sounded like thunder roaring across the valley and echoing back, but at that moment she didn't care if all of Hidden heard her. She just cried out all the louder.

"Someday I will leave this cursed valley and never come back! I swear today that I will be *free!*"

Her eyes searched over the buildings of the village far below. She recognized the slate roof and stone garden wall of the lovely cottage on the edge of town where she had lived as long as she could remember and had nurtured her precious rose garden since childhood.

Somewhere deep in the center of her heart Aidan had always known that Aunt Mara's house was not her home. It was the place where she had been abandoned as a baby and had grown up, the place where she had known beatings and imprisonment, the place where she had ached with a deep yearning to be loved and wanted. Such a place could never really be her home.

"Home," she whispered longingly. "Someday I will go home."

Aidan raised her eyes again to the snow-capped peaks and her voice grew bitter as she angrily wiped tears from her face.

"No one here has ever loved or wanted me. No one has ever even cared whether I live or die. All they care about is how they can use me for their selfish gain!"

The mountain wind blew gently now, softly fanning the spark of longing deep within her heart into bright and hopeful flame.

"But somewhere there was once a real home for me, far beyond this mountain valley where I've been but can't remember. I swear that someday I will find that place – and when I do, I will never be alone again. I will find my true family and go home. *Home!*"

The mountains suddenly seemed to be closing in on her, taunting her with the impossibility of making such a journey. She shouted at them in defiance.

"Even if I must climb over every one of these mountains, yes, and even a hundred more, I swear I'll never stop searching until I find my family! I must find out why they sent me away to this wretched place."

She stopped and breathed deeply as her heart swelled with the dreams she had carried for so long.

"Someday I will be *loved* – really, truly, forever *loved*. Oh, I swear this with all my life and breath! There *is* love for me somewhere in this world and I will find it! I will be loved and wanted!"

Aidan turned and looked up again at the Fairhaven mansion. Suddenly the memory came to her of the last picture in her favorite childhood fairy tale book. She had loved that book so much that she still knew all the words and pictures by heart. The story was very simple and the colorful illustrations exquisitely detailed.

Once upon a time there was a beautiful Princess who had a beloved rose garden. Along came an evil Dragon who threatened to destroy her garden with his fiery breath and carry her off to his cave. But just before that could happen, a handsome Prince rode up on his magnificent white horse and killed the Dragon with his sword, rescuing the Princess and saving her garden. The last picture showed the two of them together on his horse heading toward his palace high on a hill in the distance – where of course they lived happily ever after.

Struck by the similarities between the mansion above her and the illustration of the Prince's palace, Aidan now thought about that story. The pictures had been firmly rooted in her memory since she had learned to read as a very young child.

Somewhere deep inside she had always believed with all her heart that someday her own handsome Prince would come along on his white horse and rescue her, and they too would live happily ever after. Over the years she had often pictured her Prince in her imagination and had even given him a name.

Now she reverently whispered it into the wind.

"The One Who Will Love Me Forever. I swear someday I will find him – The One Who Will Love Me Forever!"

Aidan drew in a deep breath, now filled with renewed peace. As she knelt down for another drink, her eyes were drawn to the speckled stones that filled the bottom of the stream bed. There were hundreds of them, beautiful stones in many colors, worn round and smooth over time by flowing water.

Impulsively she started pulling them one by one from the stream and piling them into a heap in the tall dry grass. After awhile her arms and back ached, but she kept hauling the heavy stones until she had made a sturdy pillar about three feet tall.

"This tower is my monument, the symbol of my vow," she declared. "It stands as proof that as long as I live, I am bound to these words I have sworn. I will find my family and go home."

She stroked the smooth hard stones, drawing strength from them.

"I will not be unloved and unwanted forever. Someday I will find the love beyond the mountains that I know is out there waiting for me. I swear I will never stop searching until I find The One Who Will Love Me Forever!"

Aidan stood upright and lifted her gaze from the tower of stones to the intimidating mansion on the crest of the hill far above her. Even as her heart pounded with fear at the prospect of knocking on the door and asking to see Lady Fairhaven, she knew she simply had no other choice. Her course of action was as crystal clear as the rippling water in the mountain stream.

She either had to go up the hill and accept Lady Fairhaven's offer – or go back down into Hidden and accept Uncle Asa's.

Bending down one last time, Aidan chose another stone from the stream bed. She carried it with her as she picked her way back to the path and left it right at the edge of the grass as a marker so she would be able to find her tower again easily.

Then, taking in one more deep breath of the blustery mountain air, she began walking up the steep path to the Fairhaven mansion.

Chapter Four

Mysterious Encounter

The rising sun was beginning to lighten the sky behind the mountains, casting black shadows across the valley. There was rarely anyone else awake so early in the morning and Aidan almost always had the cobblestone main street all to herself as she hurried along the dark streets of Hidden on her way to the Fairhaven mansion. On this particular late September morning the quiet was broken only by the song of a single bird. She smiled at the cheerful sound, her heart filled with contentment. Her walk to work in the quiet solitude of dawn was the most peaceful part of every day.

Aidan had been working six days a week at the mansion since spring and for the most part had found her job to be very enjoyable. It included a noonday meal which was always more sumptuous than anything she would ever cook for herself. Finding her way around the mansion and remembering the names of the other staff members had been a huge challenge at first, but most of them were helpful and pleasant enough. There were some who were a bit unfriendly to work with and even seemed suspicious of her, so she avoided them as much as she could. She was quite used to being the outsider and in many ways felt those few inhabitants of the mansion were not unlike all the other people in Hidden.

In the beginning her job had confused her. Lady Fairhaven had said she needed help with cleaning and gardening, so she had expected to be doing heavy scrubbing and dusting and other backbreaking drudgery. She had also expected to be treated harshly, for that was what she had always known with Aunt Mara. But when she reported for work on her first day, to her great surprise, Lady Fairhaven presented her with three elegant uniforms like the other maidservants wore – lovely dresses of crisp shiny blue fabric, with starched white aprons and pretty lace collars. Then she informed Aidan that her job would be to work closely beside her as her personal handmaid.

During those first spring days Aidan had been terrified and clumsy, but Lady Fairhaven was always very patient with her. Once she overcame her nervousness, she found the work was easy and pleasant. Her mornings began by helping the noblewoman do her hair and choose an outfit and accessories for the day. Then she did light housework such as making the bed, hanging up clothes, and general tidying.

Her favorite daily task was to accompany her employer to the west wing where an extensive collection of musical instruments was kept. A most accomplished musician, Lady Fairhaven practiced for a long time every day and she seemed to like having someone there with her to listen. Aidan would quickly do some light dusting and then just sit and relax, enraptured to have a private concert to enjoy. Over the course of the summer she learned the names of every instrument and heard each one played many times, although she was not invited to try playing any of them herself.

And as summer came on, to her total delight, Lady Fairhaven decided to put her in charge of tending her rose garden. For Aidan this was not work at all, for gardening was her passion and creative gift. Nurturing the beautiful roses was a complete joy and they thrived under her exacting care.

Very often it seemed that the noblewoman just wanted a companion to talk to, someone with whom she could share and enjoy the beautiful things in the mansion. At first it troubled Aidan a great deal that her job was so easy and sometimes she wondered why she had been hired at all. She often felt guilty that she was not doing much of what she would consider actual work. But her employer never seemed to mind and before long it became clear that this was just her manner.

Eventually Aidan came to relax with her and appreciate their time together. Everything in the mansion was completely different from everything she had known with Aunt Mara, and she was grateful to be working for someone so kind and gentle.

At the end of every week Lady Fairhaven herself would pay Aidan her wages. Her generous salary seemed like a small fortune, especially since the work was not at all difficult. It had proven to be much more than enough for her to live on, especially for the summer when she had plenty to eat from her own garden.

Now not only would she soon harvest the rest of its bounty and fill her root cellar for the winter, she had even been able to save a great deal of money.

For the first time in her life Aidan felt she was accomplishing something tremendous all on her own. Her heart was filled with deep satisfaction that she had come through the summer with no financial problems despite all of Uncle Asa's apparently empty threats the day after Aunt Mara's funeral.

As Aidan walked along this particular morning and passed by Uncle Asa's bank, which of course was now shuttered and closed, the thought of him left her confused and suspicious. She was still afraid of him, but mysteriously he had made no effort to force her into his "business arrangement." It was highly unlikely that he had forgotten the threats he had made in the spring, and she was quite sure he would someday try to force his hand. Yet her only communication with him throughout the summer had been a terse note delivered to her by a messenger informing her that – "by a most fortunate coincidence" – the money from Aunt Mara's assets had been almost the exact amount needed to pay all the outstanding taxes, the lawyer's bill, the doctor's bill, and the undertaker's fees – leaving a tidy balance of close to zero in the bank.

No doubt he was lying about it all, but it made no sense to try to contest it, for she knew that would be fruitless. So she let the whole matter go, choosing to just be grateful that for right now, at least, she had a roof over her head and food to eat and a good job that paid well. She was capable and strong and would survive all on her own.

The chill of autumn in the mountain air pierced like needles through the long woolen shawl wrapped around Aidan's shoulders. Her panting breath puffed little clouds of swirling white mist into the black morning shadows as she hurried along the cobblestone street. All too soon the hard frosts would come and usher in another long dark mountain winter. She shivered from the cold and sighed wearily at the thought of the approaching season, which was always lonely and dangerously harsh in the mountains.

Then she brightened, remembering that this would be the last winter she would ever spend in Hidden.

By springtime she would have more than enough money to be able to leave the valley forever. Next winter she was certain she would be living with her family in true love and happiness. Next winter – her heart thrilled at the thought! – she just knew she would even be with The One Who Would Love Her Forever. All her dreams would soon be coming true!

Her only real problem now, never having been outside the valley, was determining how to travel the mountain roads and where to go to begin her search. But she was confident that she would figure all that out when the time came.

She paused to take in a deep breath of the autumn air as peace and contentment filled her heart once more. Then she rounded the final curve in the town's main street and hurried along the last stretch of cobblestones toward the dirt road that led across the valley and up the hill to the mansion.

And at that moment, Aidan's life was forever changed.

Just as she approached the last building before the dirt road, she was startled to realize that she was not alone on the street. Two women had evidently just come down the mountain road and were walking straight toward her into the town. Their dark forms were so lost in the shadows that they seemed to be emerging forth from them.

She could not make out their faces, but upon seeing the two women her heart gave an odd little leap, as though she somehow knew them and had indeed been waiting for them to arrive. This reaction surprised her because she had never seen an outsider in Hidden. These two women were without doubt complete strangers to her.

Nervously Aidan shrank back into the shadows to study them. They were wearing dark dresses with long full skirts and dark knitted shawls clutched tightly around their heads and shoulders to keep warm. She could see that they were tall and slender, but as they walked along they moved slowly and seemed hunched over, as though they were carrying heavy burdens. Since neither of them seemed to have anything in their hands, she guessed that they must be very old.

How had two elderly women come to be walking through the mountains so early on a cold morning with no baggage of any kind? Had they been walking all night? Who were these women and how far had they come?

She knew she would have to pass by them to get to the mansion, so she took a deep breath, straightened her shoulders, and stepped out of the shadows. Smiling anxiously, she started walking toward them. Her timid voice seemed terribly loud against the quietness of dawn.

"Good morning, ladies."

The women nodded to her and one of them returned her greeting in a weary-sounding contralto.

"Good morning, Aidan."

Aidan froze and stared in panic and confusion at the shadowy bent figures before her.

"How do you know my name? I'm sure I don't know you. You must be strangers here."

The same woman spoke again.

"We are not strangers in Hidden, and we are not strangers to you. We've known you since before you were born."

It took a stunned moment for Aidan to fully comprehend what the woman had just told her.

"Before I was born," she repeated. "Then – then you must have known my mother. Do you know my mother?"

The second woman nodded. "Oh, yes, we know her. We knew her before she was born, too."

Aidan could scarcely believe it. These women knew her mother! They knew where she was from!

Her fear of the strangers melted away into a desperate courage she had never felt before. For the first time in her life she had the chance to find out about her family!

Eagerly she began questioning the two strangers.

"What is my mother's name? Where is she now?"

The women looked at each other, then turned again to Aidan, but said nothing.

Confused, Aidan persisted.

"Why did she give me up as an orphan? Where was I born?"

Still they gave her no reply.

Tormented by their cold dark silence, Aidan begged, "Please, tell me all you know. You have no idea how much I've longed to find someone who can tell me about my mother!"

At last, speaking slowly, the first woman answered her.

"We can tell you about your mother. We know her very well."

Aidan opened her mouth to ask a thousand more questions, but at that moment the morning stillness was broken by the sudden sound of the nearby Town Hall clock tower chiming out the hour. Frantically torn between her eagerness to talk to the two women and her need to get to the Fairhaven mansion, she waited impatiently for the bells to stop.

When it was quiet again, she said, "Ladies, I'm on my way to the place where I work and I'm afraid I must hurry. But I've never met anyone who said they knew about my family and I simply have to know more. I know nothing about my mother and no one in Hidden can tell me anything either. I don't even know where I was born or why I was brought here. Do you know these things? Will you tell me?"

"We know the story well, Aidan, but it's a very long one," the second woman replied. "It can't be told in a moment or two. And you are going to be late getting to the mansion."

It was only much later that Aidan thought to wonder how they could have known she worked at the Fairhaven mansion and that she was running late, since she hadn't told them that.

But at that moment nothing in the world mattered to her as much as finding out about her past and her family. Even at the risk of losing her job in the face of the approaching winter, she would easily have chosen to hear the strangers' long story over getting to the mansion. Their slow hesitant answers were frustrating, but she was determined to learn the truth.

Smiling as graciously as she could, she said, "I understand. Please tell me, what are your names? Will you be staying in Hidden?"

"We are sisters traveling together," the first woman told her. "We have much business to attend to in Hidden and we will need to lodge here for awhile. We are on our way to the inn."

"Oh, no, no, don't go there," Aidan insisted quickly, her heart almost bursting with eager excitement. "If you were to stay with me, we'd have plenty of time to talk. Oh please, *please* say you'll stay with me! I live in a grey stone cottage at the end of the –"

The second woman was suddenly quick to interrupt her. "We know where you live, Aidan. We will be pleased to stay with you."

"Go on to your work," the other woman insisted. "We will come to your home at sundown tonight. Then we will talk, for we have much to tell you."

"Oh, thank you! Thank you so much!" Aidan cried. "I shall see you then! Good day to you, ladies!"

She left the women standing there and hurried along the dirt road and up the hill to the Fairhaven mansion.

The day passed maddeningly slowly. The only thing she could think about was meeting the two strangers. In her excitement she assisted Lady Fairhaven with an energy and exuberance she had never felt before. As she dusted musical instruments and tended the rose garden, she turned over and over again in her mind the amazing events of the early morning. The thought that she would soon know the truth about her family was more incredible than she could believe.

What a stroke of good fortune to encounter the two strangers just as they entered Hidden! Why, if they had gone on to the inn, or if someone else had offered them a place to stay, or if she had been just a few minutes earlier or later as she walked to the mansion, she most likely never would have made their acquaintance at all. They probably would have conducted their business and then gone on their way through the mountains – and she never would have even known that there were two people in Hidden who knew her mother.

What a wonderful coincidence that she had met them!

Still, something about the whole encounter was very disturbing and she tormented herself all morning with many anxious questions. The two sisters seemed so cold and mysterious that the thought of having them stay with her was quite daunting. She wondered if she should have invited them, especially since she had never entertained overnight guests before.

What possible business could these sisters have in Hidden? Where had they come from? How could two old women have managed to walk along the mountain road and make their way in the cold darkness of night?

How did they know her – and how did they know her mother?

Finally Aidan decided to set all her questions aside and concentrate on the joyful fact that she would soon have answers to them all. Her dream of leaving Hidden in the spring and finding her family was closer to reality than ever before!

Suddenly the thought struck her that perhaps her mother had actually sent these two women to bring her back to wherever she had come from. Could that be the sisters' business in Hidden?

The dream that her mother would one day send for her or come back for her was a hope that had been buried like a small seed in Aidan's heart since her very earliest memories. Now this hope abruptly sprang forth, as fully developed and sweet as a rose opening to full bloom. The thought that these women might take her home cast a rush of warm joy across Aidan's plain face. As she came inside from the rose garden she smiled happily and even started humming a little tune.

It was at that moment that Lady Fairhaven happened to see her walking down the hallway. After watching her for a moment, she beckoned to her.

"Aidan, may I have a word with you, please?"

Aidan's heart sank with dread. Already on edge from her mysterious encounter that morning, she trembled nervously before her employer.

"Is – is anything wrong, my Lady?" she asked.

"No, not at all," replied Lady Fairhaven, smiling in her regal but gentle way. "On the contrary, it would seem that something must be very right. You have been lost in thought all morning and now you seem so joyful – just radiant. May I ask what is making you so happy?"

Relieved, Aidan quickly seized the chance to tell someone about what had happened that morning.

"Oh, my Lady, you may certainly ask. I'm simply bursting to tell someone!" she cried, then immediately gasped with embarrassment and put her hands over her mouth at her impulsiveness.

But Lady Fairhaven only laughed.

"Well, then, you must tell me! Come sit and we'll talk."

They went into a nearby room and sat down at opposite ends of a velvet-covered couch. Aidan's words tumbled excitedly as she eagerly poured out her heart.

"I met two women this morning as I was walking here, strangers just coming into town. They said they were sisters traveling together and they had business in Hidden. When I spoke to them, they called me by name. They said they knew me even before I was born. They know my family – they know my mother!"

Lady Fairhaven's deep blue eyes went wide with surprise, sparkling like sapphires in her elegant face. "Well, that *is* wonderful news! Strangers in Hidden who know your family! And what are these sisters' names?"

It was not until that moment that Aidan realized she didn't know their names.

"Why, I asked them – but they didn't tell me," she said.

The strangers seemed all the more mysterious to her now, and she shivered from a sudden chill of fear as she thought of their shadowed faces again.

Lady Fairhaven looked at her with curiosity.

"Do you know from where these women have come?"

"No," Aidan admitted. "I know nothing about them at all, really. I was only able to talk to them for a moment. But I did invite them to stay with me, and they said they would come to my house this evening at sundown. I'm sure I'll find out more about them tonight – and about my family, too."

"Well, I certainly hope so, Aidan," Lady Fairhaven said sincerely. "I can imagine how anxious you must be to find out about your mother."

Her gentle encouragement suddenly made Aidan feel brave enough to confide in her for the first time about her dreams.

"I want to find her – I want that more than anything in the world," she said. "I can hardly believe that I've actually met two people right here in Hidden who know her – who can tell me where I was born and how I came here and how

I can find her. Oh, I have so much to do! I must make my house ready for my guests and prepare a meal for them."

Lady Fairhaven reached out and patted her hand.

"But of course you must," she agreed. "I can see how important this is to you. You may take the afternoon off."

Awed by her employer's kindness, Aidan whispered, "Oh, my Lady – thank you!"

Lady Fairhaven smiled. "And you must take some fresh bread from the kitchen for your guests," she said firmly. "You won't have much time before they arrive. The cooks have just finished the baking, and we have plenty. I'll send Stewart to fetch some for you."

Her eyes were serious but soft as she added, "And I do hope that you'll feel free to talk to me whenever you want to – about anything at all. In fact – if you wouldn't mind – I would really like to hear what your guests have to tell you about your mother."

"Of course," Aidan answered.

She was completely amazed that the noblewoman should take such interest in her. Lady Fairhaven smiled, patted her hand again, and then rang for Stewart, her butler, to bring the bread for her.

The early afternoon sun was warm and bright as Aidan excitedly left the Fairhaven mansion a few minutes later. Over her arm she carried a large basket containing two heavy loaves of warm dark bread wrapped in linen towels.

As she hurried down the grassy hill, she came to the marker stone that she had left at the side of the road. She stopped and looked in the direction of the stream where months before she had built the pillar of stones and had sworn to leave Hidden someday to find her family. Her heart thrilled with the certainty that she would soon be able to fulfill her vows.

Surely it wouldn't be long now before she would be home, loved and wanted at last in her mother's embrace!

Her eyes sparkling with hope, she continued on her way.

In a frenzy of nervous energy, Aidan scurried about cleaning and scrubbing her house and preparing Aunt Mara's old room for her guests. She picked vegetables from her garden and cooked a large pot of soup to serve with slices of cheese and Lady Fairhaven's fresh bread.

As the afternoon wore on, her hopes began to dissolve into anxious doubts and fears. Perhaps the women would not find her home to their liking and would refuse to stay with her. Or perhaps she had somehow dreamed the entire encounter that morning and the two women had never really existed at all. Or, worse yet – perhaps the two women had changed their minds during the day and had already passed through Hidden and left, taking all her dreams with them, never to be seen again.

As the sun sank lower and lower in the sky, Aidan found herself rushing frantically to the front window every few minutes to look for the two sisters. But the only thing she could see was her beloved rose garden, which was still stubbornly blooming despite the cold nights and approaching frosts.

After awhile she opened the windows to bring the rich scent of the garden into the front room. When the perfumed air became chilly, she built a roaring fire in the great stone fireplace. She kept glancing anxiously out the window, afraid that her guests would come at any moment – but much more afraid that they would never show up at all.

Finally Aidan settled herself on the window seat to watch and wait. Curling up on the embroidered cushions, she listened to the crackling fire and gazed dreamily at her roses, drawing strength and peace from their fragrant beauty as she nervously anticipated the arrival of the two mysterious strangers who had promised they would come.

Chapter Five

Unloved, Unwanted and Orphan

Just as the twilight shadows from the mountains reached Aidan's yard, two bent figures dressed in dark clothes came to her gate and opened it. As they entered her rose garden, she sprang up from the window seat and raced to the door, flinging it open for them. The strangers stared at her coldly, their faces like masks of stone as Aidan greeted them breathlessly, hoping her smile would hide her nervous excitement.

"Come in," she invited eagerly, "please, come in. Oh, I'm so glad you've come! I have a meal all prepared and a room all ready for you."

The two women nodded to her but neither spoke nor smiled as they stepped through the doorway.

When they passed by her, Aidan was startled to see that there was a small child walking between them, so quiet and frail that he was almost lost in their black wool skirts.

As she managed to get a good look at him, she saw that the pathetic little boy was barefoot and dressed in dusty ragged clothes. In one arm he clutched a filthy baby blanket to his chest. His thin face was streaked with dirt beneath matted and tangled brown hair. He looked up at Aidan with huge dark eyes and then quickly turned away, seemingly more sad than afraid.

"Why, who is this?" Aidan asked.

One of the women looked absently down at the child, almost as though she had forgotten he was clinging to her skirt, and then turned back to Aidan.

"His name is Orphan, and he almost always travels with us."

Upon hearing the child's unusual name, Aidan stared at him, suddenly filled with fearful tension. She looked back up at the woman.

"Was he with you this morning? I don't remember seeing him."

"Yes," the woman answered, "he was with us, but he kept himself hidden so he wouldn't be seen in the darkness. Orphan is very shy. He almost always hides from people."

Aidan took a deep breath and smiled graciously, comforting herself with the thought that she herself would soon be an orphan no longer. After all, these women were going to tell her where she could find her mother. Very soon she would be able to leave Hidden and go home!

"Well," she told them cheerfully, "he is more than welcome here. I will make room for Orphan too. Come rest by my fire and warm yourselves, and we shall have supper in a few minutes."

With that, she closed the door. She held out her hands to take their shawls and they removed them, revealing stiff dark grey blouses tucked into their black skirts.

Aidan had a sudden peculiar but definite impression that her guests were somehow devoid of all color. It was almost as though they had carried the mountain shadows inside with them, as though they were somehow wrapped in wraithlike darkness that had obscured everything about them into hazy twilight. Even their eyes seemed colorless, a dark shade of grey that looked black against their pale cheerless faces.

Now that she could see them clearly, Aidan noticed that they had strong hard features set into identical gaunt faces that were etched with deep lines. Their streaked grey hair was pulled back into tight braided coils pinned up at the backs of their necks. As she took their heavy shawls and hung them on pegs by the door, she thought her guests must be twins.

Moving with surprising strength and grace, the two old women crossed the front room and settled themselves into the chairs by the fireplace. There was something about the way they carried themselves that made it seem as though they had been living there for a long time and were coming into their own home.

Orphan clung to the skirt of the woman who had told Aidan his name, and when they took their seats he sat down on the braided rug between them. He hugged his tattered blanket tightly and kept his face buried in heavy black wool, never saying a single word. The two sisters were also silent as they sat warming themselves by the pleasantly crackling fire.

Aidan could feel her heart pounding. Quickly smoothing her apron, she hurried to the hearth and perched herself on the edge of Aunt Mara's old rocking chair.

"I'm so glad you've come," she told the women again, not knowing how to begin. "I must confess that until I met you this morning I'd never seen an outsider in Hidden – and I've never had a guest come and stay in my home. Please tell me your names."

One of the women turned to look at her and quietly replied, "My name is Unloved, and my sister's name is Unwanted."

At the sound of her guests' strange names, Aidan felt the blood drain from her face.

"Where are you from?" she asked them nervously.

Unloved looked at Unwanted and then back to Aidan before she replied.

"We haven't come far. In fact, we're from very near you, nearer than you know."

Aidan was puzzled by this cryptic statement.

"Have you come into Hidden from the place where I was born?"

"No," Unloved answered. "We've traveled much since your birth. We travel a great deal, you see."

"But we know the place very well," Unwanted added. "There are few places we do not know well."

"And my mother," Aidan said eagerly. "You said you know my mother, too. Please, as I told you this morning, I'm longing to know anything you can tell me about her – everything you know. You do know her, don't you?"

"Oh, yes," Unloved said. "We knew her before she was born."

Aidan's hands trembled with eager excitement. "What is she like? Where does she live?"

Unloved's face looked harsh in the dim firelight.

"She lives in a place very far from here, far across the mountains. A place – not of this land."

Aidan's mouth dropped open and she quickly placed her hand over her lips. She had never even imagined that her mother might be in a foreign country.

When at last she found her voice, she said, "A place not of this land – not in Davarius? Do you mean to say that she is – that I am – a foreigner?"

At that Unloved's dark eyes flashed sharply.

"You are of *this* land," she answered firmly. "You were born in the Kingdom of Davarius and this is the land where you truly belong. But she who bore you is not of this land."

"Then – then what land is she from? Where is she now?"

When the sisters hesitated before answering, Aidan began to pour out her heart to them in desperation.

"My mother – where can I find her? Oh, please, I simply must find out where she is. You see, I don't have any family or friends here. I'm a stranger here, all alone, and I want to leave Hidden to find my family. Can you help me find her?"

Unloved shook her head firmly. "No. We cannot do that."

At their reply, Aidan felt both confused and dismayed.

"Oh, but – but you said you know my mother. You're the only ones I have ever met who have told me such things. Please, *please* – you must help me. I have to find my family!"

The two women were silent for a long frustrating moment.

Finally, speaking slowly as though she were choosing her words very carefully, Unwanted replied, "We are allowed to tell you certain things that we know about your past. However, we have been warned not to tell you where your mother was born or where she is now. Our Master has strictly forbidden this."

Aidan shook her head in complete bewilderment.

"Your – your Master? I don't understand."

"Our Master is the one who sent us here, and we are his servants," Unwanted explained. "He has given us work to do, and we must be about his business."

"And – and your Master told you not to tell me where my mother lives?" Aidan asked, confused. "Who is your Master? How does he know of my mother – or me?"

The sisters were again maddeningly silent. Flickering firelight cast eerie shadows across their stony faces.

Finally in frustration Aidan asked, "What *can* you tell me about my mother? You told me you had much to tell me. Is she – is she still alive?"

Unloved nodded. "Yes, she is alive."

"She is alive," Aidan whispered, hope filling her heart at last. "What is she like? Why did she give me away when I was a baby? How did I come to live here in Hidden?"

The sisters hesitated as they seemed to consider how to answer Aidan's many questions. Then Unloved told her, "You have both a mother and a father."

Aidan stared with breathless anticipation at Unloved's dark face. At last she was hearing words she had longed to hear all her life, and she took them in with desperate eagerness, as one who was dying of thirst would drink cup after cup of fresh water.

"But your father has never known you," Unloved continued. "He never knew your mother had conceived, and he knows nothing about you to this day. By the time your mother knew she was going to have his child, your father had already left her, and he never returned."

The fire popped and crackled just then and her dark eyes glittered.

"She was very young – younger than you are now – and they were not married."

This news was an immense shock, for Aidan had never before considered such a thing.

"Not married!" she whispered. "Do you mean to say that I was – I am – a bastard? Illegitimate?"

From the folds of Unwanted's skirt, Orphan peeked out at Aidan with his round mournful eyes. Unwanted reached down and absently stroked his matted hair. He silently laid his head against her knee.

"Yes," answered Unloved. There was no trace of sympathy or understanding in her cold voice. "You are a bastard, and your mother's indiscretion would have been a tremendous disgrace to her family had they known. When she realized she was with child, she was afraid to tell her father. So she left her country and went to visit a relative who was living here, in the Kingdom of Davarius. She intended to have her baby in complete secrecy so her family would never find out."

Unwanted added, "You were born in a town here in the mountains. This Kingdom is the place of your birth. This is the land where you truly belong."

"A town here in the mountains," Aidan repeated, eager to know more. "What is the name of this town? Where is it? How can I go there?"

Unwanted ignored her questions.

"You must understand, Aidan, your mother was trapped in a very difficult situation. Fortunately, her relative was an elderly invalid who was sympathetic to her plight. She promised to help your mother and gave her a place to stay and have her baby. In exchange your mother helped take care of her."

"Soon after you were born," Unloved added, "the relative took ill quite suddenly and died, and your mother was told that she could no longer stay in her house. Her situation was quite desperate and she had no idea of what to do. To return to her own land and go back to her father's house with you – this terrified her. She knew it would be a very difficult journey and that her family would never forgive her for what she had done. It seemed impossible for her to return."

Unwanted broke in to continue the story. "Right at that time, as good fortune would have it, some old family friends happened to be traveling through the town where your mother was staying. They took pity on her and offered to help her and take you off her hands. They even gave her a generous amount of money so she could go back home. Your mother was most grateful. She was very eager to gain her life back and be free again."

"No," Aidan whispered. "Oh, no."

Hearing this part of the story was devastating. Tears welled in her eyes as she struggled to accept what the women were telling her.

"So – so you're saying she never wanted to keep me, then. She was glad to give me away to her friends. She didn't really care – she just wanted to get rid of me."

"Yes," Unloved said, again without sympathy. "She was relieved and very happy to give you away. So she wrapped you in a blanket and laid you in a large basket and handed you over to her friends, and they gave her the money for the journey home. That same day, your mother left to go back to her own land. Her family never discovered her secret."

"Her friends were on their way to Hidden," Unwanted added, "so they took you that very night and left you here on Mara Teague's doorstep."

At that, Unloved turned to Unwanted and said, "Sister, I believe Aidan already knows this part of the story."

Aidan was taking their words into her broken heart with great difficulty, fighting to keep her tears from spilling over onto her face.

"Yes," she whispered, "I know all about being left in a basket on a doorstep."

She stared again at Unloved and Unwanted and the child Orphan with them, filled with dread as she suddenly understood why her heart had leapt with that strange feeling of recognition when she had first seen them in the morning shadows of the street.

"Yes. I have always known that I am – an orphan. And I well know that I am – unloved and unwanted."

Unloved nodded.

"Yes, we've known you since before you were born."

"And we've known your mother since before she was born," Unwanted added.

Aidan wiped her eyes with the back of her hand. "But – but my mother must have been loved and wanted. She had a family."

"Yes, she did," Unwanted said. "But even those with families are sometimes as unloved and unwanted as Orphan here."

Another long silence fell between them. Unwanted was still stroking Orphan's hair. As Aidan looked at his sad countenance she noticed that he seemed to cling desperately to her, hungry for her touch. There was a tormented look in his eyes, as though he were cursed with an unspeakable yearning for love that was never satisfied – a yearning that she herself knew only too well.

There was so much more Aidan needed to know and now her questions began to flow like a torrent.

"What else can you tell me about my mother? What is she like? Is she pretty? Where is she now?"

Unloved and Unwanted returned her queries with such hard and cold expressions that Aidan felt like she had suddenly run into a stone wall.

"We can tell you nothing more of her," Unloved replied, her voice now harsh. "All that we are allowed to tell you, we have said."

"Our Master has forbidden us to speak of where she is now," Unwanted added.

"But – but –" Aidan was completely bewildered by their abrupt reply. "Then why have you come to me when you can't tell me everything I need to know?"

When they did not answer right away, she persisted.

"How did you know my mother? You told me you were from very near here. Are you of this land? Or are you from my mother's land, and foreigners here yourselves?"

Unloved shook her head.

"We are not foreigners here. We are not foreigners in any land."

Aidan was becoming quite irritated with these two cold intimidating women and was completely frustrated by their cryptic answers. Looking down into her lap, where her fists were tightly closed from tension, she breathed deeply and tried to make sense of all they were telling her.

Conflicting emotions churned within her. She was grateful to learn the truth at long last, but she was also overcome with shame, anger and grief at hearing the circumstances of her birth. The thought that her mother had abandoned her so eagerly when offered her freedom was more than she could bear. The tears she had been fighting began to spill over and flow down her cheeks.

As they fell, she quickly unclenched her fists and raised her hands to her face to brush them away. The sight of her hands opening and tears falling against them suddenly brought to her mind a picture of a rose unfolding to the soft touch of warm raindrops. She stared at her open hands for a brief second, then wiped her face, refusing to let go of the dreams she had clung to for so long.

Determined to convince the two women to help her, she looked back up at her guests, pushing away her fears and meeting their gaze.

"If everything you say is true," she said quietly, "then you can help me find my mother. You can take me to the place where she is now. You've been there, you've traveled to many places, so you know the way. I know you know where she is. I want you to take me there."

"We cannot do that," Unloved quickly replied.

"Aidan," Unwanted said impatiently, "you must remember that your mother chose to give you away so that she could return to her father's house. You must realize that she was much younger then, a child herself trying unsuccessfully to care for a child. She left you behind and went home to make a new life for herself. How can you possibly think that she will want you now, some seventeen years later?"

"My mother *will* want me!" Aidan cried stubbornly. "If I were to search for her, if I were to find her, then I just know she would see how much I long for her and she would take me back. I *need* her. She is all I have in this world, my only hope – don't you see? Oh, *surely* you can understand how I feel! I believe, I *have* to believe, that deep in her heart she really did love me and was sorry she couldn't keep me. If I could find her and tell her I love her even though she had to give me away, I just know she would take me back with joy. We would both be happy together at last. I believe this with all my heart!"

The sisters just stared at Aidan in cold silence.

"You have no idea how much I need to find her," Aidan pleaded. "You *must* tell me where she is – you simply *must* take me to her. If it's money you want, I have some saved. I'll give you everything I have! I beg of you, *please* – help me find my mother!"

"We cannot," Unloved said again in a firm voice. "We are not here to do your bidding, only the Master's."

"Our Master has given us certain work to do here," Unwanted added. "We must obey him, for we are here only to do as he commands. We are not permitted to take you out of Hidden, nor to allow you to leave."

Dumbfounded, Aidan stared at her guests.

"What do you mean, you're not permitted to take me out of Hidden or to allow me to leave?" she demanded. "I can leave Hidden whenever I please, and no one can stop me! Just what *is* your work here? What kind of a Master would force his servants to walk so far through the mountains with no baggage and a barefoot child at your heels? What work has he given you to do here – and what has it to do with me?"

The firelight cast flickering shadows across the sisters' faces as Unloved spoke.

"Our Master has sent us here to live with you in your house for a time."

"Sent you here to live with me!" cried Aidan in amazement. "But why? Who would send anyone to live with me from another place I've never seen? How does your Master even know who I am? Just who *is* this Master of yours?!"

Unwanted answered her in a deathly quiet voice that sent a chill through the room.

"We are servants of the Dark Prince."

This news, more astounding than everything else she had heard, took Aidan's breath away.

"The Dark Prince! You – you've been sent to me by Prince Bal'Davarius?"

"The Dark Prince is our Lord and Master," Unloved said.

Aidan began to tremble.

"But why – but how – what could the Prince possibly want with me? How does he even know me? Why has he told you to stay here with me?"

"We are to live with you in your house until the work our Master has given us to do is finished," Unloved said. "He will be sending other servants to join us here as well."

"Others!" cried Aidan, her heart pounding. "But why? Who else will come? What does the Prince intend to do?"

"He has not revealed this to us," Unloved said.

Panic gripped Aidan's racing heart and she could hardly breathe. What had she done that the sovereign ruler of all the Kingdom knew about her in his palace somewhere far across the mountains?

"Who are the others who will come?" she pleaded. "When will they arrive? What are you going to do?"

Her chest tightened with dread as she imagined soldiers coming to arrest her and lock her away in prison.

"Please," she insisted urgently. "I must know, for I want to be ready."

"They will begin to arrive this very night," said Unwanted.

"Tonight!"

Aidan jumped to her feet, shaking uncontrollably.

"Who will come? What are their names? And how many? Can you at least tell me how many will come?"

"Many will come," Unwanted said, "but do not worry, Aidan. You have plenty of room for us here."

"But – but I have my work for Lady Fairhaven," Aidan protested. "I must go there in the morning – I work for her all day. Will I be able to go to the mansion? How can I have many guests here in my little cottage? Guests – from the Dark Prince himself!"

Suddenly Unloved leapt up from her chair and took a quick step forward. Her abrupt movement was so like Aunt Mara going into one of her rages that Aidan gasped and cringed in horror, instinctively covering her face with one arm. Unloved reached out and grabbed her firmly by her other arm. Her surprisingly powerful grip was as strong as the piercing talons of a mountain eagle closing around its prey.

Aidan could only cry out helplessly in pain, fully expecting Unloved to start beating her, just as Aunt Mara had done so many times.

But Unloved did not raise her hand to strike. Instead, she spoke quietly but firmly in her harsh voice.

"You mustn't be afraid of our presence here, Aidan. We are going to help you sustain your life in this place. You shall see. The Master takes good care of his servants, I assure you, and he will take good care of you – as long as you cooperate with us."

Unwanted rose and stood behind her sister. In the dim light their faces were stony and threatening. Aidan cowered helplessly before them.

Suddenly her choked voice became that of a terrified child.

"Don't hurt me!" she whimpered. "Oh, please, don't hurt me!"

Unloved held firmly to Aidan's arm.

"No one will hurt you if you do exactly as we tell you. We shall need to come and go as we please, since we have a great deal of work to attend to for our Master. You have said you would give us everything you have in exchange for our help. The only thing we require of you is the key to your house."

She thrust out her other hand, waiting for Aidan to put the key into it.

Bewildered, her heart pounding wildly in her ears, Aidan stared at Unloved's shadowed face and outstretched hand. Beneath the old woman's talon grip her arm was beginning to go numb.

"The key to my house?" she repeated.

She was horrified at the mere idea that she should give these strangers the key to her cottage and allow them – and who knew how many others like them – to have free access to all that belonged to her.

If their Master really was Prince Bal'Davarius, the Sovereign Lord of all the Kingdom, he could surely provide them with whatever they needed to do his work, even lodging at the town inn.

Why should they need the key to her house?

The sisters were waiting silently for her reply, their faces cold and hard as mountain ice.

Why had the Prince ordered them to stay with her? What did they plan to do? Could they be trusted?

For the briefest of seconds Aidan's heart swelled with a surge of unexpected courage and determination, and she actually opened her mouth to refuse and tell them to get out of her house. But that impulse faded as quickly as it came.

These women were her only link to her mother, tenuous though it was. If they were staying in her house, she might yet be able to find out what she desperately needed to know.

And all the while running through the back of her mind was the chilling fear that if she were to turn them away or refuse to comply with their demands, their Master the Dark Prince might send soldiers to arrest her – to lock her into a tiny prison cell – or even, perhaps, to kill her.

It was all too much for her to bear. Weary now from her fears but completely trapped by their hold over her, she knew she really had no recourse but to give them the key. Yet still she hesitated.

"What does the Prince want with me?" she moaned. "Is he himself coming here?"

Impatiently Unloved replied, "I do not know if the Master is coming. But if he does, he shall be most displeased if he finds you haven't obeyed his orders, for he is Bal'Davarius, the Dark Prince, the Lord and Master of all the Kingdom."

Relentlessly she tightened her grip on Aidan's arm and pushed her other hand closer to her face. Her voice became insistent, filled with threatening urgency.

"The key, Aidan. You must give us the key."

Aidan gasped in pain and helpless terror, knowing she had no choice. Trembling, she reached into her apron pocket and drew out the key to her front door.

"Very well," she whispered meekly, and held it out to Unloved. "Here is the key. Take it."

Unloved's dark grey eyes glittered with triumph.

She quickly snatched the key from Aidan's shaking hand, at the same time releasing her grip and roughly shoving her away.

Aidan began to fall backwards and cried out in panic. She managed to grab hold of the rocking chair to steady herself, but her legs were shaking so badly they collapsed beneath her. As she sank unhurt to the floor she stared up at the two old women, wondering what they would do to her now.

Without a word of thanks or a moment's hesitation, Unloved slipped the key into a pocket hidden in a fold of her skirt.

"Our fellow servants will begin arriving tonight, as we told you," Unwanted said. "You will provide all of us with lodging here until our Master's work in your house is done."

"Go on about your business as usual," Unloved commanded, "and we shall go on about ours."

The two old women settled back down into their chairs. Orphan took hold of Unwanted's skirt again and rested his head on her lap. She began stroking his hair as she had before.

Tears streamed down Aidan's face as she rubbed at the red welts left on her arm by Unloved's talon grip. She put her head down into her hands and sobbed helplessly.

At last she lifted her face, wiping her tears away with her apron. She drew in several deep breaths and fought to regain her composure. Her three mysterious guests were sitting silently, gazing into the fire as though nothing unusual had ever happened.

Now that they had the key to her house, there was nothing more she could do but be as gracious a hostess to them as possible until she could find out what Prince Bal'Davarius wanted with her.

Very slowly Aidan pulled herself to her feet and gestured toward the dining room.

"I have prepared a nice meal for us," she told her guests. "Please, come to my table and eat."

Chapter Six

Fear

Late that night after the fire downstairs had dwindled to embers, Aidan lay wide awake in her bed staring up at the ceiling in the darkness. Cold silvery moonlight coming through the window cast diamond-shaped shadows across the room from panes of leaded glass. Her ears strained to hear any sound in the silence, painfully aware that her mysterious guests were right across the hall in Aunt Mara's old room. As she shivered beneath heavy layers of quilts, unable to get warm, her mind was tormented with fears and unanswered questions.

How did Prince Bal'Davarius know of her? What did he want with her? Why was he sending his servants to live in her house? Who else would be coming? Would they all be as harsh and frightening as Unloved and Unwanted?

And what did it mean that they were not going to let her leave Hidden? Would she ever be able to find her mother?

Weary from trying to focus in the pale darkness, Aidan tossed and turned. Finally she pulled the covers over her head and closed her eyes. Sleep came at last, but it was light and restless and filled with dreams about strange old women in black shawls.

She had no idea how long she had been asleep when she woke with a sudden start and bolted upright. Her body was rigid and her heart pounding as she pulled the quilts protectively around herself. For a long moment she sat frozen in the darkness, listening intently, certain she had heard a noise downstairs.

Summoning all her courage, she slipped out of bed and tied her robe tightly around herself. Cautiously she opened her bedroom door and stepped into the hall.

Aunt Mara's door was closed. The house was silent and still.

But she could see warm golden light at the end of the hall by the front staircase. The shadow of the railing flickered across the whitewashed wall.

Someone had lit a fire in the front room below.

Hardly daring to breathe, Aidan slowly walked to the stairs. Halfway down she crouched and peered through the railing.

Someone was sitting in Aunt Mara's old rocking chair by the hearth.

Her knees shaking beneath her, Aidan carefully descended to the foot of the stairs and silently entered the front room. She could only see the back of her new guest's head but she could tell it was a dark-haired woman.

The stranger immediately sensed another presence behind her and rose gracefully to her feet. She didn't seem startled in the least and moved as though she had been expecting someone.

The black wool cape draped around the woman's shoulders was so long it almost brushed against the braided rug. As she turned around it opened slightly and beneath it Aidan caught a glimpse of a silvery blue dress. Before the cape closed and covered it again, the pale fabric seemed to shimmer with a light all its own, as cold and smooth as mountain ice shining in the winter sun.

Tall and willowy, her countenance reserved and unsmiling, the woman offered no greeting. The hood of her cape had been pulled back so that it rested on her shoulders, revealing soft waves of the blackest hair Aidan had ever seen. Dark curls framed a hauntingly beautiful face flawlessly sculpted with delicate features and smooth pale skin drawn taut over high cheekbones. Framed by thick black lashes, her mesmerizing eyes were pale silvery blue, the same icy color as her shimmering dress.

Aidan froze, unable to tear her own eyes away from the woman's intent gaze. Her heart was suddenly seized by overwhelming dread. Every one of her instincts was sounding alarm, screaming at her to turn and run, but all she could do was stand there rigidly still, unable to speak, staring in overpowering fascination at the indescribable beauty of the woman standing before her.

Despite the blazing fire, a mysterious arctic chill began to seep beneath her threadbare robe and sink into her very bones. A cold wind suddenly rippled through the room, opening the woman's heavy black cape so that it billowed out all around her. The silvery dress was now plainly visible but Aidan barely noticed it, for something else arrested her attention. She gasped in horror.

For staring out at her from the darkness beneath the cape were eyes, perhaps a hundred pairs of them – pale icy blue eyes, intense and frightening.

The stranger's aloof manner never changed. She seemed completely unconcerned by the breeze and the movement of her cape. Calmly she looked down and pulled it back around herself with graceful gestures of her long slender hands.

Finding her voice at last, Aidan stammered, "You must be here to join Unloved and Unwanted. Have you – have you been sent to me by Prince Bal'Davarius?"

"I have," the woman replied. "I am Fear."

Aidan shuddered at the woman's name. So this was Fear. Now she understood the chill in the room and the pounding of her heart and her instincts clamoring to flee. She wondered how Fear had entered her house, but then she remembered she had given the key to Unloved and Unwanted.

"I am Aidan, but I suppose you know who I am already," she said.

"Yes, I know you, Aidan," Fear said.

"Are there – are there others beneath your cape?"

"Yes. My children are with me. I have many children, but you know almost all of them already."

"I know them? But – but I haven't met you before."

"Oh, but you have, Aidan," Fear said quietly. "You know us very well. And we also know you very well."

Aidan was too afraid to ask her new guest what she meant by that. She wondered how many children Fear had.

There was a moment of awkward silence between them. Then Aidan asked, "Have you also known me from my mother's womb, as Unloved and Unwanted have?"

"No. We have known you from your early youth, but not from the womb."

"Do you know my mother?" Aidan asked hopefully. "Can you tell me anything about her?"

Fear smiled coldly.

"Oh, yes, I know your mother. Really, there are very, very few people with whom I'm not intimately acquainted. But I'm not allowed to tell you anything about your mother. The Master didn't send me to you because of her. My work here is with you and you alone."

Again, Aidan was too frightened to ask what she meant.

"We'll be staying with you for awhile, as I believe you know," Fear continued.

"Yes," Aidan sighed, "and I know that you're here because your Master has given you work to do in my house. And I'm to provide lodging for you until that work is done."

Fear's eyes sparkled as she laughed. "You learn very quickly, Aidan."

Aidan glanced away from Fear to the warm dancing fire behind her. Then she noticed the time on the mantel clock.

"It's so late," she said wearily, trying to be gracious. "You must be very tired from traveling. I know I'm supposed to give you lodging, but I must confess I have very little room in my house for guests."

"Don't trouble yourself about us," Fear said. "My children and I have been traveling together near and far since long before you were born. We've lodged in some very small houses, and even the least accommodation will be more than enough, I assure you. And we aren't even tired just yet. We're accustomed to staying up very late, often all night. We'll be content to sit here by the fire awhile longer."

"Of course," Aidan replied. "You may sit here as long as you like. When you wish to go to bed, there is a room –"

Fear interrupted her with a graceful wave of her hand.

"I'll find it. I know the place where my children and I belong in your house."

At that Aidan shuddered.

"Of course you do," she said meekly.

With a derisive smile Fear said, "I can see that you're very tired. Please, don't let me keep you awake. We'll have plenty of time to become better acquainted in the days to come."

"I'm sure we will," Aidan agreed softly. "Good night to you, Fear. I'll see you tomorrow, then."

"Good night, Aidan."

Grateful to be away from her disturbing new guest, Aidan hurried up the stairs and latched her door firmly before climbing back into bed. She huddled under the quilts in the darkness, unable to escape the chill she had felt downstairs. Too tense to sleep, she again strained to hear every sound in the night.

The diamond shapes of silvery moonlight cast across her bedroom wall from the window now reminded her of a shimmering dress and hundreds of pale eyes staring out from the shadows of a black cape.

She couldn't stop wondering about Fear's children. What were they like? How many were there?

And how could it be that she already knew them all?

Chapter Seven

Fear Of Being Hurt

In the early morning darkness Aidan pulled herself out of bed with extreme difficulty. Her guests were apparently still asleep, for the house was deathly quiet. She dressed quickly in one of her lovely blue work uniforms, tied on a clean white apron and pulled a scarf around her hair, tying it at the nape of her neck.

Slowly she opened her bedroom door and looked out into the dark hall. The other bedroom doors were closed. Carrying her shoes in her hand, she tiptoed silently down the back stairs in her stocking feet and cautiously peeked into the kitchen. To her relief, no one was there.

Even in the predawn stillness Aidan could feel the presence of her mysterious guests very strongly in her house. As she moved about in the dark shadows of the kitchen she had the distinct feeling that someone was watching her. Nervously she kept looking around and over her shoulder, but there didn't seem to be anyone there.

She quickly sliced and buttered two pieces of leftover bread from the night before and decided to eat her simple breakfast as she walked to the mansion. In vain she tried to convince herself she was only doing this because she was in a hurry, not because she was really afraid.

Aidan put her shoes on and headed through the dining room. Cautiously she looked into the main room. The fire had long gone out and no one was there either. Relieved, she grabbed her warm shawl and flung it around her shoulders as she raced out the door and down the flagstone path through her rose garden.

As Aidan hurried along the quiet streets in the grey light, eating her breakfast as she went, she was still plagued by the eerie feeling that she was not alone. Faint though they were, she didn't think she could be imagining the sound of light footsteps behind her. By the time she reached the cobblestones on the main street she was quite certain that someone was following her.

Her heart was racing with panic as she wondered who might be behind her. Was it a new servant of the Dark Prince who had come quietly in the night?

Finally she took a deep breath, gathered all her courage, and whirled around to see who it was. Her demand resounded against the buildings lining the street, abruptly breaking the morning stillness.

"Who are you?!"

To her great surprise, there was a tiny child walking right behind her.

The boy immediately gasped and jumped at her rough words, putting an arm up across his face as if to ward off a blow, and whimpered pathetically.

"Don't hurt me! Oh, please, don't hurt me!"

Her heart still pounding, Aidan softened quickly at the terrified child cringing before her. She crouched down and reached out her hand to him.

"I'm sorry – I'm so sorry – I didn't mean to frighten you," she said gently. "But you frightened me terribly."

The boy cowered away from her. His panicky round eyes were pale icy blue and his thin face was creamy white beneath thick curls of black hair. She knew at once that this must be one of Fear's children whose eyes beneath the black cape had horrified her the night before.

"Why are you walking behind me? Were you following me around in my house?"

"I'm with you almost all the time," the boy told her in his timid shaking voice. "I've been close to you from long ago, from when you were a small child."

"Are you one of Fear's children?" Aidan asked quietly, although she already knew that he was.

"Yes."

"What is your name?"

"Fear of Being Hurt," he replied softly.

For a long moment Aidan stared at her little companion. Fear of Being Hurt's eyes had the same mesmerizing effect on her that she had felt staring into his mother's eyes the night before.

"Of course," she whispered. "I should have known at once who you were."

She knew she would not be able to run away from him. Still, she couldn't take a child with her to the Fairhaven mansion.

Not knowing what to do, she told him, "You must go back to my house and stay with your mother."

Suddenly Fear of Being Hurt seemed to become bold.

"No," he replied firmly. "I must come with you, for I've been sent to you by my Master."

At that Aidan felt a shudder run down her spine. Wondering how she would ever explain this to anyone at the mansion, but seeing she apparently had no choice, she sighed.

"Very well then, but keep pace with me, for I'm quite late."

They hurried together out of the town and along the dirt road that wound up the grassy hill to the mansion. When they arrived at the main entrance, the huge heavy door was opened by Stewart, the Fairhavens' pompous butler, as it was every day.

"Good morning to you, Aidan," he greeted her coldly, not a trace of welcome in his haughty voice. "You are a bit late today."

"Good morning, Stewart," Aidan replied cheerfully, stepping inside. "Yes – I'm sorry, but it couldn't be helped."

"I see," he said drily.

Although he was a young man of small stature, the Fairhavens' butler surrounded himself with an air of grand self-importance, for he also attended Lord Fairhaven closely as his valet. He frequently bullied the household staff under his authority and Aidan knew they all resented this greatly. From what various servants had told her about him, Stewart was never seen dressed in anything other than his formal uniform – a black morning coat with tails, a grey waistcoat, a starched white shirt, and neatly pressed pinstriped trousers. Impeccably groomed, his hands were soft and perfectly manicured. His dark hair was always combed and slicked back with a shine to rival that of his patent leather shoes.

In an effort to keep herself from being intimidated by him, Aidan would smile each morning and greet Stewart just as brightly as she could, trying to win a smile from him in return. But from the beginning it was obvious that he just didn't like her, for he had never once smiled back or been friendly to her.

This morning was no different.

Standing imperiously with his back perfectly straight and his shoulders square, he looked down his long nose at her. Thankfully, he never once noticed Fear of Being Hurt, who was cowering behind her hidden in the folds of her skirt.

Sighing, Aidan asked, "Is Lady Fairhaven awake yet?"

"My Lord and Lady have just left for Clearview," he informed her crisply. "My Lord decided late yesterday to take care of some business at his mill, and as usual my Lady has gone with him."

Clearview was the next town over from Hidden and some distance away along the mountain trail. The Fairhavens owned a house and some businesses there and had gone away twice before that summer. Aidan greatly disliked taking orders from Stewart while they were gone, for he seemed to enjoy giving her heavy unpleasant work to do. But she was especially disappointed this time, for she was anxious to talk to Lady Fairhaven about the events of the night before and tell her about her disturbing guests from Prince Bal'Davarius.

"Oh, I see," she said. "How long will they be gone?"

He answered her question in his usual condescending tone.

"They are not expected back for several days, and as always you are to follow my orders precisely as long as they are gone." He cleared his throat lightly as though for emphasis. "This morning Lady Fairhaven has told me that once your tasks are finished you are free to leave early. For some reason she felt she shouldn't detain you in the mansion for the full day. She seemed to think you had some kind of important business you might want to take care of at home."

Aidan ignored his obvious prying to find out what her important business was.

"I see," she said again. "And what did she want me to do today?"

"She is leaving to your discretion whether or not any care is needed in the rose garden, but she does ask that you work in the west wing as usual dusting and polishing her instruments." Stewart paused, then added firmly, "Just be sure that you take great care not to harm them."

"Of course I won't harm them!" Aidan replied indignantly. "I'm always very careful – I dust them every day!"

Taken aback at her outburst, Stewart scowled angrily. His eyes flashed with annoyance as he looked down his nose at her.

"Indeed!" he scoffed. "Well, then, after you have dusted the instruments – but not harmed them! – see that you scrub the floors thoroughly! And when you next report for work, do make sure to arrive on time!"

With that, he turned and Aidan glared at him as he stalked away.

Fear of Being Hurt followed along behind her as she gathered cleaning supplies and climbed the grand marble staircase to the second floor of the west wing. He was always near her while she worked, close by but keeping well out of her way. In fact, he kept well out of sight altogether, blending into shadows and hiding behind furniture and drapes, careful not to let himself be seen. Aidan watched his behavior and began to understand why she had not seen him earlier that morning at home before leaving for work.

It wasn't long before she began to feel great pity for the poor little boy. At one point, as he bolted into a corner to hide, she smiled and tried to reassure him.

"Fear of Being Hurt, really, it will be all right for you to be in the mansion as long as you stay with me and don't touch anything. Nothing is going to hurt you. There isn't anyone else here in the west wing but the two of us."

But Fear of Being Hurt made no reply and stayed hidden, so quiet and still Aidan herself could hardly tell he was in the room with her. He seemed so overwhelmingly afraid that she could not help but wonder why he had come with her at all.

What possible work could the Dark Prince have given this tiny frightened child to do in her life?

Yet as the hours wore on, the presence of Fear of Being Hurt made Aidan increasingly nervous. Every time there was a noise he whimpered and cowered, making her jump too, wondering what had frightened him so. This went on all morning until she found herself becoming startled at every noise and constantly looking over her shoulder.

There was something disturbingly familiar about this fear.

Deep in her heart Aidan began to understand that the little boy had been telling her the truth that morning on the cobblestone street. Although she couldn't understand it at all and had never seen him before, she somehow knew that Fear of Being Hurt had indeed been her constant companion from her early childhood.

By late morning Aidan had almost finished in the rooms where Lady Fairhaven kept her large collection of antique musical instruments. Aidan always marveled that her employer knew how to play them all, although most of the time she only worked on a few of her favorites.

Over the course of the summer she had told Aidan the names of all her instruments and had demonstrated each one for her. Some of them were most fascinating, such as the droning hurdy-gurdy and the lively hammered dulcimer, but she had only ever heard those played a few times when Lady Fairhaven was in the mood. Most of the others were more familiar and played quite frequently. Aidan especially loved the gentle lute, which was kept on a carved wooden stand next to a tufted velvet chair, and the finely crafted harpsichord, which was prominently displayed at one end of the largest music room.

Near a tall window in one corner of a smaller room stood the most impressive instrument in the collection and the one Aidan loved most of all – the great mahogany concert harp. This was Lady Fairhaven's special pride and joy, and Aidan noticed she smiled affectionately whenever she walked into the room and saw it.

Before they were married, Lord Fairhaven had commissioned the harp as his wedding gift to her. Aidan could only imagine the joy Lady Fairhaven must have felt as a bride to receive such a precious gift from her new husband. As she observed the Fairhavens together every day in the mansion it was clear to Aidan that they were still deeply in love even after many years of marriage.

The pillar of the harp was crowned by a small sculpture of the two of them as a bride and groom, making the gift a wedding portrait as well as a beautiful instrument. Lady Fairhaven had pointed out to Aidan that the bride's wedding gown was an exact copy of the gown she had actually worn, down to the last small detail. The craftsman had depicted the young Lord and Lady smiling warmly at each other, their tiny fingers entwined together in an intimate gesture around a finely detailed sprig of oak leaves and acorns. Around their feet was a carved circle of life-sized oak leaves and acorns which formed the head of a garland that spiraled all the way down the pillar to the foot of the harp.

Inlaid oak leaves and acorns made of several colors of rare and precious wood decorated the soundboard of the harp on either side of the strings. Delicately accented with subtle lines of gold, this colorful inlay had been so skillfully crafted that although the wood was perfectly flat and smoothly polished, the oak leaves and acorns looked as though they had been carved in deep relief and were emerging from the wooden surface.

The sturdy majestic oak tree was the central image of Lord Fairhaven's family crest and had been the symbol of his ancestral line for hundreds of years. It was therefore most significant that images of its leaves and acorns had been incorporated into the wedding harp. The gift had been meant to welcome his new bride into his heritage with the blessings of strength and fruitfulness to carry on the Fairhaven legacy and prominence.

But tragically, despite their love and his blessing, Lady Fairhaven had never been able to produce an heir to continue the family name.

Nothing in the mansion fascinated Aidan more than the harp, both to look at and to listen to. Its soft and soothing music was more beautiful than anything she had ever heard. As she carefully dusted the grand instrument day after day, she could only wonder how Lady Fairhaven must feel while playing it.

Working on the harp was a task she relished despite the tedious work needed to clean the deep crevices of the intricate carvings and to dust between the strings. The smooth wood of the sounding board was glorious beneath her hands and she loved making it shine. She had polished all the instruments in the music rooms many times, but just being allowed to touch the harp gave her the greatest joy.

How Aidan longed to be able to make music herself! This was a privilege she greatly coveted, but she knew it would never be within her grasp. She could never work up the courage to ask Lady Fairhaven if she could try playing the harp. Indeed, she never dared to deliberately cause any of the instruments to make a sound.

Today, however, she knew that the Fairhavens were away, and she was certain that no other servants were presently in the west wing. She and Fear of Being Hurt, who was crouched in a corner out of sight, were the only ones anywhere around. Gazing longingly at the pattern of oak leaves and acorns on the sounding board, she ran her fingers lightly along the smooth polished wood inlay. Then, impulsively, she reached up and gently stroked the strings, going from the highest to the lowest notes.

The wonderful sounds which emanated from the harp were as warm and golden as the brilliant sunlight streaming through the tall windows. Her heart pounding, Aidan glanced around nervously. Then, feeling bolder, she reached out again and plucked the strings with her fingertips in the same way she had seen Lady Fairhaven play them. She tested each of the strings one by one, marveling at their tones. The highest notes were bright and crystalline and the lowest notes were rich and resonant.

An unexpected laugh rose up from her throat. Indulging in this forbidden pleasure filled her with an intense joy she had never before experienced. She eagerly drank in the melodic vibrations of the strings as though something deep in her soul that had been dying of thirst was suddenly coming alive. Before long she was lost completely in making gentle music with the harp.

Suddenly a noise startled her and brought her back to herself.

Aidan looked across the room and saw Fear of Being Hurt stepping timidly out of the corner from behind the heavy window drape where he had been huddled. Beckoned out of hiding by the music, he began walking toward her, staring at the beautiful harp in wonder.

But something was terribly wrong. She froze in horror.

Somehow the child's appearance had completely changed.

His thin wide-eyed face had mysteriously been transformed into a perfect mirror image of her own: waves of auburn hair, blue-green eyes, slight freckles, even light smudges of dust on the cheeks and forehead.

Aidan gasped loudly, terrified by the unexpected sight of her own face looking back at her from the little boy's body. Fear of Being Hurt immediately panicked at her reaction. His body went rigid and he leapt like a startled deer back to his hiding place behind the curtain.

She whirled away from him, momentarily unable to breathe. Then, keeping her head down, she hastily finished dusting the harp, not daring to touch the strings again.

Had the music itself somehow caused the frightful vision?

Her face was hot and her heart was pounding from deep guilt and shame. It had been wrong of her, completely wrong, to play Lady Fairhaven's precious wedding harp. She had been wicked and evil even just to touch the strings, for she knew she could never be worthy of such a privilege. Making music was a pleasure she would never deserve.

Surely the vision had been the punishment for her deplorable infraction, the lesson she needed to be taught!

Aidan quickly moved to polish another instrument, working silently and industriously, careful not to bring forth a single note. She kept her eyes from looking at the corner where Fear of Being Hurt was hiding.

At last he peeked out from his hiding place. Aidan gathered all her courage to look at him and was relieved to see his pale face and black hair again. But she was still quite shaken from what she had seen, for she knew with absolute certainty that she hadn't imagined it.

Her work in the west wing finished and supplies put away, Aidan decided the rose garden could wait until another day, for all she wanted was to leave the mansion. Gratefully she stepped outside into the sunlight with Fear of Being Hurt staying close behind her as she headed down the hill into Hidden.

But after what had happened in the music room, she dreaded what she might find waiting for her at home.

Chapter Eight

Drudgery and Night Terrors

Fear of Being Hurt still at her heels, Aidan opened the door to her cottage and cautiously stepped inside. To her relief, everything seemed to be just as she had left it. She removed her shawl and hung it on a peg near the door.

A small fire was pleasantly crackling in the front room and it gave Aidan an unexpected feeling of being welcomed into her own house. She relaxed and walked over to the fireplace. Then she looked around more closely and saw that the front room had been swept and dusted. When she walked to the archway and looked into the dining room, she was surprised to see a clean tablecloth and a vase of freshly cut roses on the table. At that moment she realized that the house was filled with delicious aromas.

Someone had apparently been very busy all morning while she had been gone. But who would be cleaning her house and cooking?

Aidan turned to see that Fear of Being Hurt was standing by the front door watching her. Just then Fear came down the stairs, still dressed in her black cape and pale blue taffeta dress. When she reached the bottom the little boy hurried over to her.

"There you are," she greeted him, and with a loveless gesture swept her son beneath her cape.

"Hello, Fear. Has someone been cleaning and cooking today?" Aidan asked her.

"A new guest for you," Fear replied over her shoulder as she headed out the front door. "She arrived early this morning."

Aidan hurried to the kitchen. As she entered the warm room, the enticing smell of simmering stew made her realize how famished she was after her morning at work.

A tall slender woman was bending over a huge pot on the wood-burning cookstove, so preoccupied with stirring its fragrant contents that she didn't notice Aidan enter the kitchen. She moved very slowly, as though she were old and perhaps arthritic. Stringy light brown hair hung down her back from beneath a faded blue scarf. Her patched work dress was stained and grimy, but she had on a clean apron for cooking.

Just then the stranger became aware of someone behind her and turned around, meeting Aidan's gaze with wide hazel eyes. She didn't seem at all startled, but Aidan was quite surprised to discover that her new guest was really a very young woman whose plain round face was haggard and smudged with dirt. Her slow careworn movements made her seem much older than her years.

"Hello," Aidan said. "I am Aidan. Are you the one who has cleaned my house and lit the fire in the front room?"

"Yes," the newcomer said. "My name is Drudgery."

There was nothing about this guest that gave Aidan any kind of fright or concern, but upon hearing her name she felt a sense of weary resignation.

"Drudgery," she repeated. "I'm not surprised that you should have come to me. My entire life has been one of drudgery and hard work. Have you come from Prince Bal'Davarius too? I suppose you've known me since my youth, just like the others."

Drudgery smiled.

"Yes, I have. You've known me very well for most of your life. The Master has sent me to help you here in your house while we're lodging with you. I am to cook and clean for you."

This surprising news was most welcome. For the first time in two days Aidan felt a sense of relief that came close to joy.

"I thank you," she said gratefully, smiling at her newest guest.

"Our Master takes good care of his own," Drudgery told her.

"I've heard that before," Aidan said. "I suppose I'll be seeing it more as time goes by."

She looked at Drudgery's smudged face and thought that her hazel eyes were more green than any other color.

"You're most welcome here, Drudgery. Have you found a place to sleep?"

"Yes, I have," her guest answered. "We'll be having lunch before too long."

She turned back to the stew pot and stirred its contents with a large wooden spoon. Aidan noticed that her bony hands were rough and calloused.

The meal Drudgery had made was simple but just as delicious as the sumptuous noonday meals Aidan ate every day at the mansion. At her first bite of the savory stew she knew that the Dark Prince must have provided its ingredients, for meat was a luxury she could rarely afford. It tasted to her like it could be a dish fit for the Master himself.

As she ate heartily, thoroughly enjoying every bite after her morning of work, she tried to relax and make conversation with her guests, but they never spoke to her during the meal unless she asked them something. Even then, their cryptic replies completely frustrated her.

The only one Aidan felt she could like at all was Drudgery, yet she couldn't say why this was so, for her newest guest was just as quiet as the others.

Unloved and Unwanted sat together, their stony faces offering no clues as to what they were thinking. Little Orphan sat between them, totally silent. Aidan noticed that he only picked at his food.

Across the table from her, Fear had removed her dark cape and sat regally dressed in her pale blue gown eating her stew. Aidan cleared her throat, gathered all her courage, and asked, "Fear, where is Fear of Being Hurt and all of your other children?"

Fear looked up. Her icy stare made Aidan shiver.

"My children are here in your house. I shall give them their meal later."

"Why don't they just come and eat with us here?" Aidan asked. "There's plenty, I'm sure."

In a crisp voice, Fear told her, "My children are so many they wouldn't all fit at your table. In fact, they wouldn't all fit in this room. But don't concern yourself about my children, Aidan. They know where they belong in your house. They will eat later."

"Of course," Aidan replied meekly.

Fear went back to eating her stew. For a long moment Aidan watched her graceful movements and marveled at her flawless beauty. She wondered again how many children Fear had. Then she took a deep breath and turned to her other guests.

"Unloved, can you tell me how many more of your fellow servants will be coming and when I should expect them?"

Unloved scowled at her and answered sharply.

"I don't know who else will come or when they will arrive. That is up to the Master, and he hasn't told me."

"I see," Aidan said. "So the Prince hasn't really told you much about what you're all supposed to be doing here."

"We know very well what we are to do here," Unloved snapped. "The work our Master has given us is to stay here with you in your house for awhile."

"And how long will that be?" Aidan persisted.

The old woman's dark eyes glittered impatiently.

"We will leave your house when our work is finished and not a moment before. The Master's orders are very clear about that."

"I see," Aidan said again, then sighed in frustration and let the subject drop.

The meal was finished in uncomfortable silence.

Late that night pale moonlight shone through her bedroom window as it had the night before. Aidan again lay staring at the shadowy diamonds on the ceiling, exhausted but unable to sleep in her torment of unanswered questions. The house was deathly quiet and so still it seemed empty, but she felt the disturbing presence of her guests as though they were all right there in the room with her.

It had become clear to her by now that the servants of the Dark Prince were not ordinary people. Each of them had known her all her life – and each possessed some kind of strange power over her.

Breathing deeply, she fought hard against the surging panic that threatened to overwhelm her at the haunting memory of seeing her own face on the body of a small boy.

What could it all mean?

The next day was her day off from work. Her stomach knotted with tension as she anticipated spending the whole day at home with such intimidating company. She wondered who else would be arriving.

Suddenly, as if in answer, there was an abrupt movement in the darkness.

Aidan gasped and sat up, clutching the quilts to her chest, frozen with terror.

Someone really *was* in her bedroom with her!

But how could anyone have gotten in? The latched door had never opened, nor had the window.

"Who's there?" she demanded, her voice shaking.

The intruder stepped out of the shadows and stood over her bed.

In the dim light Aidan could see that he was an immense man whose clothes were so black it seemed he was wearing the darkness itself. A tall top hat shaded his eyes. All that was visible of his face was his black mustache and goatee that framed a glowing malevolent grin.

She cowered beneath the bedclothes, trying in vain to move away from him.

"Who are you? What do you want with me?! Don't come any closer!"

The huge man began to laugh softly, a wicked rumbling laugh filled with intense mockery. He seemed delighted at her fear of him.

"Are you – are you from the Prince?" she gasped.

The man answered in a deep voice that was slippery with evil.

"Yes, Aidan, I've been sent to you by the Master."

He moved still closer to her, a motion which seemed more of a glide than a step. He towered over her right beside the bed, now visible in the moonlight.

"But you already know me very well. I've spent many a night here by your bedside, often all night long. Yes, Aidan, I'm very close to your heart – your old dear friend."

Now Aidan could see he was wearing a tailored black suitcoat with a white silk ascot knotted at his throat. Draped around his shoulders was a shiny black cape and on his hands he wore soft white gloves.

She struggled for breath, fighting to keep from fainting dead away.

"Sir, I am certain that I don't know you."

In a deliberately sinister gesture he began tugging one by one at the fingers of his right glove, slowly pulling it from his hand.

"Ah, but you do know me, Aidan," he insisted softly. "Surely you recall that from the time you were a small child you would wake up in the night – from dreams."

Aidan felt the blood drain from her face.

"I've always had dreams," she whispered.

His grin showed his satisfaction at her answer.

"Yes, dreams, Aidan, terrifying dreams, paralyzing dreams that made you wake up screaming and sobbing. Dreams so frightening that you often fought to stay awake all night so I wouldn't come to you. But still I came – and when I did, you would dream my dreams."

She watched with trepidation as he slowly removed the other white glove just as he had the first and slipped them into a coat pocket.

"Yes, Aidan, look into your heart and you will see me there, for you know me very, very well indeed."

"Yes – I do know you," she whispered. "You are the one who brings me the dreams. You have come to me many times."

Frequent nightmares had plagued her for as long as she could remember. Now she understood for the first time that she was seeing the one responsible for them and she was filled with dread.

For she knew what he would do next.

The intruder laughed softly and leaned closer to her. He tipped his hat back on his head, revealing luminous green eyes that gleamed in the darkness.

"You see, you do know me, Aidan," he said softly. "I can see it in your eyes. Yes, you do remember your old friend Night Terrors."

"Night Terrors," she whispered. "So that is your name."

As he bent still closer, his low rumbling laugh was filled with wicked delight at the helpless way she cowered from him. The silken fabric of his cape was shining silvery in the moonlight. It slipped silently from his shoulder onto the bed like soft liquid darkness.

Something about the sight of the cape gripped Aidan's chest with sudden panic. She began crying hysterically, barely able to gasp out an incoherent plea.

"No – please, go away! I beg of you – oh, please, please – don't do this!"

At that, Night Terrors only laughed again, this time a cruel roaring that resounded like thunder and drowned out her final whimpered supplication.

"Don't hurt me! Oh, please, don't hurt me!"

In a move swifter than lightning, he pulled his cape from his shoulders and swept it through the air. It billowed out and seemed to stay floating above her for a long moment like a threatening storm cloud.

Aidan stared up at the cape in horror. Its black satin lining was glowing with vivid images, moving images that seemed to be alive. In the center was a little girl's terrified face – her face – surrounded by a jumble of scenes she remembered clearly from her very earliest nightmares.

She saw a filthy rag doll burning in a fireplace.

Apparitions emerging wraithlike from tall bottles.

Aunt Mara screaming, her face contorted with rage.

A leather belt writhing like a viper about to strike.

A slamming door shutting out the light.

And then the darkness. Suffocating, paralyzing darkness.

The silken black darkness of Night Terrors' cape.

Screaming, Aidan writhed beneath the quilts trying desperately to throw them off and escape, but in the next instant the cape fell upon her, constricting tightly around her like a snake and pinning her back into the pillows. She tried to cry out and fight against it but she was helplessly trapped.

The unbearable nightmare that she had experienced so many times began once again.

It started, as always, with a familiar tingling sensation at the back of her neck that quickly spread through her body into an icy paralysis, leaving her unable to move or speak. At the same time a rushing wind tore through the room, a gale more forceful than any mountain storm she had seen. Her body seemed to rise with the fierce wind and she was afraid it would send her crashing through the window. Night Terrors' cruel mocking laughter was so unearthly loud it could easily be heard even over the roar of the tempest.

Although no sound came from her mouth, in her heart Aidan was screaming for help, silently begging for someone, anyone, to come and save her from this enemy.

But no one could hear her – and she knew no one would answer.

The ordeal only lasted a few moments, but it seemed an eternity before Night Terrors finally pulled his cape away.

The fierce wind died away and she no longer felt like she was floating. The tingling sensation stopped and she found she could move and speak again, but her body was now completely drained of strength. She lay still against the pillows, heart pounding, breathing hard, wondering what her enemy would do now.

Still laughing, Night Terrors swept his cape around his shoulders. It settled against him in a fluid serpentine motion. Then all at once he stepped back into the shadows as quickly and mysteriously as he had come out of them and disappeared.

Aidan lay there trembling and crying, thankful he was gone but terrified he would come back. She had suffered from those paralyzing nightmares from her earliest memories. Now she knew for the first time that a servant of the Dark Prince had been the cause of them all along!

This realization was horrifying.

It meant that – like her other guests who had known her from long ago – Night Terrors was doing the work the Master had given him to do in her life.

Her nightmares had been ordained by Prince Bal'Davarius himself!

How did the Prince even know her? What did he want from her? What was going to happen to her?!

Suddenly she remembered the words Drudgery had spoken in the kitchen.

Our Master takes good care of his own.

Kind Drudgery had also been sent to her by the Dark Prince with work to do in her life – but her work cleaning and cooking was good.

How could all this be?

Goodness and evil from the same Master – it just didn't make any sense!

Aidan curled her body into a ball and pulled the quilts tightly around herself as she wept out her confusion and trauma.

"Why are these things happening to me?" she moaned. "What have I ever done to deserve all this? Oh, why did I ever give Unloved my key?!"

She brushed her tears away, shivering in the cold moonlight.

"There must be someone who can help me," she whispered into the darkness. "Can anyone free me from these wretched guests – my wretched life?"

But no answer came. The darkness was silent and still.

At last Aidan's head sank deep into the pillows and she fell into an exhausted dreamless sleep.

Chapter Nine

Gatekeeper and Grief

When Aidan awoke the next morning, she lay with her head under the covers for a long time, dreading the moment when she knew she must rise and greet the day. She was petrified that she would go downstairs and find Night Terrors at her table or in her front room. He had admitted, after all, that the Dark Prince had sent him to her, so she assumed that she must provide lodging for him. But her heart ached, wondering how long she must endure his nighttime visits, wishing she could be free of him.

It was only after a long time of hiding beneath the quilts from the day – and from her guests – that she finally, reluctantly, rose from her bed and got dressed.

But to her great relief, Night Terrors was not in the front room or in the dining room. Unloved and Unwanted were sitting by the fireplace talking quietly together. Orphan was sitting at Unwanted's feet, half wrapped in her skirts, just staring into the fire and hugging his blanket. Funny, Aidan thought, how she hardly ever noticed Orphan with them. He was so quiet she almost forgot he was there most of the time.

"Good morning, ladies," Aidan said, trying to sound cheerful.

"Good morning, Aidan," they replied. Neither of them smiled at her.

"How was your night?" Aidan asked.

Unloved nodded. "We slept well," she said.

After a brief moment's hesitation, Aidan decided to ask the sisters about her night visitor.

"Someone came to my room last night, and I was wondering if perhaps you could tell me anything about him. He is also one of your Master's servants – his name is Night Terrors. Do you know him? Have you seen him here this morning?"

Unwanted shook her head. "We know him, but we haven't seen him. He almost always stays out of sight in the daylight."

"Don't trouble yourself about Night Terrors," Unloved added. "He keeps to himself and travels alone. And he will only come to you at night."

"Yes," Unwanted agreed. "He will not harm you."

Aidan looked from one sister to the other.

"Please, ladies, can you tell me – why does he try to frighten me so?"

Unloved shrugged.

"It is just his way. It is the work the Master has given him to do in your house."

The impression Aidan always had of Unloved and Unwanted was that they knew something and were keeping it to themselves, and this conversation was no different. She eyed the two with suspicion.

"If your Master has sent this Night Terrors to me, then it must be that he is really the one who wants to frighten me. Why should this be so? What does Prince Bal'Davarius want with me?"

"The Master's plans are his own business and he has not told us what he intends for you," Unwanted answered impatiently. "We only know what he has told us to do here in your house. Don't trouble yourself about any of us. In the course of time you will understand our wise Master's purposes."

Aidan felt her face redden with frustration.

"How can you be so certain of this, if you don't know his plans?" she demanded.

Unloved and Unwanted offered no answer.

"I know you're hiding something from me. You were the first to come here, and I think you must know why your Master has sent any of his servants to me. If Night Terrors is to lodge with me, I simply can't bear it. If you know how I can keep him from staying here, please, you must tell me."

"You won't be able to keep any of us from lodging with you," Unloved said firmly. "The Master has sent us and we must do his bidding."

"And none of us is allowed to interfere with the work he has given another of his servants to do," Unwanted added. "The Master strictly forbids this."

Aidan sighed. Clearly there was no use trying to get anything more out of them.

"Will more guests arrive today?"

"I'm certain of it," Unloved said.

Aidan turned and headed for the kitchen to see if Drudgery was making breakfast. But just as she entered the dining room, there was a sharp rapping at the front door. As she turned around and went to open it, her stomach tightened with apprehension, wondering who was there.

To her surprise, she came face to face with an older gentleman standing on the step holding a large black valise.

Her newest guest was tall and slender, immaculately dressed in a dark grey morning coat with coordinating waistcoat, pin-striped trousers and a starched white shirt with a bow tie. Completing his formal outfit was a black bowler hat and a huge bright red carnation that fairly glowed from his lapel.

Aidan looked up into a long pleasant face with a beaked nose above a thick grey mustache waxed into twin elegant curls. His beady blue eyes were set beneath bushy grey eyebrows into folds of skin that crinkled as he looked down at her with a huge smile.

The gentleman put down the valise and with a gallant sweeping gesture removed his hat, displaying wisps of thin grey hair combed across his balding scalp. Holding the hat against his chest, he bowed slightly, snappily clicked the heels of his black patent leather shoes together, and introduced himself.

"A lovely good morning to you, Miss. My name is Gatekeeper."

Aidan liked this man's gracious manners at once and her dark mood quickly brightened.

"Good morning," she replied. "I am Aidan. Have you been sent to me by Prince Bal'Davarius?"

"I have indeed, Miss. Have you been expecting me?"

"Well – I am expecting guests, yes," she said, "but I'm afraid I didn't know that you personally were coming, Mr. – Gatekeeper, did you say?"

"Yes, Miss, Gatekeeper. No Mister, just Gatekeeper."

"Please come in," she said, delighted with this new guest's cheerful demeanor.

As Gatekeeper stepped into the front room, Aidan closed the door behind him. She gestured to the sisters, who were still sitting by the fireplace.

"Perhaps you know some of my other guests – Unloved and Unwanted and their companion Orphan."

The sisters nodded to him, as unsmiling as ever.

"Yes, we know Gatekeeper," Unwanted said. "It has been quite awhile, though."

Unloved frowned at the finely dressed gentleman and to Aidan's surprise greeted him with a stern rebuke.

"It is about time you arrived. You are quite late."

Gatekeeper remained cordial and bowed slightly to them.

"I came as quickly as I could, Madam. And I must say, I am charmed to see you two ladies again."

In her harsh voice Unloved told him, "I have the key."

"Very good, Madam. May I have it, please?"

He stepped toward her and held out his hand.

Unloved reached into the hidden pocket of her skirt, drew out the key to Aidan's house, and gave it to him. His hand closed firmly around it as he bowed again, clicking his heels together with a flourish. With a polite smile spreading broadly beneath his mustache, he thanked her graciously.

Aidan watched this exchange with alarm. There was something very well-rehearsed about their actions, as though they had done this many times before.

Nervously she asked, "Why are you – why are you giving him the key to my house?"

Gatekeeper looked at Aidan with mild surprise. Then he smiled again and answered her before Unloved could speak.

"Well, I should think I will be needing it, Miss. I have been sent here to be your butler."

"Butler!" In her wildest dreams she had never imagined such a thing. "The Prince has decided that I should have a butler?"

"Yes indeed, Miss, and he sent me. Now, if you will please excuse me, I shall freshen up and begin my work straightaway."

"Yes, of course," Aidan said, and gestured toward the stairs. "Oh – but I'm not sure where you can stay – there isn't any more room –"

"No problem at all, Miss," Gatekeeper reassured her. "Leave this up to me now. My job here is to take care of all of your guests and to keep the household running smoothly. I am to be a manager, or an overseer, if you will. I shall keep watch over all the coming and going of the Master's servants while they are in your house, and I shall also see to their lodging."

Aidan smiled. She liked this gentleman butler with his gracious manners more than any of the other guests she had met so far. Gatekeeper made her feel like an elegant lady, a feeling she had never known before and enjoyed immensely.

"I'm so grateful for your help, Gatekeeper, and I hope that you'll be comfortable in my home."

Gatekeeper again smiled, bowed slightly and clicked his heels together.

"I thank you most kindly, Miss. Now, if you will excuse me, I shall go up and find my room."

As he rushed up the stairs, Aidan was filled with wonder at her good fortune. A butler – and such a nice gentleman too!

In the dining room Drudgery was just setting dishes onto the table and the aromas of hot food were enticing. The breakfast she served up was delicious and filling – hotcakes with butter and syrup, fried eggs and sausages with gravy. Aidan had never seen such a breakfast. She heaped her plate with food and enjoyed every bite.

Drudgery was pouring cups of steaming tea when there was another knock at the door. Out of habit, Aidan began to rise to answer it, but Gatekeeper held up his hand to stop her.

"Allow me, Miss, that's my job now," he reminded her, dabbing quickly at his lips with his napkin before jumping up from his seat.

"Of course," Aidan said meekly, obediently settling herself back into her chair. She could see that having a butler was going to be wonderful, but it was also going to take some getting used to.

When she heard the door open and Gatekeeper's cordial greeting, she stood up anyway and went to see who was there.

The visitor that Gatekeeper was helping through the door was a tiny ancient woman. She was dressed from head to toe in black and Aidan recognized at once that her new guest was wearing mourning clothes. Her taffeta dress was covered by a long woven shawl and on her head was a small satin hat with a lace veil that covered most of her face.

The pathetic old woman was so frail and bent over that she could only totter along very slowly, leaning heavily on a twisted wooden cane and the support of Gatekeeper's arm. She was moaning as if she were in terrible pain.

Gatekeeper led the woman carefully to the fireplace in the front room. The woman thanked him in her feeble voice as she settled herself into the rocking chair. She seemed so old and weak that Aidan could scarcely believe she could have been sent by Prince Bal'Davarius to do any kind of work in her house at all. Had she walked the mountain trails all by herself?

Aidan knelt beside her and gently patted her gnarled hand.

"My name is Aidan. What is your name?"

As she bent forward to listen to her reply, she breathed in a strong floral scent which seemed to be coming from the woman's black clothes. The fragrance was not sweet but it was not unpleasant either. It was heavy and musty and something about it stirred an elusive memory.

In a shaking mournful voice, the old woman replied, "I am Grief."

Aidan shrank back at her new guest's name, suddenly feeling a cold shiver run along her spine.

"And – and you are from Prince Bal'Davarius," she said.

"Yes, from the Master," Grief moaned. She seemed to be out of breath. "Oh, I am so very, very tired. Forgive me, but I must sit here awhile and rest."

For a long moment Aidan stared at Grief, trying to remember where she had smelled that distinctive odor which clung to her clothes.

"Of course you may rest awhile," she said gently. "I know that you'll be lodging with me for a time. Gatekeeper will show you to your room when you are ready."

"You are most kind," Grief said gratefully. "Most kind to a poor old woman. Thank you, my dear, thank you."

She briefly closed her shaky crooked fingers around Aidan's hand in a grip that was surprisingly strong.

Grief rocked back and forth in the chair for a few moments until she finally seemed to catch her breath. She leaned forward and pushed her veil back over the top of the hat out of her face, revealing thin snowy white hair pulled into a tight bun at the nape of her neck. Her dry papery skin was deeply etched with a labyrinth of crisscrossing lines. Aidan noticed that her kind eyes were watery and dark, like deep mountain pools on a lonely moonless night.

There was something so deeply disturbing about Grief's presence that Aidan found herself desperately anxious to turn and leave the room. But she stayed where she was, not really knowing what to do.

"Have you known me from my youth – from my childhood?" she asked.

Grief looked into Aidan's eyes. Her mournful voice was now steady.

"Why, my dear, of course. I have been with you since you were a very small child. I always come to lodge with those who have lost something of great value – or someone they love. And you have lost so very much in your life."

"You speak of my mother, then," Aidan said softly.

Grief nodded. "Yes, your mother – and a great deal more."

Aidan pondered that for a moment. Suddenly she remembered where she had smelled the fragrance that seemed to emanate from Grief's clothes. It was the musty scent of the little lace sachets filled with lavender and sweet woodruff that she had made to tuck around Aunt Mara's body in her coffin.

She shuddered now to smell it again, as though it were the odor of death itself.

Grief was carefully studying her face. Despite her frailty, there was a piercing alertness in her gaze, a brightness that began to reach deep into Aidan's heart, threatening to illuminate secret memories that she desperately wanted to keep hidden.

Aidan thought that Grief must know her mother but she suddenly felt exhausted, overcome by melancholy despair, and just couldn't ask her about it. Trembling, she stood up, no longer able to bear her disturbing new guest's presence.

"I'm afraid I have some things I must attend to now. I hope you'll make yourself comfortable," she told the old woman graciously.

"Oh, thank you, my dear," Grief replied. "Thank you for your kindness to a poor old woman."

As Aidan turned around, she saw that her other guests, who were either clustered in the front room or still sitting at the dining room table, seemed unconcerned about the frail newcomer. It was becoming uncomfortably crowded in her house and she suddenly felt a great need to be alone.

She was grateful that Gatekeeper had come to help keep track of all the coming and going. Turning to him now, she gestured to Grief, who was slowly rocking in the chair again, her head down and shoulders hunched under her shawl.

"Gatekeeper," she said timidly to her new butler, "would you please be so kind as to ask Drudgery to fix a meal and a little tea for our new guest?"

Even as she said the words, it seemed extremely strange to Aidan to be giving instructions to a servant, apprehensive though they were. She was anxious to see how Gatekeeper would respond.

To her delight, he immediately snapped to attention. "Yes, Miss, straightaway," he answered, and headed for the kitchen.

Impressed by Gatekeeper's bustling energy and enthusiasm, Aidan smiled, thinking it wouldn't be long before she grew to like having a butler very much.

Reassured that Grief was in good hands, she took her sunhat from a peg by the door and hurried outside to her rose garden.

Chapter Ten

Fear's Children

The sunlight was comforting on Aidan's face as she closed the door behind herself and went down the steps into the front yard. Greatly relieved to be alone, she stood still and closed her eyes. The scent of her beloved roses was strong in the warmth of the morning sun and as always it soothed her troubled spirit to breathe in their heady fragrance. She could hear the lazy buzzing of bees moving from bush to bush seeking the last of the season's nectar. Somewhere nearby a bird was trilling its sweet melody.

Opening her eyes, Aidan squinted in the brilliant light. She put on her wide-brimmed straw sunhat, tied the blue ribbon that laced through it into a bow beneath her chin, and stepped into her rose garden.

The front yard was quite large. It was enclosed within a grey stone wall about four feet high that ran completely around the cottage. Two wide black iron gates offered entrance to Aidan's property, one in the front yard leading to the street and one in the back yard leading to an old stable and carriage shed just outside the wall.

Over many years Aidan had completely filled the front yard with a rustic arrangement of rosebushes in every color bloom imaginable. The stone wall on either side of the gate was covered with thick clusters of climbing roses. Masses of roses in shades of palest pink had even meandered all the way up the front wall of the cottage and partway across the slate roof, clinging to tall sturdy trellises that Samuel Teague had built long before Aidan had come to Aunt Mara.

Walking slowly down the picturesque flagstone path that ran through the center of the yard to the gate, Aidan paused here and there to caress soft petals and savor their fragrance. Nothing was more precious to her than her rose garden, and she desperately needed its comfort now that her home was overrun by her disturbing guests. She turned and looked back at the cottage, admiring all the bright colors that filled the yard and the impressive rambling pink roses on the tall trellises.

Although the stone cottage where Samuel and Mara Teague had set up housekeeping was not large, it had at one time been a very lovely home. Aidan had heard more than one person say that the cottage was the most beautiful house in Hidden. But after Samuel's death Aunt Mara had lacked both the funds for repairs and the will to tend the yard. As the cottage had fallen into disrepair, the neglected yards had become overgrown with thick tangles of weeds.

Aidan could barely remember when she had begun to care for the gardens or how she had managed that task, for she knew she had been just a small child then. But she would never forget how she had always been praised for it. Aunt Mara used to tell her that she herself had never been good at gardening and she was grateful that Aidan had a true gift for it, especially since it put food on the table.

Spurred on by this encouragement, Aidan had worked very hard to artfully arrange her garden areas all around the house. They graced the cottage with a cozy charm that was not to be found anywhere else in Hidden. It gave her immense satisfaction to know that her impressive gardens were the envy of all her neighbors. She had every reason to be fiercely proud of them, for she had spent many years nurturing each perennial and rosebush along to their present glory.

Gardening was her one great joy in life, the only creative pursuit that made her feel confident and special. And roses were her passion, bringing the finest beauty to her otherwise difficult and colorless existence.

Aidan sighed contentedly as she followed the flagstones back toward the cottage. At the front steps the path turned sharply left and took her past the rambling pink roses, ending at a tall wooden gate to her right that connected the corner of the house to the stone wall. Just behind the gate was a wooden lattice arch thickly covered with climbing red and yellow variegated roses. She opened the gate and passed beneath the arch, then continued along the path in the narrow space between the house and the wall toward a second arch of red and yellow roses that led into the back yard.

As much as Aidan loved tending Lady Fairhaven's rose garden, her day off was her special time to enjoy her own gardens. She wasn't about to let her guests' intrusion into her life keep her from them this warm sunny day, for September was almost over now and they wouldn't be blooming much longer.

But as she made her way along the narrow path to the back gardens she became aware of noise and activity up ahead. Disappointed to have her brief solitude interrupted, she stepped through the shadows beneath the second arch into the bright sunlight, squinting to see who was in the yard. What she saw made her suddenly go numb with shock.

There were perhaps a hundred children wandering through her gardens and running along the paths!

At the sight of all those children Aidan immediately panicked, thinking they would surely ruin her perennials and vegetables.

Who were all these children?!

Then something shiny and blue caught her eye and she saw that Fear was sitting on the bench in the middle of the yard.

The realization that she was getting her first good look at Fear's children filled Aidan with utter astonishment. How could any woman, especially one who seemed to be so young, have so many children?

And how could they all live beneath a wool cape?

Still staring all around in bewilderment, she began to hurry toward the bench.

In the back yard the main flagstone path ran past a small wooden shed that had been built against the back wall of the stone cottage near the kitchen door. The wide path then turned again and meandered down the middle of a rustic perennial garden, branching out into a maze of smaller paths through the flowers. In the center of the yard was a decorative wooden bench where Fear was now seated. The path then continued on between two large vegetable gardens before it ended at the back gate in the stone wall, which was shaded by another wooden arch covered with climbing white roses.

Just outside the wall near the iron gate was a little grove of apple trees which were now heavy with ripening fruit. Nestled among them was a large stone stable and carriage house that had four stalls. Aunt Mara had sold Samuel's horses and carriage years before Aidan had arrived on her doorstep and the empty old building had stood unused for as long as she could remember. As a child she had played in it often. Now it was so overgrown with vines that its roof sagged beneath their weight.

Beyond the carriage house and the apple trees was the grassy valley where herds of goats and flocks of sheep were grazing. And off in the distance, stretching across the horizon like a majestic ever-present backdrop, were the rocky snow-covered mountains.

In the warmth of the morning Fear had removed her black wool cape and had draped it neatly over the back of the bench. It almost hurt Aidan's eyes to look at her silvery blue dress, for it sparkled and fairly glowed in the sunlight, as brilliant as fresh snow on a bright winter day.

She called out and Fear turned around at her approach.

"Fear, please be careful of my gardens and have your children keep to the paths!"

As Aidan reached the bench, Fear looked at her reproachfully.

"My children are keeping to the paths, Aidan. They are quiet and very well behaved. Don't trouble yourself about your gardens."

Afraid she had said the wrong thing, Aidan timidly slipped onto the bench beside Fear.

"I'm sorry – I didn't mean to offend you. It's just that my gardens are most precious to me – they're my favorite thing in the whole world. I find my greatest joy in the beauty of growing things, and I – well – until this moment I hadn't realized just how many children you have."

Fear did not reply. Aidan sat next to her in silence for several minutes, watching the children at their play. They were indeed quiet and well-behaved as they darted about – eerily quiet, in fact, slipping in and out of the garden spaces with hardly a sound. There was no doubt that they were playing, yet there was no childlike joy in their faces and no sweet laughter in their voices.

Aidan began to look for Fear of Being Hurt, but it was hard to pick him out in the crowd, for all of Fear's children looked alike. One small boy was standing alone watching a butterfly as it flitted among the flowers, and she thought she recognized him.

"Is that Fear of Being Hurt?"

Fear glanced over at the boy.

"No, that one is Fear of Failure."

She gestured to the other side of the garden. "Fear of Being Hurt is over by the stone wall. See him there? He's the one playing ring-around-the-roses with two of his sisters."

For a moment Aidan watched the three children Fear had pointed to. They were dancing in a little circle and she could hear them singing, but there was no music in their soft voices. The boy did look like Fear of Being Hurt, but so did all the other boys and she still wasn't sure.

"Fear, all of your children – they look very much alike, don't they?"

"At first glance, I suppose they would seem to," Fear replied. "But just watch them for a moment or two, Aidan. As each one becomes more familiar to you, you'll be able to recognize one from another right away."

At that moment Aidan got her first good look at the boy with the two girls. To her surprise Fear was right, for she recognized him at once as Fear of Being Hurt.

"Now I see – it is him," she said.

She looked at his two sisters closely. They were identical in every way, from their wide blue eyes to their long black braids. Even their blue gingham play dresses were identical.

"What are the two girls' names?" she asked. "Are they twins?"

"Yes, they are," Fear told her. "Their names are Fear of the Unknown and Fear of the Future."

Fear went on to tell the names of some of the other children, and the more of them Aidan saw, the more uneasy she became.

As each was pointed out, something deep in her heart responded with the same mysterious little leap of recognition she had felt at her first sight of Unloved and Unwanted in the dark street. She had never seen any of these children before – yet somehow it was becoming clear that she knew them all.

What could it mean that Fear and all of her children had come to lodge with her?

Fear gestured toward a few of her children playing near the back gate in the far end of the yard where Aidan's vegetable gardens were located. Three children were climbing along the stone wall near the vine-covered shed while a fourth stood nearby watching.

"The boys on your wall are Fear of Being Accused and Fear of Retribution, and their sister Fear of Humiliation is with them," Fear said. "The boy watching them is Fear of Betrayal."

Next she gestured to a little group in the corner of the yard who seemed to be huddled tightly together watching the group of children climbing on the wall.

"That group stays together most of the time. The older boy is Fear of Being Alone, and the two little girls are Fear of Abandonment and Fear of Rejection. Fear of Loss is the smaller boy with them and next to him is his sister Fear of Losing Someone You Love."

As Fear kept pointing to various children and listing their names, Aidan was beginning to feel overwhelmed with dread.

"Over there near the hollyhocks are Fear of the Dark and her brothers Fear of Small Enclosed Spaces and Fear of Being Trapped – the boys are also twins. That girl by the sunflowers is Fear of Punishment and the boy with her is Fear of Imprisonment."

Fear gestured in another direction.

"Over this way looking at your herb garden is Fear of Falling. And his two sisters with him, the twins – their names are Fear of Being Found Out and Fear of Being Known."

Just then a little boy broke away from a group and started running across the yard. As he sped past the back gate, Aidan's attention was drawn to a large boy who was standing in the shadows beneath the wooden arch.

There seemed to be something very different about this boy.

She pointed to him and asked, "Fear, that boy there beneath the white roses – what is his name?"

Fear looked at him for a long moment before turning back to Aidan. In a very quiet voice she replied, "That is my firstborn, Fear of Death."

Aidan quickly turned away from her chilling stare and looked back at Fear of Death. She shuddered as that feeling of recognition made her heart leap once again.

Even in the shadows beneath the roses, she could see now that Fear of Death was much older than his siblings, a teenager grown almost to manhood. He was tall and slender with the same round icy blue eyes, black hair, and pale skin as all of Fear's other children. Other than his age, Aidan wondered why it had seemed to her that this boy was different from the rest.

Then he stepped out from under the arch, and as he came into the light she was astonished to see that he was limping badly. His body was twisted and he supported himself with a homemade wooden crutch.

"Why, he – he is crippled," Aidan gasped. "What happened to him?"

There was no trace of emotion on Fear's face as she watched her firstborn stumble along the path.

"Fear of Death has always been crippled. He was born that way."

She turned and looked directly into Aidan's eyes.

"And all who embrace him become crippled as well."

Aidan stared at her, feeling the blood draining from her face. Her heart began pounding and she shivered as she turned to look again at Fear of Death.

Fear saw her reaction and a mocking half-smile cast a pale coldness across her delicate features.

"Would you like to know the names of the rest of my children, Aidan?"

"No, thank you," Aidan said softly. "I'm beginning to understand now that I already know them all."

For a long silent moment she watched the activity in her yard.

"And I'm beginning to see that they have played in my gardens before."

Fear nodded with satisfaction as she turned and looked again at her children.

"Indeed," she agreed softly. "Many, many times."

They sat there in silence watching the busy children for several more minutes. Then Aidan sighed with deep resignation. She wanted to work in her gardens but had no desire to be where Fear's children were at play.

At last she smiled as graciously as she could and stood up.

"Well, I hope you and your children enjoy the morning, Fear. If you will excuse me, I have things I must do."

Fear nodded again. "As you wish."

Aidan hurried back toward the house. She pulled open the door of the shed and turned to look back at her gardens.

Across the long yard she saw that Fear of Death was leaning on his crutch watching her intently.

For the briefest of seconds their eyes met. His face was hard and his accusing stare never flinched. Something in his manner caused Aidan to be overwhelmed by a rush of cold panic. Suddenly she couldn't breathe.

It was all she could do to tear her gaze away from him, but at last she turned and escaped into the shed. As her eyes adjusted to the darkness, the driving rhythm of her pounding heart resounded like thunder in her ears.

She grabbed gardening shears, gloves and a basket before stepping quickly back into the sunlight, keeping her head down and not daring even to glance into the back yard again. Then, without even pausing to latch the shed door, she raced around the corner of the house, desperate for the solace of her rose garden.

Chapter Eleven

Depression, Anger and Abuse

Something in Aidan's heart urgently needed to gather her roses close to her and hold them in her hands. Instinctively she found herself choosing warm colors in an effort to overcome the cold fear that was still making her heart pound. Blooms of fiery red, yellow, creamy white and coral were quickly snipped and laid carefully into her basket. Their scent was like a soothing tonic for her soul and she breathed deeply.

Suddenly a thundering clatter from the street made her gasp and jump. Roses and basket went flying as she dropped down behind the bushes in a panic and covered her head with her arms.

The noise grew louder. Then she heard hoofbeats and a horse snorting. It was just a carriage in the street.

Aidan breathed deeply, feeling foolish at having been so frightened, but her heart was still racing. Quickly she gathered her roses back into the basket, then straightened up and peeked cautiously through the tall bushes.

An open black carriage drawn by twin bay horses was just pulling up outside her wrought iron gate. As Aidan watched, the driver of the carriage reined in his horses, calling to his passengers that they had arrived at their destination.

A thin weary-looking man dressed in rumpled grey trousers and a gaudy grey plaid jacket stepped down from the carriage. Aidan could see that there were two finely-dressed ladies still seated inside. The man turned and offered his hand to the closest one. The woman grabbed it impatiently and with a loud sigh of annoyance stood up and flounced heavily onto the sidewalk.

Everything about the woman seemed to snap and blaze like fire. She was short and stout and her ample bosom was fashionably covered by a vibrant red-orange velvet jacket. Perched atop the woman's brunette coiffure was a stylish black hat accented with a red velvet band and three fluffy red feathers.

Her showy taffeta dress was elaborately enhanced with a lace bow at the throat and several tiers of ruffles that cascaded down the back of the skirt. Its shiny material had an iridescent quality as it caught the sunlight and as the skirt swept around the woman's legs it seemed to flare and recede in flamelike swirls of orange, crimson and gold. It even sounded like a crackling fire as it rustled over layers of stiff petticoats.

As soon as both of her feet were on the sidewalk, the woman snatched her hand away from the man. Throwing him a poisonous look, she began brushing furiously at her jacket and smoothing imaginary wrinkles from her skirt.

The man stepped back and watched her for a moment. He was slightly bent over and moved very slowly, giving the distinct impression that he was carrying a heavy unseen burden. In contrast to the flamboyant woman, he seemed to be surrounded by shadows, as though an unseen cloud was hovering over his head and following him wherever he went. When he turned his head slightly, Aidan saw that his countenance was most gloomy and pensive.

The woman glared at the man.

"I thought we would never get here!" she snapped heatedly, her voice shrill. "A fine mess you've made of things as usual, I must say. Had we not hired this driver who knew the way, I expect we would have wandered the mountain roads and the streets of this detestable little hamlet forever!"

The man nodded meekly and said nothing to deny her accusations. He turned resolutely away from her and reached up into the carriage, hoisting two large valises and one small carpetbag from the seat.

Before he could set the luggage on the sidewalk, the woman began shouting at him.

"Oh, for pity's sake! Where are your manners? You should help Mother down before getting the bags!"

The man never protested or argued with her, but Aidan noticed he also did not apologize, not saying a word either to the fiery woman on the sidewalk or to the older woman still in the carriage. He shrugged his shoulders slightly and then, moving with resignation, obediently set the valises and carpetbag on the sidewalk and reached up to offer his hand to the second woman.

As the mother of the fiery woman stood up, Aidan could see that their faces were nearly identical except for the difference in age. Their outfits were similar in style as well but the colors were very different. The older woman was wearing a copper-colored velvet jacket over a gold blouse and a shiny dark brown taffeta skirt with a ruffled hem. On her head she wore a wide-brimmed gold velvet hat accented with a spray of bright crimson silk flowers and a large brown ostrich plume. Aidan had never seen such a feather before and for a moment it fascinated her.

The older woman was apparently a lover of hats, for rather than take the man's hand she immediately flung four immense hatboxes over the side of the open carriage for him to take. He reached for them but wasn't quick enough. They knocked roughly into his face, causing his own hat to fly off his head as he lost his balance. Hatboxes went flying and the poor man landed hard in the street, the round boxes rolling all around him.

Aidan gasped as the man fell but she stayed hidden behind the rosebushes. She could see him sitting on the pavement through the ironwork of the front gate.

Furious, the younger woman shouted at him again.

"You clumsy swine! How dare you throw Mother's hatboxes into the street like that!"

Momentarily dazed but apparently not seriously hurt, the man rubbed the side of his face where the boxes had hit him. Then he put his hat back on before pulling himself slowly to his feet. After brushing dust from his rumpled suit, he reached up again to help the older woman down from the carriage.

To Aidan's amazement, instead of apologizing for her part in the accident, the older woman drew herself up and glared down at him with fire in her eyes. Her deep contralto voice was strident with open contempt.

"You worthless dog! Pick up my hatboxes! You'll pay dearly if you've damaged any of my hats with your clumsiness!"

The man was clearly shaking now as he submissively picked up the hatboxes and stacked them neatly on the sidewalk. The older woman, still waiting for him to help her down from the carriage, turned to her daughter and vented her wrath at her.

"I knew years ago it was a grave mistake for you to marry this good-for-nothing fool, even if the Master did choose him for you! But I suppose I shouldn't have been surprised. You never did have one bit of sense either. The two of you deserve each other!"

Aidan was completely appalled at the vile exchange taking place between these three sorry people. The man seemed resigned to the women's abuse and spoke not a word of defense, but just reached up again to help the older woman down from the carriage. She stepped heavily onto the sidewalk and began fussing at her clothes as her daughter had done.

The man turned from them and slowly took out a large wallet from a pocket inside his plaid suitcoat. With great dignity he walked up to the driver of the hired carriage, who seemed most anxious to take leave of these finely dressed but dreadfully mannered passengers. He snatched his pay out of the man's hand, tipped his hat quickly to him, and drove off without a word, his horses almost at a gallop.

As the carriage clattered noisily away up the street, the two women stood by without lifting a finger to help as their pitiful companion struggled silently to pick up all the hatboxes and luggage. Then, to Aidan's horror, they turned toward her gate!

Surely these three pathetic people weren't more of the Dark Prince's servants sent to live in her house with her!

But her heart filled with dread because she knew they must be. Why else would they have come?

Speechless, Aidan stared as the two ladies stood outside the gate and waited impatiently for the man to open it for them. The poor burdened man, who looked as though he didn't have an ounce of strength left in his thin body, had to put down all the luggage again to open the heavy iron gate for them. Not offering a single word of appreciation or thanks, they flounced gracelessly past him, their noses in the air. The man slowly gathered the hatboxes and the heavy suitcases into his arms again and followed his wife and mother-in-law into the yard, kicking the gate shut behind them and stumbling up the flagstone path that wound through the roses.

His repeated efforts carrying the luggage would have been comical if it hadn't been for the ghastly treatment he was receiving from his companions.

Reluctantly Aidan stepped out from behind the rosebushes where she had been hiding.

"Hello. I am Aidan. Can I help you?"

The women stopped short and condescendingly eyed her up and down. Then without a word they turned to the man, waiting pointedly for him to be a gentleman and make their introductions.

The man put down all the luggage again and stepped wearily toward Aidan. He politely removed his hat and held it in front of his chest with both hands like a shield as he bowed formally to her. His utterly cheerless eyes were dull grey like his rumpled suit and there was no trace of a smile on his solemn face as he spoke for the first time in a meek nasal tenor.

"Good morning, Aidan. My name is Depression."

Aidan was apprehensive but somehow not greatly surprised to learn the man's name.

"Have you come to me from Prince Bal'Davarius?"

"Yes, we have," he said. He gestured to the two women, his manners flawless. "Allow me to present my wife Anger and my mother-in-law Abuse."

Upon hearing their names Aidan felt all her strength wither, for she had known anger and abuse only too well throughout her life.

"Hello," she said warily, but the two women didn't even nod back. They just stared coldly at her, not saying a word in greeting.

How appalling, Aidan thought, that they should be so adamant that the man treat them with good manners and respect when they themselves were so horribly rude.

Then Depression spoke the dreaded words she had already anticipated.

"We are to stay with you until the Master gives us further instructions."

Before Aidan could open her mouth to answer, Abuse spoke up. She was looking around in disgust at the house and yard.

"What a dreary little hovel the Master has sent us to this time! A veritable pigsty with a garden!"

Completely stunned at the blatant insult, Aidan froze.

"If you can call this overgrown mess a garden," Abuse went on. "Oh! *Roses!* – no, no, no! This simply won't do at *all*. I absolutely detest roses! Nastiest little flowers on earth, they are. They attract so many dreadful little bees, and the thorns always catch on one's clothing and prick one's fingers. Simply nasty, I say!"

She turned and looked Aidan directly in the eye as if daring her to say anything.

"And the stench – they simply *reek* – just revolting! Syrupy sweet enough to make me retch! It's turning my stomach even as I stand here."

Speechless, Aidan felt her hands turn icy cold and her body tremble. How dare this stranger insult her beloved roses!

Abuse tilted her head back and looked down her short tipped nose at Aidan with open contempt.

"Well, there's nothing to be done about your nauseating little weed patch now, is there? The Master has decided that we are to lodge here with you and his orders must be obeyed. I suppose I'm forced to endure your loathsome roses – for now."

Aidan could feel her face flaming with indignation and her heart pounding. But she was still so shocked that she couldn't even begin to find words to answer her newest guest.

Abuse looked up at the cottage again and sighed loudly.

"Tacky little shanty, isn't it? Needs a lot of work – just like the garden. Well! Evidently we're stuck with it."

Turning again, she frowned at Aidan.

"I trust that there will be enough room somewhere in your ramshackle little hovel so that I can hang up all my hats. They must be well cared for. I simply won't have them crushed in some filthy drawer or wardrobe!"

"Mother, really!" Anger snapped. "All you ever care about is your hats! Let's just get inside and freshen up from that dreadful carriage ride. Hurry along, Depression, bring the valises. Let's get on with this."

She looked haughtily at Aidan.

"Take us to our rooms at once. And they'd better be clean."

No one had ever treated Aidan quite like this. By now she was shaking with such intense rage that it took all her strength to keep from slapping Anger and Abuse right in their faces.

Suddenly she realized with horror that she had actually begun to lift her hand to do just that. She quickly drew it back and clutched the handle of her rose basket, appalled more at her own savage reaction than at her new guests' vile behavior.

Aidan knew beyond any doubt that as long as these people were lodging in her house she would never be free from the pain and suffering that had been inflicted upon her by Aunt Mara's drunken fury. But she also knew there was nothing she could do but invite them in and hope their stay would be very short.

She dared not lose her temper. They were, after all, the servants of the Dark Prince, the sovereign ruler of the Kingdom.

Clenching her teeth, she gestured toward the cottage.

"This way, then."

But as she turned to lead them to the door, Gatekeeper opened it and with bustling energy stepped outside. Aidan immediately noticed with surprise that her house key was now attached to a long heavy gold chain which hung down from his neck.

Bowing and clicking his heels together, her butler greeted the three as cordially as he had greeted everyone else.

"Good day, Abuse, Anger, Depression! Charmed to see you again, I must say!"

He quickly reached out and took the two heavy valises from Depression, who looked relieved to be free of his burden.

"Allow me to take you right upstairs. I have already prepared your rooms for you."

"Rooms?" Aidan cried. "What rooms? How are you going to fit everyone in?"

But Gatekeeper didn't hear her, for he was already inside and heading up the stairs. Anger and Abuse swept haughtily past her to follow him as poor Depression stumbled after them, struggling beneath the four hatboxes and the carpetbag.

It was not until they were all well out of sight that the full meaning of Gatekeeper's comment came to her.

I have already prepared your rooms for you.

Already prepared?!

Had Gatekeeper anticipated their arrival? Did he know in advance who was coming to stay?

As she turned back to her roses, Aidan was alarmed to see that her hands were still trembling with rage.

Chapter Twelve

Talking With Gatekeeper and Drudgery

Late that afternoon, Aidan came into the kitchen from the back yard and found Gatekeeper sitting at the table drinking tea with Drudgery. They were casually talking and laughing as though they had worked together in the same house for years. Drudgery was apparently busy with dinner preparations, for a large pot was simmering on the stove and the room was filled with delightful aromas. Aidan quietly walked to the pump at the sink and began washing her hands.

Gatekeeper snapped to attention and jumped to his feet, bowing slightly. "Good afternoon, Miss," he greeted her. "Drudgery and I were just having a spot of tea. What can I do for you?"

"Oh, please, don't let me interrupt you," Aidan replied. "Just enjoy your tea."

"Thank you, Miss," Gatekeeper replied. "Would you care to join us?"

"Why, yes, thank you, I think I would," Aidan said, drying her hands on a towel. "I'll just get another cup."

"No, no, Miss, I shall get it for you," Gatekeeper insisted quickly, and pulled out a chair for her. "Please sit down."

"Oh –" Aidan hesitated for a moment. It felt very strange to have someone wait on her. "Well – thank you."

She settled herself into the chair Gatekeeper held out for her. He helped her push the chair in and hurried to the cupboard to get a cup and saucer.

Drudgery got up and went to the stove. She opened the oven door and peeked in. "Not quite done," she said softly, more to herself than anyone else, and closed the door. Then she lifted the lid of the soup pot and stirred its contents with a long wooden spoon. The aroma of whatever she was cooking was unfamiliar to Aidan but very enticing.

"I don't mean to interrupt your tea," she apologized.

"It's no imposition at all, Miss," Gatekeeper replied cheerfully as he poured her tea. "We are here to serve you."

"Thank you," Aidan said. "Whatever are you making for dinner, Drudgery? It smells wonderful. You're such a gifted cook."

"Thank you," Drudgery replied as she sat back down. "We'll be having beef and barley stew tonight. The bread is in the oven."

"Beef and barley stew!" cried Aidan, amazed. "Has this meat come from the Prince?"

"Of course," Drudgery told her. "Our Master takes good care of his servants."

Aidan had heard this several times in the past few days, and somehow it reassured her now to hear Drudgery say it again.

"That must be true," she said softly.

She picked up her cup and sipped her tea. It was strong and fragrant, much better than any tea she had ever tasted, and she was surprised at how good it was.

"This tea is lovely," she said. "Has it too come from your Master?"

"That it has, Miss," Gatekeeper told her. "It is the Master's finest tea."

As Aidan sipped her tea again, she began to relax and enjoy herself.

"I must say, out of all my guests, I especially appreciate the two of you. I'm so grateful for all your hard work."

Drudgery smiled and shrugged. "That's the reason we were sent here, Aidan," she said. "To serve you well."

"But – but I don't understand why," Aidan said. "What is the purpose of all this? Why should the sovereign Prince of all the Kingdom be sending his servants to me – or expensive meat, or his finest tea?"

She turned to her butler.

"Gatekeeper, I thought perhaps you could tell me. Earlier today, you seemed to know – before they arrived – that Depression, Anger, and Abuse were coming. I thought perhaps your Master has told you who else will be joining you."

Gatekeeper seemed surprised at her questioning.

"Well, yes, Miss, of course I knew they would arrive. As I've told you, I'm the one who takes care of all the coming and going here, and all the lodging arrangements. The others must pass by me on their arrival or departure."

It was reassuring to think that Gatekeeper would be like a guard to her, for Aidan liked him very much.

"Do you know who else will be coming?"

"Yes, Miss."

"Did Prince Bal'Davarius give you a list of some sort?"

"No, Miss, he gave me no list."

Aidan was puzzled. "Then how do you know who will arrive next?"

He seemed genuinely taken aback that she should need to ask that question at all.

"Why, Miss, it's very simple. I just look into your heart, and then I know. You have the list in your heart."

Aidan was stunned by his answer.

"In my heart? How – how do you look into my heart?"

Gatekeeper smiled patiently beneath his mustache and held up the gold chain around his neck. The key to Aidan's front door dangled before her.

"Have you forgotten, Miss? I have the key to your house. It opens everything in your heart to me. As the saying goes, the home and the heart are one."

"I see," Aidan said, although she wasn't sure she understood at all. "But how does looking into my heart show you who the next guest will be? How can I have a list in my heart?"

Gatekeeper paused for a long moment. Aidan could see he was collecting his thoughts and weighing out how to explain. When he finally answered, he spoke slowly and deliberately, as though he were taking great care to tell her what she wanted to know but not to say too much.

"Well, Miss, surely you must have realized by now that all the Master's servants who are lodging here have really known you since long ago."

Aidan nodded. "Yes, just about all of them have told me something like that."

"You must have seen, then, that we have not just come to you in the last few days. Each of us has actually been with you for a long while. But it was only recently that the Master decided to make our work plain to you. So you are now meeting us face to face for the first time."

He paused again.

"So, Miss, when I look into your heart, I see your list – if you will – for we are already there. And then I know who will be arriving next."

Nothing that had happened in the previous two days had prepared Aidan for what Gatekeeper was now telling her. Even though she liked and trusted him, it gave her a sudden creepy feeling inside to think that he – or anyone – could somehow see into her heart and know what was there.

"And – so – when you know," she stammered, "when you know who is going to come next, can you – are you allowed to tell me in advance?"

"There is no need, Miss," Gatekeeper said. "When I know, then they are here."

"But Gatekeeper – if you have all really been with me from long ago – why couldn't I see any of you before? If the Prince has had plans for me for so long, why is he only now making all of you known to me?" Aidan paused, collecting her thoughts. "I suppose what I really want to know is – what does he want with me?"

Gatekeeper chuckled beneath his bushy mustache. The little crinkles at the corners of his eyes when he smiled made him seem grandfatherly.

"Why, Miss, those things I can't tell you because I don't know. The Master gives us our orders, but his ultimate plans are his own business. I just know what I need to do, and so I do my job."

"What would happen to you – or any of the other servants – if you refused to obey your Master's orders?" Aidan asked.

Gatekeeper was visibly startled by this question and seemed to be at a complete loss for an answer.

At last he said, "Well, now, Miss, I don't rightly know. I suppose he would punish us somehow, perhaps throw us into his prison. I've heard a great deal about the Master's prison and I can tell you I wouldn't want to be locked up in there."

He seemed to almost shudder at the thought.

"But no, I have never heard of one of his servants being punished for disobeying – I'm not even sure it could ever happen. You see, we all know it's to our advantage to serve the Master as best we can. He takes good care of us, as you yourself have seen."

Before Aidan could reply, Drudgery spoke softly.

"Oh, but there's much more to it than just that. It gives us our meaning to serve him."

"I'm afraid I don't understand, Drudgery," Aidan said.

"Our meaning," Drudgery repeated, struggling to find the words she wanted to say. "As though we were born to it. Serving the Master is simply what we were meant to do. Our lives would have no meaning if we didn't have the Master to serve."

Aidan was quiet for a long moment. Drudgery was such a simple kind of person that the depth of this idea seemed quite profound.

At that moment Gatekeeper placed his empty teacup in its saucer and drew out a large gold pocket watch from his vest.

"Dear me, look at the time! If you will excuse me, Miss, I must be attending to my duties."

"Of course," Aidan said. "Thank you, Gatekeeper."

"You are most welcome, Miss," he replied in his businesslike but gracious manner. He stood up and bowed slightly, clicking his heels together with his usual flourish. "Thank you for the tea, Drudgery. Good afternoon, ladies."

He hurried out of the kitchen. Aidan watched him leave, then turned to Drudgery.

"When you say you would have no meaning, do you mean you would have no purpose in life?"

"Yes, that's it," Drudgery replied, nodding. "Our lives would have no purpose. It's good for us, like Gatekeeper said, to work for the Master. He takes care of us. But – he also gives us our purpose in life."

"I see," Aidan said, smiling at her earnestness.

Shyly Drudgery smiled back. She hesitated, then said, "Aidan, I think – I think he wants you to serve him, too."

Aidan's smile froze on her face.

"You think – he wants – *me?* Prince Bal'Davarius?"

Drudgery nodded, laughing at the look on Aidan's face.

"Yes, Prince Bal'Davarius. The Master. Oh, I don't know any more than Gatekeeper what plans he has for you, but he must want you for something or he wouldn't have sent us here to stay with you. I think he wants to prepare you for his service."

Aidan was astounded by this idea.

"I can't imagine that such a thing could be true. What on earth would he want with the likes of me? Isolated here in Hidden, with no family or friends or wealth or – or anything. Why, I can scarcely understand how he knows I'm alive at all."

Drudgery's eyes suddenly sparkled as she talked of her Master.

"Oh, no, Aidan, you simply wouldn't believe what the Master knows. He is the most powerful ruler on earth, more powerful than you could imagine – but you mustn't be afraid of him. He sees and cares for everyone in his Kingdom. I just know he has a very special plan for you, and we seem to be a large part of that. I think this is why he is making us known to you now."

Aidan just stared at Drudgery, dumbfounded by what she was saying.

"Then – Drudgery – what about my mother?"

"Your mother?"

"Well, yes, my mother." Aidan slipped her teacup into its saucer. "Oh Drudgery, with all my heart I want to leave Hidden and find her. When I first met Unloved and Unwanted they said they knew her, and that was why I invited them here. They told me that she was a foreigner who lived in Davarius for awhile and that I was born here in the mountains. But she left me here and went back to her own country when I was just a baby and –"

"You were born here in the Master's Kingdom?" Drudgery asked.

"Yes. I thought all of you coming to stay in my house would somehow lead me to this other land and to my mother. But now you're telling me you think the Prince wants me to serve him here in some special way. I don't understand how all of this could fit together."

All at once Drudgery became very excited.

"Oh, but Aidan, this just proves it! It doesn't matter that your mother was a foreigner. All who are born in the Master's Kingdom are born into his plans for them. Your mother had you here and left you behind because you were meant to be here to do the Master's bidding. It must be your meaning, too – your purpose in life. Whatever the Master wants from you – it's what you were born to do."

Aidan stared in awe at the sudden change that had come over Drudgery. Her smudged face, so drawn and weary a moment before from all her hard work, had come alive and taken on a radiance that almost made her look beautiful. There was a burst of fire in her eyes, an intense blaze that burned from the depths of her great devotion to her Master.

Looking into those eyes, Aidan felt the fire begin to burn in her own heart as she caught Drudgery's excitement.

"Do you really think so?" she asked.

"Oh, I am *sure* of it," Drudgery insisted. "He has a great work for you to do. Our presence here *must* be to prepare you for it."

Aidan considered this for a long moment. Then she asked, "Tell me, Drudgery – have you ever seen him?"

"Seen the Master? Of course," Drudgery replied. "All of his servants have seen him."

"Is he – is he handsome? What does he look like?"

Drudgery's face took on a dreamy look as she thought of him.

"Oh, I couldn't begin to describe the Master. He is – well, he is incredibly beautiful. More beautiful than a god."

"A god!" Aidan exclaimed.

"Well – yes, a god."

Drudgery was again struggling to find the words she wanted.

"It's as though light comes from him. He shines with colors – brighter than a rainbow. His eyes sparkle with all the brilliance of jewels. The Master is much more lovely than any of the sons of men."

Aidan was stunned by her description of the Dark Prince.

"I have never before heard of a such a thing," she said. "A man as radiant as a god – how can this be?"

"I don't know, Aidan, but I have seen him, and I tell you I speak the truth," Drudgery replied earnestly. "But sometimes he looks like an ordinary man. A tall man with long black hair and dark eyes and a black beard – that's why they call him the Dark Prince."

"I have heard that about him," Aidan said. "But I have never heard that he is beautiful."

Drudgery suddenly leaned closer to Aidan and dropped her voice to a whisper, as though what she had to say next was a great secret.

"I once saw the Master when he was a lion."

"A *lion*?" Aidan gasped.

"Yes, a lion. I was in his court at the palace one day, and something made him angry, fearsomely angry. Suddenly he – he just turned into a huge lion. I saw him change right there, right in front of me. He roared with such mighty strength it shook the whole palace."

Aidan stared at Drudgery, speechless with amazement. She remembered seeing pictures of ferocious lions in her childhood story books.

"How can a man turn into a lion?"

Drudgery smiled.

"Oh, he's so much more than an ordinary man, Aidan, much, much more. He is strong and powerful and awesome – but he is good and kind to those who serve him. Someday you will meet him face to face, I'm sure of it, and then you shall see for yourself. I have no doubt that you have been chosen for a special purpose in the Master's Kingdom."

Aidan took a deep breath. She found herself almost wishing that Drudgery's convictions were true. But it was hard to believe this when all her fellow servants kept saying they didn't know his plans for her.

"Well, thank you for telling me all this," she said. "I suppose only time will tell if it comes to pass."

She looked down at her empty teacup and sighed reluctantly. "I should let you get on with cooking supper, but I must say I have enjoyed our talk."

When she looked up again, she saw that the beautiful radiance on Drudgery's countenance had faded away. Once again she looked like an old woman, with her face all lined beyond her years and darkened with dirt from hard work.

Aidan could not understand why she suddenly felt a grateful swelling in her heart as she looked at Drudgery.

Shyly she said, "I don't know why it should be that out of all my guests, you seem to be the one I can talk to most easily. You are – the closest thing I have to a friend."

Drudgery smiled sadly. In her quietly profound way she replied, "I have been your only friend for most of your life, Aidan."

Aidan thought about that and realized it was true.

Her toils, her labors, her drudgery all those years slaving for Aunt Mara had at times been the only thing that had kept her sane. Concentrating on physical work and pushing away all other thoughts had often been the only escape she could find from her broken heart when despair completely overcame her and all hope was gone. So in a very real sense Drudgery *had* been her only friend.

And now her only friend was serving her well.

"Thank you," she whispered, her voice thick with tears. Then she rose and hurried out of the kitchen.

Chapter Thirteen

Pride and Greed

The next morning Aidan opened her eyes to the grey light just before dawn. She sat up, yawned, and stretched luxuriously. Exhausted, she had gone to bed quite early and her sleep had been very deep and satisfying, the first good rest she had experienced since Unloved and Unwanted had come to her. Night Terrors had not shown himself, and for that she was extremely grateful.

Retiring early had also been a convenient way to escape from Anger and Abuse, whose presence at her dinner table had been simply unbearable. They had spoken rudely to everyone, argued loudly together, and berated poor Depression throughout the meal. Their ill manners were so upsetting that she could hardly eat the wonderful beef and barley stew Drudgery had so artfully prepared.

As Depression had sat there in silence so pathetically defenseless, Aidan had felt great pity for him. She wondered why he had ever married Anger and how he now managed to survive. By the time the meal was over, he was bent low over his almost untouched bowl of stew, and Aidan was shaking with disgust and rage.

Anger and Abuse were utterly contemptible and she could hardly contain the hatred she felt for them. She feared that at some point in time she would lose all control in their presence and do something she would greatly regret. If only she could be rid of them forever!

Reluctantly Aidan pulled herself out of bed, lit an oil lamp, and slowly began to dress. There was a gnawing pain in the pit of her stomach and she realized she was dreading opening her door and going downstairs, even just to leave the house and head for the mansion for her workday. She tied a scarf around her head and smoothed the apron of her uniform, then sat on the edge of the bed for a long time, breathing deeply to try to calm herself and wondering what she should do.

Suddenly a knock at her bedroom door made her jump.

Heart pounding, she called anxiously, "Yes, who is there?"

"It is I, Miss." Gatekeeper's voice was muffled by the wooden door. "I have brought your tray."

"Tray?" Aidan hurried to the door and opened it.

To her astonishment, there stood her butler in the darkness of the hallway holding a huge covered silver tray.

"Why, what is this?" she asked.

"Your breakfast, Miss," Gatekeeper replied in his pleasant but businesslike manner, bowing slightly.

"I don't know what to say," Aidan said. "I have never in all my life had a meal brought to me on a tray. Whatever made you do this?"

"Orders from the Master," Gatekeeper announced as he swept past her and carried the tray into the room. He set it on the bedside table next to the oil lamp. "Here you go now, Miss. You do need to hurry, though. We haven't much time to get you to work, I'm afraid."

"No, I suppose *we* don't," Aidan answered, amused at the familial way he had phrased his last sentence. "Thank you."

Snappily clicking his heels together with his usual little bow, Gatekeeper smiled at her, then turned and rushed out of the room.

Aidan sat back down on the edge of the bed. For a very long moment she just stared in amazement at the tray he had brought. She had never seen such a fancy thing in all her life. The gleaming silver tray and its lid were polished to mirrored perfection and ornately decorated with an intricate pattern of engraved flowers.

When at last she cautiously lifted the cover, she was astonished to find delicate white porcelain dishes filled with steaming food. A white linen napkin and a cup and saucer had been placed next to a tiny pot of tea. There was even a crystal bud vase containing a freshly cut rose.

Delighted, Aidan set the lid aside on the bed and reached for the napkin, which was rolled around the eating utensils. To her amazement, the heavy fork, knife, and spoon that slipped out onto the tray were made of real silver as well.

As she turned her attention to the food it was clear that Drudgery had been quite busy in the kitchen. There were poached eggs on fresh warm biscuits topped with a rich creamy sauce that smelled quite delicious and spilled over a bit onto slices of smoked sausage and a pile of fried potatoes. A small bowl contained some kind of fruit mixture topped with cream. It was a much more sumptuous breakfast than she had ever before eaten.

Aidan smiled with complete delight. How grateful she was for a dear thoughtful friend like Drudgery!

As she dug into the food, she looked out the bedroom window. Far off in the distance she could see the rose-golden dawn just beginning to lighten the sky behind the majestic wall of mountains that surrounded the valley. She found herself wondering when she had last taken the time to look at the beautiful sight before hurrying off to her job at the Fairhaven mansion.

In the back of her mind she also began to wonder what time it was.

Still, she couldn't help but linger over the meal before her, especially savoring the fruit with cream. She poured steaming tea from the tiny pot into the cup and was just beginning to sip the fragrant drink when Gatekeeper's words suddenly came back to her.

Orders from the Master.

At that thought Aidan almost dropped the cup into its saucer. When had Gatekeeper gotten a message from Prince Bal'Davarius about her breakfast?!

She stared again at the tray and dishes. Where had they come from? Why should the Dark Prince care whether she ate breakfast on a fancy tray in her room or on Aunt Mara's old chipped dishes at the dining room table?

In that moment she noticed light sparkling from the crystal bud vase and she picked it up to examine it more closely. It was a most elegantly cut design, almost like a carved jewel, flashing with intense rainbow colors that seemed to radiate from within the vase itself even in the dim lamplight.

It was then that Aidan had her first good look at the rose.

She had naturally assumed it was one of her own cut from a bush in the front yard, but now she saw clearly that it was not. Many different kinds of roses were growing in her garden, but never had she seen one like this.

It was huge and gorgeous, fully open and much too large for the little vase, so heavy it leaned over its edge. Round and perfectly shaped, it was thickly layered with petals colored such a dark shade of burgundy red that they looked black. Both its color and its fragrance reminded her of the sweet wine Aunt Mara used to like. She noticed with surprise that its short stem was grey, almost woody, and bore neither leaves nor thorns.

Delighted, she pressed her fingers into the velvety soft petals. The rose released its heady perfume, so exquisitely sweet that for a moment she felt lightheaded, almost intoxicated, by the sheer joy it gave her. She breathed in deeply, savoring its rich fragrance and beauty.

If I could grow a rose like this, it would be the crown jewel of my garden, she thought. *Where has it come from?*

Suddenly Aidan gasped and came back to herself, realizing she must be late for work. She carefully set the vase back onto the tray, then bolted for the door and raced down the front stairs.

Gatekeeper was standing at the bottom waiting for her.

"There you are, Miss! I have given orders for your –"

Aidan cut him off with a wave of her hand as she grabbed her shawl and swept it around her shoulders.

"I'm much too late to stop now, Gatekeeper! Thank you so much for the lovely breakfast! I must be on my way – I'll see you later!"

"But Miss – wait!" Gatekeeper called, hurrying after her.

Aidan pulled open the door and dashed down the path to the sidewalk, but when she reached the iron gate she stopped short and gasped at what she saw.

For there, directly in front of her, stood a magnificent carriage!

Her immediate thought was that this was a hired carriage and that new guests were arriving, and her heart sank.

Not more guests – not now! I'm already so late!

Stewart would surely scold her without mercy – and what would Lady Fairhaven say?!

The enclosed carriage was lacquered in shiny black and crimson and lavishly decorated with elaborate gold scrolls. Hitched to it were two elegant black horses, snorting impatiently and stamping their polished hoofs against the cobblestones. A footman wearing an elaborate uniform in the same colors as the carriage stood waiting at attention holding the door open.

Aidan stared at the amazing spectacle, at first dumbfounded and then completely horrified as she suddenly realized this was a royal carriage – and it was empty.

It's the Prince! He's actually come – but where is he?!

Her butler quickly came up beside her.

"Gatekeeper, what is this?!" she demanded. "Why didn't you tell me?!"

"But Miss, I did try to tell you," he said.

"Where is he now? Did he go into the house? He must be furious that I've kept him waiting!"

Confused, Gatekeeper replied, "Waiting? I don't understand, Miss. Whom?"

"Prince Bal'Davarius – your Master!" Aidan gestured frantically to the coach. "This *is* his carriage, isn't it?!"

Gatekeeper suddenly understood her agitation and gave a hearty laugh.

"Oh no, Miss, no! The Master isn't here. If he were, I surely would have told you at once. No, Miss, this is your carriage."

At this Aidan could hardly speak.

"My – *my* carriage?!" she stammered. "But – but how can this be?"

Just then a pleasant baritone voice called out a greeting from far above her.

"Good morning, Milady! And such a fine morning it is too!"

Aidan looked up to see who had spoken. It was the coachman, who was perched high above the street in the driver's seat with a crop and the reins in one strong gloved hand. As she stared up at him, he smiled down at her and politely tipped his cap with his free hand.

Obviously a man who took great care in his appearance, the portly driver had a perfectly trimmed streaked grey beard beneath a thick waxed and curled mustache. He was dressed in soft black suede breeches and a crimson satin coat resplendent with gold braid, buttons, and epaulets. His black leather boots had been polished until they shone brightly. As he set his cap back onto his head, Aidan noticed that it too was black leather and trimmed with gold braid.

"As I started to tell you, Miss," Gatekeeper said, "I have given orders for your carriage to take you right to the Fairhaven mansion."

"Don't fret about a thing, Milady," the coachman reassured her. "My fine horses are swift as mountain streams in springtime and we know the way very well. Step right into my coach and we shall have you there straightaway."

Completely dazed and confused, Aidan turned to stare at Gatekeeper. Finding her voice at last, she said, "I don't understand – what is this all about?"

"Well, Miss," Gatekeeper explained patiently, "this is your carriage. It arrived last evening after you were asleep. The driver will take you anywhere you need to go."

"*My* carriage." Aidan felt herself go numb with shock.

"Sent by the Master for your personal use," the driver called to her. "Now please get in, Milady. I'm afraid I can't take you anywhere unless you get in."

Aidan could only protest incoherently.

"But I – I – I can't – I don't know – I've never ridden in a carriage!"

"Orders from the Master, Miss," Gatekeeper insisted. He took her arm gently but firmly and ushered her through the open gate toward the waiting coach. "Come along now, you must hurry!"

Obediently, feeling as though she were in a dream, Aidan stumbled toward the ornately decorated coach. The spirited black horses snorted again, anxious to start moving, and made her jump in fright.

When she reached the carriage door, which was still held open by the footman, she looked inside and gasped in awe. It was more luxurious than anything she had ever seen. The seats, the walls and even the insides of the doors were covered with dark crimson velvet, all thickly padded and tufted with gold buttons. The windows in the doors could slide open and were framed by black velvet curtains held back with heavy gold chains.

Frozen with wonder, Aidan was sure she was staring at a vision come to life from a picture in one of her childhood fairy tale books.

"Miss, you must hurry," Gatekeeper urged her again.

He gestured to the footman, who bowed and reached out to her. Aidan hesitantly took his hand and carefully stepped up into the carriage. She settled herself very lightly on the cushioned seat and gently ran her fingers across the velvet. It seemed to her that she had never before felt anything so soft.

The footman quickly shut the door and the carriage bounced as he leapt up onto its rear perch. The movement startled Aidan and she reached out to steady herself, clutching nervously at the cushioned door.

Through the open window she could hear Gatekeeper issuing orders to the driver. "Make haste and take her right to the mansion. Now off with you!"

Aidan could see the driver's shoulders and back through a small upper window directly in front of her. With a flourish he shook the reins and tapped his crop against the horses' flanks, calling sharply to them. The spirited animals were eager to move, and as the coach lurched forward she was abruptly thrown backwards into the velvet padding behind her.

Grabbing the wall to steady herself, she listened in panic to the jangling of the hitches and the unfamiliar rhythms of the horses' snappy hoofs clipping along the cobblestones. Outside the windows to her right and left, the houses on the street seemed to race past her at dizzying speed.

Her heart pounded in a mixture of elation and terror. Although she was fearful at this new experience, Aidan felt thrilled beyond words at this incredible turn of events. She wondered why the Dark Prince would ever give her a royal carriage.

Then the thought struck her that Lord and Lady Fairhaven – or even worse, Stewart – would see her drive up to the mansion. How would she ever explain all this when she herself could hardly begin to understand it?

But then she was even more horrified to think that her neighbors might also see her. She sank back into the velvet padding, realizing with dread that she – who was such an outsider as it was – would no doubt soon be the object of all the town's latest gossip.

The carriage bumped and jostled noisily all the way through the town and up the Fairhavens' hill. To Aidan's great relief, when it finally pulled up outside the mansion, there was no one in sight.

The driver pulled hard on the reins and called affectionately to his horses.

"Whoa, now! Whoa there, my lovelies!"

Neighing in protest, the magnificent animals came to a halt. The coach bounced again as the footman jumped down from his perch and opened the door, reaching out a hand to help her.

Aidan's knees were shaking so badly she was afraid she would fall as she carefully stepped onto the ground. She turned and as the footman closed the door she saw for the first time that the royal crest of Prince Bal'Davarius was prominently displayed on the door, carved in relief and overlaid with gold.

The driver tipped his hat to her again. "I trust your ride was perfectly comfortable, Milady," he called to her.

"Oh, yes, thank you," Aidan replied, looking up at him. "Tell me, please, what is your name?"

He smiled beneath his mustache, revealing perfectly straight white teeth.

"My name is Pride."

"It's nice to meet you," Aidan said, and turned to the footman. "And you, sir, what is your name?"

The footman bowed slightly and smiled at her, but there was something sinister in his eyes that made Aidan shiver.

"I am Greed," he answered.

Aidan smiled back at him but felt uneasy at the look in his eyes.

"Well – I thank you both again. I must go right inside. I'm terribly late."

"Good day to you, Milady," Pride said with a last tip of his cap.

Greed went to the front of the carriage and climbed up into the driver's seat next to him. Pride called to his horses and turned the carriage around, then headed swiftly down the hill.

Aidan watched them go. "Good day," she replied softly, knowing the driver could not hear her, for they were already too far away. She turned and raced up the steps to the front door.

The Fairhavens' intimidating butler greeted her with a pompous announcement, his voice quite brusque.

"Good morning, Aidan. My Lord and Lady have not yet returned from Clearview, so I have decided you shall work in the library this morning. Lord Fairhaven's books need a thorough dusting."

Aidan was completely disappointed to receive this tedious and dirty assignment – and greatly annoyed, for she was sure Stewart was just being mean to her. But there wasn't much she could do, for he would surely report any protest to Lady Fairhaven.

"Yes, Stewart," she sighed.

"Some of the volumes are extremely old and fragile," he continued crisply, "so you must be sure to take the greatest of care." Then he looked pointedly down his nose at her and with thick sarcasm added, "But, of course, I am *quite* sure that you would *never* harm my Lord's precious books any more than you would harm my Lady's precious musical instruments!"

With that, he spun on his heel and marched stiffly away from her, leaving her speechless with indignation. She started angrily down the main hallway to gather cleaning supplies.

To her amazement, as she passed Lord Fairhaven's huge antique floor clock, she discovered that she was not late for work at all and in fact had arrived five minutes early!

Staring at the clock in bewilderment, she wondered how this could have happened. Her heart swelled with gratitude for the arrival of Pride's coach with its swift black horses, and she quickly forgot all about Stewart's unkindness.

Aidan had never set foot in the library before and she entered cautiously, extremely intimidated at the privilege even though she knew Lord Fairhaven would not be there.

Her first sight of the room completely took her breath away.

Ornately carved oak shelves filled with books were built into the entire length and height of three walls, even surrounding the heavy door that was the only entrance into the room. Tall sliding ladders on wheels could be moved along the walls of books, enabling one to reach the very highest shelves. The fourth wall featured two tall leaded glass windows set high above oak wainscoting that flanked a huge dark green marble fireplace.

It was clear even at first glance that this was Lord Fairhaven's private refuge, a very masculine room that housed his extensive collection of books acquired over centuries by many ancestors. Spacious and stately with a high ceiling and an oak parquet floor, the library exhibited a pervasive strength and a sense of order that reflected its owner's personality in every way.

Aidan almost tiptoed to the center of the room, just staring up in awe. She had never even imagined a room like this with so many books!

Had Lord Fairhaven actually read them all?!

As she looked around the impressive room she steadied herself by putting her hand on the immense oak desk next to her. Arranged very precisely across its top were a brass oil lamp, an inkwell and various other writing supplies. The desk faced the fireplace. Its chair was cushioned in dark green leather and two more green leather chairs were by the stone hearth. One of these had a matching hassock and was positioned beside a small table and a reading lamp on a brass stand. Aidan assumed this was where Lord Fairhaven relaxed to enjoy his books.

She walked over to the elegant fireplace. To her amazement she found that the upper part of the wall surrounding the windows was completely covered with soft brown suede. Under one window was a liquor cabinet offering crystal glasses and sparkling decanters full of various drinks.

Centered above the thick wooden mantel was a large ornately framed picture that seemed very strange indeed – an ancient yellowed piece of vellum filled with finely drawn meandering lines. She puzzled over it for a long moment before turning to look again with trepidation at the many books she had to dust and the tall ladders she would have to climb to get to them all.

The warmth of polished golden oak and the smells of wood and leather made Lord Fairhaven's library seem entirely different to Aidan than any other place she had ever been. Suddenly she found herself wondering what it must feel like to have such a room in one's house – a private haven for a man with whom one was deeply in love.

She was completely taken aback at this notion and wondered whatever could have prompted her to think of it, for she had never had such a thought before.

But a deep wistful longing overwhelmed her as she realized – once again – that she would never know the quiet joy of that kind of intimacy. There were few eligible young men in Hidden, and none of them had ever shown any interest in the likes of her, a poor orphan and an outsider in the town.

Then she brightened, remembering the vow she had sworn right there on the hill below her that she would not be alone forever. Someday she was certain she would be loved and wanted. Someday soon she just knew she would find him – The One Who Would Love Her Forever!

Aidan paused for another moment to admire the masculine elegance of the room, then went right to work. There were hundreds, perhaps thousands of books, and she knew she had no small task ahead of her.

She carefully climbed up the ladder to the top shelf on the left wall. Although the books were quite dusty, the work went fairly quickly. There was no need to remove them any further than tilting them forward a bit whenever necessary. Mostly she was able to slide a cloth along the tops and spines of the volumes while they were still in place on their shelves, especially on the uppermost rows where she was close to panic to be so high up on the ladder. Dirt smudged her apron and dust landed on the floor far below as she worked.

Lord Fairhaven's vast collection of books was fascinating to Aidan. Some of them were ancient and crumbling and she dusted those very carefully. She didn't dare open a single book but she did read some of the titles, many of which were stamped in gold. Most of them she didn't understand, for they mainly seemed to be about wars and history, leather-bound volumes of subjects that would appeal more to a man's literary taste than a woman's. Still, she thought, it must be wonderful beyond measure to have so many books to read – and so much free time in which to read them.

Books had been a treasured luxury in the Teague household. As Aidan dusted Lord Fairhaven's volumes she remembered the beloved picture books she had read as a young child, especially her favorite fairy tale about the Prince rescuing the Princess in her rose garden and killing the Dragon.

The stories and pictures were still vivid in her mind. She had begged Aunt Mara to read the books to her over and over again. Indeed, she had loved them so much that she had quickly learned to read the words herself at an unusually young age. It was one of the very few things Aidan could remember having done so well that Aunt Mara had boasted about it to her friends.

As she grew older, she had read whenever she could find a book to borrow. Books had been her dearest escape from the pain and drudgery of her life with Aunt Mara.

By the time Aidan stepped down from the ladder against the third wall, her chore accomplished, late afternoon sunlight was coming in through the windows. Her body ached and she realized gratefully that it had been a long time since she had done such strenuous work. Her hands and her pretty uniform were covered with grime and she scowled with resentment that Stewart had given her such a harsh and dirty task. She quickly swept the floor and wiped a clean cloth over the desk and leather chairs.

As she came to her final task and reached up to dust the mantel, her attention was again drawn to the strange framed picture hanging above it. She looked more closely and saw that the odd meandering lines were dotted with circles next to ornately scripted words. There were also little drawings scattered somewhat randomly across the picture that looked like tiny hills and groups of relatively large pine trees.

Suddenly the word "Hidden" leapt out at her. Its circle was almost in the center and had a wavy line going through it which branched into more lines on either side. The next circle to the right from this one, close to the edge of the picture, was labeled "Clearview."

Clearview! she thought. *Why, that's where Lord and Lady Fairhaven have gone!*

Aidan had never seen a map before but now she quickly realized the circles were places and the meandering lines must be the roads going through the mountains that connected them. Clearview was the next town along the road to the northeast of Hidden. More wavy lines branched out across the map and contained many other circles. She read the unfamiliar place names with great fascination.

This strange yellowed picture was Aidan's very first glimpse into the world that was outside Hidden. She had no way of knowing it then, but the ancient vellum map showed the towns and mountain territories that had once been ruled by Lord Fairhaven's powerful ancestors over the centuries.

Aidan studied it for a long time before she remembered her workday was over and she could go home. She took one last wondering look at the grand library before stepping into the hall and softly closing the door. Then she quickly put her cleaning supplies away and headed for the door of the mansion.

Chapter Fourteen

Lust and Vanity

To her complete joy, Aidan stepped out of the mansion to find her royal carriage waiting for her. It looked even more spectacular than she remembered. The afternoon sunlight was reflecting brightly from the ornate gold decoration and the royal crest of Prince Bal'Davarius on the door. Feeling a fresh surge of energy and excitement, she hurried down the stone steps, calling to Pride and Greed.

"Good afternoon! I'm so glad to see you."

One of the horses sniffed loudly and flicked his long black tail as Aidan approached the carriage. Greed pulled open the door and stood at attention, waiting for her. Pride smiled and tipped his cap.

"Good afternoon, Milady," he said. "Climb right on in now, and these fine beasts will have you home straightaway."

Greed reached out a hand to help her, and as Aidan thanked him she looked closely at him for the first time. He was dressed in an outfit similar to Pride's. His greasy black hair was slicked down beneath his leather cap and his dark eyes glittered as he smiled beneath his black pencil mustache. She felt herself shiver beneath his gaze, for his look seemed to communicate that he wanted something from her and would stop at nothing to get it. When he closed the door behind her and climbed up onto his perch at the rear of the coach, she felt a curious sense of relief.

Pride snapped his crop and called to the horses, and with a lurch they started down the hill. Aidan leaned back against the plush interior of the coach, feeling much more at home there now than she had that morning, and let her aching body relax. How wonderful to feel so pampered and to have such a pleasant rest after her hard day at work!

As Aidan's eyes moved across the tufted walls and thick velvet drapes, she could feel their rich softness without even extending her hand. All at once a triumphant laugh rose unexpectedly from her throat as it occurred to her that she, a common servant, was riding home from the Fairhavens' mansion in a carriage much more grand than any they had ever owned despite all their great power and wealth!

Drudgery must be right, she thought. *The Prince must have a special plan for me. He has given me servants and fine food on a silver tray and now this carriage. Just look at me! A proper lady, riding in a royal coach!*

Aidan laughed again, utterly contented in the midst of luxury. Reaching out to stroke one of the black velvet window curtains, her attention was drawn to the heavy gold chain that held it open. She sat up and looked at it closely, enjoying the way it caught the light. It was attached to a small golden hook at the side of the window and could be unfastened to close the drape for privacy, but not removed completely from the door.

Letting the curtain fall closed, Aidan draped the chain across the back of her hand and wrapped it around her wrist like a bracelet. Judging from its weight she guessed that it must be pure gold. She had never before held anything that was so precious and found herself wondering what she would look like wearing fine jewels and gold every day as Lady Fairhaven did.

She laughed again, feeling regal and rich, the gold chain gleaming and warm against her wrist. Delicious brand-new feelings of elegance and prestige washed over her for the first time.

Oh, I could grow to love all this, she thought. *Wealth and power! I've never even dared to dream of it – but wouldn't it be fine!*

Then Aidan stopped, suddenly noticing how calloused and dirty her hand was beside the gold chain.

A surge of tremendous guilt rose in her heart as she remembered she didn't deserve any of this. She quickly removed the chain from her wrist and fastened it back around the curtain. Then she wiped her hands on her grimy apron, wondering why all this luxury should have been given to her, of all people – nothing more than a poor common servant girl with no real hope of ever being anything else.

When they arrived at the cottage, Greed opened the carriage door for Aidan and helped her step down onto the sidewalk. Turning back to the carriage, she thanked the two men. Greed jumped back onto the coach and Pride tipped his hat to her before driving around the cottage to Samuel Teague's old carriage house.

Gatekeeper opened the door for Aidan. As she stepped inside, he took her shawl from her and hung it up.

"Good afternoon, Miss," he said.

"Hello, Gatekeeper," she replied.

It was an odd but lovely feeling to have her gentleman butler greet her at the door. The front room was all clean and tidy and she could smell dinner cooking in the kitchen. What a joy not to have to worry about caring for her own house or preparing her own meals! And Drudgery was such a good cook, too.

Gatekeeper gestured to the main room. "If you would like, Miss, I shall have Drudgery prepare tea for you so you may relax awhile by the fire."

Surprised and thoroughly delighted at this, Aidan smiled up at him. "Why – that is so thoughtful of you, Gatekeeper. I'll just run up and change first."

"Very good, Miss." He bowed slightly as she hurried up the stairs.

In her bedroom Aidan quickly removed her filthy work uniform and laid it on the bed. When Lady Fairhaven hired her, she had been thrilled to receive three uniforms like the other servants wore. Although they were sturdy and practical dresses made for work, she thought they were the loveliest clothes she had ever owned. Each was made of dark blue material with a white collar and cuffs and included a starched white apron that partially covered two deep pockets on the front of the skirt.

Aidan kept her uniforms meticulously clean and neat so she would look nice attending Lady Fairhaven every day. But today's dress and apron seemed quite ruined and she hoped they would come clean when they were washed and ironed. Once again she was greatly annoyed that Stewart had given her such a dirty job.

She felt better after she cleaned up and dried herself at the washstand in the corner of her room. Then she put on one of her old dresses, which was patched and worn but clean and very comfortable.

As Aidan brushed the dust out of her long waves of auburn hair, she peered closely at her reflection in the mirror and was alarmed to see dark circles under her eyes. The thought came to her that – just like Drudgery who was young but seemed so old and arthritic from all her hard work – tiring days like this one were likely to age her beyond her years as well.

Then she brightened, thinking of how pleasant it would be to relax by the fire with a cup of tea, and hurried downstairs.

Her butler was waiting for her as Aidan sank into Aunt Mara's old rocking chair by the fireplace. He bowed respectfully, hovering over her with grandfatherly concern.

"Did you have a difficult day, Miss?"

Aidan smiled at him.

"No, not really that difficult. It was very quiet – it was almost rather pleasant, dusting all of Lord Fairhaven's books. But I'm quite tired now."

Gatekeeper picked up a small wooden table and moved it over next to her chair. On the table was her breakfast tray, now bearing a gleaming silver tea service and a plate heaped with little pastries. He poured some steaming tea into a white porcelain cup.

"Your tea, Miss," he said, bowing and handing it to her.

"Oh, this is so kind of you, Gatekeeper," Aidan said gratefully as she took the cup and saucer. She breathed in the fragrance of the Master's best tea, feeling that she had never felt so completely pampered in all her life. "Thank you so much."

Then Gatekeeper held out the plate. "This is delightful!" Aidan exclaimed as she chose a sweet roll that was sticky with sugary glaze. "Did Drudgery bake these?"

"That she did, Miss."

He handed her a white linen napkin and stood by attentively while she ate her pastry and then chose a second. Feeling thoroughly decadent, Aidan licked her fingers, wiped them with the napkin, and sank back into the cushions of the rocking chair, relaxing as the tension left her aching muscles. Gatekeeper refilled her teacup and she took it from him, sighing with contentment.

"This is all so wonderful," she said. "Having a carriage to ride in and tea waiting for me when I arrive home – especially today when I'm so worn out – it's just so lovely. Did you say this morning that the coach arrived last night?"

"Yes, Miss, after you went to bed."

She sipped her tea thoughtfully, rocking gently in the chair.

"And I take it you found room for Pride and Greed upstairs?"

"Yes, Miss, they've been taken care of, and their wives with them."

"*Wives?!* Goodness!"

Flustered, Aidan bolted upright in the chair.

"You didn't tell me their wives were here too! Where are they? I should greet them."

Gatekeeper took her cup and saucer and placed them on the tray.

"I believe they're out in the gardens back of the house, Miss. Shall I summon them for you?"

Aidan's legs were still stiff, but she felt she needed the solace of her gardens to greet more new guests.

"No, I'll go to them, Gatekeeper. Thank you so much for the tea and please thank Drudgery for the pastries too."

Gatekeeper bowed, clicking his heels together with his usual flourish. "Very good, Miss."

He picked up the silver tray and carried it toward the kitchen. Aidan rose carefully from the rocker, straightening up slowly, and followed behind him, heading for the back yard.

Even though many of her guests were enjoying the gardens, the newcomers to her household were not at all hard to pick out. They were standing together talking at the far end of the yard watching through the open iron gate as Pride and Greed brushed the horses outside the carriage house. Aidan was not surprised that one woman was older and the other younger, but she was astounded at the bright colors they were wearing. For a long moment, unnoticed by her new guests, she stood near the cottage staring at their outfits, the fanciest dresses she had ever seen.

The older woman was ostentatiously dressed in a flawlessly coordinated ensemble. Her bright emerald green silk dress had elaborately gathered ruffles cascading down the back of the skirt, which flared slightly at the bottom. Over the dress she wore a darker green velvet jacket with a peplum at the waist that spread out in the back above the ruffles. Perched atop her head was a dark green velvet hat with a narrow brim. Rising from the back of the hat were three showy peacock feathers, something Aidan had never seen before.

The younger woman had her back to Aidan. Her light blonde hair was pinned back on top of her head leaving a cascade of loose curls tumbling softly against the back of her neck and shoulders. She was wearing a gown of scarlet satin. Its skirt was tight but had a gentle flair at the bottom and accentuated the shapely curves of her tiny waist and round firm buttocks.

But Aidan's attention was not on the skirt of the dress so much as on the bodice – or lack thereof, for the woman's back was exposed almost all the way to her waist and it appeared that she was wearing only a skirt with no top at all. The sight was so shocking that Aidan froze, afraid to approach the newcomers.

Just then the woman in the green outfit turned and glanced at her. She said something to the woman in scarlet, who quickly turned around. As Aidan caught sight of the front of her, she immediately felt her face flame as bright red as the woman's outfit.

For the dress did indeed have a top, but not much of one. It was a halter made of the same scarlet satin as the skirt. Its shockingly low cut plunged to just below her cleavage, exposing a great deal of the woman's large round breasts. As if the top of the dress weren't revealing enough, the tight flaring skirt was slit all the way up the right side almost to the hip, and Aidan could see a black lace stocking covering the woman's shapely leg. The curves of her body were emphasized by thin black vertical stripes running down the halter to just below the fitted waist.

The woman smiled, turned again and said something to the woman in green. Staring at the outrageous red dress, Aidan suddenly felt naked and exposed herself, yet at the same time she was fascinated by this new guest. She took a deep breath, trying to hide her complete embarrassment as she walked the length of the yard to where the pair was standing. Hoping she wouldn't seem rude, she kept her face steadily focused on the woman in the green outfit to avoid looking at the woman in scarlet.

"Good afternoon, ladies. You must be my latest guests from Prince Bal'Davarius."

"Yes, of course," the older woman replied, her voice deep and haughty. "The Master has decided that we are needed here. You must be Aidan."

She held out her left hand. Aidan was intrigued by the dark green lace gloves she wore that covered her hands from her wrists to her knuckles but left her perfectly manicured fingers and ornate gold wedding rings uncovered.

"How do you do? My name is Vanity. I am the wife of Pride, the driver of your coach."

Vanity was a strikingly aristocratic woman. Her pepper-and-salt grey hair was pulled neatly back beneath her green velvet hat into a perfectly coiled bun with not a single hair out of place. Her long oval face was graced by a powdered apricot complexion that was obviously well pampered. She peered down her long straight nose at Aidan through heavily lidded dark green eyes which were set off to perfection by her green outfit.

"How do you do?" repeated Aidan as she nervously bowed slightly, completely intimidated by this imposing woman. She reached for the outstretched gloved hand and was puzzled when Vanity barely rested her limp fingers against her own for an instant before quickly withdrawing them.

"I must apologize that I haven't met you until now," Aidan said shyly. "I do hope you've made yourselves comfortable. I've just come home from work."

"Oh!" Vanity sniffed pompously. "A *working* girl. How very droll." She eyed Aidan up and down and gestured with obvious disdain toward her patched and threadbare dress. "Well! No wonder the Master has sent us! I can see that we're most needed here."

Aidan was taken aback by the insult, but before she could even react, her attention was caught by the large brooch nestled amid the lace ruffles of Vanity's collar. Diamonds and emeralds flashed in the sunlight like green flames. She had never seen anything so spectacular in all her life.

At that same instant the woman in red reached out and put her hand on Aidan's arm. As she moved, the narrow black stripes running down the bodice of her dress glittered and Aidan now saw that they were actually rows of faceted black glass beads.

"Oh, now, don't you listen to Vanity," she scolded amiably, speaking to Aidan but directing her comments to the older woman. Her soft contralto voice was friendly and cheerful. "She's always so full of herself that she doesn't think of others' feelings. I'm Greed's wife. My name is Lust."

Turning to Lust, Aidan carefully kept her eyes on her face to avoid looking at her bosom. She saw that her hair had somehow been lightened to its pale blonde color, for it was darker at the roots. Her soft curls had been loosely pulled away from her face and secured above her ears with small gold combs sparkling with rubies.

Beneath Lust's curls Aidan could see long cascades of flashing diamonds hanging from gold wires pierced through her earlobes. She found herself at the same time fascinated by the showy earrings and horrified at the thought of having holes in one's ears, something she had never seen before.

At Lust's throat was a necklace not as showy but just as beautiful as Vanity's emerald brooch. Three large square diamonds accented by several small rubies hung on a gold chain resting against her collarbone, setting off her long thin neck and elegant chin to perfection.

Lust's face was delicately beautiful with a small tipped nose and high dark pink cheekbones framing a bright red rosebud of a mouth. On the left side of her chin, just beneath her full sensuous lips, was a small black mole.

But Aidan was most fascinated by her pale eyes, which were violet-grey, an eye color she had never seen before. Lust's thick black lashes seemed to be accented by subtle black lines drawn around her eyes and by light streaks of shiny gold across her eyelids. This was greatly intriguing to Aidan, who couldn't know that she had used cosmetics because these, like pierced ears, were totally unknown in Hidden.

Aidan had never met anyone like this and couldn't understand her own reaction to her. Even though she felt deep embarrassment in the presence of Lust's blatant sensuality and revealing dress, she was also drawn to her beauty – beauty as hot and alluring as Fear's was cold and aloof, a sophisticated beauty borne worlds away from the valley where Hidden was nestled in complete isolation.

It was difficult for Aidan to keep her voice steady as she struggled to find something to say. She breathed deeply and said, "It's nice to meet you, Lust. Did – did all of you travel together in the carriage?"

If Lust noticed Aidan's uneasiness, she never let on. The smile on her face was open and sincere.

"Yes," she replied, "and it was such a long wearisome trip from the Master's palace through the mountains. But we've taken the entire day to freshen up. Your gardens have been the most lovely place to relax. Such beautiful roses!"

"Why – thank you," Aidan said, surprised and flattered by her compliment.

"Yes, it's very quaint," Vanity interjected in her haughty tone. Then she reached out and rested one gloved hand on Lust's arm. "But enough of this small talk, Lust. We must get busy and attend to the work the Master has given us to do here."

Turning to Aidan, she announced crisply, "The Master has sent us to help you with your wardrobe."

"My – my *wardrobe?"*

Aidan could scarcely begin to imagine how these two incredibly dressed women might help her with her wardrobe!

"Yes, Aidan," Lust said excitedly. "Come see what the Master has sent for you!"

She tucked her arm through Aidan's and began to lead her up the path toward the house.

"The Master has sent me clothes?" Aidan asked, astounded.

"Oh, yes, clothes and much, much more," Lust replied. "So many wonderful gifts! Come at once and see!"

The rustle of petticoats and ruffles accompanied the three as Lust ushered Aidan through the back door into the kitchen, Vanity following close behind.

Chapter Fifteen

Aidan's New Wardrobe

Lust and Vanity led Aidan upstairs to Aunt Mara's old bedroom. When they opened the heavy wooden door and ushered her inside, Aidan gasped in shock.

There were sturdy cardboard boxes stacked everywhere: hat boxes, shoe boxes, dress boxes, coat boxes, beautifully wrapped boxes of all sizes and shapes. The heady scent of roses permeated the room from a huge crystal vase filled with dark long-stemmed blooms that took up most of the space on a table by the window.

Vanity carefully removed her hat and began to pick fussily at it, removing bits of invisible lint and fluffing the peacock feathers. Then she turned and pointedly ran her finger along the top of the bureau checking for dust before placing the hat on it.

But Aidan was barely even aware of Vanity in the room with her. She was staring in complete awe at all the boxes.

"What is this?" she whispered, leaning against the doorframe for support. "Are these – for me?"

"Every one," laughed Lust. "All for you, and all from the Master."

She began picking up boxes and looking them over, trying to decide which one Aidan should open first.

Aidan shook her head in confusion. "But – but why?"

Vanity was patting gently at her pepper-and-salt hair, but at Aidan's question she stopped and turned to look at her.

"Obviously, my dear," she sniffed, "the Master has decided you should look more like a fine young lady and less like a scullery maid."

Lust's eyes glinted enticingly as she chose a box and held it out to Aidan.

"Come, Aidan, open this one first. Let's see what the Master has sent for you."

Like a confused child at her first birthday party, not at all sure what to do, Aidan reached out uncertainly and took the gift. The fancy box was printed with brightly colored flowers and tied shut with a pale blue satin ribbon. She gazed in wonder at it, hardly able to believe it was really for her.

"I've never received such a lovely box in all my life," she whispered. "I've never received a gift like this at all – never mind a whole roomful of them." She looked at Lust in bewilderment. "This is more than I can believe."

Lust smiled.

"Don't be afraid to believe, Aidan. The Master has personally chosen each of these gifts for you. He ordered them wrapped in beautiful boxes just for your pleasure. Go ahead – open it!"

Moving slowly, as though in a daze, Aidan sank down onto the edge of the bed. She pulled at the bow, which untied easily. The ribbon slipped away from the box and Aidan set it gently aside onto the bed. Then she carefully opened the box.

Inside were several layers of crisp white tissue paper. She carefully folded back the paper and gasped at the sight of a filmy silk blouse. Gently, as though it would break, she lifted it out of the box and held it up.

Creamy white, trimmed with delicate lace, it had shiny round buttons running down its front and accenting the cuffs of its long fully gathered sleeves. She looked more closely at the buttons and found to her amazement that they looked like pearls.

"Oh my goodness," she gasped, touching one with her finger. "These buttons – are they real?"

"Yes, those are real pearls," Lust said, holding out a larger box. "Open this one next. I think they might go together." She seemed as excited as Aidan over the gifts.

Aidan carefully laid the blouse back in the first box as though she were putting a newborn baby into a cradle. Then she took the second box from Lust and untied its ribbon. Inside, also wrapped in white tissue paper, was a skirt of navy blue taffeta, long and full with wide ruffles at the bottom.

"Oh! Isn't it lovely!" she exclaimed. She jumped to her feet, holding the skirt up to her waist, laughing and twirling to see how it would fall. It looked to be just the right size.

Lust laughed along with her, obviously enjoying Aidan's delight. Vanity turned up her nose haughtily at their excitement, as if she herself were above such girlishness, and handed Aidan the next box.

By now Aidan was becoming very curious about what was in all the boxes. She took the one Vanity was holding and opened it quickly. Gasping in awe, she pulled out a navy blue velvet jacket that was a perfect match for the taffeta skirt. The buttons along the front of the jacket looked like they were made of silver. As Aidan fingered the soft velvet she thought of the plush tufted interior of the carriage.

Lust held out another box, the largest yet, and Aidan took it greedily. Her shock and amazement were quickly turning to great joy and covetousness at all the beautiful new clothes. She eagerly tore open the box and pulled at the white tissue paper to see what else Prince Bal'Davarius had sent for her.

Her heart leapt at the sight of an elegant blue-grey taffeta dress. Aidan pulled it out of the box with a loud squeal of delight and held it up. It had long sleeves with puffed shoulders and a fitted bodice. Adorning the dress were a wide sash around the waist and cascading tiers of ruffles running down the back of the skirt, all of shiny red, blue and green plaid taffeta. Such a fancy, showy dress!

"Oh, but that does set off the color of your eyes, Aidan," Lust declared approvingly.

"Does it really?" Aidan asked, holding it up against her chest, amazed that the beautiful colors would look so fine on her.

"These two go with it," said Vanity.

She held out a hatbox. Inside there was a tiny hat of the same blue-grey fabric with a wide plaid ribbon to tie under the chin. Rising from one side was a soft blue ostrich feather. Aidan had never seen a hat like it and she stroked the feather in wonder before she excitedly placed it on her head. It felt to her like a crown, and she giggled at Lust's encouraging nod. Then Vanity handed her a shoebox containing a pair of coordinating blue-grey silk pumps.

"I've never had an outfit that matched from head to toe," Aidan told her guests as she tried on the shoes. They fit perfectly, as though they had been made for her.

"It will be a stunning outfit, just perfect," Lust insisted. "Here, now open these." She held out two boxes tied together with a pink ribbon.

Reaching for the boxes, Aidan tossed the hat and shoes aside onto the bed, which caused Vanity to gasp and frown with disapproval as she quickly retrieved them. She fussed at the feather on the hat with obvious annoyance before carefully replacing it into its box.

The top box contained a white silk petticoat with two tiers of ruffles and fine lace around the hem. With the petticoat was a white silk camisole trimmed with satin ribbon and the daintiest lace Aidan had ever seen.

The second box contained a floor-length linen nightdress. She cried out in awe and delight when she saw it. It was pure snowy white trimmed with handmade white lace and pink satin ribbon at the collar and the edges of the puffy sleeves. Large embroidered roses in all different shades of pink, red, and yellow were scattered across the upper front of the nightdress, which hung loose and full to its lacy ruffle around the hem.

Aidan had never imagined anything like this exquisitely made garment designed just for sleep. Speechless, she stroked the soft linen and looked closely at the roses, which were flawless. It was much more exacting handwork than any she had ever seen, even Aunt Mara's, which had been very fine indeed.

"The Master has excellent taste in women's clothing, does he not?" Vanity commented approvingly.

Speaking as though she knew about this intimately, Lust replied softly, "Yes, he certainly does know how to pamper a maiden."

At that, Aidan stared at Lust and suddenly came back to herself. Blushing crimson, she gently folded the nightdress, replacing it reluctantly but firmly into its box.

"I can never accept this," she whispered, shaking her head sadly and pushing the box away on the bed. "I just can't. It isn't proper to accept such intimate clothing from – from a man. Not even from a Prince."

Lust looked at Aidan with her beguiling violet-grey eyes and said very quietly, "You know you want that nightdress very much, Aidan. Just like all the other clothes."

"Oh, more than anything," Aidan agreed, and longingly caressed the soft embroidered rosebuds again. "But to take gifts of – of petticoats and nightdresses from a man I've never met, Prince or not, why, it's – it's indecent."

She looked longingly at the boxes she had opened and their elegant contents.

"Perhaps it isn't right for me to accept any of this."

Lust laughed derisively at her comment.

"How absurd! You know how deeply you've yearned all your life for such a fabulous wardrobe. Hasn't this always been one of your heart's greatest desires?"

Aidan stared at her, wondering how she knew that having fine beautiful clothes had indeed been one of her fondest dreams.

"And here it's been placed right into your hands! Beautiful clothes with all the accessories, all more wonderful than you've ever imagined – all yours just for the taking. Don't be a fool, Aidan. You want them – you know you want them very much – and the Master has gladly given them. So just take them!"

Completely torn, Aidan moaned, "But I just can't! I – I know I don't deserve anything like this!"

She looked imploringly into the haughty face of Vanity and the enticing face of Lust.

"How does Prince Bal'Davarius even know me? Why is he giving me all these things? What does he want from me in return? I simply can't accept these things unless I know."

Vanity cleared her throat.

"We don't know what the Master ultimately intends for you, Aidan, but we do know that he has selected each piece of this wardrobe for you with his own hand, out of his great generosity. He has given us the task of presenting them to you, and our orders are very strict. He will not take kindly to being refused. I give you fair warning – you must never risk angering the Master."

Aidan stared at her in shock, astounded to learn that the sovereign Prince of all the Kingdom had gone to the great trouble and expense of personally choosing a luxurious wardrobe for a common servant girl he had never before laid eyes on. Something in her heart was telling her that no matter how generous the Dark Prince might be, such gifts were rarely offered without strings attached. What would he want from her in return?

In that instant she remembered Drudgery telling her that in his great anger the Prince had once turned into a huge lion.

Suddenly she felt trapped and afraid – afraid to accept any of his gifts, but just as afraid not to.

Seeing her tension, Lust smiled, her eyes warm and alluring.

"Don't be afraid, Aidan," she urged. "Only the Master knows why he has decided to bestow his great blessing upon you. What does it matter? All you need to do is accept his fine gifts. Just take them all! You know you want to, more than anything. So why not do it?"

Aidan trembled with an intense yearning she had never known and didn't fully understand. The temptation to just give in and accept everything was overwhelming, yet still she hesitated.

"I'm sorry. Somehow this just feels wrong to me. I'm – I'm afraid."

Lust picked up a tiny box and stepped close to her.

"How can it be wrong to accept gifts from a willing giver?" she whispered persuasively. "There's nothing wrong with taking your heart's desire. Look here, Aidan – let me show you how truly generous the Master can be."

Aidan looked down at the box, intrigued because she had never seen one like it. It was an oval-shaped box that just fit into Lust's palm, covered with soft black velvet. Lust flipped open the top, which was hinged to the bottom at the back of the box.

A flash of light caught Aidan's eye. Suddenly her mouth dropped open and she gasped loudly as she found herself staring at a circle of small sapphires surrounding a huge oval bluish-white diamond on a gleaming chain of gold. Sparks of rainbow fire glittered from the priceless treasure that was being offered to her.

All her resistance to temptation melted.

She reached breathlessly for the box, which Lust readily gave, removing the necklace for her. Aidan held it up in her shaking hand as though it were so delicate it would break.

Lust laughed.

"It's not glass, Aidan. Every stone is genuine, and I can assure you they won't break. Here, let me fasten it for you."

She took the treasure and Aidan eagerly turned around and held up her hair. The weight of the stones felt heavy and foreign against her throat, for she had never worn a necklace before, but the rich feeling it gave her was the most glorious sensation she could ever remember experiencing.

Trembling with excitement, gently caressing the necklace with her fingers, she turned and faced Lust and Vanity.

"How does it look?"

"Aidan, it's as though it was made just for you," Lust replied. "You were born to wear diamonds."

Flushed with pride, Aidan giggled excitedly. "Do you really think so?"

"Oh come now, Lust, *really!*"

Vanity's face was twisted with irritation. She waved a hand in disgust toward Aidan, whose patched dress looked strange indeed paired with a priceless necklace.

"Right now she hardly looks as though she were born to wear diamonds! Let us not waste a single moment on such idiocy. We may not have enough time to accomplish our work for the Master as it is."

While Aidan was wondering what she meant by that, Vanity turned to her and announced, "Aidan, after dinner I shall have Drudgery draw you a hot bath.

There can be no doubt that soap and water will help tremendously. And we shall need to do something with your hair as well."

She frowned thoughtfully, eyeing Aidan up and down.

"While I'm certain that each of the outfits the Master has chosen will be perfect, we have a great deal of work ahead of us before you will be able to carry yourself as a lady who truly seems born to wear diamonds."

"A lady," whispered Aidan. The necklace made her feel like one already, even in her threadbare dress. "But – but why are you doing all this? Why do you want to turn me into a lady?"

"Mercy, child!" Vanity exclaimed in frustration. "So many questions! I would venture to guess that the Master is planning to come here himself and you surely can't meet him in filthy rags. You must be ready."

Aidan gasped, but part of her had been expecting this news all along.

"So the Prince *is* coming here!" she cried. "When will he come? I must know!"

Vanity sighed impatiently.

"As I told you, I cannot say for certain what the Master's intentions are, for I don't know them. Nor do I know for certain if he will actually come here, for whatever he chooses to do is his own business. But it would seem reasonable that eventually he intends to meet you in person. Our task is simply to give you these clothes and other gifts and prepare you for when that might happen."

Lust was busily picking over the piles of gifts that remained to be opened.

"There are still many more boxes here, Aidan," she commented. "I think this one might be perfume."

Aidan turned around to look and caught sight of the bouquet of long-stemmed roses on the table by the window. They were of the same dark variety as the one that had been placed on her breakfast tray. She walked over to examine them closely.

"These roses are just gorgeous," she said. "I've never seen anything like them before. Where have they come from?"

"They are exquisite, aren't they?" Lust replied, looking at the vase. "These are the Master's prized black roses. He cut them himself from the bushes in his private palace garden, and we brought them with us in the coach. The Master knows you have a passion for roses, so he sent you his finest – just for your pleasure."

Aidan bent over the crystal vase and looked closely at the perfectly shaped and heavily scented blossoms. The unusual roses were every bit as precious to her as the jewels at her throat. Their fragrance was intoxicating and their beauty unrivaled.

Curiously, there was no greenery in the vase, for like the one that had been on her tray that morning, the huge blooms were supported by thick woody stems that apparently had no leaves. As she carefully lifted a rose from the vase, she could see that its stem had been scraped, for there were no thorns on it either.

"Does your Master have other roses in his garden, too?" she asked.

"Oh, of course, hundreds of different varieties," Lust said. "But this is his favorite – the finest of them all."

"There are no leaves," Aidan commented. "How odd."

"Yes, this variety grows without them," Lust replied. "That's one of the things that the Master loves most about his black roses. Nothing to distract from the beauty of the blossoms."

Aidan stroked the dark velvety petals thoughtfully, her fingers lingering in pleasure at their luxurious softness. Looking up at Lust, she said quietly, "I still don't understand. Why would he send these beautiful treasures to the likes of me?"

Lust laughed.

"My, Aidan, but you do ask a lot of silly questions! Why trouble yourself so about it? Isn't this better than what you had before? Do you wish to stay the way you are forever? As I said a moment ago – it can't be wrong to take gifts from a willing giver."

"But you don't understand," Aidan said, wistfully sliding the black rose back into the crystal vase. "I'm not royalty. I'm not wealthy. I'm just a poor orphan girl – a common servant. I know I don't deserve any of this, no matter how much I might want it."

"The Master chooses to do whatever he will, Aidan, and he won't change his mind once it is made up," Vanity told her firmly. "He is extremely rich and powerful, and he will take good care of you if he so chooses. And he does seem to have chosen you – for whatever reason. So we must get on with the work he has given us to do here in your house."

Aidan laughed nervously. Perhaps Lust and Vanity were right. Now that she had tasted such riches, wouldn't it be better to take and enjoy them than to live out her life without them?

Lust held out another box for her to open.

In her final moment of hesitation, she caressed the velvety black roses one last time. Then she moved her hand from the roses to the jewels at her throat, needing to convince herself that it was really all right for them to be there.

Finally, all resistance crumbling at last, Aidan smiled broadly and reached eagerly for the box in Lust's hand. Giggling delightedly, she threw herself with complete abandon into the intense pleasure of opening all of her gifts from the Dark Prince.

Chapter Sixteen

Aidan Shows Off

Much later that evening, after she had eaten a sumptuous meal, Aidan stepped carefully into a large metal tub of hot water thick with bubbles. At Vanity's strict instructions, Drudgery and Gatekeeper had set up the tub in a corner of the kitchen behind makeshift curtains and had drawn the steaming bath for her. Now she settled into the fragrant water and relaxed, savoring the luxurious feeling of being pampered, thoroughly enjoying her good fortune at the hands of Prince Bal'Davarius and his servants.

Surely life could be no finer!

It had taken a long time to open all the boxes Lust and Vanity had brought, but her closet was now filled with the most beautiful clothes she had ever seen – dresses more elegant than she had ever imagined, with shoes, hats, and expensive jewelry to match. As Aidan sat in the tub washing herself and thinking about her new wardrobe, her mind was still trying to grasp that every gift she had unwrapped upstairs was really *hers.*

The Prince had thought of every minute detail and had spared no expense – and all of it, Lust kept reminding her, was just for her pleasure. It was for her pleasure that he had lavished upon her a fortune in fine clothes. It was for her pleasure that he had sent that fabulous diamond necklace and several other pieces of fine jewelry. It was for her pleasure that he had sent his most precious roses, cut by his own hand from the bushes that grew in his palace garden.

No one had ever cared about her pleasure before. Now Aidan sighed with complete contentment, giggling as she played with the soap bubbles in her bath. Could there be any greater pleasure than she was enjoying at that moment?

It seemed like a lifetime ago that Aidan had labored so hard dusting Lord Fairhaven's books. Hanging over a nearby chair was the patched threadbare dress she had put on after work. As she looked over at the dress, Vanity's words floated back to her.

I would venture to guess that the Master is planning to come here himself and you surely can't meet him in filthy rags. You must be ready.

The thought that Prince Bal'Davarius himself might be coming to meet her made Aidan's heart pound with dread, yet at the same time the anticipation of his arrival was the most delicious and exhilarating part of everything that was happening to her. It felt like one of her beloved childhood fairy tales was coming to life before her eyes. She had somehow found favor with a handsome Prince!

Just then, on the other side of the curtain, the kitchen door opened and Aidan heard Gatekeeper and Drudgery enter the room. Their conversation was rushed and their voices low. Aidan could tell that they were hurrying around the kitchen in a bustling of activity. She heard the clattering of dishes and then the door opened again and Gatekeeper's quick tapping footsteps disappeared.

"Drudgery," she called, "is something wrong?"

Drudgery came around the curtain carrying a cake of perfumed soap and some fresh towels, which she laid on the chair.

"Aidan, I don't want to rush your bath, but some new guests have just arrived. Gatekeeper and I are setting out a meal for them."

"More guests!" exclaimed Aidan. "At this hour?"

Then a terrible thought came to her, and with a sudden flurry of soapsuds and water splashing onto the slate floor she whirled around in the tub to look at her friend.

"Drudgery, it isn't – it couldn't be, could it?! – I mean, you would tell me at once if it were, wouldn't you? It isn't – *him* – is it?!"

Drudgery stared at Aidan in total bewilderment, then burst into sudden laughter.

"Do you mean the Master? No, of course not! I would tell you right away if the Master were here. I certainly wouldn't let you sit here in the bath and keep him waiting! No, this is a family of six."

"Oh my goodness!" cried Aidan. "How many more will come? How will Gatekeeper ever find room for everyone?"

"Don't worry, Aidan, he's already taken care of everything. Gatekeeper is a master at arranging lodging for us, even in the smallest of houses. Here, we need to wash your hair. Lean your head back."

Drudgery took a pan and poured water over Aidan's head. Then she dipped the perfumed soap into the bath and worked a lather into her wet hair, gently scrubbing her scalp.

"Will you meet your new guests tonight, or wait until morning? The choice is yours."

Aidan sighed. How she longed to slip right into that lovely linen nightdress and go right to bed!

"I think I'd best meet them tonight – there won't be time in the morning," she replied.

Then she brightened at the thought that this would give her a chance to try on one of her new outfits.

"Do try to hurry, Drudgery. It's getting so late and I must be up early for work tomorrow. Lord and Lady Fairhaven are due back and I need to be on time."

Drudgery dried her hands with a towel and went around the curtain to where she was heating rinse water in a kettle on the stove. Her voice floated up over the curtain.

"Aidan, I've been meaning to ask you about that."

"About what?"

"About your work at the Fairhaven mansion. You don't mean to continue working for them, do you?"

"Why, of course I do," Aidan replied, surprised at the question. "It's my job. How would I support myself if I didn't work for Lady Fairhaven? She pays me very well and she has been so kind to me – I can't let her down. I couldn't just quit."

Drudgery came back around the curtain and stood looking at her mistress for a long moment.

"Aidan, the Master will give you whatever you need. He'll take good care of you, don't you see? Didn't today's gifts prove this to you? He's given you more than you could ever need – even everything you need to be a lady yourself."

Aidan laughed aloud at the thought. She looked at her red workworn hands, which, although softened now by the sweet bath, were still thickly calloused from a lifetime of hard work.

"Me, a lady? A fine lady, as regal as Lady Fairhaven? Oh Drudgery, how absurd!"

But she smiled as she said the words, for she'd been thinking all evening long that this must be what the Dark Prince had in mind.

"It seems much more absurd to me," Drudgery replied very quietly, "that you should work as a servant for another when the Master has chosen to bless you with your own."

Aidan's mind was still on her new clothes. Then she thought of her work uniforms hanging upstairs, including the dirty one that Drudgery would wash for her. Up until now those dark blue dresses had been the loveliest she had ever owned.

"I hadn't thought of it that way, Drudgery, and what you say is perfectly true. Still, I don't think I should quit my job. Not yet, anyway. I think I should wait – at least until the Master lets me know what it is he wants with me."

Drudgery nodded. "That's probably wise, Aidan, but I think you'll soon discover that you don't need to work for the Fairhavens any longer."

She went back around the curtain to see if the rinse water had heated.

Aidan settled back into the sweetly scented bath and thought about what Drudgery had said. She could scarcely even imagine what it would be like to live as Lady Fairhaven did. How pleasant life would be if she never again had to tidy someone else's rooms – or even her own! She wondered how she would fill up the lovely long hours of each day if she were the mistress instead of the servant.

What would it be like to live in a fine mansion, with servants of her own to clean and cook for her?

Perhaps she could have music rooms like Lady Fairhaven's where she could learn to play instruments of her own – even a fine carved wooden harp. Perhaps she could have a library like Lord Fairhaven's that was filled with hundreds of books about interesting people and places. Perhaps she could travel in her fine carriage out of Hidden to places far away – and make her long-awaited journey at last to find her mother.

Aidan thought again of her desire to find out more about her past. Surely Prince Bal'Davarius knew where her mother was, for he had told Unloved and Unwanted specifically not to reveal that to her. She wondered if he would be coming to meet her and tell her himself. If he cared about her as much as he was demonstrating, he would certainly help her in her greatest need!

The idea seemed perfectly logical to Aidan. In fact, it was the only possible explanation for all of this that she could imagine.

Yet threads of doubt and discouragement continued to weave their way through her thoughts. She wondered if receiving help from the Prince would mean she'd have to live with all these guests of hers forever. Thinking of Abuse's shrill voice and Night Terrors' malevolent eyes, Aidan shuddered. She knew she couldn't bear that.

Steam rose over the curtain as Drudgery poured hot water from the kettle into a bucket partially filled with cool water. She brought the bucket around the curtain to the bathtub. "Close your eyes tight, now," she warned, and as Aidan tipped her head back, she slowly and carefully poured the pleasantly warm water over her mistress' soapy hair.

Face dripping, Aidan held out her hand. "A towel, please."

Drudgery set the empty bucket on the floor and picked up a soft towel from the chair. She reached over and gently patted Aidan's face dry. Then she twisted her wet hair into a rope, wringing the water out of it. Next she wrapped the towel around Aidan's head and knotted it up into a turban.

Soapsuds slid down Aidan's wet body as she stood up and stepped carefully out of the tub onto a rug. Drudgery handed another large towel to her and she wrapped it around herself.

Aidan smiled shyly at her friend. She was embarrassed to have someone help her take a bath, but she loved the feeling of being so pampered. While it was true that some of her guests from the Dark Prince were hard to endure, she knew she wouldn't at all mind having Drudgery serving her in her house forever.

Drudgery wrapped a soft warm robe around Aidan's shoulders and handed her an oil lamp that was already lit.

"I can't wait to see you in one of your new outfits, Aidan," she said. "But I need to clean up now and see to your new guests."

"Of course," Aidan said. "Please tell them I'll be down in just a few minutes. And thank you so much for the bath!"

Carrying the lamp carefully, Aidan darted up the back stairs and through the hallway to her room, where Lust and Vanity were waiting for her. Two more lamps were already burning and there was plenty of light to see by. She was terribly nervous, but she greeted her guests with a smile.

"I'm so excited," she told them breathlessly. "What do I do first?"

"We must do something with your hair," Vanity said. "We wouldn't want your wet hair to ruin one of your new dresses. Come, child, sit here in the light. Lust, bring that perfume bottle over here."

Aidan sat down in a chair and Vanity removed the towel from her head, pressing as much water out of her hair into it as she could. While Lust liberally sprinkled drops of rose-scented cologne, Vanity gently untangled the long damp tresses with a silver comb. Then she worked with deft fingers, plaiting and pinning the perfumed hair up off of Aidan's neck with silver hairpins.

"Which of your new dresses will you try on tonight?" asked Lust, who had moved to the door of the closet.

Aidan had already made up her mind.

"I'd like to try on the blue taffeta with the plaid sash."

"Oh, that's my very favorite," Lust said approvingly. "Yes, do let's try that one."

She pulled the dress from the closet as Vanity set out the matching pumps and said, "We won't put on the hat tonight while your hair is still wet."

As Aidan stood up she noticed that the silk undergarments she had received were already lying on the bed. She took off her robe, embarrassed to be naked before Lust and Vanity, but the feeling quickly disappeared as soon as she felt the luxurious soft undergarments against her clean bare skin. She slipped into the ruffled petticoat and waited while Vanity fastened it around her waist.

Aidan held her breath with excitement as Lust and Vanity supported the dress for her. She carefully stepped under it and raised her arms as shiny blue fabric fell all around her. It felt lovely to slide her arms into the puffed sleeves. The cool smooth material moving against her skin made her shiver with delight. This elegant dress was heavier than any garment she had ever put on, but the weight of her new finery was hardly a burden.

Vanity fastened the buttons up the back as Aidan slid her feet into the little blue silk shoes. The entire ensemble fit her perfectly, leaving no doubt that it had somehow been tailored especially for her.

"How does it look?" she asked anxiously.

"See for yourself, child," said Vanity, gesturing to the mirror.

Crisp blue taffeta and ruffled petticoats rustled as Aidan turned around. She gasped in astonishment at her reflection, which was completely different now than it had been hours earlier. No longer did she look anything like the weary servant girl with dark circles beneath her eyes who had spent the day dusting grimy books!

The cut of the dress flattered her slender figure and made her look elegant and charming. Her pale skin took on a creamy warmth against the blue fabric, and, although it was still wet, the way her hair was arranged made her plain face look regal.

Aidan was completely shocked at the transformation. She had never dared to think that she could look so pretty and sophisticated.

But the most amazing thing of all was the change in her eyes. Instead of blue-green, they had taken on the same beautiful shade of blue-grey as the dress. Somehow now they seemed two sizes larger than they had been before, and as she smiled they sparkled and danced with energy and joy.

Vanity came up behind her and began fussing with the plaid ruffles, arranging and rearranging them until she was satisfied. Then she tugged at the puffed shoulders until she felt they were just right. Finally she picked meticulously here and there at pieces of invisible lint before fluffing the ruffles one last time.

At long last she stepped back, clicking her tongue and frowning uncertainly as she scrutinized Aidan's appearance.

"Well, I suppose it might do," she declared pessimistically in her understated way. "What do you think, Lust?"

Lust's response was anything but understated. She smiled broadly with open admiration and lavished Aidan with praise.

"It's *marvelous!*" she gushed. "It's *perfect!* Just look at the change in her, Vanity! She even carries herself like a lady. And wasn't I right about the color?" She turned to Aidan. "Aidan, this dress sets off your eyes and skin to absolute perfection! You look positively *gorgeous!*"

Aidan giggled with all the excitement of a bride on her wedding day. "I've never felt so beautiful!" she cried, twisting around to see every angle of the lovely dress in the mirror.

Vanity was still frowning thoughtfully.

"No, no, no, Lust, it will never do. It's just not right. It still needs something."

Lust looked carefully at Aidan again, then nodded.

"I know just what's missing," she said.

She went to the bureau and came back with the diamond and sapphire necklace. It flashed and glittered like brilliant blue fire in her hand.

Aidan felt her heart beat faster with anticipation at the sight. She held her breath as Lust fastened it around her neck again. Its weight against her throat was dearly precious, like the presence of an old friend, and it went perfectly with the fine dress.

Vanity nodded and clicked her tongue again, this time with approval as she looked at Aidan again.

"Yes, that was just what it needed," she decided. "Now it will certainly do."

Lust smiled with satisfaction.

"Aidan, now you truly look as though you were born to wear those diamonds. Don't you agree, Vanity?"

Vanity looked down her nose at Aidan. "They certainly look better with the Master's fine dress than they did with that horrid old rag she was wearing this afternoon," she declared drily.

"Oh, we'll tell Drudgery to burn that old thing," Lust said. "Aidan, all you need to do is trust the Master and you'll never have to look like that again!"

Aidan's eyes shone, her face flushed with elation. "I never want to look like that again," she replied firmly. "I only want to look like this – forever!"

She twirled before the mirror, laughing with delight as the skirt swished around her legs and the ruffles flew out behind her like royal banners in the wind.

Vanity watched her for a long moment. Then she smiled for the first time since Aidan had met her.

"Aidan, it certainly does surprise me, but I think you shall make a fine lady after all. The Master will be most pleased."

Aidan thrilled at Vanity's smile and words of approval as though she had just won the finest trophy of all.

"Thank you," she whispered gratefully.

At that moment there was a knock at the door. "Yes, who's there?" Vanity called.

"It's Gatekeeper, Madam," came a muffled voice.

With a flurry of petticoats, Aidan turned excitedly toward the door and struck a stately pose. Trying to match Vanity's haughty tone, she called, "You may come in, Gatekeeper."

The door opened and her butler stepped into the room. He stopped short with amazement when he saw Aidan. His face broke into a delighted smile and crinkles appeared at the corners of his bright blue eyes.

"Why, Miss! How lovely you look! Well, well! I must say, Lust and Vanity have certainly done a fine job here with you this evening."

Filled with a surge of pride, Aidan barely suppressed a laugh of pleasure as she answered regally, "Thank you, Gatekeeper."

He bowed slightly to her.

"Your new guests have finished their meal and are waiting for you. Shall I tell them you'll be detained a bit longer, or will you be down presently?"

"My new guests!" She had forgotten all about them. "Oh my goodness! I'll come down right away."

"Very good, Miss."

Aidan descended the front stairs with Lust, Vanity, and Gatekeeper right behind her. Delighted to see that a number of her guests were seated in the front room, she couldn't help but relish the chance to show off her outfit, for it was the first time she'd ever been able to do such a thing in her entire life. The diamond necklace sparkling merrily at her throat and taffeta rustling softly around her dainty blue pumps, she picked up her skirt with a demure gesture and swept into the front room with a proud flourish.

Her entrance could not have caused more excitement if she had been wildfire bursting through a forest. Hushed silence fell like a weight across both the sitting and dining rooms as all her guests stopped talking and turned to stare. Every man present jumped quickly to his feet.

Nothing like this had ever happened to Aidan before. In fact, she had never received any attention of any kind from men at all. A flush of delight reddened her face and her ladylike demeanor was spoiled when she could no longer hold back a girlish giggle of nervous excitement.

Pride was the first to speak. He bowed to her in his pompous way and said, "How beautiful you look tonight, Milady. Such an elegant dress!"

Laughing brightly, Aidan twirled around before him. Pride smiled and nodded to Vanity, who answered him with a single prim nod in return.

"My wife has done an excellent job with your wardrobe, hasn't she? How fine you'll look riding in my carriage wearing that outfit! And I must say, a lovely lady like yourself certainly deserves everything the Master has sent to you. Why, just think of it! Soon everyone in town will be talking about you! They will wonder if a queen has come to Hidden!"

Everyone in town! What *would* they say?

That old familiar fear began gnawing at Aidan's heart, but she was so taken up with all her new finery that she suddenly didn't care. She smoothed her skirt and turned up her nose.

"Oh, who cares about what anyone in this wretched town says!" she pouted. "I hate them all! They've never been kind to me. Nothing would make me happier than to see them all just drop dead!"

Her own words shocked her the moment they were out of her mouth. She had never acted so arrogantly before, never spoken with such cruelty. How her new clothes had changed her already!

Fear spoke up quietly in her icy voice.

"You do look lovely, Aidan, but surely you are afraid of the gossip this will cause?"

"No, not one little bit," Aidan declared grandly.

But deep inside she was practically quaking at the thought. If the townspeople scorned her, her lonely life in Hidden would be more unbearable than ever.

Still, after a lifetime of being an outsider in the town, she couldn't help but relish the idea that all of Hidden would soon be envious of her, for she had been singled out by Prince Bal'Davarius himself for this special royal treatment!

Aidan covered up her fear with a show of fresh arrogance.

"Just imagine! I'll ride up and down the streets of Hidden in my royal carriage, and the whole town will bow down with respect and reverence – bow down to *me*, as if I were Lady Fairhaven herself! Can't you just picture it? Lady Aidan – doesn't it sound wonderful?"

She pranced around the room, swishing her skirt, grinning with triumphant glee.

"And Uncle Asa! Just think of how green with envy his face will turn when he sees how rich I am! Richer than he ever dreamed of being! Richer than I ever would have been if I had agreed to his horrible 'business arrangement!' He'll have to treat me very respectfully – if he knows what's good for him."

She laughed loudly.

"Revenge – sweet revenge at last! Uncle Asa bowing to me, yes, even trembling before me – yes, that will be the very best thing of all!"

Greed stepped over to her, grinning darkly.

"Yes, it's true, Aidan. You are the Master's chosen one. All of Hidden will indeed bow down to you, but this is only the beginning!"

Aidan listened to Greed with intense interest as he continued.

"If you trust in the Master, he'll give you even greater glory. He offers you riches and power beyond your wildest dreams. Now that you have found favor with the Master, you can have anything – *anything* – your heart desires."

His eyes glittered with consuming fire.

"Yes, this is only the beginning, Aidan."

Only the beginning? What greater glory could there possibly be than the glory she had at that moment?

"Riches and glory beyond my wildest dreams! Why, my wildest dreams must be quite tame," she laughed. "Until today I couldn't imagine having even as much as this! And now are you telling me that your Master wants to give me still more? I can have *anything* I want?!"

The idea that she could have all she had ever yearned for and much more was completely intoxicating. She had savored her first taste of riches and now she knew for certain that she would take all she could have if the Dark Prince were willing to give it.

Greed nodded, and the fire in his eyes pierced into her heart.

"Yes, Aidan, my words are utterly true. There are worlds of riches and glory out there just waiting for you if you will but serve the Master. Once you've found favor in his sight, he'll hold nothing back from you. He'll lay his very kingdom at your feet. All of it – yours just for the taking!"

"The entire *kingdom?*" Aidan gasped. "Mine just for the taking? How can this be? Why should your Master do such a thing for the likes of me?"

"Greed is right, Milady," Pride chimed in. "The Master has taken a special interest in you. You're a very special young lady indeed. Why, I would even venture to say you are blessed above all other women!"

Aidan stared at Pride, hesitating for a brief second at his words. She ran her hands along the smooth sleeves of her fine new dress and reached up to caress the diamond necklace.

Then she nodded, her heart swelling with conceit as she completely embraced everything Pride and Greed were telling her.

"You're right, Pride," she agreed. "You *must* be! It would seem I'm very special indeed to your Master! Why else would he be doing all this? Yes, I think both of you must be right! I am the Prince's most favored one. I must be the most blessed woman on earth!"

At that moment one of her new guests spoke up, a dark-haired girl of perhaps twelve who had been sitting at the dining room table with her family quietly watching all the fuss over Aidan's new finery. Abruptly she cried out in a loud voice.

"Surely you don't actually *believe* that! Why, you're just a poor little maidservant! Don't you scrub floors and dig garden dirt and dust furniture to earn a living? Perhaps you ought to prepare yourself for the possibility that all of this might just be a huge mistake!"

Chapter Seventeen

Doubt's Family

Aidan froze with indignation at the insolent words of the dark-haired girl. How dare she speak so rudely!

Her childish voice had sounded completely innocent, as though she were merely asking questions rather than passing judgment, but Aidan felt completely humiliated just the same. She turned in anger with every intention of rebuking the girl firmly.

But as she looked into the faces of her newest guests for the first time, she suddenly came back to herself. Her arrogance quickly melted into overwhelming embarrassment for getting so carried away with herself that she had forgotten all about them. She began to make apologies, her face flushed with deep shame at her self-important behavior.

Whatever had come over her?!

"Oh my goodness!" she stammered. "Where are my manners tonight? Please forgive me. I should have introduced myself before."

She smiled graciously and held out her hand as she moved quickly to the dining room table, where the new arrivals had just eaten dinner and were now finishing their tea.

"I'm Aidan. And your names are –?"

The father of the family was still on his feet, having stood when Aidan made her entrance. A tall slender man with a narrow clean-shaven face and a mild-mannered expression, he had the same dark hair and dark eyes as his daughter who had just spoken. He leaned forward over the table and as Aidan shook his hand, she noticed it was soft and well-manicured. In his other hand he was holding a pipe.

"My name is Doubt," he said, "and this is my wife, Discouragement."

With his pipe he pointed to the woman who was seated next to him. Discouragement was an attractive woman, polished and fashionably dressed, with round blue eyes and dark smooth hair piled loosely into a coil atop her head. Her lips curled into a gracious smile as she spoke in a pleasant soprano voice.

"So nice to meet you, Aidan. Allow me to present our children."

She gestured with unabashed motherly pride to her brood, pointing first to the girl who had spoken out so boldly.

"Our eldest, False Hopes."

False Hopes was still staring at Aidan without smiling, her large dark eyes filled with curiosity. She was a lovely girl somewhere just beyond childhood but barely reaching into adolescence. Her lightly freckled face was round with innocence and bore an intensely serious expression, as though she were constantly trying to understand things that remained just beyond her grasp. As she stood politely and quickly dipped into a perfunctory curtsy, Aidan nodded warily back to her, still feeling annoyed.

Discouragement continued enthusiastically with her introductions.

"And these are our twins, Despair and Self-Pity."

The girls who pulled themselves petulantly to their feet were perhaps eight or nine, two smaller versions of False Hopes. After a brief curtsy Despair and Self-Pity plopped gracelessly back onto their chairs and scowled at Aidan. With their identical pouting faces and matching dresses, it was not clear which girl was which.

Her voice now overflowing with maternal ardor, Discouragement patted the head of her fourth child, which was in her lap.

"And our youngest – our only son – Vain Imaginings."

Vain Imaginings was perhaps six. He occupied the chair next to her but had slumped over to use her lap as a pillow. Half asleep, he resisted with annoyance as she gently but firmly prodded him to his feet. When he finally did stand, he glared resentfully at Aidan from dark eyes set into a handsome but sullen freckled face. Then he quickly flopped back onto his chair and fell over into his mother's lap again.

Discouragement tittered with delight as though her beloved son had just done something marvelously clever. She began stroking his thick dark curls with obvious fondness. There could be no doubt that Vain Imaginings was his mother's special little darling.

Upon learning her new guests' names, Aidan's heart sank. She wondered why this dreary-sounding group should be arriving on the same day Pride's carriage had come bringing all her beautiful gifts from their Master. But she hid her dismay and tried to be cordial.

"I'm so sorry to have kept you waiting," she apologized again. "I do hope that Gatekeeper and Drudgery have taken good care of you. I see that you've eaten."

"Yes, thank you," Doubt said. "Gatekeeper has shown us our room, and Drudgery has served us an adequate meal."

He placed his pipe in one corner of his mouth and patted at his pockets in search of matches.

Aidan guessed that Doubt's family must be fairly wealthy, for they were all wearing fine linen clothing in pastel colors and looked as though they had just stepped out of a family portrait.

Doubt was dressed in a natty blue suitcoat with white trousers, a blue and white striped shirt, and a red bow tie. Discouragement wore a peach-colored dress trimmed with fine lace and a wide ivory satin sash. Prim and proper, she moved with aristocratic grace and had obviously worked at preening each of her children until they looked perfect.

Her three daughters all wore their straight dark brown hair in the same style. Thick bangs shadowed their eyes and the rest hung long and loose down their backs, tied with huge satin bows perched at the crowns of their heads. Their dresses had puffy sleeves, starched ivory collars, wide satin sashes tied into large bows at the hips, and gathered dropped-waist skirts that came to just below the knee. The twins' dresses were vertically-striped in ivory and lavender while False Hopes wore a dress printed with tiny blue and pink flowers.

Vain Imaginings looked miserable in rumpled blue knickers and a starched white shirt with a red bow tie like his father's. All four children wore white knit stockings and soft leather shoes.

Aidan could see that this man and his wife lacked for nothing and had given their family every fine thing they could ever want. But the opinion she was forming of their children – that beneath their fine appearance they were all quite spoiled – was confirmed in the next moments by their shockingly rude behavior.

One twin spoke up first in a whining voice.

"I just have to tell you that your cook's meal was absolutely dreadful! I couldn't eat a bite of it. It just turned my stomach!"

Flustered, Discouragement quickly scolded her. "Despair! Hush now!"

"But Mother, Despair is right," Self-Pity agreed. "It was awful! Why did the Master have to send us here anyway? Other families get to live in fine homes and have servants of their own. Why can't we?!"

"Yes, that's right," Despair chimed in. "Why do we have to travel for the Master all the time? Why do we have to live in other people's houses and eat their disgusting food?"

"Oh, I'm sure I shall *never* get used to this!" moaned Self-Pity.

"Girls! That's enough now," Discouragement said firmly. "You know we must do whatever the Master commands."

She turned to Aidan and smiled apologetically.

"You must excuse my daughters, Aidan. We've had such a long journey today, and we're all quite exhausted."

"I do understand," Aidan said graciously, but inside she was appalled at these ill-mannered children. She wished that she didn't have to give this family lodging in her home.

False Hopes was still quietly staring at Aidan with her intense but naive expression. As she spoke up there was no trace of guile in her innocent voice.

"You *are* just a maidservant, aren't you? Don't you clean house for some rich person?"

Aidan felt her face redden with indignation.

"I work for Lady Fairhaven as her personal attendant," she replied crisply. "What is that to you?"

False Hopes seemed not to notice Aidan's annoyance.

"That *is* a lovely dress you're wearing," she said sincerely. "But a dress can't change who you really are inside."

Doubt put his arm around his daughter's shoulders. A cloud of fragrant pipe smoke rose up and obscured his face for a moment, then cleared as he agreed.

"That's quite true. None of us can ever change who we really are, no matter how hard we may try."

Although his words were spoken convincingly, Aidan wasn't so sure. Dressed in her fine new clothes, she felt and acted like a completely different person than she ever had before. The conceit and arrogance which had filled her heart moments earlier were brand new to her, yet now she wondered at the ease with which her haughty words had slipped from her tongue.

Had she always been so fiercely proud, despite the fact that she had never owned anything of value?

Suddenly Aidan realized that the words False Hopes had so impudently declared were really a reflection of the fears and doubts that were in her own heart.

Perhaps all this really *was* a huge mistake. Perhaps the Dark Prince's generosity came at a cost she would not be able to pay.

Perhaps her newfound finery was only filling her heart with false hopes and vain imaginings.

"Mother, I'm *soooo* tired," Self-Pity whined loudly. "I want to go to bed!"

"Perhaps I should be getting my children upstairs now," Discouragement said.

"Yes, perhaps that would be best," Aidan agreed, grateful at the opportunity to be free of her rude children. She hoped that their behavior would improve after a good night's sleep, but she doubted very much that it would.

Discouragement gently pushed Vain Imaginings from her lap. He sat up sleepily in his chair as she stood and began gathering her daughters.

"Come, my darlings," she urged cheerfully, "quickly now, upstairs to bed."

She prodded the girls up the stairs. Their voices floated back down behind them.

"Oh, Mother," Despair complained, "do we *have* to? I just know it will be *dreadful* in that horrible attic!"

"I wish we'd *never* come here," pouted Self-Pity. "Why can't we just go back to the Master's palace? It's beautiful there!"

"And his rose garden is so much prettier!" Despair added.

Doubt wished everyone a good night as he calmly lifted Vain Imaginings from the chair into his arms. The boy laid his head on his father's shoulder and closed his eyes. A pungent trail of pipe smoke wafted behind them down the stairs as they followed the rest of the family.

"Good night, Doubt," Aidan called graciously. "I hope your family sleeps well."

"Oh, I don't imagine we'll sleep a wink, but thank you just the same," he replied pleasantly as he disappeared into the darkness of the upstairs hallway.

Aidan took a deep breath, feeling better the moment they were out of the room. Some of the self-confidence she had felt moments earlier came back as she turned around to see Lust smiling at her.

"Don't trouble yourself about them, Aidan," she said. "You really do look marvelous. That outfit does wonders for you."

"Thank you, Lust," she said gratefully.

From the rocking chair by the fire, a feeble old voice spoke up.

"I know that family well."

Aidan looked at Grief with interest.

"Have their children always acted that way?" she asked.

"Oh yes, they are always just as they were tonight," Grief said slowly. "Doubt's family has a way of making sure you listen to what they have to say. Even when they whisper, they speak so that they cannot be ignored."

"Well, I must agree with that," Aidan said.

She sighed and smoothed the skirt of her fine taffeta dress with her hands. Then she thought of the beautiful linen nightdress waiting for her upstairs.

"It's getting so late, and I must be on time for work in the morning. I suppose I should be going up to bed myself. Good night, everyone."

Aidan turned and headed toward the stairs, but at that moment the front door opened and three more of her guests stepped inside.

Chapter Eighteen

Confrontation With Abuse

Abuse and Anger flounced through the door, Depression following gloomily at their heels, and stopped short at the sight of Aidan in her fine new clothes.

As always, Abuse was wearing a fancy hat. This one was dark maroon with bright flowers and a narrow brim, and although Aidan was sure she had never seen it before, there was something strangely familiar about it. But this was not surprising, for there seemed to be something strangely familiar about every one of Abuse's hats.

As Depression closed the door, Abuse pointedly eyed Aidan up and down.

"Well, look at this!" she exclaimed in her shrill voice. "Our ugly little duckling has actually turned into a swan!"

Aidan's mouth dropped open, speechless at the blatant insult. Her face flamed scarlet with deep hurt and humiliation.

Personally offended, Vanity quickly came to her defense. She clicked her tongue indignantly and stepped forward, looking down her long powdered nose at Abuse.

"What a dreadful thing to say, Abuse! How rude of you!" she scolded sharply. "It's a fine outfit and she looks stunning. You are disgracing the Master by insulting the clothing he has chosen for her."

Anger quickly stepped forward and rebuked Vanity.

"How dare you speak to my mother that way!"

Aidan was shocked when Abuse abruptly turned on Anger and shoved her aside.

"Oh, shut up, you little fool!" she snapped. "I can fight my own battles!"

Anger's hurt was clearly visible by the rejected look on her face as she withered beneath her mother's rebuke. In spite of herself, Aidan suddenly found herself feeling sorry for her. She quickly stepped back, pouting, and stood next to Depression, taking his arm and leaning against him for support. He patted her hand, trying in his own clumsy way to comfort her.

To Aidan this gesture was the most astounding thing of all after the cruel way she and Abuse constantly treated him. For an instant she stared at Depression, feeling more sorry for him than for anyone else, wondering how this pitiful excuse for a man had ever ended up married to someone like Anger.

Abuse turned back to Vanity and smiled with mock sweetness. Gesturing to Aidan, she said, "I never said anything to insult the Master's choices, dearie. Obviously you weren't listening to what I did say. I said the ugly little duckling has finally become a lovely swan. And so she has!"

Vanity drew in a sharp breath.

"Come now, Abuse! Don't think you can take me for a fool! I'm fully aware of what you meant by your dreadful insult. Lust and I have worked very hard today. You ought to apologize."

At that, Abuse laughed with scorn.

"Apologize? *Me?* I never apologize for anything! And there is no need to. You know as well as I do that I'm merely doing the work the Master has given me to do in Aidan's house – the work I must continue until it's fully completed. I am not interfering with your work here, dearie, and you aren't allowed to interfere with mine – so just shut up and let me be!"

Vanity drew in another frustrated breath but was silenced. She stepped back and stood next to Pride. With a triumphant sneer Abuse turned to Aidan, her eyes ablaze with malicious delight.

"Yes, Aidan, you certainly do look the part of the lovely swan tonight. No one can argue with that. But you and I both know, don't we, that wearing the feathers of a swan can never turn you into one. Beneath that dress and those lovely jewels, you're still a scrawny ugly little duckling – and you always will be!"

Aidan felt her face burning and she clenched her fists so tightly her knuckles went white. Her knees were shaking beneath her petticoat, but she knew she couldn't back down from this confrontation. Depression might be a weakling with no backbone, but she was determined not to suffer at Abuse's hands any longer.

Glaring at her enemy with bold fury, she took a quick step forward.

"How dare you speak to me this way in my own home! I've endured your tyranny long enough, Abuse! You're not welcome here! I *order* you to take your things and get out of my house!"

"My, my, my! Just *listen* to you!" Abuse replied with a derisive laugh. "So grandly dressed tonight that you think you can issue orders to *me*? You common little scullery maid! You have no power over me. I take orders from the Master alone – and he has commanded that I live with you."

Suddenly Aidan became aware of an icy breeze blowing through the room.

She turned to see that Fear had stepped close behind her. Her hauntingly beautiful face was emotionless as she opened her black cape and some of her children began to rush out from beneath it.

Fear of Being Hurt was the first to emerge. He hurried straight over to Aidan and grabbed hold of her skirt. She looked down at his timid face with alarm, wondering what he was doing.

Then two more of Fear's sons ducked out from under the cape and stood next to their brother. Aidan recognized them immediately as Fear of Being Accused and Fear of Retribution. The last to join them was their sister Fear of Humiliation.

Aidan stared at the children in helpless confusion as they clustered around her. None of them spoke a single word, but she saw that their presence now made her openly vulnerable before her enemy, removing all pretense and revealing her true heart.

Looking pointedly at Fear's children, Abuse smiled triumphantly and quickly pressed her advantage. Motioning to Aidan's dress with both hands, she began to play against her fears.

"Let me remind you, Aidan, that everything you've received today has come from the Master. Yes, out of the generosity of his heart, our good Prince himself gave you that fine blue dress and those fabulous jewels. But don't you ever forget that if you fail to please him, he can take it all away just as quickly as he gave it. You are in the Master's debt forever!"

It didn't surprise Aidan in the least to learn that all of her suspicions had been correct. The Dark Prince's gifts had indeed been given with strings attached.

"I warn you, Aidan," Abuse went on, "you'd better treat all of us with the utmost respect, or you'll be very, very sorry. If you should cross the Master – or any one of us – he could take back everything he's given you."

Her eyes narrowed threateningly.

"Or perhaps do something much, much worse."

Aidan stood there helplessly subdued before her enemy. She suddenly recalled Drudgery telling her about the Dark Prince turning into a roaring lion in his fury. The thought sent a powerful shudder down her spine.

Standing up to Abuse had clearly been the biggest mistake she could have made.

With a smug grin, Abuse crossed her arms over her ample bosom.

"But I tell you what, ugly duckling. Don't worry your elegant little head over what happened tonight. You were inexcusably rude to me, but just this once I'll forget about it – and accept your apology."

She stood waiting pointedly for Aidan to respond.

Not sure what to do, Aidan glanced hopefully at Vanity, but she was standing quietly by, waiting to see what would happen next. There was now nothing in her elegant powdered face that offered a trace of support.

Her other guests were all standing or sitting around in silence, watching the whole ugly scene unfold, and she realized she would receive no help from anyone in the room. There was no graceful way out of this confrontation.

As much as she hated the mere idea, Aidan knew she had no other recourse than to back down, even though Abuse had started the whole thing. She began to turn, reluctantly opening her mouth to apologize.

But before she could say a single word, Pride stepped silently behind her and gently laid his hand on her arm.

Startled by this gesture, Aidan stared at his hand and then looked into his impassive face. Suddenly she knew she couldn't back down without suffering great humiliation.

Tapping her foot impatiently, Abuse said, "So what do you say, little swan? I'm waiting for your apology."

Pride tightened his grip on Aidan's arm.

His presence behind her seemed to offer the support she needed. Aidan clenched her fists and bristled with defiance. In a surge of foolhardy recklessness she turned and faced Abuse.

"I see no reason to give you one. You insulted me first, here in my own home. You ought to apologize to me, whether you're a servant of Prince Bal'Davarius or not!"

Abuse's face darkened with rage.

"You wretched little fool!" she cried. "You'll live to regret crossing me! Don't you know I could have you thrown into the Master's prison and given over to his torturers?!"

Suddenly four more of Fear's children darted out from under her cape and rushed to join their siblings standing around Aidan. She immediately knew them all – Fear of Punishment, Fear of Imprisonment, and the twins Fear of Being Trapped and Fear of Small Enclosed Spaces.

By now Aidan could barely breathe from panic. But Pride's grip on her arm was unyielding.

"Surely your Master would never allow that!" she declared stubbornly. "He gave me all these gifts and he won't take them back. He's good and kind and takes good care of his servants – that's what the others have been telling me! They said I've been chosen for a special purpose!"

At that, Abuse's eyes flashed with fury.

"So now I'm a liar, am I? Listen here, you disgusting little wench, I'd say I know the Master far better than you ever will! And I know you because I've been with you all your life. You always were a wicked and evil child – and apparently you still need to be taught a lesson!"

Those cruel words Aidan had heard so many times from Aunt Mara cut into her heart now as sharply as the beatings that had always followed them.

"I happen to know that the Master does indeed have special plans for you, but they have nothing to do with a fine new wardrobe and expensive jewelry."

"What do you know of his plans?" Aidan demanded.

Abuse smiled tauntingly.

"He has commanded that my family dwell in your house forever."

Aidan's courage withered within her chest. So what she had dreaded from the first moment she had seen Abuse at her gate was true. She would never be free of her tyranny!

"You see, Aidan," she continued, "the Master has sent my family through the generations to you and we will never leave you. And should you ever find someone stupid enough to marry you, should you ever actually have a family, we'll be right there with you to help you raise your children. We'll teach you as we taught Mara and her mother and grandmother before her. You'll raise your children just as you were raised – and they in turn will raise their children exactly as they were – and on and on through the generations to come, for we will never leave them either."

She grinned with triumph.

"Yes, Aidan, my ugly little duckling – *this* is the Master's special purpose for you!"

Horrified at the mere thought, Aidan cried, "No! You'll never touch my children! I will never treat my children as Aunt Mara treated me!"

"Oh, but you will, Aidan," Abuse insisted. "I know you will, because the Master has sent my family to you with his orders to make sure of it."

At that moment Anger spoke up eagerly in her shrill voice.

"Mother, tell her about Father and my brothers who will be coming soon to join us!"

Aidan stared at Anger in shock and disbelief. There couldn't still be more of Abuse's hateful family coming to lodge with her – could there?!

"Yes, of course," Abuse said, her smile dark and wicked. "How forgetful of me! I've neglected to mention to you, Aidan, that my dear husband and sons are due to arrive any day now. They're on a hunting trip and late, as usual. But they will surely be here very soon."

This news was more devastating to Aidan than anything she had endured all evening. She began to shake uncontrollably from panic.

"Who will come?" she demanded. "How many? What are their names?"

Looking her right in the eye, Abuse answered.

"There are five. I believe you'll find you know them all very well already. My husband's name is Wrath. Our four sons are Rage, Strife, Neglect – and Murder."

This was too much for Aidan. At the sound of their names, her chest constricted and she was suddenly unable to breathe. All at once the room became dim and foggy. She felt the floor start to pitch and sway and the walls begin to spin all around her. Before she knew what was happening, her knees buckled beneath her.

As if coming from a great distance, she heard Gatekeeper's voice call out in concern.

"Miss? Miss, are you all right?! *Miss!*"

As she fainted, the last thing Aidan remembered was Abuse's shrill raucous laughter and someone's strong arms catching her before she hit the floor.

Then everything went black.

Chapter Nineteen

In The Garden With Lust

The next thing Aidan knew she was lying on the cushions of the window seat and the air was bitingly cold.

Slowly she moved her head and looked around. All she could see were vague wavering shadows, as though the room had somehow filled with fog. Others were clustered around her, but their voices were muffled and seemed far away.

Someone was bending over her, gently nudging her shoulder and patting her hand.

"Aidan, are you all right?"

Lust's face suddenly came into sharp focus above her.

"Yes," Aidan whispered, struggling against the fog. Her body was shivering uncontrollably in the chilly air. "Where am I? It's so cold."

"Just relax," Lust said, smiling and squeezing her hand. "You'll be all right. I opened the window to bring in some fresh air."

"What happened to me?" Aidan moaned. She began to rub her hands along her arms to warm them. The smooth feel of taffeta sleeves was somehow reassuring. "Did I fall? I can't remember –"

"Yes, you fainted, but you'll be fine in just a moment."

Lust reached over Aidan and closed the window, then helped her sit up.

Now Aidan could see that Gatekeeper was standing beside them. In his hands he was holding a glass and a tall bottle, which she immediately recognized had come from Aunt Mara's liquor cabinet. He handed the glass to Lust, who held it out to Aidan. It was half full of golden liquid.

"Here now, you need to drink this," Lust told her.

"What is it?" Aidan asked uncertainly.

"It's brandy. It will make you feel better."

Aidan had looked at all the bottles in the liquor cabinet many times out of curiosity but had never dared to open any of them. She always remembered how she dreaded what would happen whenever Aunt Mara started drinking and she was too afraid to try it herself.

"But I've never drunk this," she moaned in feeble protest.

Lust held the glass to her lips.

"You must, Aidan," she insisted. "It will help you now. Trust me."

Obediently Aidan sipped the brandy. It burned her throat and she shuddered, wondering how it could possibly help her and thinking again of Aunt Mara's rages. What would this drink do to her?

Lust gently prodded her to finish it, so she took the glass and drank slowly.

As she started to get used to it, she thought the brandy didn't taste that bad after all. It actually began to give her a strange peaceful feeling that was unexpected but rather pleasant. Still, she was glad to finish it, and gratefully handed the empty glass back to Lust.

Lust immediately turned to Gatekeeper and told him to refill it.

"You need to drink some more, Aidan. It will warm you up."

Aidan took it from her and drank the second glass, this time more eagerly. A curious warmth was indeed seeping into her chest and the fog in her head was starting to lift. The sensation of soothing fire spreading gently through her shivering body was most pleasurable.

As Lust handed the empty glass to Gatekeeper, Aidan remembered what had happened before she fainted and looked around the room. Abuse, Anger, and Depression were nowhere to be seen.

"What happened after I fainted?" she asked. "How did I get here?"

"Pride caught you when you fell and carried you here to the window seat," Lust said. "I opened the window because I thought the fresh air would help."

"Where did they go? Abuse and Anger – where are they?" Aidan demanded.

"They've gone up to bed, Miss," Gatekeeper told her.

"Let's go out to the garden for a few minutes," Lust suggested. She tugged at Aidan's arm. "Do you think you can walk?"

Aidan struggled unsteadily to her feet, leaning heavily on Lust's arm, and they went slowly to the door. Lust pulled Aidan's shawl from its hook and draped it around her shoulders.

"You must excuse us, everyone," she said. "It's been such a difficult evening for poor Aidan."

As they stepped out of the warm house onto the front steps, the chill of the late night air made Aidan shiver again and she pulled her shawl up tightly around her head. The scent of roses was strong and as always just being in her garden was a comfort. The weakness in her knees left her as she breathed deeply, gulping in the perfumed air as though it were a refreshing tonic.

"Come, Aidan," Lust urged her, "let's walk around to the bench in the back yard."

She slipped her arm through Aidan's and they headed for the wooden gate. In the perennial garden Aidan sank heavily onto the bench as Lust settled herself lightly and gracefully beside her.

"Are you all right now?"

"I'm not sure," Aidan replied.

Lust was quiet a moment. Then she said sympathetically, "I know Abuse and her family very well. We work together quite often, but she's so difficult we don't always get along. And she was in rare form tonight."

"I hate them!" Aidan was surprised at the snarling vehemence in her own voice. "They're unbearable. I must find a way to get them out of my house!"

She turned accusingly to Lust.

"Why were the rest of you so silent?! I felt so alone! How could all of you just stand by and let her humiliate me like that? Why didn't someone stop her?!"

Lust looked into Aidan's eyes. Her face bore no trace of sympathy now.

"The Master has sent us to you, Aidan, and he has given each of us a special job to do in your house. We couldn't interfere with Abuse tonight because she was doing the work the Master gave her to do. He is very strict about that."

She let that sink in, then added, "And as for finding a way to get them out of your house, I must warn you that you'll never be able to do that. None of us can leave here as long as we've been ordered to stay with you."

Aidan was quiet. She couldn't stop trembling, but she wasn't sure if it was from the chilly night air or from what had happened to her or from the effects of the brandy.

Turning away from Lust's face, she looked up at the clear moonless night. Far above the stars glistened silently, a scattering of a thousand celestial diamonds against a black velvet sky.

At the thought of diamonds, Aidan suddenly remembered the necklace at her throat and moved her hand to see if it were still there. She was relieved to feel the cold hard stones beneath her fingers, yet she felt no comfort at their presence. Suddenly her eyes welled with uncontrollable tears.

"Oh, Lust, why is all this happening to me? I just don't understand! I thought all the wonderful things you and Vanity brought – the clothes and the beautiful carriage – I thought they'd make my life better. I was so happy tonight, all dressed up in this lovely outfit, so excited, so proud – a feeling I've never known before. It was glorious to feel that way! And then False Hopes spoke up and ruined everything. And then Abuse came in and –"

She brushed at the tears on her face and tried in vain to regain her composure. "Now my life seems more wretched than ever – and I'm so confused!"

Lust chuckled and patted Aidan's arm.

"Why, Aidan, I do believe that brandy has gone right to your head!"

She smiled and slid her arm around Aidan's shoulders. Her soft voice was low and patronizing.

"Oh, but you mustn't cry. Your life will be better, you'll see. Remember what Greed told you. You've found special favor with the Master. He'll give you anything your heart desires if you please him – even half of his kingdom. Think of the things he's given you already – those fabulous jewels – and his prized black roses."

Aidan pulled away from her.

"But none of this makes any sense! I'll have to live with Abuse and Anger and their horrible family forever. How can that possibly make my life better? I can't bear them in my house another moment!"

She wiped her eyes with a quick motion of her hand as her voice abruptly filled with savage fury.

"Unloved and Unwanted tricked me into giving them the key to my house! They said they knew my mother, and I thought they would tell me how to find her. And then the rest of you came – Fear and Abuse – and Night Terrors – and all the others – and still more are coming! I'm so confused – I don't know what to think anymore!"

At that, the dam of her control burst and she bent over in an overwhelming flood of despair and torment, her body convulsing with loud sobs.

"There must be some way to make them all go away!" she moaned.

"There, there, hush now. It's going to be all right."

Lust wrapped her arms around Aidan and gently pulled her close, offering tender whispers of comfort.

Aidan could not stop crying. She shook helplessly from the intensity of her emotions and sank into Lust's embrace, covering her face and sobbing desperately into her hands.

"I hate them! They lied to me and I hate them! If only I could kill them – I'd kill them all! Then I'd be free!"

The moment Aidan heard her own words, she froze in horror and came back to herself. Suddenly mortified to find herself in Lust's embrace, she stiffened and pulled away, breathing deeply and nervously smoothing her skirt with her hands.

Lust calmly released her, not surprised at all by this last outburst.

"You'd kill them, Aidan?" she whispered softly. "Who is it that you'd like to kill?"

"Why, I – I would kill no one," Aidan declared quickly.

But burning guilt and shame were engulfing her like flames, for deep inside she knew that the incriminating words she had just spoken were completely and undeniably true.

Lust smiled knowingly. Leaning gracefully back against the bench, she crossed one leg over the other. It slipped through the slit in her skirt and, uncovered to the hip, revealed her black lace stocking.

Flustered, Aidan stared at the lace and then quickly tore her eyes away. Desperate to conceal everything in her heart that now felt as completely exposed as Lust's leg, she looked down at her lap and swiped frantically at her tears.

"What did I say? I don't even know what I just said. Oh Lust, I'm so tired. I think you're right about the brandy – it's making me say strange things, things I don't mean."

She looked up again. Pale starlight fell across Lust's face, neck, and breasts. It seemed like a long time ago that Aidan had been so shocked by her scandalous dress at their first meeting. With a start, she realized it had only been that afternoon.

As Lust met her gaze, the piercing look in her violet-grey eyes suddenly made Aidan think of a cat about to leap upon a mouse.

She shivered nervously.

"Lust, aren't you cold out here in that dress? You'll catch a chill."

Lust laughed ever so softly. Her intense gaze never left Aidan's face.

"Oh, don't worry about me, Aidan, I'm fine. Believe me, I've been out late in the evening air on many a night much colder than this."

Aidan wondered what she meant by that but was too afraid to ask her to explain.

She turned her face back to the velvet sky. The diamond stars far above the black mountains glittered like a tantalizing treasure that was just out of reach.

Pulling her shawl more tightly around her head, she gazed in awe at the intense beauty of the night.

"Such a wonderful sky," she whispered. "How I wish I could leap into those stars and fly far away from here!"

Lust leaned her head back and looked up at the stars. After a long thoughtful moment she said, "Did you know, Aidan, that the stars control your destiny?"

Confused, Aidan turned to look at Lust, whose face had a dreamy expression as she gazed at the sky.

"Control my destiny? What do you mean?"

"They determine everything you'll be and do – all your future."

"I've never heard of such a thing," Aidan said. "How can this be?"

"The stars – their position in the sky when you are born and all their movements afterwards – they determine what you'll become and what you'll do in your lifetime. They even control the number of your days. Your entire life, from birth to death, is right there in the night sky at the moment you are born."

Aidan shook her head, wondering why Lust was telling her all this.

"I don't understand how such a thing as a star can control my life," she replied. "How can they determine my future?"

"You only need to know how to read them. The Master teaches many of his servants how to do this."

Lust was quiet for a long moment. Far above the stars glittered silently. Then she turned and again looked Aidan directly in the eye.

"The stars can also reveal your past – if you wish to know," she whispered.

Aidan felt her pulse begin to race with excitement.

"My past! Can they really? Do you know how to read the stars? Oh, Lust, I want to know about my past more than anything! I need to know about my birth – about why my mother left me here. I want to – I *need* to find her."

The intense catlike look in the depths of Lust's pale eyes suddenly made Aidan shudder.

"Then I shall tell you about your past, Aidan, and about your destiny as well," she whispered. "The stars were shining very much like this – on the night your mother conceived you."

Aidan gasped in shock.

"I was there that night and I remember it well. You see, Aidan, like Unloved and Unwanted – I knew your mother, too."

"Oh Lust," Aidan whispered, her heart torn between fear and hope. "My mother – how can I find her? Please, you must tell me – what land was I conceived in? Where was I born? Where is my mother now?"

Lust's eyes narrowed. "I have been ordered by the Master never to tell you those things," she replied sharply.

At that Aidan was filled with frustration.

"No!" she cried. "I don't care what the Master ordered! If you knew my mother, you must tell me what I want to know!"

Lust laughed again, a throaty musical sound, and looked back up at the stars.

"Yes, I did know your mother – but I knew your father much, much better. He was quite a bit older than she was, a journeyman who wandered from town to town in search of odd jobs to support himself. His travels brought him to your mother's town the winter she turned sixteen. Your mother's father needed some carpentry work done, so he hired your father and provided him a room in his house for the winter."

Aidan was shivering intensely, but she sat very still, listening eagerly to Lust's story.

"Oh, but your mother was a beautiful girl, Aidan," Lust went on, "just about the loveliest girl in town – but she was very young and very foolish. She had tried all her life to earn her father's favor, but he was a cold and distant man, and she was never quite able to win his affection. This wasn't her fault, but she couldn't know that. He was simply a man with no love for his children. But your mother blamed herself – she thought she must be unworthy of his love."

"Yes, go on, please," Aidan urged.

"Her father's indifference left a huge emptiness in her heart that demanded to be filled. And so your mother grew up craving love and affection from a man. By the time your father entered her house, she was ripe for love – like a forbidden fruit just waiting to be plucked – and savored."

In the starlight Lust's delicate features took on a dreamy look as she remembered.

"Oh, she had such a deep curiosity about men. How she longed to be held in a man's arms! She yearned desperately to know what it's like to be kissed and desired – and to make love."

Lust abruptly turned her face from the sky and looked at Aidan.

"You wonder about those things quite often, too, Aidan – don't you?"

Aidan felt her face suddenly flame crimson in the darkness. She ignored Lust's question.

"What happened to my mother?" she demanded.

Lust smiled and went on with her story.

"Your father was warm and friendly and seemed to like her. And he was so handsome, Aidan, so attractive – so strong and masculine. Your mother fell deeply in love with him as only a sixteen-year-old girl can. She set about flirting, teasing him – quite innocently, really, for she was still a child in so many ways. She didn't understand what such teasing can do to a man."

"Yes," whispered Aidan, although she didn't understand that herself.

Lust's eyes were sparkling now. She seemed eager to tell Aidan everything.

"One night he invited her to go for a walk. It was a starry moonless night, a beautiful night much like this one, but in early spring. They walked and he held her hand and she was thrilled that he wanted to be alone with her. She thought her heart would burst for joy when he told her he had fallen deeply in love with her – and would love her forever."

Aidan shivered as she imagined the scene. So her mother, too, had yearned to find The One Who Would Love Her Forever! She could only imagine the happiness she must have felt to be alone in the night with the man she loved.

"Yes, she believed him with all her heart," Lust went on, "for he was telling her exactly what she had longed to hear all her life. He said he wanted to marry her. Then he held her close and kissed her – and when they went back to the house he sneaked her into his bedroom and – well – I think you know what happened next."

Aidan quickly looked down at her hands in her lap.

"Yes, Aidan," Lust continued quietly, gazing up at the sky, "she believed with all her heart that he loved her and would marry her, and she gave herself eagerly to his caresses with complete joy, thinking they would be together forever. She came to his room many a night after that."

Lust took a deep breath.

"Poor thing. She was so foolish – so naive."

At that Aidan's heart sank. Unloved and Unwanted had already told her that her mother wasn't married when she gave birth to her. She suddenly dreaded hearing the next part of the story.

But Lust went on relentlessly.

"Soon after that, his work for her father was done and he received his wages. He told her again that he wanted to marry her and they had one last night together. But the next morning when she went to find him – he was long gone."

She looked into Aidan's eyes.

"His bags were packed and waiting even as he was making love to her. Your mother never saw him again."

The terrible impact of Lust's words pierced Aidan's heart more sharply than a dagger, but she was too shocked to cry.

"No," she whispered. "Oh, no! He promised to marry her – when he *knew* he was going to leave town that night?"

Lust nodded.

"Your father knew exactly what he was doing right from the beginning."

"So – so he never really loved her at all. He only said he did."

"He desired her. He could see it would be easy to get what he wanted from her. But no. He never loved her."

Aidan was struggling to understand.

"My mother was deceived by my father. He lied to her, knowing he was going to leave her."

"Yes."

"He – he just lied to her – so she would let him – let him make love to her."

"That's right."

A swell of fury rose up in Aidan's heart.

"How could he *do* that? She loved him! She really *loved* him!"

Lust shrugged her shoulders.

"She wanted him. She needed him. But no, Aidan, she didn't really love him either. Your mother was too young, too filled with her own needs, to understand what real love was all about."

Aidan barely heard Lust's comments as she kept on ranting.

"How could anyone be so cruel – so completely selfish! To use a young innocent girl that way!"

"Your father was a lonely traveler – a lot older, and very experienced. Your mother wasn't the first woman he had been with by any means. He knew how to get what he wanted from a woman, and she was desperate for affection from a man."

Lust shrugged again.

"In other words, Aidan, she wanted him – and he wanted her. It was that simple. Love had nothing to do with what happened between them."

Still Aidan couldn't understand.

"How could he just lie to her – just deliberately *lie* about such a thing – and break her heart like that?!"

Once again Lust looked her directly in the eye.

"People who want something from someone else – and who have no intention of giving anything in return – frequently lie to get what they want. That is just the way of the world."

Aidan was silent.

"And someday you too will lie to get what you want from someone. You'll see."

"Oh, no," Aidan declared firmly. "Not me. I would never hurt anyone like that. I would never deceive anyone. Not ever!"

Suddenly Lust's eyes seemed to flash with fire.

"And just what makes you so pure and undefiled that you think you're so far above the rest of the world? Believe me, Aidan, I know about this better than anyone else alive! Every person has one thing that means more to them than life itself, something they crave with absolute passion. Someday you'll find that thing for yourself, be it the love of a man, or great riches, or power – or something else. And when you find it, whatever it is, the craving to have it will burn in you like fire. It will utterly consume you day and night until you let nothing stand in your way – nothing. You will lie and cheat and steal, and you too will break someone's heart – but you won't even care. You'll sell your very soul to have your heart's deepest desire. You're not above doing that, Aidan. No one is."

Aidan was horrified at the mere idea.

"No! That isn't true! I don't believe you! I can't believe that!"

Lust smiled at her vehemence.

"My words are utterly true. You'll believe me someday, Aidan. You'll come to understand. I promise you that."

"No," Aidan moaned, fighting tears. "I'm not like that!"

But deep inside she already knew that Lust was speaking the truth. She knew very well that there were things she wanted and needed so desperately she could even kill for them and not care.

"It was true for your father," Lust said. "And it was true for your mother."

Wiping at her tears, Aidan said, "What do you mean?"

Lust smiled and resumed her tale of the past.

"After your mother found out your father had left, she was brokenhearted. She was ashamed of what she had done and told no one about it. She clung to the hope that he would return, but deep inside she knew he wouldn't. And then, as if having a broken heart weren't bad enough, before very long she realized she was also going to have you. But if I'm not mistaken, you already know this part of the story, don't you?"

"Yes, I do," Aidan sighed sadly. "Unloved and Unwanted told me. She was afraid to tell her parents, so she left her own country to stay with a relative here in Davarius to have me in secret. They said some old friends of her family gave her money to go home, so she gave me away to them and they brought me here."

Her voice shook with pain and bitterness.

"They said she didn't want me – all she wanted was to be free and start her life over again – but I can't believe that."

Lust nodded.

"They told you the story well. That's exactly what happened, whether you believe it or not."

Aidan was quiet for a long time, staring up at the sky. The flickering stars were glorious but so cold and distant, offering no comfort for her broken heart. Her mind was filled with questions as she fought to sort through all the things Lust was telling her.

How could the stars so far above control her destiny from the moment she was born until the day she died? Had the stars truly ordained everything that had ever happened to her and everything that was to come? How could a star, so distant and unreachable, have that kind of power over her life?

Aidan could hardly begin to understand such a thing.

Then other thoughts came to her. If the powerful stars had already determined her separation from her mother, was there any hope that Aidan would ever be able to leave Hidden and find her again?

And what about love?

Aidan could not even imagine what it would be like to love a man who would truly love her in return. It seemed hopeless to think she would ever be loved and wanted.

Lust's heartbreaking story about her mother and father had brought back to her all over again the intense loneliness of her wretched life.

Even her very conception had come not from love but from selfish desire, deceitful promises, and false hopes. Long ago a young girl had given herself completely to an older man she thought would love her forever, but he had only used her for his own lustful pleasure. Aidan had been born out of one kind of cruelty to live her life in a different kind of cruelty.

Suddenly she thought of the vow she had made on the hillside to find The One Who Would Love Her Forever.

She shivered again, not from the cold but from the familiar haunting fear that she would never know love at all. Perhaps love had never been ordained for her in all those cruel stars that controlled her destiny. Perhaps she would always be alone – an orphan, unloved and unwanted.

Perhaps The One Who Would Love Her Forever only existed in her false hopes and vain imaginings.

Breaking into her thoughts, Lust turned to her.

"Yes, Unloved and Unwanted told you the story very well. But tell me, Aidan, did they also mention the names of those old family friends who carried you here to Hidden in the basket?"

"No," Aidan replied softly, "they didn't. Who were they?"

In the starlight Lust's face suddenly looked hard and cruel, as though it had been chiseled from stone.

"It was Unloved and Unwanted who brought you here."

Aidan winced and doubled over as though this were the fatal blow that she knew would surely come. She closed her eyes and covered her face with her hands.

"Of course," she moaned wearily. "I should have known."

They were quiet for a long moment. Then Lust spoke again.

"As I told you, Aidan, everyone has something they want so badly that they will do whatever it takes to get it. Your mother was trapped in a desperate situation. The one thing she wanted more than anything else was to go back home and forget about what happened – to start her life over – to somehow forget all about you and be free again."

Aidan yanked her hands from her face and glared at Lust.

"No!" she cried. *"No!* That's not true! My mother *loved* me – she wanted to keep me! I know she did!"

Lust just laughed again.

"No, I'm afraid not, Aidan. Your presence in her life reminded her every day of her one awful mistake and the man who broke her heart. She knew she would suffer the consequences of that mistake for the rest of her life. No – she desperately wanted to be free again."

"I can't believe that!" Aidan shouted, clenching her fists. "I *won't* believe it! It was Unloved and Unwanted! My mother never wanted to lose me! I *know* she never once thought of giving me up – until they came and *forced* her to!"

The memory came back to her of her struggle with Unloved. She could still feel the talon grip on her arm and hear the harsh voice demanding the key to her house.

"No, Aidan," Lust insisted. "Your mother wanted her freedom. It was only then that Unloved and Unwanted came to her – when she fully understood how trapped she was. There was no other way out. She was ready to do anything to be free of the past and start her life over – even get rid of you."

"You're *lying!* It was Unloved and Unwanted!" Aidan cried bitterly. "Just like they made me give them the key to my house. They forced my mother to give me away!"

Lust shook her head firmly.

"Unloved and Unwanted never forced your mother to do anything she didn't really want to do. They offered to pay the price of her freedom – and she was eager to take it."

Tears glistened on Aidan's face.

"I don't believe you," she declared between sobs. "I *can't* believe you! They *must* have forced her! I just know my mother loved and wanted me more than anything! She couldn't bear to give me up! Don't you see – I *have* to believe that!"

Sighing loudly, Lust rolled her eyes in disgust.

"My, but you are stubborn! Well, believe whatever you will, Aidan, but the fact is, your mother did indeed give you up. She exchanged her wretched life for the Master's money. She packed you into a basket and handed you over to Unloved and Unwanted – for whatever reason – and they brought you here to live with Mara."

Aidan wept softly into her hands. Those were facts they both knew she could never deny.

Lust leaned closer to her ear and whispered, "So you see, Aidan, what I said before is true. Everyone has their passion – the one thing they will do *anything* to have, no matter who they hurt. Freedom was your mother's passion, and she didn't care whose heart she broke to get it – even yours."

"Stop, stop!" Aidan groaned. "Please, I beg of you, stop tormenting me! I can't bear to hear any more!"

She put her hands over her ears, but Lust went on without mercy.

"A simple exchange, and she had what she most wanted. Unloved and Unwanted did the work the Master gave them to do in your mother's life, and she had her freedom. Yes – the Master took good care of your mother."

"Why are you hurting me this way?" Aidan moaned. "Why are you telling me all this?"

Lust straightened up and leaned back against the bench again.

"I'm telling you all this so you will know that you were brought to Hidden by the will of the Master himself. Living here in Hidden with Mara Teague was the destiny written for you in the stars on the very night you were conceived. Yes, and you'll live here in Hidden until you die – your future has already been decreed. But our kind and wise Master, out of the abundant generosity of his heart, has sent us to you to help you sustain your life here."

"No," whispered Aidan.

At Lust's words she suddenly felt all of her hopes and dreams shriveling and blowing away like late summer rose petals sunburned in the dry mountain wind.

"No, that can't be. If that is true, then – then I can never be free. I'm trapped here with all of you forever – and I can never be free!"

Lust laughed.

"Oh, honestly, Aidan, it's not as bad as all that. Have you forgotten everything the Master has given you – the carriage, the clothes, even his prized roses? And like Greed said, there is plenty more where those came from. The Master is good and kind and he will take very good care of you."

Aidan looked down at her elegant taffeta dress shining in the starlight. It was so lovely and she had been so thrilled to wear such finery – but at that moment it was very poor comfort indeed.

She shook her head firmly and looked Lust in the eye.

"I don't want the Master to take very good care of me. All I want is my freedom – just like my mother wanted hers."

Lust laughed again.

"Well, Aidan, you can want anything you like, but don't waste your time waiting for someone to come pay the price for your freedom as the Master paid for your mother's, because it will never happen. Freedom is not in the stars for you. Your destiny is to live here in Hidden with all of us – until the day you die."

Aidan bent over in complete despair, her head in her hands. She was so overwhelmed that she could no longer even weep. Her heart felt dead inside, fatally crushed beneath the heavy burden of all that Lust had told her.

She pulled her shawl tightly around her head and sat hunched over on the bench for a long time. At last she looked up and realized with surprise that Lust had left her and she was alone. Had she fallen asleep? She wasn't sure.

Wearily Aidan rose and left her garden, chilled to the bone and eager to get out of the darkness.

Chapter Twenty

The Mysterious Knight

The next morning Aidan came slowly to awareness at the sound of a gentle tapping and opened her eyes with great difficulty. There was a dim rosy light shining in from the window and in a surge of panic she wondered what time it was. She sat up in bed, her body still heavy from sleep, and for a moment the room seemed to spin around her.

The tapping came again and Drudgery's gentle voice outside the door sounded like thunder.

"Aidan, are you awake? I have your tray."

"Yes, come in," she replied.

The door opened and Drudgery entered carrying the domed silver tray. "Here you are," she announced brightly, and hurried to the table by the window seat. After setting the tray down, she turned around and took a good look at Aidan.

"Why are you still in bed? Do you feel all right? You don't look well at all."

The room had stopped spinning. Aidan rubbed her eyes.

"I'm just very tired. It was a late night."

Drudgery bent over Aidan and felt her forehead.

"You were out in the cold air for a long time last night with your wet hair," she said. "No fever, but you do look pale. Here, perhaps a nice breakfast and some good hot tea will wake you up and make you feel better. It's the Master's best!"

Moving very slowly, Aidan struggled to pull herself out of bed and take two steps to the window seat while Drudgery poured a cup of steaming tea. “Thank you,” she said as her friend busied herself making the bed.

The fragrant vapor that rose against her face was a comfort. After taking a few small sips of tea Aidan thought perhaps she was beginning to feel a little better. But the delicious food Drudgery had prepared wasn’t appealing at all. After a few small bites she had to stop eating. She put her fork down and wrapped both of her hands around the warm teacup, bringing it carefully to her lips.

Drudgery was laying out a clean freshly pressed work uniform on the bed. “Do you feel any better now?”

“Yes, a little,” Aidan said.

“Do you need anything else?”

“No, I’ll be all right. You can take the tray.”

Making no comment about how little Aidan had eaten, Drudgery picked up the tray and went out of the room, closing the door softly behind her.

Aidan rose and slowly put on her uniform. It took her a long time to brush out her hair, which was still a bit damp, and secure it under a white scarf. At last, moving a little more steadily, her eyes now fully focused, she opened the door and went downstairs.

Her butler was waiting for her by the front door, his grandfatherly face a study of concern.

“Gatekeeper, is the carriage ready? I’m late for work.”

“Yes, Miss, everything is ready for you.” Gatekeeper frowned at her. “But are you quite certain you feel up to working today? Drudgery told me you were ill, and you do look a bit pale.”

“No, I don’t feel well at all, but I must go,” Aidan said resolutely. “The Fairhavens will probably come back today, and Stewart will no doubt scold me severely for being late.”

“Very well, Miss,” Gatekeeper replied as he opened the door for her. “On your way, then.”

“Thank you,” Aidan said gratefully, and headed out the door.

Greed had the carriage door open before she reached the gate. Pride’s spirited black horses were snorting and impatiently flicking their tails.

“Good morning, Milady,” he called to her. “You’ve kept us waiting quite a spell this fine day. These beasts are most anxious to get started.”

“Well, you can have them hurry right along, then. I’m very late today,” Aidan called back as she climbed carefully into the coach.

Greed latched the door and jumped up onto his rear perch. Leaning back into the plush velvet tufting, she closed her eyes and braced herself as the carriage lurched forward.

Pride took her at her word and had the horses canter through town. His deep voice urging them on and the clatter of hoofbeats and clanking hitches seemed unbearably loud. The coach bumped over the cobblestones and the few bites of breakfast she had eaten jostled in her stomach right along with it. She had never before felt this way. How she longed to be able to just go back home and climb into bed again!

Aidan slid the windows open for fresh air. The snow on the mountain peaks glowed brilliant white, for the sun was now fully risen. She knew the Fairhavens' pompous butler would scold her without mercy for being so late. Dreading Stewart's rebuke and whatever dirty task he had planned for her only made her feel worse.

She pulled her feet up and curled herself into a ball on the padded seat, wondering how she would ever make it through the day.

Although the carriage reached the edge of town within minutes, to Aidan the jarring ride over the cobblestones seemed to take forever. Pride reined in the horses to slow them down as they turned onto the road that crossed the valley and headed toward the mansion. As they picked up speed again, she rested her head upon her knees and closed her eyes. The inescapable rhythm of horses' hooves relentlessly pounding against dirt road seemed loud enough to be echoing back from the mountains.

After just a few seconds the animals' steps sounded strangely out of rhythm. It seemed to Aidan that either Pride's horses were failing to keep pace with each other or she was hearing the hoofbeats of a third horse.

Suddenly she bolted upright to listen more carefully. She really *was* hearing another horse! It was running much faster than Pride's horses – and the sound was getting louder.

Aidan leaned over and looked out the window. Not far behind them a magnificent white horse was racing across the grassy field and heading straight toward her carriage.

Her first thought upon seeing this was that a picture from one of her beloved childhood fairy tales was actually coming to life before her eyes, for mounted on the white horse was a Knight wearing a suit of gleaming armor.

She blinked in shock. Riding at full gallop, his perfectly fluid movements were confident and graceful, as though he and his beautiful steed were one entity and his armor weighed nothing at all.

Dumbfounded, at first Aidan felt no fear, thinking he must be another servant of the Dark Prince who had been sent after her for some unknown reason.

Even across the distance that separated them, she could clearly see that the Knight's piercing gaze was fixed directly upon her, for the visor of his helmet was raised and his face exposed. She noticed that the breastplate of his armor bore some kind of colorful design. With his left hand he firmly controlled the reins of his horse while in his right hand he held a huge gleaming sword.

There was something about the sword that immediately drew her full attention. It seemed to be ablaze with large flames of golden fire. Confused by this, she thought at first that sunlight was flashing off the highly polished metal blade, but after a second she realized the sword was somehow actually burning.

It was at that moment – staring at the strange fiery sword which was pointed directly at her as he advanced at high speed toward the carriage – that she was suddenly seized by a grip of terror that took her breath away.

At that same instant Pride and Greed apparently saw the Knight as well, for her footman suddenly let out an unearthly shriek unlike anything she had ever heard.

Her heart stood still as she whirled to look out the opposite side of the carriage just in time to see Greed throw himself down from his rear perch. She screamed, but she couldn't see how he landed or if he was hurt. The sound of his piercing shriek lingered in her ears.

But the Knight paid no attention to Greed. His eyes remained fixed upon Aidan as he continued racing toward the carriage.

Pride frantically snapped his crop and bellowed to the horses, who bolted into a frenzied gallop. The carriage lurched violently forward and careened dangerously from side to side. Aidan gasped and braced herself, thinking it was about to topple right over.

They were swiftly approaching the base of the Fairhavens' hill as Pride was evidently trying to outrun the Knight. But this desperate attempt was futile, for not only could a single rider on horseback easily overtake a carriage, there was nowhere they could go on the hill or anywhere else in the valley to escape.

Sure that they were about to crash, Aidan jumped to her feet and pounded frantically on the little front window, screaming and begging Pride to stop. But her cries were lost beneath the thundering cacophony of horses' hooves and the ominous creaking of the swaying coach. Nearly hysterical, she turned back to the window to see where the Knight was.

To her horror, he was now right there outside the carriage, riding close enough that she could easily stretch out her arm and touch him.

She stared in astonishment at his strong handsome countenance, a face harder and colder than chiseled stone. Beneath a neatly trimmed dark beard, his square jaw was set with fierce determination and the focused intensity of a warrior's pursuit.

Fighting to breathe, she trembled helplessly before him. She could see the flames of his fiery sword and feel their intense heat. There was no doubt in her mind that within the next few seconds she was about to die at his hand.

The Knight slackened his pace and skillfully kept his horse galloping right alongside the carriage, his face framed by the window. He never once took his eyes from her.

And then, all at once – for the most unforgettable moment of her life – Aidan's gaze locked with his.

Suddenly the churning of her stomach, the lurching of the coach, the clamor of horses and hitches and Pride shouting, all of this completely faded away. Time seemed to stand still as the only things she could see – indeed, all that existed in her entire world at that moment – were two wide dark eyes more incredibly beautiful than anything she had ever imagined.

How was it even possible that such soft and tender eyes could be set into the formidable hardness of a warrior's face?

Most intriguing of all was that deep within them Aidan could plainly see strange radiant flames mysteriously flaring with rich jewel colors, which immediately reminded her of the stained glass windows she had seen in the mansion.

All her fear dissolved into wonder. Staring at the rainbow fire in the Knight's dark eyes, she was completely mesmerized and felt herself irresistibly drawn into the depths of his heart.

Instantly she knew that her pursuer was carrying a burden of great pain. She knew this because she somehow felt his pain in her own heart – a torment of excruciating yearning and sorrow, so intense she could hardly bear it.

And at the same time she clearly understood that the fascinating colors in his eyes and the terrible aching in his heart were both there because of her.

With a jolt her own heart responded, suddenly and inexplicably wanting to be very close to him, even somehow to comfort him. She could not understand her strange desire, yet she wanted this more than she had ever wanted anything in her life. To her own shock and bewilderment, she actually found herself lifting her hand and reaching out to touch his face.

But in that same instant, never taking his eyes from hers or changing his expression, the Knight raised his burning sword and struck the carriage door.

All at once the world came thundering back to Aidan as a roaring explosion of white fire shot up in the wind and burst through the window. She screamed and fell backwards against the seat, thinking her dress had caught fire. Frantically she began beating at her clothing until she realized that the inferno had not hit her.

She looked back up at the window. The Knight was still there, keeping perfect pace with the motions of the carriage as his white horse galloped beneath him. Yellow flames and black smoke blew around his face and Aidan realized with horror that he had just set the carriage on fire.

With one quick graceful motion the Knight slid his sword into its sheath at his left hip. As he turned back to the window Aidan found her voice at last and cried out in a desperate plea for mercy.

"Who are you?! What do you want with me?! Don't hurt me! Oh, please, don't hurt me!"

She could tell by his face that the Knight had heard her, but he spoke no word of reply.

Instead he reached beneath the pommel of his saddle and pulled out something small and dark. Then, undaunted by the burning door, he leaned sideways and thrust his arm through the open window, holding the dark object out to her and indicating with a single nod of his head that she should take it from him.

Aidan stared in shock at the hand of her attacker reaching toward her and shrank as far back from him as possible. All the emotion she had felt for him a moment earlier was now replaced by panic and confusion. She could not identify what he was trying to give her, but she was sure she wanted nothing to do with it. Shaking her head emphatically, she silently begged him with her eyes to go away.

The Knight leaned over further and tossed the dark object right into her lap. Screaming hysterically, she immediately reacted by swatting it away with her hands. It landed on the seat opposite her.

As she stared at the dark object he had thrown, she realized it hadn't hurt her. In fact, it was so light that she had barely felt it hit her at all.

The Knight pulled his arm back through the window and straightened up in the saddle. She looked up at his face and for another brief instant their gaze locked.

Now there was a look of complete triumph in the depths of his beautiful dark eyes. The cold hardness of his face melted into warm joy as he broke into a jubilant smile. The softening of his countenance drew her heart to him again so strongly that she could hardly bear it.

At that moment, looking again at his handsome face, Aidan had that strange feeling that she had experienced with all of her guests – that somehow she actually knew him. And this bewildered her because of course that was impossible.

But one thing was crystal clear to her – this mysterious Knight was not at all like the Dark Prince's servants.

She opened her mouth to ask him again who he was, but at that moment he nodded one last time to her and without warning reached up to his helmet and snapped the visor down over his face. Then he abruptly reined in his horse and disappeared from the window as the carriage bolted ahead of him.

Barely a heartbeat passed before Aidan realized what had happened. She leapt to the window. Through the flames and smoke she could just see that the Knight had already turned his horse around and was galloping swiftly back down the hill.

She was suddenly shocked to hear her own voice screaming after him.

"Wait! Come back! Who are you?!"

But he was already much too far away to hear her, heading across the valley toward the mountain road.

With great confusion Aidan watched the Knight disappear into the distance. She was both grateful and relieved to see him go, yet at the same time she had the strangest feeling that her only friend had just left her.

Just then she realized Pride had slowed his horses considerably. A dark shadow fell over the carriage as they rolled under the huge oak trees. The mansion was just ahead and the terrifying carriage ride would be over within a moment.

Aidan sat back down and looked at the dark object the Knight had thrown to her. Her hand was shaking as she reached out cautiously and touched it.

The unexpected softness that met her fingers was warm and inviting. Her fear again melted into wonder as she gently lifted the little object and set it onto her lap.

The Knight had thrown her a small pouch made of dark purple velvet that was thicker and more luxurious even than the fabric of the carriage cushions. It was tightly closed with a knotted drawstring of braided gold cord from which hung two small tassels. She could tell there was something inside the pouch, but whatever it was seemed to be weightless.

Intensely curious, she stroked the soft velvet and then turned the pouch over. On the other side, exquisitely embroidered in threads of gleaming gold, was a family crest. It was not familiar to her and she knew at once that it belonged neither to the Fairhavens nor to Prince Bal'Davarius.

The gold threads flashed in the sunlight as the carriage came out from under the oak trees. Pride called to his weary horses and reined them in as they drew close to the mansion steps.

Just as the carriage came to a full stop, Aidan had the strongest impression that she should not let Pride know about the pouch. She quickly stuffed it into one of the large deep pockets of her work uniform beneath her apron.

After the frenzied chase it felt strange to be stopped, for Aidan's heart and mind were still racing. Pride yanked on the brake lever and leapt down from the driver's seat to check on his horses and examine the carriage door. It was still smoldering, but no longer aflame.

"Are you all right, Milady?"

He waved the thick smoke aside, pulled open the door and reached out to help her down. Aidan clutched his hand, her whole body shaking uncontrollably as she stumbled out of the coach. The feel of her feet against the solid earth was instantly comforting, but as she tried to speak her words tumbled out incoherently.

"Pride, what just happened? Who was that man? Are you all right? Are we – was he – how did –?!"

Then she glanced up at the mansion and her heart stood still.

For there on an upper balcony, looking tiny against the facade of the huge building, was Lady Fairhaven!

Wrapped in a robe, the noblewoman had no doubt been watching and waiting for Aidan to arrive and attend to her. Now she was staring down in shock at the fine royal carriage with black smoke rising from its door.

Aidan suddenly felt faint with fresh panic. Everything that had happened to her that morning had been horrifying enough, but how was she ever going to explain any of this to Lady Fairhaven?

As she turned back, she saw that Pride was studying the damage to the carriage. The smoke was coming from the edges of a gaping hole that had been seared through the door just below the window.

Plainly visible now was the back side of the cloth padding beneath the tufted velvet interior, but oddly enough the fabric wasn't even scorched. Even more strange, the hole was exactly the same shape and size as the gilded royal crest of Prince Bal'Davarius, which was now completely burned away.

Flustered, Aidan turned again, looking from the carriage back to the balcony. Lady Fairhaven had gone inside.

"Are you certain you're all right, Milady? Were you harmed in the fire?"

Pride was looking steadily at her, his brow furrowed with concern. Strangely, he showed no apprehension about the burned hole in the carriage door and seemed not at all surprised that it was there.

Aidan looked down again at her dress and then back at the smoldering door.

"No, I never felt a thing," she stammered. "It didn't come near me. Pride, who was that man? What did he want with us?"

The strangest look passed like a shadow across his face. When he answered he spoke slowly, as though choosing his words very carefully.

"I can't say for certain who it was, Milady, but I do know he is one of the Master's enemies."

"Enemies?!"

Aidan suddenly felt lightheaded. It had never occurred to her that Prince Bal'Davarius had enemies. Now she was terrified to learn that he did indeed – and she herself had evidently become a target for them, since his servants were lodging with her.

An enemy! The thought took her breath away.

But then the memory of the Knight's beautiful eyes and warm smile flashed into her mind, leaving her utterly confused.

The Knight might be the Dark Prince's enemy – but did that make him her enemy too?

Before she realized she was doing it, Aidan instinctively moved her hand to her apron where it covered her dress pocket. As she felt for the soft velvet pouch, she wondered with dread what this enemy Knight had thrown to her.

Pride caught her gesture and the odd look on her face. She knew at once that she had done the wrong thing and could see the suspicion in his eyes.

"Yes, one of the Master's enemies," he repeated. "We've been through such attacks before. Now, Milady, I don't mean to frighten you any more than you've already been, but I must give you fair warning. The Master's enemies are ruthless and dangerous scoundrels who will stop at nothing to harm us. You see what this one did to the coach!"

He gestured to the burned door.

"And so I must ask you, Milady, did he speak to you, or – give you anything?"

Aidan hesitated. There was something about the look on Pride's face and the urgency in his voice that suddenly made it clear to her that she must keep the pouch a secret.

She quickly smoothed her apron and turned away from him, moving her hand from her pocket as she did so, and looked again at the coach.

"Milady," Pride said, more insistently this time, "I must ask you again – did the Knight speak to you or give you anything?"

Suddenly Lust's words from the night before floated back to her.

You will lie and cheat and steal . . .

Aidan turned back to Pride and looked him boldly in the eye. Then she told a deliberate lie – something she could never remember doing before.

"No," she said firmly. "I called out to him, but he wouldn't answer me. He said nothing to me – and he gave me nothing. What makes you think he would give me anything?"

Pride studied her face, not even blinking.

"Milady, not meaning to frighten you, but – these attacks have been known to be much worse than this. The Master's enemies have thrown powerful weapons at times that have – well – let's just say I've seen some things happen that have been horribly gruesome."

His words chilled Aidan to the core. It took all her self-control to keep from reaching for the velvet pouch, for she was suddenly filled with panic at what might be inside her pocket.

But she could tell he was watching carefully to see what her reaction would be, so she kept very still and quickly changed the subject.

"I see. But – Pride, what about Greed? He jumped from the carriage – do you think he's hurt?"

Pride shook his head.

"Greed will be fine. He wasn't hurt. I saw him running toward Hidden."

Then he laughed gruffly, breaking some of the tension between them.

"Ah, don't trouble yourself about us, Milady. As I told you, we've been through enemy attacks many times, often far worse than this. My fine horses are a bit lathered, but they'll take me home again. Have no fear now. The Master always takes good care of us, and he'll take good care of you. Shall I return for you this afternoon, as usual?"

"Return for me!" cried Aidan. "Do you mean you're just going to leave? We don't know where that Knight went! Suppose he's planning to attack again! Perhaps he's waiting to attack you on your way home!"

"No, Milady," Pride said firmly. "I assure you, he is gone now. If he'd wanted more from us, he wouldn't have run off."

Aidan realized Pride was right. If the Knight had wanted to harm them further, he could easily have done so. Apparently he had done exactly what he had intended to do, which was to burn the crest of the Dark Prince on the carriage door and to give her the velvet pouch – and whatever was inside it.

"Shall I return for you later, then?" Pride repeated, now anxious to leave.

It occurred to Aidan that he wanted to warn her other guests of the attack. It also occurred to her that he knew full well that she had lied to him – and would tell the others about that too.

"Yes, very well," she agreed.

"Very good, then," Pride said, and tipped his cap to her. "Good day, Milady."

He climbed back up into the driver's seat and took the reins, calling to the horses. Thinning smoke from the door left a wispy trail behind the carriage as it turned around and sped away down the hill.

Aidan watched it go, then turned and headed for the mansion, wondering how she would ever get through the day now that all this had happened.

She was halfway up the steps when she saw with dismay that Stewart had just come outside and was standing above her. At first his face wore a look of astonished confusion, but that was quickly replaced by an angry scowl.

"Aidan! What are *you* doing here?" he demanded.

She sighed. There would be no cheerful greeting trying to coax a smile from him today.

"I'm here for work as usual," she replied. "I know, I'm late."

"Indeed you are – extremely late!" Stewart accused. "You have kept my Lady waiting a long time!"

"I'm sorry, Stewart. It was unavoidable."

She came up the steps and stood on the landing before him. He glared down at her, his eyes narrowed with suspicion.

"I was sent out here to greet a carriage. Lady Fairhaven saw it from her balcony. She said it looked like a very fine carriage – and it was burning. Do you know anything about this?"

Aidan sighed again, not at all sure how to answer.

Finally she said, "Yes, I do. It's my carriage and it brought me here. And yes, it was burning. But my driver is taking it home now."

Stewart's eyes became huge. Then he straightened up and squared his shoulders, regaining his arrogant composure.

"My Lady has informed my Lord of the situation," he said crisply. "I have been instructed to bring our visitors to the parlor. I suppose that means I must bring you. Come along quickly, then."

Aidan was filled with dread but there was nothing she could do.

"Yes, Stewart," she replied meekly, and followed him into the mansion.

Chapter Twenty-One

The Knight's Gift

With the stride of a marching soldier, Stewart led Aidan through the corridors of the mansion to the oval-shaped ballroom on the first floor. At the far end of this grand hall was the door to the room Lady Fairhaven called the parlor. Aidan had been in both rooms many times and never ceased to be fascinated by their opulence.

Huge and ornate with lavish gold decoration and sparkling crystal chandeliers, the ballroom featured a polished wood dance floor and pale blue walls rising to a high ceiling. Along one side of the room sunlight was streaming in through tall windows framed by long heavy draperies of rich gold and ivory brocade. The same shiny fabric covered benches and chairs that had been placed around the edges of the room, leaving the main space open for dancing.

A massive fireplace of veined white marble took up the central space between the windows. Above its mantel was an immense oil painting, a life-sized double portrait of Lord and Lady Fairhaven that Aidan knew had been painted soon after their wedding.

On the other side of the room a row of large niches had been cut into the wall, each framed by sculpted garlands of oak leaves and acorns covered in gold. These niches contained finely carved marble busts of some of Lord Fairhaven's male ancestors. Between them were tall mirrors framed in gold that reflected light into the room.

But by far the feature Aidan found most fascinating about the ballroom was its domed ceiling. It had been decorated long ago with an enormous fresco done in glowing colors. The elaborate scene was one of sky and clouds, so skillfully rendered that upon seeing it for the first time she had gasped, thinking the room had no ceiling at all and she was actually looking up at a celestial vision.

In the center a golden chariot pulled by a magnificent white horse was emerging from fluffy clouds as if streaking across the heavens. The chariot seemed to be ablaze with yellow and orange flames that surrounded its driver, whose rosy-gold skin looked like it had been burnished by the fire. His thick dark hair was crowned with a wreath of golden leaves and his body was draped in loose white garments that billowed out around him, leaving much of his muscular shoulders and torso exposed.

White doves were flying through the sky all around the chariot. At the edges of the painting, flitting in and out of the clouds, were playful pink-cheeked little boys with softly feathered white wings on the backs of their plump naked bodies.

Aidan had stared up in wonder at the fresco many times. The silly winged children sometimes made her laugh, but her attention was inevitably drawn to the handsome face of the charioteer. His impassive countenance featured large dark eyes that always seemed to follow her as she walked across the room far below him. Who was he supposed to be?

It was a complete mystery to her as to why anyone would have a painting on their ceiling, of all places, especially one as strange as this. She had asked Lady Fairhaven about it, but the work had been created so long ago that its meaning was now lost both to her and to her husband.

As Stewart led her to the parlor, Aidan glanced up at the painting as she always did. All at once she froze with a loud gasp that echoed across the cavernous emptiness of the hall as the image brought all the morning's trauma back to her. In a rush of panic, unable to move, she was completely arrested by the scene high above her and stared at its every detail with new perception.

Blazing fire. A white horse. A strong warrior.

Dark eyes with piercing gaze.

What could it all mean?

Stewart yanked open the double doors of the parlor, then turned and glared at her with annoyance.

"Whatever is the matter with you, Aidan?!" he snapped impatiently. "Come along!"

"Yes, Stewart," she said meekly. She tore her eyes from the painting and ducked her head down, carefully studying the floor as she hurried past him through the doorway into the parlor.

"My Lord and Lady shall see you presently," he said haughtily, and quickly closed the doors behind her.

Aidan whirled around and stared at the closed doors, her heart pounding and her stomach churning, suddenly feeling like a prisoner closed into her cell awaiting a terrible fate.

The parlor was hardly a prison cell, however. She knew that it was used as a sitting room and also as Lady Fairhaven's private library and office. Decorated in the same colors and flamboyant style as the ballroom, it was much smaller and more intimate than the grand hall but just as impressive with its pale blue walls, ornate gold decoration, and carved white marble fireplace. The drapes and all the chair cushions were made with the same shiny brocade fabric as was used in the grand hall.

Two tall windows flanked the fireplace and above the mantel were two large portraits which Aidan knew were of Lord Fairhaven's parents. In the middle of the room on a rug with a gold and dark blue floral design, a settee and two coordinating chairs surrounded a low table. A cushioned rocking chair and a tall wingback chair with a hassock were positioned in front of the fireplace, completing the conversation area.

At one end of the room were shelves built into one wall that contained Lady Fairhaven's collection of books. In front of them was her ornately carved wooden desk, painted white and trimmed with gold. At the other end of the room was a tall liquor cabinet with leaded glass doors and a square oak game table with four chairs.

Grateful to be alone, Aidan hurried to the settee and sat down. Carefully she drew the purple velvet pouch from her pocket. Despite Pride's frightening words to her, it was oddly reassuring to feel the warm fabric so richly soft in her hand. As she tugged at the knot in the drawstring, the gold threads of the embroidered crest glittered in the morning sunlight pouring in through the windows. She was afraid to open the pouch but didn't hesitate, for by now her curiosity was burning within her to find out what it contained.

The pouch opened easily and she cautiously peeked inside, but all she could see was something that looked like soft shiny cloth.

Holding her breath, she reached in and pulled out a neatly folded piece of lustrous gold silk wrapped around something small and very light. She set the pouch on the table, then gently laid the silk next to it and pulled back the corners.

To her utter astonishment, Aidan uncovered a tiny white rose.

"Oh my," she whispered in awe.

Her heart melted with complete delight at the sight of the unexpected treasure, which was smaller than any rose she had ever seen. It measured perhaps four inches from the top of its flawless bud to the end of its freshly cut stem, which bore several dark green leaves but not a single thorn.

Reverently she lifted it between her thumb and two fingers. Then she jumped up and hurried to one of the windows to examine it more closely.

The little rose was perfectly formed and exquisitely beautiful. It was not bright white but richly cream-colored, its petals delicately edged with dark crimson that cast a hint of blush across the top of the blossom. Two petals were just beginning to curl back from the bud, invitingly soft and looking as fragile as the finest porcelain. In the bright sunlight the rose seemed to shimmer with faint iridescence as though it had been dusted with subtle flecks of gold like a velvety pearl.

It was the most incredible rose Aidan had ever seen, much more beautiful even than the Dark Prince's showy black roses. She was astounded that such a dainty little thing could have survived so completely undamaged by its rough ride wrapped up inside a pouch stashed beneath a galloping horse's saddle.

Now exposed to the air, the rose released a strong sweet fragrance quite unlike any she had ever smelled before. Bringing the blossom to her face she inhaled deeply, marveling that such a tiny bud not even fully opened should have such a heady scent.

As Aidan savored the exquisite perfume, the strangest thing happened.

A surge of warmth and strength suddenly seemed to pour into her body. The dread in her heart and tightness in her stomach gave way to the most amazing sense of peace she had ever known. The beauty of the rose filled her with such intense joy that she even felt laughter rise up in her throat.

Startled by all this, she pulled the rose away from her face and stared at it again. It glistened softly, its very presence in her hand a silent mystery.

Thinking again of the Knight and his handsome face, Aidan remembered how all her fear had melted away as she gazed into his beautiful eyes. Now his incredible gift was filling her with the same peace and comfort.

"Why should I be feeling this way?" she whispered to the treasure in her hand. "Are you a healing rose?"

At that moment Aidan heard voices and footsteps in the ballroom.

She ran to the table, where she quickly wrapped the rose in the silk square before carefully slipping it back into the pouch and pulling the drawstring tight. Then she hid the pouch safely in her pocket beneath her apron.

As she sat back down on the settee, her mind was racing with questions.

Who was that mysterious Knight? Where had he come from? Why had he chased her carriage and burned its door with his fearsome sword?

What was this wondrous rose he had thrown to her?

Why were all these disturbing things happening in her life?!

And most importantly, was the Knight her enemy – or her friend?

Chapter Twenty-Two

Explaining To The Fairhavens

Just then Aidan heard the parlor doors open and turned around to see Lord and Lady Fairhaven quietly staring at her from across the room. All the peace she had felt a moment before left her. She leapt to her feet, her heart pounding with dread at the sight of them, and smoothed her apron with trembling hands.

Lord Malcolm Fairhaven was tall and slender, a powerfully built man with broad shoulders and muscular arms. His handsome wide face boasted a ruddy complexion that was framed by a neatly trimmed auburn beard and wavy dark red hair that was beginning to turn pale gold at the temples. He had always spoken to her in a cordial manner and his bright blue eyes sometimes even seemed to twinkle with mischief, but Aidan was still greatly intimidated by him. Now as they stood together in the doorway, Lady Fairhaven seemed tiny and frail next to her husband.

They entered the room and Stewart closed the doors behind them. Aidan stood anxiously by the settee waiting for one of them to speak first. As they walked to the chairs by the fireplace, Lord Fairhaven greeted her in his rich baritone voice.

"Good morning, Aidan. Come sit with us."

"Thank you, my Lord."

Lady Fairhaven settled herself gracefully in the rocking chair, smiling warmly at Aidan and silently inviting her to sit in the chair next to hers by patting its carved wooden arm. Aidan moved quickly to the chair but waited until Lord Fairhaven had taken his place in the wingback chair before sitting down herself.

He cleared his throat, regarding her with curiosity.

"Stewart tells us you have arrived in a carriage this morning."

"Yes, my Lord," Aidan answered meekly.

"My wife saw this. She said it looked like a royal carriage but that its door seemed to be on fire. Please explain how you came to be riding in a royal carriage that was burning."

Aidan felt her face flaming as hot as the carriage door had been. She was at a complete loss to be able to explain what had happened that morning when it made no sense to her at all. Fear made her throat constrict and her mouth go dry. She began to speak with difficulty.

"Yes, my Lord. I will try to explain. You see, I –"

"*Try* to explain?" Lord Fairhaven's deep stern voice seemed to resound throughout the room. "That will not be good enough. I will require a full explanation."

At that Aidan became even more flustered and couldn't answer. Helplessly she smoothed her apron again, trying to think of what to say.

To her relief, Lady Fairhaven quickly broke in.

"Malcolm," she chided softly, "you're frightening her. Please be gentle. She's done nothing wrong." Turning to Aidan, she spoke calmly. "Aidan, please tell us as best you can what has happened to you. It would seem that you have had a frightful experience. Are you all right?"

Aidan took a deep breath, grateful for her employer's kindness.

"Yes, thank you, my Lady. Yes. It was a very frightful experience. I thought – I thought I would surely die."

Lady Fairhaven's sapphire blue eyes became very round with alarm.

"Do try to tell us what has happened to you, child. Start from the beginning. Tell us about the carriage. It was very beautiful. Where did you get such a carriage?"

Aidan took another deep breath.

"It is mine – and yes, it is a royal carriage. It was given to me with a driver and horses –"

She stopped, not sure how much she should tell them about everything that had happened to her in the last few days.

"Given to you? By whom?" Lord Fairhaven said.

Aidan gathered her courage and told him.

"By Prince Bal'Davarius."

Lady Fairhaven gasped and Lord Fairhaven's eyes went wide with shock. He sat up and leaned forward in his chair.

"Prince Bal'Davarius? How can this be? Has our Prince come to Hidden while we were away and I was not told?"

"No, my Lord, he hasn't come here," Aidan said. "He sent the carriage to me with the driver and a footman. Their wives came with them too."

"But how does he know of you? Why would he give you a carriage?"

"I don't know, my Lord," Aidan replied, "but he has sent many of his servants to me – and they brought me the carriage – and many other gifts as well."

Slowly Lord Fairhaven leaned back in his chair, looking completely stunned.

"And when did this happen?"

"Just in the last few days," Aidan said. "While you were away."

"Aidan," Lady Fairhaven said, "those two strangers you told me about – you said you met them in the morning on your way to the mansion that day I let you go home early – the day before we left. Were they also from the Prince? Are they still staying with you?"

"Yes, my Lady," Aidan replied. "They were the first to come."

"Did they tell you about your mother, as you had hoped?"

"Well – they told me some things, yes," Aidan said. "And they said Prince Bal'Davarius would be sending more of his servants to me. And then they started arriving that same night."

"How many have come?" Lady Fairhaven asked.

Aidan glanced down into her lap, then looked into the noblewoman's kind eyes and began to unburden her troubled heart.

"So many I can't even count them all. Some of them are really helpful to me – there is a butler and a maidservant to cook and clean, and the carriage and driver – but there are others who are completely dreadful and unbearable and – and they don't seem to be ordinary people – and I'm so confused and frightened, my Lady! I don't know what to do."

"There, there, child, of course you are frightened," Lady Fairhaven said sympathetically. "Tell us more about the Prince's servants. If there are so many, how do they all fit into your little cottage?"

"I don't know," Aidan replied. "But my butler seems to be able to fit them all in. He's the one who oversees all their coming and going." She looked down again and spoke to her hands in her lap. "Each one says they have been ordered by their Master to do some kind of work in my life and can't leave until it's done."

"Remarkable," Lord Fairhaven said, stroking his beard thoughtfully. "I wonder what his purposes are – and how he knows of you."

They were quiet a moment. Then he said, "Aidan, you said you had a frightening experience in the carriage this morning and that you thought you were going to die. What happened? How was the carriage burned?"

Suddenly Aidan found herself strangely more afraid to tell Lord Fairhaven about the Knight than she was about her guests.

At last she said, "We were attacked, my Lord."

"Attacked!" he repeated. "By whom?"

Aidan took a deep breath. She knew that what she was about to tell them would sound crazy, especially since she could hardly make sense of it herself.

"A Knight riding on a white horse. He was wearing silver armor – and he had a flaming sword. He used that to burn the carriage."

"Indeed! A flaming sword!" Lord Fairhaven said, incredulous. "And how can this be?"

"I don't know, my Lord, but it really was burning," Aidan said earnestly. "I saw the flames and I thought he wanted to kill me, but when the fire came at me it never touched me – just the carriage. He burned away the Prince's royal crest that was on the door, and nothing else."

She decided not to tell them about the Knight's kind eyes and the yearning she still felt for him, nor about the rose in the velvet pouch he had thrown to her. Moving her hand over her apron to her pocket, she gently felt for it to be sure she hadn't imagined it.

Lord Fairhaven's bright blue eyes were now huge.

"Just the royal crest, you say! Then surely this Knight is our Prince's enemy!"

"Yes, my Lord, that is what my driver said," Aidan replied.

"So it would appear that your Knight was only interested in burning your royal carriage," he said thoughtfully. "Did you see if he was wearing a coat of arms or a crest of any kind on his armor?"

Aidan was too afraid to show him the pouch with the embroidered crest.

"I think there was a design on his chest," she told him. "I could see colors but I couldn't see it very well. He was moving too fast."

"Can you tell me anything more about this Knight? Can you describe the attack?"

"Well –" Aidan was at a loss for words. "He was riding on a beautiful white horse – it looked just like the horse in your painting on the ceiling. And he chased us – and he rode alongside the carriage – he was riding right next to us. And then he burned the door – and just turned around and rode away down the hill."

Lord Fairhaven's face suddenly turned crimson.

"Down the *hill?* Do you mean to tell me that this Knight attacked you *here?* On *Fairhaven property?!"*

Aidan was terrified by his sudden anger. Thinking he was about to jump up and go into a rage, she raised her hands to her face and cowered back into the chair cushion.

"Yes, my Lord," she whimpered meekly.

Lord Fairhaven did not go into a rage, but his deep voice seemed to Aidan to roar like thunder as he scolded her.

"You should have told me this right away! I would have sent out the guards!"

Aidan could barely whisper in reply.

"I'm sorry, my Lord. I didn't think of that. I'm so sorry!"

"But of course you didn't think of that, child," Lady Fairhaven said, reaching over and grasping her husband's arm. "You were too upset – too afraid."

"Yes," Aidan said frantically. "Yes, I was terrified!"

Lord Fairhaven closed his eyes. He quickly put his large hand over his wife's on his arm and was quiet for a long moment, regaining his composure.

Opening his eyes, he said, "There hasn't been an act of warfare in this valley for centuries. And right here on our hill! This is most upsetting to me."

He looked at Lady Fairhaven and squeezed her hand. Then he turned to Aidan and his voice became very quiet and gentle.

"Aidan, I did not mean to frighten you. I apologize. Please forgive me."

Shocked that he should apologize to her and not knowing what else to say, Aidan replied, "Yes, my Lord, of course."

He took a deep breath. "You say the Knight rode away."

"Yes, my Lord," Aidan said. "He rode off before we reached the oak trees. I saw him heading across the valley toward the road. My driver said he won't be back – that if he had wanted more from us, he wouldn't have run off."

"Yes, I must agree," Lord Fairhaven said. "I suspect this Knight is heading for the border right now. But he is obviously our Prince's enemy and we really have no idea what he wanted or why he attacked you – or if he will come back – or if there are more such knights working with him. Whatever the case, clearly this was a blatant act of aggression."

Abruptly he stood up and Aidan jumped to her feet.

"I must alert the guards to be on the lookout for him should he return. If you will excuse me, ladies."

Lady Fairhaven rose gracefully and extended her hand to him. The diamonds that adorned her heavy gold wedding rings flashed in the light from the windows.

"Of course, Malcolm," she said.

Folding his powerful hand around her small one, Lord Fairhaven lifted it tenderly to his lips as though it were fragile crystal. At the sight of their hands together in such obvious affection for each other, Aidan was immediately reminded of the carved bride and groom on the wedding harp.

He turned to Aidan and bowed slightly.

"Aidan, I am terribly sorry that you have had such a frightening experience here on my hill, and I am glad that you are all right. I wish to know more about all this. We shall talk again."

"Of course, my Lord," Aidan replied.

He turned and strode across the room, gently closing the doors behind himself as he left.

Chapter Twenty-Three

Tea In The Rose Garden

When they were alone and seated again, Aidan turned to Lady Fairhaven and said, "My Lady, I'm sorry that I made him so angry. This is all my fault. I'm so sorry."

Lady Fairhaven looked at her in surprise.

"There is no need for you to apologize, Aidan. What happened to you this morning was not your fault – you've done nothing wrong. Lord Fairhaven was understandably upset to think that this strange attack happened on our hill. But sometimes he's much too quick to become angry. I'm sorry he frightened you."

Then she laughed quietly.

"Alert the guards!" she repeated in amusement. "Our guards are useless! They've had nothing to do for years, but we keep them because their families have served us for generations. Life is so very quiet here. This will be the most excitement they've had in a very long time, I'm sure, even though your Knight seems to have run off."

At that moment she stopped and began to sniff the air.

"What is that scent?"

Her eyes were filled with curiosity. She bent forward and sniffed again, and Aidan sniffed too, although she wasn't sure what it was that Lady Fairhaven was smelling.

"Why, Aidan, are you wearing perfume?"

"Perfume?" It was a few seconds before Aidan remembered that Vanity had combed drops of perfume into her hair the night before. She smiled with embarrassment. "Oh – why, yes – I guess I am."

"Is it rose? It suits you," Lady Fairhaven said.

"Thank you," Aidan said.

There was a brief silence between them. Then she asked, "What did Lord Fairhaven mean – that the Knight is heading for the border?"

"Well, he must be from across the border," Lady Fairhaven told her. "There is only one other country that is anywhere near to us, and it is our enemy. That's why Lord Fairhaven asked if you could describe the Knight's crest. He is most certainly from the Kingdom of Everestaal."

"Everestaal," Aidan repeated in a reverent whisper.

Suddenly she was filled with a surge of excitement as a realization came to her.

Everestaal! Why, that must be where my mother is!

"How close is this border?" she asked eagerly. "How can a person go to the Kingdom of Everestaal?"

Lady Fairhaven seemed quite startled by her questions.

"It's not far. Clearview is right on the border – you can see into Everestaal from the cliffs. But we're not allowed to go there. It's forbidden to cross over into an enemy country."

"Clearview," said Aidan. "That's where you and Lord Fairhaven have gone."

"Yes, we go frequently when the season is fair. We have a house there and Malcolm owns a mill and some rental properties, so he collects payments and conducts his business. And we have dear friends in Clearview, so I always travel with him when he goes."

Aidan tried in vain to imagine what it would be like to ride in a carriage over the mountain road, to view scenery that was different from the valley where she had always lived, to own a second house in a town where one could look right into a foreign country. But now her resolve to leave Hidden in the spring and find her mother was greater than ever.

"It must be so wonderful to travel," she said longingly.

At that Lady Fairhaven laughed lightly, a musical sound that rippled like a mountain stream.

"Oh my dear, I would hardly call it wonderful – it's just a long tedious trip across that bumpy mountain road! But I do love visiting our good friends. Frankly, I much prefer our house in Clearview. I so wish Malcolm would agree to living there permanently, but he won't – he loves this mansion where he grew up."

"How far is Clearview from Hidden?" Aidan asked.

"It's perhaps half a day's journey. The road can be quite treacherous in certain seasons – we never go there in late fall or winter. But in summer the scenery is so lovely going through the valleys and over the hills – such beautiful forests. And we always stop at a lake along the way."

"I've never been outside Hidden," Aidan confessed. "What is Clearview like?"

"Oh, the shops there are just as dismal as those here," Lady Fairhaven told her. "But it really is a lovely town – much larger than Hidden, with so much more to do. It's right on the steep cliffs at the very edge of the mountains. There's a large river that runs through the center of town with a beautiful waterfall. Malcolm's grandfather took advantage of that river over a century ago and built the mill and our house there."

Her sapphire blue eyes suddenly became wistful.

"And the view of the great plain beyond the mountains as you look into Everestaal – why, it just takes my breath away whenever I see it. I dearly love that view."

Aidan was quiet, listening in rapt fascination to Lady Fairhaven's description. She had seen spring waterfalls of melting snow, but never a large river or a lake or a plain. Indeed, she was not even sure she understood what a plain was.

"If you look down from the cliff across the river below, you can see for miles into Everestaal," Lady Fairhaven continued dreamily. "Oh, the view, Aidan, the view! It's the most incredible sight. You can look all the way across the great plain and rolling hills to lakes and forests and the mountain range far off on the horizon. It's a most beautiful country, so green and fruitful – not at all like these cold barren mountains."

"It sounds wonderful," Aidan said in awe. "Have you ever gone there?"

"Oh, my dear, no," Lady Fairhaven replied quickly, shaking her head. "That would be quite impossible. As I told you, Everestaal is our enemy and it's strictly forbidden to cross the border. But even if it were not, the cliffs are steep and rocky and the river below is quite wide. I'm not even sure how you could get there."

She sighed.

"But I do confess that there have been many times when I've looked at that glorious sweeping view of the plain and with all my heart I've longed to go there."

From the melancholy look on her face, Aidan could sense the great depth of her yearning. Then she resolutely shook her head.

"But it's just not possible. No, I know I can never follow my heart down out of these mountains."

Aidan was becoming completely convinced that Clearview must be where she had been born and that her mother must have come from Everestaal. But suddenly Unwanted's words came back to her so forcefully it was almost as if the old woman's harsh voice was whispering into her ear.

This Kingdom is the place of your birth. This is the land where you truly belong.

Could she ever hope to follow her own heart down out of the mountains?

At that moment the parlor doors abruptly opened and Stewart entered. As he strode toward them, Lady Fairhaven frowned with clear annoyance at the intrusion.

"Yes, Stewart, what is it?"

He bowed with his usual pompous flair.

"Forgive me for interrupting, my Lady, but your morning tea is ready."

Lady Fairhaven's face brightened. "Oh, excellent," she said. "I shall take tea in the rose garden, and Aidan will be joining me."

Stewart's eyebrows went up as his eyes widened with surprise, but he quickly composed himself.

"Yes – very good then, my Lady. I shall see to it at once."

With a stiff bow he turned and left the room. Aidan had caught his expression and suddenly panicked.

"Oh, my Lady – this is so kind of you – but shouldn't I be starting work now?"

Lady Fairhaven rose to her feet and fussed at her skirt, smoothing it with her hand as Aidan quickly stood up.

"Not this morning, my dear. You've had a terrible fright – and I wish to know more about these guests of yours. Come have tea with me."

The Fairhavens' extensive and carefully maintained gardens grew food and provided beautiful landscaping for the mansion. The formal flower gardens were separated by finely sculpted hedges and decorated with arbors and sculptures. But all the garden activity at present seemed to be among the rows of vegetables, where servants were beginning to reap the autumn harvest and fill the root cellars in preparation for the long mountain winter.

Rising up in the midst of the vegetable gardens was a huge glass-enclosed greenhouse. This ornate structure fascinated Aidan, for nothing like it existed in Hidden and she had never seen such a wonder before coming to work at the mansion. The greenhouse was the hub around which all the gardens were planned. She had spent much time that summer learning how the vegetable plants and annual flowers were started from seed there weeks before going into the ground.

But most amazing of all to her were the flowers that grew all year round in the greenhouse. Flowers in the midst of winter was a luxury she had never even imagined.

Aidan was especially glad that Lady Fairhaven had chosen her to take charge of her rose garden, which was just a step outside one of the mansion's many doors. Some of the rosebushes were rare and precious specimens, and she had worked carefully and diligently to nurture the garden to the fullness of its beauty. She took great pride in knowing that her employer was well pleased with what she had done that summer.

Lady Fairhaven's rose garden was much like Aidan's with its flagstone paths that meandered through bushes of every size and shape, but the similarity ended there due to its most unusual setting. It was completely enclosed and protected by the ancient broken-down stone walls of what had once been a very large room connected to the mansion. Two long parallel walls formed its length, each in various states of ruin and containing tall arched windows which no longer held any glass. Climbing roses of many colors trailed across these stone walls and out of the open window spaces.

On the end opposite the mansion was the adjoining wall that was still mostly intact and rose to a high point. In the center of this wall was an open archway that had once contained a wooden door. Above this arch was a large circular window which like the other windows had long ago lost its glass.

The roofless room and broken walls seemed to Aidan to be an extraordinary space. Compared to the manicured formal gardens, it was simply charming and beautifully rustic. She loved Lady Fairhaven's rose garden almost as much as she loved her own.

A stone terrace right outside the mansion door contained a table and cushioned chairs nestled cozily beneath a large shady arbor covered with rambling roses of various colors. The terrace was a few steps higher than the rest of the garden, offering a perfect view of its beauty, and the shady space beneath the arbor was fragrant and private.

Although Aidan had often worked in the garden, she had never before taken tea with her employer or even sat at the terrace table. But she knew it was one of Lady Fairhaven's favorite places in the mansion, and as she settled into her chair she immediately understood why.

"This is so beautiful," she said in awe. "What a lovely place to have tea!"

"Why, thank you, my dear," Lady Fairhaven replied. "I do love this terrace table. And you have done such wonders with the garden this summer."

"Thank you, my Lady," Aidan said, then asked, "Why are there broken walls with open windows all around your garden? I have often wondered."

"Oh, this was once a room of some kind," Lady Fairhaven explained. "It was built centuries ago, probably with the original part of the mansion. At some point long before our time the roof fell in, but the walls were left standing, as you can see. It seemed the perfect place to plant my rose garden, protected from the winds. I had this terrace built and the garden started right after I married Malcolm."

Stewart appeared just then followed by footmen carrying trays bearing a silver tea service and porcelain plates heaped with food. There were dainty tea sandwiches on small flaky rolls, thin slices of sausage and cheese, clusters of grapes, and tiny frosted cakes.

"Will that be all, my Lady?" he asked.

"Yes, this is quite fine," Lady Fairhaven told him. "Thank you, Stewart, you may leave us now."

"Very good, my Lady," he answered with a haughty bow. He turned and Aidan was sure that the look he then gave to her was a resentful scowl, but he spoke cordially. "Good morning to you, Aidan."

He gestured to the footmen and they all went back inside the mansion, leaving her alone with Lady Fairhaven.

The noblewoman shook out her linen napkin and placed it on her lap. As she poured tea for them both she said, "Help yourself, child."

Aidan nervously picked up her napkin and copied Lady Fairhaven's movements.

"Thank you, my Lady. It all looks delicious."

"Well, I do hope you will enjoy it, my dear. Have as much as you like."

Aidan was very hungry and began heaping food onto her plate. Then she noticed Lady Fairhaven hadn't taken any food for herself. She feared she had been too greedy, but her employer didn't seem to mind.

They sat quietly for a few minutes while Aidan ate tea sandwiches and grapes, then took some cakes. Lady Fairhaven sipped her tea and gazed thoughtfully at her roses. At last she turned to Aidan and broke the silence.

"Aidan, my dear, I would like to hear more about your guests. Those first two that came to you – what did they tell you about your mother? Do they really know her?"

"Yes, they have told me they do," Aidan said. "And some of my other guests say they know her too. But they are not allowed to tell me anything about her, not even her name. I'm certain they also know where she is now, but they all keep saying that Prince Bal'Davarius has strictly ordered them not to tell me that."

"How odd! I wonder why," said Lady Fairhaven. "I wonder how he even knows of her or you at all. Have they told you anything about your birth or why she gave you up?"

"They told me that my mother is from a foreign land and that I was born in a town here in the mountains," Aidan said.

"A foreign land!" Lady Fairhaven repeated, surprised. "Why, that must mean she is from Everestaal!"

"Yes, I think so. When we were talking just now, from what you were saying – I was thinking that my mother must have come from there and that I must have been born in Clearview."

"That would seem very logical," Lady Fairhaven agreed. "But my goodness, why would your mother leave Everestaal to come to an enemy country? How could she have crossed that river or climbed those cliffs?"

Her face reddening with shame, Aidan looked down at her teacup to avoid Lady Fairhaven's eyes.

"I don't know how she did it, my Lady, but I'm told she was desperate to come here. You see, she – she wasn't married. She was very young – and all alone. She had to run away from her family before they found out what she had done. So she came to stay with a relative here in the mountains – and I was born in Davarius."

Aidan was deathly afraid that Lady Fairhaven would despise her upon learning that she was illegitimate, but to her surprise there was no reaction other than a brief silence followed by a gentle question.

"What of your father? Did they tell you anything about him?"

Remembering her conversation with Lust in the starlight – had it really been just the night before? – Aidan felt herself shiver as though she were still sitting in the cold night air.

"Yes, one of my guests knew him too. He – he was a deceiver. He lied to my mother and told her he wanted to marry her. But then he left town and she never saw him again. By the time she knew she was going to have me, he was long gone and she was afraid to tell her family."

"Of course she was," Lady Fairhaven said sympathetically. "Oh my. Such a difficult situation for a young girl! And she couldn't take care of you all by herself. No wonder she wanted to find another family for you. But I wonder why she chose to give you to Mara Teague – a poor widow with no real means to bring up a child."

Grateful that her employer was so understanding, Aidan finished the last sips of her tea and put her empty cup back into its saucer. She kept her eyes on it while she continued with her story.

"My mother never met Aunt Mara. She lived with her relative until that person died, but then she couldn't stay there. The first two guests who came to me – the two sisters I met that first morning – they were the ones who brought me here to Hidden in the basket."

"Oh my!" Lady Fairhaven said, her voice filled with amazement. "So you were brought to Hidden by two servants of Prince Bal'Davarius himself? And these same two women are now living in your house with you?"

"Yes, my Lady," Aidan replied. "Their names are Unloved and Unwanted. They have a little boy who travels with them named Orphan. Prince Bal'Davarius sent them to my mother, and they took me in the basket and gave her money so she could go back home."

Lady Fairhaven was clearly shaken by this. She stared at Aidan for a long moment before answering.

"I see. Unloved and Unwanted – and Orphan," she repeated slowly. "Sent from the Prince himself. And these servants of his paid money to your mother – and took you away – as though they were buying you."

Her words were suddenly as heavy and brightly illuminating as the crystal chandeliers hanging in the ballroom. Aidan stared at her in complete shock, realizing for the first time that she had been sold – like a slave.

There was a long uncomfortable silence between them. Lady Fairhaven dabbed at her lips with her napkin.

"Please tell me more, Aidan."

Looking back down at her plate, Aidan continued.

"Unloved and Unwanted told me that the Prince would be sending more of his servants to me. They insisted they needed the key to my house to come and go as they please. Then they grabbed me – I was scared to death. They forced me to give it to them. Now there are so many of them I don't know what to do! I'm sorry I ever invited them – but they have my key – I can't get them to leave."

She looked back up, eager to unburden her heart to Lady Fairhaven, who had only ever been kind to her. In a rush, her words began to tumble out like water in the mountain streams in springtime.

"They keep telling me they have work to do in my house for their Master and they can't leave until it's finished. Some of them have brought me good things, like fine clothing and expensive jewelry – and fancy food and dishes – and the carriage and horses. The Prince has even sent a servant to cook and clean for me – and a butler who brings me breakfast on a silver tray, as Stewart did just now with the tea."

Lady Fairhaven was quiet, her eyes huge as she listened intently.

"Some of them have told me the Prince has chosen me for some special purpose and he will give me whatever I need and will take good care of me. But then there are others – they are just unbearable and cruel – and they terrify me – they all seem to have strange powers. And I just want them all to go away – but they won't. None of them will. And they won't tell me how to find my mother, as I had thought they would."

She looked into Lady Fairhaven's eyes and dropped her voice almost to a whisper.

"I think – I think some of them would kill me if they could."

At that Lady Fairhaven gasped in horror.

All the morning's trauma was now flooding back to Aidan as she went on.

"I don't know what the Prince wants with me, for good or for bad – I'm so confused. And now my carriage has been attacked by some kind of enemy! Why is all this happening to me? I'm so afraid, my Lady, so afraid! What can I do?"

Lady Fairhaven reached out and clutched Aidan's hand on the table. Her heavy diamond wedding rings flashed brightly and Aidan could feel them pressing into her skin.

"Aidan – Aidan, my child," she murmured soothingly.

Her face was pale with concern. Aidan was surprised at the tender softness in her voice and wide eyes.

"I'm very worried about you," she said. "My goodness, of course you're afraid. These cruel servants of the Prince – telling you all these things and frightening you – and now this wicked enemy Knight chasing you, attacking you – so much has happened to you in the last few days since we've been away!"

Aidan was too stunned to reply. No one had ever been worried about her before in her entire life. She had no idea how to respond and felt terribly guilty to be the cause of such concern.

Lady Fairhaven looked right into her eyes.

"Aidan, I want you to understand that if you don't feel safe, you can always come here," she said firmly. "Any time of the day or night – just come to the mansion."

Amazed at this invitation, Aidan stammered, "Oh, my Lady – that is too kind of you – but – I wouldn't want to impose."

"No, I'm quite serious," Lady Fairhaven insisted. "It would be no imposition at all. This old mansion has been a refuge for many people throughout generations who needed safety. Nothing can hurt you here. I want you to come."

She hesitated, then added, "You see, Aidan – I have become quite fond of you. I want you to consider me your friend."

This was more astounding to Aidan than anything else her employer had said.

"Oh my," she whispered. "I don't know what to say, my Lady. I have never had a friend."

At that, Lady Fairhaven seemed completely shocked.

"Never, Aidan? Not one friend?"

"Not one. Well – except for Drudgery."

"Drudgery?" Lady Fairhaven repeated.

"She is my maidservant from the Dark Prince," Aidan explained. "She has really been with me for a long time and is just about the only friend I have ever had. Now she is cooking and cleaning for me."

Silently Lady Fairhaven withdrew her hand, staring at Aidan in bewilderment.

"I see. Drudgery." She took a sip of tea. "Tell me the names of your other guests."

"Oh," Aidan replied, "I hardly know where to begin." She took a deep breath. "My butler is Gatekeeper. I like him very much – he is a kindly old gentleman. Then there is Fear. She is very beautiful and she keeps her children with her under her cape – there must be a hundred of them."

"A hundred children?!" gasped Lady Fairhaven, her eyes huge. "Under a cape?! How can this be?"

"I don't know, my Lady, but I have seen them. One day they were all out in my gardens. She has a long cape and they all seem to live there beneath it, and you can see their eyes staring out at you – and her firstborn –"

She shuddered, remembering Fear of Death leaning on his crutch and staring at her from across her yard.

"The Dark Prince's servants are not ordinary people, my Lady."

Lady Fairhaven was quiet for a long moment, clearly struggling to understand. Finally she said, "Tell me more. Who else has come to you?"

Aidan took another deep breath.

"There is Grief – she is a very feeble old woman who comes to those who have suffered loss. Then Pride and Greed came with the carriage and horses. Their wives Vanity and Lust brought me all the new clothes and jewelry. And then there are families – Doubt and Discouragement with their four terribly rude children, and –"

She stopped and looked down at the table.

"Go on, Aidan," Lady Fairhaven prodded gently. "Who else?"

"And then the worst of them," Aidan finished bitterly. "The ones I just can't bear. Night Terrors comes to me with horrible dreams in the night. But I have had his dreams all my life."

"Dreams?" Lady Fairhaven asked in surprise. "Nightmares?"

"Yes. Nightmares."

"Aidan – why do you have nightmares?"

Aidan kept looking down at her plate.

"I don't know. I just always have. As long as I can remember."

"Night Terrors," Lady Fairhaven whispered. "My dear child."

She seemed visibly upset. Nervously Aidan watched her as she sipped her tea quietly for a moment. Then she set the empty cup down and dabbed thoughtfully at her lips with her napkin again before looking directly into Aidan's eyes and speaking kindly but firmly.

"Aidan, please don't be afraid to tell me anything – anything at all. It's all right."

"Thank you, my Lady," Aidan whispered gratefully.

"Is there anyone else?"

"Yes," Aidan said. "There is Abuse – and her daughter Anger and son-in-law Depression – and more of their family will be coming soon. They are just unbearable – just horrible – the worst of all."

She looked down at the table again.

"I'm very afraid of them. They are the ones who I think would kill me if they could."

"Anger and Depression," Lady Fairhaven whispered. "Abuse!"

She reached across the table and grasped Aidan's hand again. Aidan looked up to see that her sapphire eyes were filled with panic and her face had gone completely white.

"Aidan, I meant what I said. You must come to the mansion at once if you ever feel threatened by these people. Tell me you will come. Please."

Flustered, Aidan stammered, "Well, I – of course. I will come here every day for work."

"No," Lady Fairhaven said adamantly. She was squeezing Aidan's hand very tightly. "No. I mean come here to stay – to live with us. I don't care if they are the Prince's servants. You are clearly terrified of them and I want to be sure you are perfectly safe. Nothing can hurt you here."

Aidan was dumbfounded. Every instinct in her knew she was completely unworthy to accept such an incredible offer, but she also knew it was given sincerely and it would not be right to hurt Lady Fairhaven's feelings.

Finally she replied, "My Lady – thank you – that is so generous of you. I don't really know what to say. This is the kindest thing anyone has ever done for me."

As Aidan said this, she thought she saw tears welling in Lady Fairhaven's eyes, but she couldn't quite be sure.

Just then the mansion door opened behind them and Lord Fairhaven stepped onto the terrace.

Chapter Twenty-Four

Talking With Lord Fairhaven

As Lord Fairhaven approached the table Aidan leapt to her feet. Lady Fairhaven quickly dabbed at her eyes with her napkin and composed herself, then turned to him with a smile.

"Dear husband," she said, extending her hand to him, "are you joining us for tea?"

"Yes, I thought I might. If you will have me," he replied teasingly.

"Malcolm," she said affectionately, "of course I will."

He bent down and gently kissed her hand. Then he nodded to Aidan as he pulled out his chair.

"Hello, Aidan. I hope you have recovered a bit from your frightful experience today. I am hoping to continue our conversation."

"Yes, my Lord," Aidan said nervously.

"Very good," he said.

She waited until he was settled, then sat down herself.

Stewart came out of the mansion just then followed by two footmen carrying trays with more food and a fresh pot of tea. He hovered over the table with a frown while the footmen did the serving. Then, after sending them back into the mansion with an impatient wave of his hand, he smiled and bowed graciously to Lord Fairhaven.

"Will there be anything else, my Lord?"

"Nothing for now, Stewart. You may leave us."

"Very good, my Lord."

Stewart bowed again and walked back into the mansion.

Lord Fairhaven shook out his napkin and laid it on his lap as he helped himself to the food. In contrast to his wife, he ate heartily. Lady Fairhaven poured his tea, then chose a bunch of grapes and three pieces of sliced cheese for herself.

"Aidan has been telling me about her guests from the Prince," she said. "She has learned that the first two women who came to her are the very ones who took her from her mother and brought her here to Mara Teague's doorstep."

"Indeed!" Lord Fairhaven said in surprise, then turned to Aidan. "So it was the servants of Prince Bal'Davarius who brought you to Hidden."

"Yes, my Lord."

"Most interesting," he said. "So our Prince has apparently somehow known about you from the time you were an infant. And from where did they bring you?"

"They wouldn't tell me that, my Lord," Aidan told him. "But they did tell me my mother came here from another country – so I think she must have come from Everestaal and I was born in Clearview."

"From Everestaal!" He seemed completely astounded by this. "Our enemy! I've known of people who have left Davarius to go there, but I have never heard of anyone from Everestaal coming here. Have you learned why she would do such a thing?"

Aidan hesitated to answer. Lady Fairhaven saw her reluctance and broke in gently.

"Malcolm, her mother was very young and not married. She came to Davarius to have her baby in secret and then left to go back home after the Prince's servants brought Aidan here."

To Aidan's relief, Lord Fairhaven seemed much more interested in where her mother was from than about her marital status. He stroked his beard thoughtfully.

"I see. So she came here from Everestaal – and then went back there. Truly remarkable! I wonder how she could have managed such a thing."

"I should think it would be impossible for a young girl expecting a child to make such a journey at all," Lady Fairhaven said. "There is the river, and of course those steep cliffs."

"It's actually not as difficult as it looks," Lord Fairhaven replied. "The river is wide but not particularly turbulent and I don't think it's very deep. And I know there is a trail northeast of Clearview going through the cliffs that is quite long but not terribly steep – it's actually fairly easy to climb."

He picked up a bunch of grapes and pulled one from its stem.

"Halfway along that trail is a flat place that marks where you pass from one country into the other. Some years ago I went to this place with a friend and I won't soon forget it. It was just a few days before I met you, Eleanora."

Lady Fairhaven smiled.

"Well," she agreed, "that certainly was some years ago."

Lord Fairhaven grinned at her as he popped the grape into his mouth.

Aidan thought about her guests who kept refusing to tell her where her mother had come from and where she was now. If her mother was from an enemy country, that would explain why they were so secretive about her.

"My Lord," she asked timidly, "if my mother was from Everestaal – if she is there now – does that make her an enemy of our Prince?"

"Well, now, that is a very good question," he answered. "Perhaps it does. A citizen of Everestaal would no doubt be considered an enemy."

Aidan hesitated, then asked, "Well, then – am I an enemy?"

Lord Fairhaven looked at her with surprise.

"You say you were born here, in these mountains – you are then a legal citizen of Davarius," he said. "No, I wouldn't think you could be considered an enemy of our Prince, no matter who your mother was. But I am quite sure that the Knight who attacked your carriage was an enemy. He must have been from Everestaal. That can be the only explanation for why he would burn the royal crest."

Aidan thought about the Knight and the rose he had given her. It was hard to think of him as her enemy, even though he had attacked her coach. Remembering the look in his eyes, she couldn't believe he had thought of her as his enemy either.

Once again she put her hand over her pocket, reassured that the rose was still there, but completely bewildered as to why it had been given to her.

"I have never even heard of this country until today," she confessed. "Why is Everestaal our enemy?"

Lord Fairhaven lifted his teacup and took a sip.

"I don't know all the details," he said, "but legend has it that centuries ago the Kingdom of Davarius was actually once part of the Kingdom of Everestaal. The story goes that at some point in time there was a conflict between two princes that caused an uprising against the King – some kind of rebellion that escalated into a war. It was a most terrible war, as I've read about it, very long and devastating. Presumably Everestaal was divided at that time and these mountains became the borderland of Davarius. We are not actively at war now, of course, but we have never been on friendly terms. And so our countries are enemies of each other."

"Even if we are enemies, I long to find my mother and learn more about my family," Aidan said. "If she is in Everestaal, I would go there."

"I would advise against that," Lord Fairhaven said firmly. "To go there would be considered an act of high treason. If the Prince's authorities caught you trying to defect, you would no doubt be arrested and imprisoned. And if you did make it there safely, you would never be able to come back here."

The thought of being locked into a tiny prison cell made Aidan shudder. Yet with all her heart she knew she must go to Everestaal. Not only had she made a vow to find her mother, now she also wanted to find the Knight.

Lord Fairhaven sat back, frowning thoughtfully and stroking his beard again.

"Aidan," he said, "tell me – about this Knight that attacked your carriage – did he speak to you – or give you anything?"

His question startled her, for Pride had asked her exactly the same thing. She wondered why this seemed to be so important.

Hesitantly she replied, "No, my Lord, he didn't say anything to me. And – if he had given me something – what would that matter?"

He looked at her intently.

"The way you have answered leads me to believe he did," he said. "It matters a great deal. Did he give you something?"

Aidan didn't know how to answer. She was afraid to lie to him but even more afraid to tell him the truth.

At last she said, "Yes, my Lord," and drew the velvet pouch from her pocket. "He gave me this."

Lord Fairhaven leaned forward and took the pouch from her with great interest. Lady Fairhaven looked surprised but sat quietly watching the two of them.

"After he burned the carriage door, he pulled this out from under his saddle and threw it to me through the window – and then just turned around and ran off without saying a word."

Studying the pouch carefully, Lord Fairhaven stroked the soft purple velvet and then turned it over. The exquisite gold embroidery caught the sunlight and flashed in his hand.

"This crest," he said reverently, staring at it in fascination. He held the pouch in his open palm and felt its lightness. "Is there something inside?"

"Yes, my Lord," Aidan replied. "Open it and see. You won't believe it."

He handed the pouch back to her. "Show me," he said.

Eager to see the white rose again, Aidan opened the pouch, took out the gold silk square, and unfolded it. She was relieved to find that the rose was just as fresh and pristine as it had been when she first saw it. As soon as it was revealed, its strong sweet fragrance was released into the air.

Lady Fairhaven gasped at the sight.

Aidan handed the rose to Lord Fairhaven, who took it and examined it carefully.

"Remarkable," he said slowly, turning it around in his hand. "A tiny cut rose, wrapped in a piece of silk and stored in a velvet pouch, thrown to you by a Knight on horseback chasing your carriage." He handed it to his wife. "Exquisite, isn't it, my dear? Lovely little rose."

"Gracious," Lady Fairhaven said in awe, cradling the rose in both of her open palms as though it were so fragile it might break. "I have never seen such a perfect rose. So tiny – and still fresh – not crushed or even wilted. How can this be?"

Taking the rose between her thumb and forefinger, she lifted it to the light. Its iridescence seemed to shimmer as she brought it close to her face to inhale its fragrance.

Then she turned to Aidan, her eyes wide with surprise.

"Why, this is the scent that I thought was your perfume!"

Lord Fairhaven took the rose from his wife and carefully scrutinized it again.

"It is a most extraordinary rose indeed," he said at last. "And delivered in a most extraordinary manner."

He handed the tiny rose back to Aidan and picked up the velvet pouch from the table to study the embroidered crest again. For a long moment he gently stroked the gold threads with one finger as though in complete wonder at what he was seeing.

At last he raised his face and looked Aidan directly in the eye. His voice was gravely serious.

"Aidan, this crest belongs to the Royal House of the King of Everestaal."

Aidan gasped. "The King!"

"I had suspected this to be the case when you first told me about the attack," he said. "Your Knight must be in his service, and I am quite certain that a rose as beautiful and unusual as this could only have come from a King's garden itself."

Aidan stared in great fear and wonder at the rose in her hand, baffled as to what it could all mean.

Lady Fairhaven was struggling to understand as well and quickly voiced the questions they were all thinking.

"But Malcolm – why would a Knight from Everestaal come all the way here to Hidden? And why would he attack and burn Aidan's carriage – only to throw this rose to her and then leave? It makes no sense."

"No, it doesn't, does it?" Lord Fairhaven said. "But clearly it was an act of aggression. The Knight may have thought he was attacking Prince Bal'Davarius himself and stopped when he realized that it was Aidan in the carriage."

Aidan had never thought of that. But she knew he had already seen her clearly when he burned the carriage door.

"But how did this Knight come here?" Lady Fairhaven asked. "He must have come up that trail through the cliffs and ridden through the mountains all the way from Clearview, as you said. That is quite a distance."

"Indeed, that is true," Lord Fairhaven said. He stroked his beard in thoughtful musing. "And this happened early in the morning. He must have set up camp somewhere in the forest along the mountain road. There could be other knights with him. Perhaps the King of Everestaal plans to invade our area. Perhaps he intends to start a war."

Lady Fairhaven shuddered.

"Oh, Malcolm, that is a very frightening thought!"

Aidan looked again at the rose in her hand, completely bewildered. The thought of a war starting was terrifying indeed, but how could the Knight be an enemy when his eyes had been so beautiful and he had given her such a precious gift? Surely the rose she was holding was clear evidence that he had meant her no harm.

"I love this rose so much," she said softly. She looked at Lord Fairhaven and spoke earnestly. "I don't care if Everestaal is our enemy. I want to go there and find where it grows."

Lord Fairhaven looked at her with concern.

"To go there would be an act of high treason, as I said."

"Yes, my Lord. But my mother must be there and I need to find her." She looked again at the dear little rose. "And – I want to find that Knight. I want to find out why he gave this to me."

She looked up. Lady Fairhaven was staring at her with a look of alarm.

"Aidan, that Knight is clearly an enemy," she said.

"Yes, my Lady, I know – but I don't think he is *my* enemy," she replied. "I don't understand why all these things are happening to me – I don't understand any of it. But now that I have heard about Everestaal, now that I have seen the Knight – now that I have received this rose – I want to go there. It must be a wonderful place. I want to go there with all my heart."

"No, Aidan," Lady Fairhaven said fervently. "You must never do that. It would be far too dangerous!"

"But my Lady – if only you could have *seen* him – his face when he was riding alongside the carriage – his eyes – they were so beautiful. He looked so kind."

"Kind?! How can such a thing be?" Lady Fairhaven said. "Aidan, he was a trained warrior. He was armed. He attacked you. He might have killed you!"

Aidan struggled to find words to make her understand.

"But no one has ever looked at me like that. And this rose is such a precious gift. He was just so – so kind to give it to me. Something in my heart is telling me I *have* to go there."

She turned impulsively to Lord Fairhaven.

"Could you help me, my Lord? If you know the way to get there – will you help me go to Everestaal?"

Lady Fairhaven broke in firmly.

"No, Aidan! I *must* forbid this! We don't know anything about –"

Lord Fairhaven abruptly leaned forward toward Aidan, gesturing with his hand and gently cutting off his wife in midsentence.

"Aidan," he said firmly, "I don't believe you understand the significance of what you are asking of me."

The ominous look on his face made Aidan freeze with fear, thinking she had said something very wrong.

"Our Prince's servants are living with you in your house because he has sent them to you with some kind of business to attend to. They would be obligated to do everything in their power to keep you from defecting to an enemy country. Should you try to do this, you will be putting your life in extreme danger. If you are apprehended, as I have just told you, you will be declared guilty of high treason against the throne. The penalty for this crime is most severe – either permanent imprisonment, with torture, or death by execution."

Aidan's heart began pounding with horror at what he was telling her. The paralyzing thought of being beaten and locked away in a tiny dark prison cell was one of her very worst fears.

Suddenly she realized her life must already be in danger because she had already told her guests she wanted to find her mother – and they knew she was in Everestaal. No wonder they had told her she was not allowed to leave Hidden!

"I understand that, my Lord," she answered. "But what other hope do I have? I must go there. I need to find my mother."

Lord Fairhaven glanced at his wife's pale face, then looked again at Aidan.

"I admire your determination and courage, Aidan," he said patiently, "but I think you still don't quite understand. You have been placed into the center of a situation that goes far beyond you."

He paused, letting that sink in, then continued.

"The King of Everestaal has sent one of his knights across the border into Davarius. This Knight made a violent attack on a citizen of our Kingdom who happened to be riding in a royal carriage – and who happens to have servants of Prince Bal'Davarius living in her house. He may have thought he was attacking the Prince himself – we simply don't know. But we do know he purposely burned the royal crest on the carriage door. This Knight seems to have known exactly what he was doing. He has made it clear that his harmful intention was really against our Prince – perhaps even to assassinate him. You must understand that this can only be considered an act of aggression – a deliberate act of war."

The blood drained from Aidan's face. She suddenly felt her whole body go weak with dread to think that a war could be starting – and that she was now somehow at the center of the conflict.

Lady Fairhaven covered her mouth with trembling hands, her face white.

"But – but he gave me this beautiful rose," Aidan whispered hopefully.

"Yes, he did – and that complicates matters even further," Lord Fairhaven replied. "I told you that it is considered high treason for a citizen of our Kingdom to go to Everestaal. What you might not know is that it's also considered high treason for a citizen to possess anything that comes from there, and the penalty for this crime is the same as I mentioned before – death or permanent imprisonment."

He gestured toward the pouch.

"The Knight who attacked you gave you a rose that not only came from there, it has clearly been identified with the Royal Crest of the King of Everestaal himself."

Aidan stared at the incriminating golden embroidery gleaming against the dark purple velvet. She could barely breathe for the panic constricting her chest.

"So you see, Aidan, this is very, very serious indeed. As long as you possess that rose from our Prince's worst enemy, even if you never go to Everestaal, you are still guilty of high treason – you are guilty right now. Do you fully understand what I have said?"

She nodded. "Yes, my Lord," she replied softly.

"Aidan, you must get rid of those things at once," Lady Fairhaven insisted. "The Prince's servants must never know you have received them."

The precious little rose almost seemed to glow in Aidan's hand and its fragrance was powerfully strong.

"I think they already know," she confessed. "When we arrived here my driver asked me if the Knight had given me anything. He was very insistent – I couldn't understand why he wanted to know that so badly. It made me afraid, so I hid the pouch in my pocket and told him the Knight hadn't given anything to me. But I'm sure he knows I was lying."

"Then you can still save yourself," Lady Fairhaven said firmly. "If you destroy the rose now, your servants can't prove you ever received anything at all. We'll burn everything the Knight gave you – no one will ever know. Malcolm, call for Stewart and have him start a fire in the parlor fireplace."

"Oh, no!" Aidan cried.

She trembled and cradled the rose protectively to her breast as though it were a newborn baby. The thought of destroying it was more agonizing than she could bear.

"I can't burn this rose. It gives me such peace – I think it's a healing rose. I love it so much. Won't it wither on its own soon enough? I'll keep it hidden until it dies, but I just can't destroy it."

Lady Fairhaven seemed on the verge of hysteria.

"No, Aidan! It's much too dangerous to keep it. That rose must be destroyed at once. You must save yourself!"

"Now, Eleanora," Lord Fairhaven broke in, "the rose was given to Aidan and it is hers. No matter the consequences, you can't force her to destroy it if she chooses not to."

He turned to Aidan.

"It was not your fault that the Knight attacked your coach. You do understand that."

"Yes, my Lord," Aidan replied, although somewhere deep in her heart she was quite convinced that she was completely to blame for everything that had happened.

Lord Fairhaven hesitated for a long moment. Then, speaking very slowly and carefully, he told her, "It would be an act of high treason on my part if I should in any way help you defect. Do you understand that? It would put my life in danger and jeopardize the Fairhaven legacy – all that I am and all that I have."

Aidan hadn't thought of that. She nodded miserably and looked down at the rose.

"I understand that now, my Lord. I shouldn't be causing you such trouble. It was wrong of me to ask you. I'm very sorry."

"Aidan," Lord Fairhaven said very softly.

She looked up at him in complete surprise at the gentleness of his voice.

"Just how determined are you to go to Everestaal?"

"It's my only hope," Aidan replied earnestly. "I'm terrified of what Prince Bal'Davarius will do to me now and I'm afraid of his servants – but I must try to find my mother. I need to find my family. What other choice do I have?"

She hesitated for a brief second.

"There is something else I haven't told you. I have to go because I am under an oath to do so."

"An oath?" Lady Fairhaven said. "Please explain what you mean."

Aidan was deathly afraid to tell them but continued with her confession.

"Months ago I made a vow that I would leave Hidden someday to find my family. I swore this with all my life and breath. I have been saving money and planning to leave in the spring."

She did not tell them about the stone tower she had impulsively built on their hillside as a testament to her vow.

"So you see, I have no other choice. I swore I would find my mother, and if she is in Everestaal, then that is where I must go. I am bound by my vow as long as I live."

At this confession, Lady Fairhaven looked stricken, as though her heart would break. Lord Fairhaven glanced at his wife and then back to Aidan, answering her quietly.

"Under those circumstances, I must agree with you. If you are bound by such a vow, then you have no choice but to try to fulfill it. If you manage to get to Everestaal, you may actually be able to save yourself by seeking asylum from their King. He should grant refuge to you freely, I would think, since he himself must have dispatched his own Knight to bring you that rose."

He paused for a very long moment. Then he spoke again in earnest.

"Aidan, I too am bound as long as I live, not by an oath but by the honor of the Fairhaven family name. It would be an act of treason for me to help you leave the country. But it would be far worse for me to withhold my help, for that in effect would be sealing the death sentence of an innocent person. And in good conscience I cannot let a young girl go to prison or die for receiving a rose through no fault of her own."

Lady Fairhaven stared at him in shock.

"No!" she cried, frantically grabbing his arm. "You aren't really going to help her defect, are you? It's too dangerous! Why, we could all be killed! This could start a war! Please, beloved – don't do it!"

Lord Fairhaven squeezed his wife's hand.

"Hush now, my dear one. There will be no war. Everything will be all right."

Lady Fairhaven was on the verge of tears.

"Malcolm, I have already told Aidan that she can come here to the mansion to live if her guests become too much to bear. She could take sanctuary here. That should be enough to save her. She doesn't need to go to Everestaal. Nothing can harm her here."

"Perhaps, my dear, perhaps. But she may not be safe anywhere as long as she has that pouch with the royal crest."

Lord Fairhaven turned to Aidan.

"I'm afraid there is nothing I can do to help you leave at this time of year. As you know, once the autumn frost falls, the weather becomes most unpredictable. It will be much too dangerous to travel to Clearview now. We will take you with us when we make our spring trip, and at that time I will show you where the trail is. In the meantime, if it becomes necessary, you may certainly seek refuge here. You are always welcome in my house."

Aidan was awed to have found such favor in his sight – and thrilled at his invitation to travel with them to Clearview in the spring.

"Thank you very much, my Lord. I'm so grateful for your kindness."

"Remember, you must keep that rose and the pouch hidden from the Prince's servants."

"Yes, my Lord." Aidan quickly wrapped the rose in the piece of silk and slipped it back into its pouch, then returned it to the safety of her deep uniform pocket.

Lord Fairhaven took a sip from his tea and quickly dropped the cup back into its saucer, his face grimacing.

"Well, ladies, the tea has turned quite cold," he said. "I believe I shall retire to my library. If you will excuse me then, beloved."

He stood up and Aidan again jumped to her feet.

"Of course, Malcolm," Lady Fairhaven said.

He kissed her hand, then turned to Aidan.

"Good day, Aidan. Remember all that I have told you."

"Yes, my Lord. Thank you again."

He went back into the mansion. When they were alone, Lady Fairhaven turned to Aidan and said fervently, "I beg of you again, Aidan, *please* – burn that rose. Destroy it and save yourself."

Aidan wasn't sure how to respond to Lady Fairhaven's emotional plea.

"I'm sorry, my Lady," she said at last. "I promise I will keep it hidden. But I can't destroy it – I just can't."

Visibly upset at her refusal, Lady Fairhaven quickly folded her napkin and dropped it onto the table.

"Its fragrance is so strong, your guests will surely smell it even if you can keep it hidden. I'm certain they will find it. But I see your mind is made up." She looked imploringly at Aidan. "I shall be so worried about you. Remember that you must come here if you need to. Please."

"I will remember," Aidan promised softly, feeling uncomfortable at the older woman's anxious concern for her. "Please, my Lady – don't worry about me. I will be all right."

She folded her napkin as Lady Fairhaven had done and set it on the table.

"You'll see. Tomorrow I will come to work as usual. And really – I should be starting my work now, shouldn't I?"

"No," Lady Fairhaven said, shaking her head firmly.

There was a shadow of pain in her dark eyes that suddenly frightened Aidan.

"No, Aidan. You mustn't concern yourself with serving me any longer. Under the present circumstances, I feel that I must release you from my employ."

Nothing could have prepared Aidan for the numbing shock she felt upon hearing Lady Fairhaven's decision. Then, as its full impact became clear, her heart broke and her eyes filled with tears.

"Release me? But – but why? I've served you faithfully."

Lady Fairhaven seemed to be as brokenhearted as Aidan.

"Yes, most faithfully, and I am so grateful for that. I wish every member of my staff would serve me as you have. But now it would seem everything has changed for you. Not only has our Prince taken special notice of you, so apparently has the King of Everestaal."

Aidan was struggling to take in what Lady Fairhaven was saying.

"How can I ask you to remain my servant now? Can I expect that you'll dust my instruments for me after you ride to the mansion in your royal carriage? Or that you will make my bed and hang up my clothes after your butler brings you breakfast on a silver tray?"

She shook her head again.

"No, it just doesn't seem right. I must let you go."

Aidan was holding back her tears with great difficulty. Being Lady Fairhaven's handmaid had been a wonderful job. Dusting her elegant instruments every day had been a pleasure and more than worth the effort to gain the privilege of listening to her music.

She looked out at the beautiful rose garden, devastated to think she would no longer have the joy of caring for it, and quickly brushed her tears away with the back of her hand.

"I don't know what to say, my Lady. I would gladly continue serving you. I don't want to leave you. You've been so kind to me – kinder than you'll ever know."

Lady Fairhaven smiled, her eyes soft and gentle. She reached out and grasped Aidan's hand.

"Dear child, I don't at all mean for this to be goodbye. Even if you are not working for me, I want you to feel welcome here always. I would like to believe that you enjoy my company as much as I enjoy yours. I want you to come see me often – not as my servant, but as my friend."

Aidan was speechless at these unexpected words of affection.

Lady Fairhaven withdrew her hand.

"You say you have never had a friend. It is also terribly lonely for me here in the mansion."

Upon hearing this confession, Aidan was completely shocked. She had never considered that her wealthy employer might be anything but perfectly happy in her fine house with her loving husband. But suddenly it was very clear.

Like her rose garden, Lady Fairhaven was sheltered and safe, yet completely isolated behind stone walls. Surrounded only by servants, there was really no one who could be her trusted friend.

And now Aidan also understood why it had so often seemed that she had just wanted to spend time together and talk. She was just as lonely as Aidan was herself.

"Come to me tomorrow at noon for lunch," Lady Fairhaven insisted. "I'll be worried about you tonight and I will need to know you are safe. Yes, we shall have lunch together tomorrow – and then perhaps we could enjoy my instruments. I could give you a music lesson."

"That would be wonderful," Aidan replied, her spirits lifting.

"Splendid! I shall see you tomorrow at noon then."

They left the rose garden and walked together through the mansion. In the front entry hall Lady Fairhaven took Aidan's hands in hers and squeezed them tightly.

"Do be careful, my child," she implored. "Be sure to keep that rose hidden from your guests."

"I will, my Lady," Aidan promised. "Please don't worry about me."

Timidly she withdrew her hands and smiled awkwardly, then opened the door and stepped outside. At the bottom of the steps she turned to look back.

Lady Fairhaven was watching her from the doorway, her dark eyes wistful.

Chapter Twenty-Five

The Second Stone Tower

Aidan walked away from the mansion. As she passed through the shade of the oak trees lining the path and then came back out into the sunlight, she breathed deeply of clean cool mountain air. So much had happened to her that morning, leaving her with a great deal to think about, but the afternoon that now stretched before her was completely free of commitments. For the first time in days she was all alone, her guests nowhere in sight, with no work to do.

It seemed too incredible to believe that Lady Fairhaven was now her friend instead of her employer – and even more unbelievable that Lord Fairhaven had invited her to go to Clearview with them in the spring! A wonderful sense of joy and freedom rose up in her heart, rejuvenating her spirit. As she hurried down the path she even hummed a little tune.

The sun and the wind and the majestic mountain views reminded Aidan of the day of Aunt Mara's funeral. She had felt that same sense of joy and freedom then too, when all of life lay stretched so hopefully before her. Then she remembered the day after, when everything had seemed so hopeless again and she had stood on this very hillside and made her vows to leave Hidden.

At that moment she realized that in the last few months, although she had passed this way twice daily on her way to and from the mansion, she had never taken the time to visit her stone tower since the day she had built it.

Now she stopped and began to look for the stone she had placed at the side of the path as a marker. It wasn't long before she found it.

Aidan waded into the tall grass that rustled softly in the gusts of wind. In the spring it had been brown and dead from the winter, but now it was green and alive and fragrant with late summer wildflowers. She sank down onto the ground and stretched out lazily on her back, filled with a fresh sense of being alive as well.

Once again the grass rose up around her like the walls of a tiny room and the sky arched over her head like its bright blue ceiling. Wispy clouds danced together high above her, swirling and flowing in rhythm with the sweet hopeful music of the wind. She lay there for a long time at peace, feeling deliciously carefree.

After awhile she thought again about her tower and wondered what had become of it. At last she pulled herself up from the ground, brushed dirt from her dress, and began wandering through the field in search of her pillar of stones.

It would be easy to get lost in the tall grass all around her, but Aidan thought she heard running water and began to follow the sound. Before long she came upon the stream sparkling in the sunlight. It was a mere trickle compared to what it had been in the early spring rushing from melting snow, but it was still flowing.

She took a few more steps up the hill – and there it was.

Her monument was just as she had left it, a neatly constructed tower of colorful stones from the stream bed. Looking uphill at it now, it seemed much taller than she remembered – quite a considerable pillar for a young girl to make with such heavy stones.

Aidan rejoiced to see it again as she walked slowly around it, examining it closely. The rounded grey, tan and red stones were really very beautiful, most of them speckled with dark spots and even some with bright flecks that seemed to sparkle like gold in the sunlight.

As far as she could tell the only things that had touched her pillar had been the mountain wind and rain. She reached out and laid her hand on it. The stones were cold and smooth, just as she remembered.

"My tower still stands, and so does my vow," she declared aloud to the stones. "Somehow I'll get through the winter without my job and I'll leave Hidden in the spring just as I had planned – but now I know I'll be traveling to Clearview with the Fairhavens. And when Lord Fairhaven shows me the path down from the mountains to Everestaal, as he has promised, I will go there and never come back! Then I will search until I find my mother – and The One Who Will Love Me Forever."

She sighed with great satisfaction and a thrill of excitement. Spring was a long way off, but she just knew all her dreams were about to come true.

Surely my life couldn't be any better! she thought happily.

Aidan turned and knelt by the stream bed to dip her fingers into the trickling water. It was still pure and icy cold. As she had so many months before, she cupped her hand to take several sips. Once again the water chilled her inside and made her shiver in the wind.

Then her eyes fell upon another stone in the stream bed. Like the others, this small stone had been rounded and polished by the water rushing over it, but it was the only one she had seen that was pure white and not speckled at all. She turned it over, rinsed it clean, and carried it to her monument.

Lifting the beautiful white rock to the very top of the tower, Aidan secured it in place. Then she stepped back to admire her work again.

"This completes my tower – this symbol of all my vows," she said softly, reaching up and laying her hands on the white stone. "With this rock I swear that no matter how perilous it may be, I will make the journey to Everestaal. Even though my life is in danger because of my guests, even though I have no idea who that Knight was or why he attacked my carriage, even if I have to make my way through the midst of a terrible war, I swear that I will go there – or I will die trying. I refuse to remain a prisoner of the Dark Prince!"

For a moment she gazed longingly at the delicate wisps of white swirling against the bright blue sky above her. Unexpectedly it brought to her mind the painting on the ballroom ceiling of the burning chariot soaring so freely into the clouds. She thought about the white horse, the flames, and the burnished skin and dark eyes of the charioteer. The memory only reinforced the fervency of her oaths.

"I will finally be *free,*" she swore, "free of this wretched lonely town – free of all my painful memories – and free of my terrible guests. Oh, I swear this with all my life and breath! I will be *free!*"

A gust of wind suddenly came up strong, catching Aidan's skirt and hair. She felt in her pocket for the velvet pouch and pulled it out.

The threads of the embroidered crest caught the sunlight and suddenly flashed as bright as the golden fire that had blazed from the Knight's sword. She now knew that the crest belonged to the Royal House of the King of Everestaal, the enemy of Prince Bal'Davarius – but somehow she wasn't afraid.

Aidan opened the pouch and peeked inside. The tiny white rose was still there with the golden silk folded around it. She drew it out and carefully unwrapped it, pinching the rose tightly between her thumb and two fingers.

With her other hand she slipped the silk and the pouch back into her pocket. The velvety rose glistened softly in the sunlight, perfectly fresh and fragrant, and so light she was afraid it would blow away in the wind.

Had this precious rose indeed come from a King's garden, as Lord Fairhaven had said?

As she inhaled its heady perfume, an image of the mysterious Knight's handsome face came into her mind. She would never forget his magnificent white horse keeping pace with her carriage in a wild ride, or how terrified she had been of his flaming sword. The memory of his dark eyes flashing with colorful fire would surely stay with her forever – his beautiful eyes that had seared into her soul with all the intensity of the inferno that had burned her carriage door.

All at once that strange unbearable yearning she couldn't understand rose up and overcame her with such force that for a moment she could hardly breathe. Staring at the tiny rose, she laid her other hand on the stone tower and whispered one last oath into the mountain wind.

"I also swear with all my life and breath that I will find the Knight from Everestaal – and learn why he attacked my coach and gave me this rose."

Aidan carefully wrapped the silk square around the rose again and slipped it into the pouch and back into her pocket. She sighed happily as she walked around her monument to look for the way back to the path.

As she turned, she noticed for the first time that there was something strange rising in the tall grass just a few feet uphill from her. Wondering how she could have been so close to this and not seen it before, she carefully took a few steps alongside the stream and spread the grass apart with her hands.

To her complete astonishment, she discovered a second stone tower!

For a long moment Aidan stared in shock at this mysterious pillar. It was much shorter than hers, also built with the round smooth stones from the stream bed. Her heart began pounding with dread, wondering what this could mean.

Suddenly she realized she was looking at *her* tower – the one she had built!

Aidan whirled and stared in horror at the taller tower that she had just crowned with the white rock – and upon which she had just sworn her oaths.

Frantic questions began to flood her bewildered mind.

What was this other tower? Who could have built it? How long had it been here? Why had it been placed so close to hers?

Had it also been built as a monument to a vow?

And if so – what was the vow?

But the tower offered no answers. It loomed before her, cold and heavy and eerily silent, her white stone perched solidly now upon its summit.

The singing of the wind that had been so glorious only moments before suddenly became a moaning cry. The warm peace and joy that had filled her heart froze into breathless panic.

All at once Aidan wanted to be very far from this place.

Slowly she backed away from the two stone towers as though they were threatening to attack her. At that moment she noticed that the grass nearby had been trampled. She stopped and looked down at her feet.

There, clearly stamped into the moist dirt, was the fresh impression of a horse's hoof.

Aidan gasped. Now she saw more hoofprints and noticed that clumps of grass had been torn away in several places. A horse had recently been grazing there by the pillars.

In that moment everything became frighteningly clear.

She stared at the two stone towers standing side by side. There could only be one explanation.

The Knight from Everestaal had been here on his beautiful white horse. He had found her stone monument – and had built his own next to it!

And she had just laid her hand on his tower and sworn an oath to go to Everestaal and find him!

Chapter Twenty-Six

Sweet Revenge

Staring up at the Knight's tower, Aidan felt the blood drain from her face and her hands start to shake. Lady Fairhaven's words came back to her as if carried on the wind.

Aidan, he was a trained warrior. He was armed. He attacked you. He might have killed you!

Despite all her bold words vowing to find him and every emotion she had felt for him only moments before, she was suddenly reminded that the Knight was from an enemy country. She had only seen him for a few frightening moments and he hadn't even spoken to her. If she were ever to actually meet him face to face, she knew she would be terrified of him – just as terrified as she was now, trembling before his silent stone tower on a grassy hillside.

What did she really know about this mysterious Knight from Everestaal? What could one look into his dark eyes tell her about him – even eyes so kind and beautiful? What did it mean that he had chased and burned her carriage just to give her a remarkable rose in a velvet pouch?

Had it been an act of warfare – or of love?

At that moment Aidan considered for the first time that all of her dreams and musings might really be just false hopes and vain imaginings. Perhaps it was time to stop believing in fairy tales and face the reality Lord Fairhaven had described to her. Through no fault of her own she had somehow become involved in the conflict between two Kingdoms – which could possibly escalate into a war because of a Knight's act of aggression involving her carriage – and her life was in real danger.

Fully overcome by panic, Aidan backed away from the towers, then turned and began to run toward the dirt road. As she stumbled through the tall grass on the steep slope, she searched the hillside all around her to see if the Knight was anywhere in sight. What if he were to find her now, when she wasn't even behind the protection of a carriage door?

Looking ahead, she saw that she was close to the road. But at that moment she heard a noise and froze, listening intently. There was a distant thundering sound coming from down the hill – and it was growing louder.

An approaching horse!

By now Aidan's fears had completely gripped her. Her heart was pounding so hard she thought she would faint dead away right there by the road.

There was nowhere she could hide. Whimpering and gasping for breath, she dropped to the ground, stretched flat on her stomach, and lay very still, hoping she couldn't be seen in the tall grass. The smell of the moist earth right under her face was strong and the wind whipped hard all around her as though a storm were approaching.

The sound of hoofbeats was steadily getting louder.

But now she heard other noises – the rattling of wheels, the clanking of hitches, and above it all the bellowing of a familiar deep baritone.

Relieved, Aidan jumped to her feet and ran to the dirt road, waving to Pride with both arms. From his high driver's seat he immediately saw her and quickly pulled hard on the reins.

"Whoa!" he shouted. "Whoa there now, my beauties!"

His horses protested with loud neighing as the carriage slowed down and came to a stop right in front of her.

Hastily brushing grass and dirt from her apron, Aidan hurried to the carriage. Greed quickly climbed down from his seat next to Pride.

Her coachman tipped his cap. "Good afternoon, Milady!"

"I'm so glad to see you!" she cried. "But why have you come so early?"

"Why, I came because I knew I was needed. What are you doing out here on the road?"

"Lady Fairhaven let me go home early. So much happened to me this morning that – well, work was just not possible. I was walking home when you drove up."

She did not tell him she had been released from employment.

Pride's mouth curled into a smile beneath his waxed mustache.

"See, I knew you needed my services, Milady. I'm almost never wrong. Get right in now, and we'll have you home straightaway."

As Greed reached for the door to open it for her, Aidan saw to her surprise that the golden royal crest of Prince Bal'Davarius was gleaming in the sunlight as though nothing had ever happened to it.

"Pride, how did you manage to fix the door?" she asked. "It looks like it was never burned!"

He chuckled.

"Well, of course I would repair the door, and without delay. It is my responsibility from the Master to take care of his carriage and horses. We can't have you riding in a damaged carriage, now, can we? That would reflect quite poorly upon our good Prince! But don't trouble yourself about the door, Milady. Climb right in so we can take you home."

As she stepped toward the door, she turned to her footman.

"Greed, are you all right? I was so worried when you fell!"

He grinned. "Ah, don't be concerned for me," he said modestly. "I've taken harder falls than that without injury."

Aidan climbed into her carriage, still shaking from the fear that had overcome her moments earlier. Greed quickly shut the door behind her and jumped up onto his rear perch. Pride shook his reins and tapped the horses with his crop. Slowly they turned around and then made their way down the hill toward Hidden.

As the carriage bumped and jostled along across the valley, she couldn't help but search anxiously out the window for the Knight. To her relief, there seemed to be no sign of him anywhere.

After a few moments her fears subsided and she calmed down. She sighed and breathed deeply, relaxing back against the tufted velvet padding. How she loved this carriage! She would miss it very much when she went to Everestaal.

They entered the town and made their way along the main street, clattering over the cobblestones. Aidan saw that people were gasping and staring, straining to see who would be riding through Hidden inside a royal carriage. She quickly shrank back into the shadows, hiding behind the velvet curtains so that no one would know it was her.

But then the bank came into view – and right at its door she caught sight of Uncle Asa stepping out onto the sidewalk.

It was actually the first she had seen of him since that fateful day in the spring when he had offered her a part in his "business arrangement." Now she saw him raise his head in surprise at the approaching carriage.

Aidan peeked out cautiously from behind the velvet curtain to see what he would do. She was delighted to see his eyes widen with complete astonishment when he realized her coach bore the crest of Prince Bal'Davarius.

Suddenly she couldn't resist having some fun with him.

Impulsively she flung open the curtain just at the moment the carriage began to pass him. She poked her head and arm out the window and called loudly to him, grinning cheerfully and waving.

"Uncle Asa! Good day to you!"

It was absolutely delicious to see the old man's face go completely white and his mouth drop open as he realized who was greeting him from inside the royal carriage.

She continued waving all the way down the street, thrilled at his response. Several other townspeople stood frozen as well, staring in shock with mouths wide open.

A feeling of complete triumph rose up in Aidan's chest as she basked in their reactions. She pulled her head back into the carriage and laughed gleefully all the way home. Her first taste of revenge had been sweeter than she ever could have imagined.

As she stepped onto the sidewalk outside her cottage, Gatekeeper held the iron gate open for her. He greeted her without his usual smile, his voice serious.

"Good afternoon, Miss. You're home early, I see. We heard about what happened this morning."

Still savoring the joy of pride and revenge, Aidan swept grandly past him into her rose garden.

"Yes, it was a morning like I've never had before," she declared. "So Pride and Greed told you about the Knight who attacked us?"

"Indeed they did, Miss," he replied. His grandfatherly face was filled with concern. "They showed us what that scoundrel did to the Master's carriage. A dreadful thing, I must say, just dreadful."

"Yes, it certainly was dreadful!"Aidan agreed. "I was so frightened – I thought he would kill me!"

Her butler closed the gate and followed her as she walked up the flagstone path.

"Miss, I must caution you to take great care whenever you are out riding. The Master has many enemies, and they are always lurking about, thinking to do him harm. No doubt that scofflaw who chased you thought you were the Master himself!"

Aidan carefully said nothing in reply as Gatekeeper reached around her to open the front door.

"Drudgery is just setting out the midday meal, Miss."

"Oh, how nice," she said. "Have any new guests arrived?"

"No, none yet today. But some are expected later."

Aidan sighed, wondering who else would be coming, but she didn't ask.

Inside the house, the enticing smells of food drew her straight to the dining room, where she found Drudgery had laid out a lace tablecloth and was carefully arranging two place settings of fine white porcelain dishes, crystal stemware, and polished silver. Savory foods in an array of serving dishes were sending clouds of steam and the most wonderful blend of aromas into the air.

"My goodness, Drudgery!" she gasped. "I've never seen so much food in one place at one time before in all my life! Why, you've cooked enough for an army!"

Drudgery smiled.

"A feast for the Master's most favored one. Yours to enjoy, friend Aidan," she said, then turned and headed into the kitchen.

Gatekeeper held her chair as Aidan sat down. She spread a linen napkin across her lap and stared in awe at the table. There was a covered soup tureen surrounded by large serving bowls containing potatoes, a variety of cooked vegetables, applesauce, biscuits, gravy, and still more foods she didn't recognize. Off to one side was a platter with a domed silver cover.

"Is someone going to join me?" she asked. "You've set two places. Surely this isn't all just for me!"

"We'll have a bit to eat later, Miss," Gatekeeper assured her. "You go ahead and take whatever pleases you, as much as you like."

He lifted the lid from the platter and set it aside. A cloud of steam rose up, revealing a large roast.

"Is that roast beef?!" Aidan exclaimed.

"That it is, Miss," he replied.

He picked up a carving knife and a long meat fork and began to slice the roast. Aidan's mouth watered as she watched the razor-sharp blade slide almost effortlessly through the savory meat.

Gatekeeper placed a large slice of beef onto her plate and poured gravy over it just as Drudgery came in with a pot of tea. Aidan dug greedily into the serving dishes and heaped food onto her plate.

"This is just wonderful!" she cried.

She felt like a queen as she began to eat, but she wasn't more than a few hearty bites into the incredible meal when there was a loud rapping at the door.

When Gatekeeper hastened to answer it, she thought her new guests must be arriving, but to her surprise she heard him say, "Very good, sir. May I tell the Mistress who is calling?"

A familiar reedy tenor voice answered him impatiently.

"Asa Maxwell. I demand to see Aidan at once!"

Aidan stifled a laugh. The old miser must have scurried all the way to have arrived so quickly after she had passed him in the carriage!

"Drudgery," she whispered, "it's Uncle Asa. I don't trust him at all. You and Gatekeeper must stay close by in case there's trouble."

"Yes, of course," Drudgery replied, nodding as she poured two cups of tea.

When Gatekeeper and Uncle Asa appeared in the wide arched doorway, the old man's face was flushed and his dark eyes were huge beneath a confused frown. Aidan didn't wait for her butler's introductions.

"Uncle Asa!" she gushed, her voice lavish with overplayed warmth. "How very nice of you to drop by! Do come in. Gatekeeper, take Uncle Asa's hat. Please, Uncle, won't you sit down and join me? There's plenty. As usual, my cook has made such a marvelous feast! Here, she's even poured your tea – it's all ready for you."

"Well, thank you, Aidan," Uncle Asa replied slowly. He seemed completely flustered by everything he was seeing in his sister's old house. Hesitantly he handed his hat to Gatekeeper, who took it from him with a bow and rushed off to hang it up.

Slowly he sat down, looking with disbelief at all the serving dishes spread across the table. Aidan was watching his bewilderment with complete delight.

Gatekeeper quickly returned and bowed graciously to him.

"May I serve you, sir?"

Uncle Asa stared at him suspiciously for a long moment. At last he pushed his plate away and replied, "Nothing, thank you. Just the tea."

"Very good, sir." Gatekeeper turned to Aidan, clicked his heels together with his usual flourish, and bowed to her. "Will there be anything else, Miss?"

"No, thank you, Gatekeeper. You and Drudgery may leave us, but stay close by in case I need you for anything else."

Her two servants quickly retreated to the kitchen, leaving Aidan alone at the table with Uncle Asa.

Chapter Twenty-Seven

Uncle Asa's Cruelty

Aidan turned to Uncle Asa and smiled sweetly. She began to pick at the food on her plate, feeling both nervous and smug at the same time.

"I'm surprised you haven't stopped by before this, Uncle," she said patronizingly. "You did promise me at our last meeting that I hadn't seen the last of you."

Uncle Asa's dark eyes flashed with annoyance.

"Oh, stop this nonsense, Aidan, and tell me at once what is going on here," he demanded. "How did you come to be riding through the streets in a royal carriage? The town has been buzzing about it since it was sighted yesterday, and today we are treated to the spectacle of you hanging out its window! I've come here to get some answers. What kind of charade is this?"

At that it was all Aidan could do to keep from bursting into ripples of delighted laughter. So her neighbors were now discovering her good fortune! To her own surprise she felt no fear at the thought of the whole town knowing what was going on. Instead she felt gloriously triumphant and maintained her composure as she answered him with a proud boast.

"It is my carriage, Uncle, sent to me just for my pleasure, along with those beautiful horses and a driver and footman who will take me anywhere I want to go. Prince Bal'Davarius himself gave it to me."

He stared at her in disbelief, his eyes huge.

"How can this be possible? Our Prince has never been to Hidden. How does he even know who you are? Or that you exist at all!"

Aidan didn't answer him right away. It was intoxicating to see him so upset and she wanted to savor this delicious new feeling of revenge.

She put down her fork and reached for the basket of hot biscuits Drudgery had set out. With carefully measured gestures, she chose one and broke it open, releasing a small puff of steam into the air. Then she picked up a silver knife and scraped it across the top of the sweet butter in the dish by her plate, bringing up a little yellow curl that perched delicately on the rounded tip of the blade.

Annoyed by her stalling, Uncle Asa demanded, "Answer me, Aidan! Where did you get all this food? How do you have a butler and a cook? Where did that carriage of yours really come from?"

Barely able to stifle her delight at his reactions, she gently slid the butter curl from the tip of her knife onto the hot biscuit. It quickly melted into pale yellow liquid.

At last she looked up at him, aware that his frustration was growing. She met his gaze and replied very sweetly.

"To be honest, dear Uncle, I don't know how the Prince knows about me. But I have told you the truth. Everything you see here is from his hand. He has sent his servants to me, and they tell me he is good and kind and will take very good care of me. And as you can see, he has been most generous."

She held out the buttered biscuit to him.

"Are you sure you wouldn't care for something to eat, Uncle? It's all so delicious. Why don't you try some of this wonderful roast beef?"

Uncle Asa scowled angrily as he lost all his patience.

"Don't put on airs and warm up to me," he snapped. "We both know perfectly well that you despise me. So stop all this nonsense and tell me the truth!"

Aidan glared back at him, dropping her pretentious airs and letting her hatred show openly.

"Very well," she said coldly, tossing the biscuit onto her plate. "What do you want to know? How the Prince knows of me? As I told you, I have no idea, and that is the absolute truth. What his intentions are? I don't know that either – but my servants tell me he might be coming here soon to meet with me personally."

Uncle Asa's mouth dropped open at her words.

"Prince Bal'Davarius – coming here, to Hidden? To meet with the likes of you?!" he sneered. "You must be joking! What could our Prince possibly want with you?"

"I told you, Uncle, I don't know," Aidan repeated firmly. "But it's all true."

She gestured to the steaming food and fine dishes spread across the table.

"Lady Fairhaven has paid me well, but do you think I could afford any of this on a servant's salary? The Prince has sent dozens of his servants to wait on me hand and foot. As you can plainly see, I lack for nothing. My butler even brings me breakfast on a silver tray."

He stared at her, speechless.

"And even if I could have somehow afforded all this myself as some sort of joke, where would I ever have gotten a royal carriage and fine horses except from the Prince himself? Where else could I have gotten the wardrobe full of fine clothing that he sent for me?"

Suddenly she couldn't resist seeing Uncle Asa squirm a little more. Her eyes narrowed and she dropped her voice to a dramatic whisper.

"Or the riches he has sent me, Uncle. Riches beyond your wildest dreams. So much gold and silver and so many precious jewels their value can't even be counted! And it's all mine just for the taking, with much more to come. You see, I have found favor in our Prince's sight, and my servants have told me he will not withhold any of his wealth from me."

Despite the fact that Greed had actually told her all those things just the night before, Aidan was deliberately stretching the truth. Her clothing and jewelry were valuable, to be sure, but their worth didn't add up to the immense amount she was describing, and of course there was no gold or silver.

But Uncle Asa had no way of knowing this, and at that moment her burning desire was to take revenge on the old man for suggesting she enter into his "business arrangement" and for stealing whatever might have been left over from Aunt Mara's estate. She knew the one thing he wouldn't be able to bear was the thought that she had come into much more wealth and power than he himself could ever expect to have.

It felt strange to be telling such a blatant lie, but she felt no guilt whatsoever. She was in fact enjoying it immensely, and to her own surprise was carrying it off perfectly. His facial expression was still one of skepticism but the look in his eyes convinced her that in spite of himself he wasn't quite sure whether or not he should believe her.

Lust's words came back to her then.

Someday you too will lie to get what you want from someone. You'll see.

At last Uncle Asa said slowly, "I see. Riches and fine clothes and jewels, you say. How very interesting. All I can see of these fine clothes and jewels is your dirty servant's uniform from the mansion."

Aidan glared at him.

"How thoughtless of me," she said haughtily. "I was so eager to enjoy this marvelous feast that I neglected to change when I arrived home."

He slowly stroked his goatee, studying her face with deep suspicion.

"Tell me, Aidan, will you be putting all your gold and silver in my bank? I shall be pleased to maintain accounts for you, if you wish."

"There is no need," she replied arrogantly. "I am more than capable of managing my great wealth, thank you. And if I should need help, my servants will provide it."

Uncle Asa scowled at her with complete derision.

"Ah, yes, of course, your servants who have been given to you just for your pleasure," he mocked. "So just where *are* these dozens of servants you spoke of? I have only seen two of them, and I must say, Mara's old house is awfully quiet to have so many people living in it now. Wherever do you keep them all in this tiny cottage?"

"My butler takes care of their lodging," she replied. "We actually manage quite well."

He stroked his beard again, watching her face very carefully. Then he abruptly changed the subject.

"Aidan, have you notified the Mayor and the town council that Prince Bal'Davarius may soon be coming to Hidden to pay you a visit? They will want to make official preparations. This will surely be the biggest event that has ever happened here."

Caught off guard by his question, Aidan said, "Why, no."

"Have you told anyone at all?" he asked.

"Yes," she replied, wondering why he would want to know. "I talked with Lord and Lady Fairhaven about it just this morning."

"Oh, yes, of course. Lord and Lady Fairhaven," Uncle Asa repeated. "And how have you enjoyed scrubbing the mansion floors all summer? I should have looked in on you long ago to make sure you were faring well in their employ, but I knew I had no reason to worry. I know Lady Fairhaven is very kind and pays very well."

Aidan chose not to mention that she had lost her job that morning.

"I don't scrub floors, Uncle. Lady Fairhaven hired me to be her close personal servant and handmaid. And now our Prince is taking good care of me – treating me like royalty."

The intense gaze from Uncle Asa's dark eyes, which were so much like Aunt Mara's, was beginning to make her very nervous. She covered this up with another saucy comment.

"So you see, Uncle, I have done very well for myself after all. I had no need to take you up on your generous 'business arrangement' of last spring."

To her surprise, Uncle Asa displayed no anger at that. Laughing softly, he picked up his teacup and leaned back in his chair, casually crossing one leg over the other. He sipped his tea, holding the cup in both hands and staring at her over its rim. A lascivious grin spread across his face and his eyes glittered in an open leer.

"A great pity, my dear," he said. "It would have been a fine arrangement. Once you had gotten used to being my mistress, I have no doubt that you would have enjoyed it – very much."

Aidan felt her face suddenly flame crimson. She leapt to her feet in a rush of hatred.

"How dare you!" she cried. "You are vile, just vile! Get out of my house! Get out – and don't ever show yourself at my door again!"

Making no move to leave, Uncle Asa calmly finished his tea and slipped the empty cup back into its saucer.

"Why, Aidan," he said, feigning indignation. "Are you taking back your kind invitation to lunch? How very rude of you!"

Trembling with fury, Aidan shouted, "Gatekeeper! Come at once!"

Her call resounded through a house that suddenly seemed overwhelmingly quiet and empty. The echo faded but nothing happened. Her heart began to race as her faithful butler failed to appear. She called for him again.

In the ensuing silence Uncle Asa began to laugh wickedly.

"A very poor butler indeed, Aidan! You should send him back to the palace at once – and demand that our Prince give you a better one."

Frantically Aidan cried out for Drudgery, but she did not come either.

Where had all her guests gone? Most of the time she couldn't get away from them. Now the house was deathly still, its palpable silence eerily foreboding.

Slowly Uncle Asa stood up and leaned across the table toward her.

"Are all of your servants so negligent of their mistress?" he taunted. "Call for all the others, Aidan. Call for all your dozens of servants to come and throw me out the door!"

Aidan froze, all her smug pride and vengeful haughtiness of a moment earlier fading quickly into helpless panic. Uncle Asa knew he now had the upper hand and grinned triumphantly at her.

She could feel him undressing her with his eyes.

"I take it we are alone, then. Just you and I – all alone in the house."

He beckoned to her with his hand.

"Come here, my dear Aidan. Come to me – and I will give you a little taste of what you have scorned."

He quickly stepped to one end of the dining room table, positioning himself strategically to block both the wide archway leading into the front room on the left and the narrow door leading into the kitchen on the right.

Aidan's heart pounded as she carefully weighed her options. No matter which way she tried to escape, she would somehow have to make her way past him.

She stood her ground, still hoping one of her guests would come to her aid.

"Don't you dare come near me," she warned.

Uncle Asa laughed, for he knew she was helplessly trapped.

The piercing look in his eyes suddenly reminded her of a cat about to pounce upon a mouse. She knew she had seen that look somewhere before, but in her panic she couldn't remember when or where.

His gaze was steadily fixed on her as he moved very slowly, taking a single calculated step around the table toward the wide archway. Immediately she seized her opportunity and bolted for the kitchen door, not realizing that she was doing exactly what he expected she would do.

Amazingly quick and agile for his many years, he changed direction and rushed at her. His hand closed like a hawk's talons around her arm. She screamed in terror and tried to yank it away, but he grabbed her other arm and roughly pulled her to him.

He tried to kiss her but she twisted her head away. His hot breath burned against her neck.

"You're mad!" she gasped. "You're insane! Why are you doing this? Let me go!"

Aidan was shocked that the old man could be so strong. She writhed, struggling in vain to free herself. He laughed wickedly and wrapped his arms tightly around her, pulling her close. She cringed at the feel of his body against hers, his hands on her back, his mouth on her neck.

Suddenly a flash of scarlet caught her eye.

Aidan looked over Uncle Asa's shoulder. There in the wide archway stood Lust in her revealing satin dress.

Relieved to see one of her guests at last, she cried out, "Help me!"

But to her dismay, Lust merely smiled and leaned against the doorframe. She folded her arms over her breasts and crossed one foot over the other so that the slit in her tight skirt opened, leaving the outside of her right leg with its black lace stocking exposed to the hip.

Aidan froze with horror as she recognized the look in her pale violet eyes.

A cat about to pounce upon a mouse.

A hunter going in for the kill.

Her heart sank with a sick feeling of dread as she suddenly understood why Lust was standing there.

"No!" she cried. "You can't be so cruel! Don't let him do this to me!"

Startled, Uncle Asa straightened up and stared suspiciously at her face.

"Who are you talking to?" he demanded.

"One of my guests," she said. "Right there – in the doorway – oh!"

Aidan gasped, for in that same instant she saw Greed step up behind his wife and passionately pull her into his arms. She watched as Lust threw her head back, laughing wickedly as Greed swept her aside into the front room, disappearing from sight.

Uncle Asa didn't turn around to look. He glared at her and shook her firmly by her upper arms.

"Don't think you can trick me, Aidan! If you had all the servants you say you have, one of them would have rushed in here by now to help you. But perhaps your cook and butler have run off with all that gold you say you have!"

"I do have servants!" she shouted in furious desperation. "They will come at any minute – and they'll tell the Prince – and you'll pay dearly for this!"

He just laughed and pulled her closer. She could feel his hand sliding up the back of her head, his fingers deep in her hair as he tried to kiss her mouth. Aidan fought with all her strength and managed to turn her face away from him again.

At that moment Abuse stepped into the archway.

She was wearing yet another hat Aidan had never seen before. This one was black with several orange and yellow feathers rising above it, huge fluffy plumes looking exactly like tongues of fire. From beneath its wide brim her enemy grinned at her with a look of purest hatred in her eyes.

The blood drained from Aidan's face. "No," she whispered helplessly, suddenly realizing she was powerless to stop whatever was about to happen next.

The servants of the Dark Prince were all doing the work their Master had given them to do in her life – and nothing could stop them.

Uncle Asa shook her roughly. "You little fool! I shall have you whether you want me or not!"

He shoved her backwards and trapped her against the wall, pressing his body close to hers. In desperation she tried to hit him with her fists and kick him.

In her struggle she caught a glimpse of the doorway again only to see that Abuse was gone. In her place now stood little Fear of Being Hurt staring frantically at the two of them, his icy blue eyes huge with panic.

Chilling shivers ran down her spine.

The next seconds would always be a vicious blur in her memory but Aidan would never forget the wild look on Uncle Asa's face or the grating sound of ripping fabric or the cold air hitting her exposed neck.

"No," she whimpered helplessly, her voice like a child's. "Don't hurt me! Oh, please, don't hurt me!"

But he only laughed wickedly and pulled at her torn dress, his hands moving across her bare skin.

Terrified, Aidan looked once again at the archway only to see that Lust, Greed, Abuse, and Anger were now clustered around Fear of Being Hurt. They all stood there quietly, just watching the two of them struggle, making no move to interfere in any way. Fear of Being Hurt trembled, his face ashen, and the adults grinned with evil delight.

Suddenly her terror turned into rage and hatred. She began to fight Uncle Asa with renewed vigor, kicking and hitting and clawing like a snarling animal.

"Curse you!" she screamed, both to her guests and to her abuser. "Curse all of you! I'll have the Prince throw you into prison when he comes for me! I swear to you I will see you hang for this!"

Uncle Asa held her tightly against the wall and laughed with derision.

"There is no Prince coming for you, Aidan! You can curse me all you want, but it won't help you. I've wanted you for years – and nothing will keep me from having you now!"

Aidan feared she would faint dead away from horror but she knew that if she weakened even for an instant he would easily overpower her. She kicked furiously at his legs. Her foot hit his shin hard and he gasped and jumped in unexpected pain. In that instant he let down his guard and she wriggled free and broke loose.

But before she could get more than two steps away he grabbed for her again, his strength only multiplied by fury. His fingers tightened around her hair with a vicious yank. Her head jerked violently backwards and she screamed in pain, bumping hard against the table. She could hear dishes rattling as they knocked against each other behind her.

He held her by her hair so that her head went back and chin lifted, exposing her neck and chest where her torn dress was hanging down from one shoulder.

Unable to move her head without pain, she felt his arms around her again, his body close against hers, his panting breath steamy on her neck.

She struggled desperately but she knew it was completely hopeless. Sobbing now, she begged him to stop.

"No, Uncle, please don't do this! Don't hurt me! Oh, please, don't hurt me!"

She was pinned awkwardly between him and the table, one arm completely trapped and the other arm half free, her head pulled backwards and slightly to one side. As she reached back to steady herself, her hand brushed against a serving dish. Out of the corner of her eye she saw a flash of metal and realized it was the silver platter containing the roast beef.

Right beneath her hand lay the carving knife, its razor-sharp blade gleaming like a sudden ray of hope.

In that instant Aidan knew that the only way she could save herself would be to kill Uncle Asa.

In the midst of her frenzied thoughts, she reached out ever so slowly and cautiously, her hand inching toward the knife. Yes, she would kill him! She would send him to his grave and be free of him forever!

Her fingers closed tightly around the handle. In her mind she was calculating how hard and how fast she would need to raise the knife and thrust it back down. She knew she would only have one chance to kill him.

Failure could not be an option.

Holding her breath, she tensed, eagerly anticipating what it would feel like to actually shove the blade deep into his flesh and watch him die.

But at that moment Uncle Asa saw what she was trying to do.

Enraged, he jerked savagely at her hair. Aidan screamed in pain and lost her balance. She fell against the table and dishes went flying. Porcelain and crystal shattered into pieces and cold food splattered against her legs.

The carving knife clattered to the floor, far out of her reach.

Uncle Asa yanked at her arms. Suddenly Aidan felt herself hurtling across the room. She landed hard against the wall and slid to the floor gasping in agony, her breath completely knocked out of her.

Now livid, he bent over her, his eyes narrow black slits ablaze with raging fire. Helplessly she stared up at him, whimpering in terror and lifting one arm to protect herself. His contorted face was a twisted mask of evil.

"So now you think you can kill me!" he roared.

Quickly he undid his belt and yanked it from his pants. Aidan was horrified, thinking he was about to force himself upon her. But then he folded the leather strip in half – and she knew what was about to happen next.

She saw his arm fly up and begin to come down fast. Gasping, she twisted her body around in a quick well-practiced movement and covered her head with her arms just as the belt struck hard on the back of her shoulder. Screaming out at the first cutting shock of pain, she braced herself for more blows that she knew were coming.

The belt rose and fell again and again as he beat her, cursing her, his rage out of control.

"First you lie to me and now you try to kill me! *Murderer!*"

All Aidan could do was hold her arms over her head trying in vain to protect herself from his savage cruelty, sobbing helplessly beneath the brutal pounding of his agonizing blows on her back.

Then suddenly he stopped, tossed the belt aside and yanked her roughly to her feet. She was shaking and gasping for breath, barely able to stand as she stared up at his face.

The fury of his countenance and the wild look in his eyes were suddenly so like his sister's that she saw the old woman's face in front of her instead of his. In that terrifying instant Aidan actually thought Aunt Mara had come back from the dead.

But it was Uncle Asa's rasping voice that snarled at her now.

"All those years Mara had you, she would tell me what a wicked little girl you were. Now I see she was right! You are evil, Aidan! You are accursed!"

Aidan shook her head, her incoherent whimpering the only sound she could make. Aunt Mara had told her she was wicked and evil so many times that the words were etched deep into her heart and she knew they were true. She *was* cursed, the most wretched person alive, a guilty criminal – and if she were the guilty criminal, that made Aunt Mara and Uncle Asa her innocent victims!

He pulled her through the archway into the front room and toward the stairs.

"You don't deserve to live!" he roared. "A liar, a cheat – a killer! *Murderer!!*"

Barely able to breathe, Aidan was helpless to fight him. In her deepest heart she knew she really *was* a murderer, through and through. She had wanted so desperately to be free of Aunt Mara that she would have sent her to her grave dead or alive. Now she knew for certain that if she had been able to reach the carving knife, nothing would have stopped her from killing Uncle Asa.

And even if he killed her now, she knew she deserved whatever punishment he would give her.

She was wicked. She was evil. She needed to be taught a lesson.

And suddenly she knew exactly what Uncle Asa was about to do to her.

"I know Mara had her own special way to teach you a lesson when you needed one!" he cried. "Now I'll teach you a lesson you'll never forget!"

He reached out and flung open the door to the little broom closet under the stairs.

The torment of being locked in that tiny closet came flooding back to Aidan, her most dreaded punishment at Aunt Mara's hand for a multitude of childhood infractions. She writhed in panic at the thought of being trapped in there again and tried desperately to pull herself from his grasp, but she was so weak from pain and trauma that all she could do was sob helplessly.

"No, Uncle, no! Don't do this! Please, *please,* I promise I'll be good! Just don't put me in there! *Please!*"

With all his strength Uncle Asa shoved her through the doorway.

There wasn't even enough space beneath the stairs in which to stand up straight, and as she fell roughly against the back wall of the closet she hit her head against its tilted ceiling. Dazed, she bumped against brooms and buckets as she went down, finally landing on top of them in a heap.

The door closed with a deafening slam. Aidan heard him firmly twist the latch, sealing her mercilessly into the suffocating blackness of her childhood prison.

Excruciating pain pulsed through every inch of her bruised body. Weak and exhausted, she felt herself go limp amid the dusty brooms and rags, all her resistance gone. Her hot face came to rest against the cold strings of a filthy damp mop. She sobbed pathetically into it, trapped without hope in that tiny black world once again.

In the midst of her suffering, wondering what Uncle Asa would do next, Aidan knew she must force herself to calm down. She stopped crying and breathed deeply, drawing in the stale black air and forcing it back out, listening intently, waiting.

After a long tense moment she heard footsteps and rustling movements, then the sound of a belt buckle fastening as Uncle Asa's voice taunted her through the heavy door.

"Well, Aidan, make yourself comfortable, because you'll be in there for awhile. I must be going now, but don't worry, my dear. I'll come back for you – in a couple of days."

Aidan gasped as though he had beaten her all over again.

"Perhaps by then you'll have learned to be a good girl. Perhaps by then you'll have learned not to lie or cheat or kill. A day or two in there will break the curse of evil over you."

There was a pause. Then he added, "And when I come back, I have no doubt you'll stop fighting me – and be more than willing to join me in the generous business arrangement I offered you in the spring."

To be left all alone in that tiny black space even for two minutes was the one thing Aidan feared above all else. The thought of two days in her prison was more unbearable than all the pain throbbing through her body.

"No, Uncle! Don't leave me here!" she moaned, barely strong enough to whisper. "I'm sorry! I'm sorry! Please, Uncle! I'll do whatever you want – I'll be your mistress, I'll do *anything* – just please, *please* don't leave me in here all alone!"

But Uncle Asa never heard her. His merciless laughter was already fading away along with his quick footsteps.

Suddenly, wrenching agonizingly through the darkness, a child's pitiful sobs rose in desperate supplication.

"I'm sorry, Aunt Mara! I promise I'll be good now! If you'll just let me out, I'll never be wicked again! I'll be a good girl, you'll see! I promise!"

Then she heard the front door open and firmly close, and she knew she was completely alone.

Chapter Twenty-Eight

Locked In The Darkness

The suffocating blackness closed in against Aidan like an oppressive weight. Even if she could have found any strength left in herself to try to escape, she knew from years of experience that her prison door was heavy and the latch on the outside very strong. So she lay still, weak and trembling, her wounds throbbing, waiting in the darkness and hoping that help would come soon.

But she knew that even if her guests were to return and find her now, she couldn't expect to receive aid from a single one of them. All the events of that afternoon had been part of the terrible work their Master had given them to do in her life.

In spite of knowing this, Aidan still hoped against hope that her two most trusted and faithful servants would rescue her. Unable to pull herself up from the floor, she called out weakly for Gatekeeper and Drudgery.

She thought fondly of Gatekeeper's grandfatherly face and Drudgery's kind smile. Yes, these two were her good friends! At any moment they would surely come back and save her and make everything all right again. Gatekeeper would hasten to bring her breakfast on the silver tray while Drudgery would quickly prepare another bath.

A hot bath!

At that moment Aidan had never wanted anything so badly. She was desperate to purge away forever the filth of that closet floor and to scrub off the lingering sinister feeling of Uncle Asa's mouth and hands that still crawled across her skin.

How wonderful it would feel to immerse her bruised and aching body into a steamy tub of fragrant water! Drudgery's gentle hands would take the cake of perfumed soap, cleanse her wounds, and rinse away all her trauma.

And then, when she was clean again, Gatekeeper would bring her the brandy bottle. Her dry mouth and shivering body suddenly ached with an unexpected craving for the golden liquid. Its warm fire would offer soothing comfort and make her forget all her pain and suffering.

Aidan began to call out again more loudly for Gatekeeper and Drudgery, but then she stopped. They hadn't answered her calls when she had needed them most. Why should she believe they would come for her now?

Suddenly her heart froze as a revelation came to her.

Gatekeeper had said that more guests were expected later that day. Drudgery had made enough food for a dozen people – but had set the table for only two.

They had both known Uncle Asa would come.

They had known all along.

And they had purposely left her alone with him!

Far worse than the injury of being beaten and imprisoned was this bitter agony of betrayal. Aidan drew her legs painfully to her chest and curled herself tightly into a ball, her head still resting against the damp cushion of filthy mop strings. She covered her face with her hands and began to weep, softly at first, then harder and harder until her body convulsed with tormented sobs so deep and intense she could barely breathe.

At last, gasping, she moaned into the darkness.

"Why is all this happening to me? What does the Dark Prince want with me? What did I ever do to deserve this wretched life of suffering?!"

Suddenly a volcanic torrent of flaming rage erupted from somewhere deep in her heart and she cried out with all her might.

"Curse you, Uncle Asa! Curse you, Aunt Mara! I curse you both that you left me here to suffer all alone in this dark prison! I curse you that you didn't just kill me and release me from this torment long ago!"

In a rush of complete fury, Aidan found renewed strength to pull herself to her knees. She began pounding on the door, beating out her frustration with her fists until they ached, but it was immovable as a wall and never so much as shivered beneath her blows. An anguished groan rose up in her throat. She struck the door one last time and then leaned her head against it, sobbing helplessly.

"Curse this darkness – this prison – this wretched grave! If only it *had* become my grave the first time I was locked in here! Then I would never have been freed so long ago only to end up imprisoned here again and again!"

Trembling and completely exhausted, Aidan wept into her hands, wishing with every fiber of her being that she could die at that very moment.

But her heart continued to beat and her lungs continued to pull in the stale air and release it as though her suffering would go on forever. The death she yearned for eluded her, leaving her feeling betrayed all over again.

Was there any hope for her?

Would she ever be free?

Aidan brushed hot tears from her face and wiped her wet fingers on her apron, wondering what she should do now.

At that moment her hand encountered a lump in the fabric of her dress.

There was something small and soft in her pocket. With a start, she suddenly remembered what it was.

The embroidered pouch with the tiny white healing rose from Everestaal!

Of course! Aidan had forgotten all about it. Reaching into her deep pocket, she felt for it eagerly. It was still there, still safe. She drew it out and held it in the palm of her hand.

Even though she couldn't see it in the darkness, the thick velvet pouch was comforting beneath her fingers. She opened it, took out the rose, and unwrapped the silk square. Taking care to hold the rose tightly between thumb and forefinger, she slipped the silk and the pouch right back into her pocket so she wouldn't lose them.

The fragrance of the rose came powerfully to her nostrils and she breathed deeply. Nothing had ever smelled so incredible to her as its sweet perfume in the darkness of the hated closet. It completely drove away the stale musty air that filled her tiny prison. For a brief hopeful moment it brought back to her the warmth of the sun in her beloved rose garden.

Aidan's fingers caressed soft petals and smooth tiny leaves for a long time. She couldn't see the rose, but she could tell that it was just as fresh as it had been that morning. Its healing scent brought an intoxicating sensation of peace that seeped like a warm balm into her aching heart, soothing her bruised body and soul until she no longer felt any pain at all.

She closed her eyes, just drinking in the rose's fragrant tonic and stroking its delicate softness, almost wishing that this serene moment would never end.

Eventually exhaustion overcame her and she slumped against the wall, her legs curled beneath her. She felt herself drifting through a blur of time and space, floating in a world of tranquility, no longer sure if she were awake or asleep.

Suddenly something startled her and she jolted fully awake. She listened carefully but heard nothing.

Then she looked at the rose in her hand and gasped in shock.

Faint light was shining from deep within its delicate petals!

It was no brighter than a tiny candle flame, just enough so that she could make out the rose's lovely shape in the darkness. As she stared at it, the light slowly grew brighter and brighter until the rose almost seemed to be on fire, burning but not consumed, bathing her black prison in a warm golden glow.

How could such a thing be happening? Was this a dream?

At that moment Aidan realized to her astonishment that she no longer seemed to be inside the closet.

It was early morning and she was riding in her carriage up the hill to the Fairhaven mansion. She could even feel the soft tufted velvet cushion beneath her and the warmth of the sunlight coming in through the curtained window, but she could hear nothing, for there was no sound. It was as though she were back in the coach, yet seeing it all from somewhere outside herself, from two places at once.

She couldn't understand what was happening to her, but there were two things she somehow knew for certain: she was watching what had happened to her that very morning, and her carriage was about to be attacked again by the Knight from Everestaal.

As the dreamlike scene came into sharp focus before her eyes, her reaction was to resist it. Hadn't she suffered enough that day? Must she endure this trauma all over again?

Just as when Night Terrors came to her bringing his dreams, Aidan now fought to rouse herself from this strange silent vision. She wasn't paralyzed, but she had no strength to control it or even to move. Yet strangely she felt no fear, only that drifting sense of comforting peace.

There he was, the Knight from Everestaal, riding so swiftly and gracefully on his white horse right outside the carriage window, close enough that she could reach out and touch him if she chose to. And there she was, huddled back in the coach, shrinking from him in terror, yet at the same time irresistibly drawn to his kind handsome face and beautiful dark eyes.

Suddenly Aidan felt herself floating through the air, moving right through the door of the carriage until she was outside looking in. Where and how she was positioned in space, whether standing or sitting or flying or even riding on the white horse, she couldn't tell. The only thing that was somehow clear was that she was about to see what had happened that morning from the Knight's point of view.

He raised the burning sword in his right hand, its bright flames reflected in his polished armor. Her own face, frenzied and pallid, stared helplessly at him through the window with wide terrified eyes. As he brought his sword down she saw that all he had done was touch the carriage door with just its tip. The huge inferno of white flame rose up and blew through the window toward her, but this time it seemed to unfurl very slowly.

She watched in fascination as the fire ignited the center of the Dark Prince's royal crest and burned outward until it had eaten a perfect oval-shaped hole completely through the wood of the door, totally obliterating every trace of the crest – but nothing else.

At that moment Aidan knew for certain that the Knight had never meant to harm her at all. Somehow it made perfect sense to her, even though the reason behind his attack was still a mystery. It was now obvious that his intention all along had indeed been to destroy the royal crest on the door.

Her Knight in shining armor was the Dark Prince's enemy – not hers!

Now Aidan felt herself moving again, floating back through fire and smoke, back into the coach and into the events of the morning. Through the window she watched again as the Knight sheathed his sword. He pulled the pouch from beneath the saddle – the pouch that she now knew contained the tiny rose – and held it out to her. Again she drew back from him in terror. He leaned through the flames and smoke surrounding the window and tossed the pouch into the carriage. It landed in her lap, as it had before, and she screamed and swatted it away onto the seat across from her.

Then the Knight stared at Aidan one last time with his incredible dark eyes blazing with tiny rainbow-colored flames. Awestruck, she gazed back into them, again feeling herself drawn into the very depths of his heart, into a world strangely filled with both overwhelming joy and unspeakable longing.

With all her heart now she responded, aching all over again with that terrible yearning to be close to him that she couldn't understand. It rose up like a fresh torment, this time consuming her until tears flowed down her cheeks and she groaned in agony.

How Aidan wished she could change what had happened that morning!

If only she had known then the things she had learned from Lord Fairhaven, if only she had known what was going to happen to her that afternoon, she would easily have found the courage and the strength to jump right through the flames and smoke, to leap right out of the carriage window and into the Knight's arms. She would have ridden away with him on his magnificent white horse to Everestaal, never once fearing what lay ahead or looking back at what she was leaving behind.

But she hadn't gone with him that morning – and she couldn't do so now.

Suddenly Aidan found herself on her knees on the cushioned seat, stretching out both her hands in desperation toward the burning window. How she craved to touch his face or take his hand – anything to be close to him!

Finding her voice at last, she cried, "O Knight, I need to know who you are! Please – I want to be with you! I beg of you, take me with you to Everestaal!"

He was right there, tantalizingly just beyond her reach, yet much closer than she remembered, so close she could somehow feel his heart beating even through his silver armor. She could see in his eyes that he had heard her plea.

But before he could respond a shadow fell across his kind face, obscuring it like a hazy shroud. Suddenly she knew that a vast distance lay between them, a huge expanse of time and space that she was unable to cross.

Then, as it had happened that morning, the Knight suddenly reached up and snapped his visor down over his face – and the mysterious vision faded away.

Aidan's heart wrenched unbearably within her. She watched, stricken and helpless, as he disappeared into the shadows through that immense gulf of time and space. Warm sunlight darkened into cold blackness and the plush carriage seat beneath her again became the tangled damp strings of a filthy mop in a locked broom closet.

"No – *no!*" she screamed. "Don't leave me! Oh, *please* – don't leave me here alone in this darkness!"

But the Knight was gone.

Still trapped inside her cruel prison, Aidan came back to agonizing reality, left only with another amazing memory of him – and his precious gift.

Bewildered, she stared at the white rose in her hand. It was still glowing, still no brighter than a candle flame – a tiny light battling the immensity of suffocating darkness that continued to close in all around her.

"What *are* you?" she whispered to the tiny rose. "Who is the Knight who gave you to me? Why do I feel that somehow you are my only hope?"

The rose shimmered softly but offered no reply.

Aidan knelt in the darkness without any answers, her heart desperately longing within her for something she couldn't begin to understand.

Chapter Twenty-Nine

Abuse's Family

There was still no sound from outside the closet door and Aidan wondered again where all of her guests were. Her pain now gone, she knelt there in the rose's dim light, savoring its scent for several more minutes before she decided to call again for help.

Stronger now, it seemed to her that her voice rang out loudly, but the house was so strangely silent that for one frightening moment she felt as though the entire world had somehow been reduced to the black interior of the closet. Was anything out there at all?

Finally, in a desperate attempt to make enough noise so that someone would hear her, Aidan clenched her hand into a tight fist. She took a deep breath, pulled her arm back, and struck the heavy wooden door as hard as she could.

To her astonishment the impact of her blow forced the door all the way open. It swung around so fast on its hinges that it banged hard against the outside wall of the closet and bounced halfway back again. Aidan jumped in shock as bright daylight flooded the closet and for a startling instant stung her eyes.

How could this be?!

Only moments before, it had not yielded even one shiver to all her pounding. Now it was wide open, as though it had never been latched at all.

Trembling, she peeked out of the closet. No one was there. No one had unlocked the door from the outside that she could tell. In the shock that thoroughly dulled her thinking, she couldn't understand how the door had opened so easily. Then all of a sudden a surge of relief filled her heart and she didn't care how it had happened.

All that mattered was that her prison door was wide open.

She was free!

Aidan lifted her hand and stared again in awe at the wondrous rose from Everestaal. In the daylight it no longer appeared to be glowing and now looked exactly as it had the first time she had seen it. She lifted it gently to her face and pressed it gratefully against her cheek. Then she softly kissed it.

"Thank you for setting me free!" she whispered fervently, knowing she was speaking not so much to the rose as somehow to the Knight who had brought it to her.

Then, mindful that she must keep it hidden, she quickly wrapped the rose in the silk, put it into the velvet pouch, and slipped her most precious treasure back into the safety of her pocket.

Very slowly, with great difficulty, Aidan pulled herself to her feet. Her knees were shaking badly as she yanked at her torn work uniform and pulled it back up onto her shoulder. She held the two halves of the bodice together against her chest as she stumbled out of the closet. Barely daring even to breathe, suspicious at the eerie silence, she looked all around in wonder as though seeing the world outside her prison for the very first time.

Still grasping her torn dress together, Aidan stepped through the archway into the dining room. The untouched food of the midday meal had long since gone cold. Directly in front of her she could see broken dishes and spattered food on the floor. Feeling as though she were moving through a dream, she stared at the huge mess for a long moment.

Where *was* everybody?

"Hello!" she cried. "Is anyone here? Gatekeeper! Drudgery! Please answer me! Where are you?"

But the only reply she received was the silence, that palpable silence that loomed heavily in the house like the threatening calm before a storm.

Then her eyes fell upon the carving knife.

It seemed to mock her as it lay gleaming on the floor amid all the mess. She walked over to it, reached down, and picked it up. Her heart pounded as she stared in horror at the long sinister blade. Disturbing thoughts filled her mind, chilling questions much colder and heavier than the knife's polished silver handle.

Had she actually come so close to killing Uncle Asa?

What would have happened in the next seconds if he hadn't seen what she was doing?

Was she really so easily capable of committing murder?

At that moment the deathly quiet of the house was broken by the front door opening. Aidan jumped and whirled around, clutching her dress tightly with one hand and lifting the carving knife with the other.

Quick tapping footsteps approached. She stood tensed and wild-eyed, knife poised and ready to strike, just as Gatekeeper stopped short in the archway with a large valise in each of his hands.

Her butler stared in shock at the scene before him.

"Miss! What's happened in here? Are you quite all right?"

"Gatekeeper." Aidan breathed with relief, her knees still shaking. She relaxed her grip on the knife and placed it gently beside the meat platter on the table.

As she turned back to him, before she knew what was happening, a torrent of unexpected rage suddenly erupted from somewhere deep within her and she heard herself shouting at him in a savage voice.

"Where *were* you?! Uncle Asa attacked me! I cried and called and screamed, and you didn't come to help me! None of you came – except for the ones who stood in the doorway and watched him do it!"

Gatekeeper was as flustered by her hurled accusations as an old gentleman could be.

"Why, I was detained, Miss, for there are –"

"Detained! How could you be detained?! The Master has sent you here to serve me. Where were you when I needed you most? He tore my dress and beat me! I thought he would kill me! And then – and then –"

The trauma of it all came flooding back to Aidan as powerfully agonizing as the blows from Uncle Asa's leather belt had been. She began shaking uncontrollably as she hurled accusations at him.

"But you knew he would do that, didn't you? You knew he would come here today before he arrived! You *knew* what would happen – and you just welcomed him in the door!"

"I am sorry, Miss," Gatekeeper replied sincerely.

He bent over and set the two heavy suitcases down on the floor. In her ranting, Aidan had not even noticed them in his hands until that moment.

"More guests have arrived. Their rooms are all prepared and I've been outside greeting them. They shall be coming inside presently."

She stared at him in horrified disbelief.

"Oh no," she moaned, "no, not more. Not more of you! I can't bear anymore! Who is here now?"

Before Gatekeeper could answer, the front door opened. Aidan could hear many voices and the footsteps of a small crowd entering the house, and she knew she was about to meet her new guests.

Her heart sank when she heard a shrill voice rising above the others.

She could feel Abuse's grating presence long before she saw her flounce gracelessly through the dining room archway. Perched brightly on her head was the black hat with the flamboyant orange and yellow feathers.

Aidan felt her heart skip a beat at the sight of that hat.

Anger and Depression came in behind Abuse, and then, to Aidan's absolute horror, five huge formidable men stepped through the archway.

At that moment Aidan knew that her greatest fear had come upon her. She thought she would faint dead away at her first sight of Abuse's husband and four sons.

"Oh no," she whispered, her knuckles white as she clutched her torn dress tightly together with both hands. "No, not you! This can't be happening. Not you. Not now!"

Gatekeeper picked up the two valises, bowed, and excused himself. His quick footsteps disappeared up the stairs as Abuse fixed her eyes upon Aidan with a taunting smile on her face. She reached out and touched a shred of shiny blue fabric hanging from Aidan's shoulder.

"Well, well, well! Just look at our lovely swan today!" she sneered. "Such a fine dress, Aidan. This torn rag is perfect on you – so much more fitting than that foolish little thing with the ruffles and jewels you had on last night!"

Aidan yanked herself away and took a step backwards, glaring poisonously at her with intense hatred. Abuse and her wretched family were without doubt the ones responsible for all the pain she had suffered that afternoon.

"Don't you dare touch me!" she snarled.

She turned to the men standing behind Abuse, mustering all her faint courage and faltering dignity.

"I know who you are," she said quietly to the older man. "I have been expecting you, for Abuse and Anger told me you were coming. You are Wrath, are you not?"

The man was immense and intimidating, lean but powerfully built with broad shoulders. His hideous smoldering features were set with the cruelest expression Aidan had ever seen, a countenance made even more fearsome by an old scar running across one cheek. His large square jaw was rough with several days' growth of silver whiskers.

Like all four of his sons, Wrath was dressed in a dirty plaid flannel shirt with the sleeves rolled partway up, revealing thick muscular arms and powerful rough hands. His heavy tan trousers were wrinkled and stained and his feet were clad in high leather work boots.

He removed his tattered black hat, revealing unkempt streaked grey hair that was matted and greasy. Beneath his thick pointed eyebrows, his burning eyes were as dark as black smoke from a fire. His deep voice rumbled softly and slowly like distant threatening thunder as he spoke to her with a coarse drawl.

"Yes, ma'am, ye spoke correct. I be Wrath, and these be me boys. Pardon us that we ain't dressed all fancy-fine fer meetin' womenfolk and all. Fact be, ma'am, we ain't seen no folks t'all fer quite some spell now. The Master done sent us out to the deep woods to do a leetle huntin,' so thet's what we been doin.' Y'see, me and the boys, we was born to hunt. Yep, thet be a fact. Huntin' big game fer the Master – it be what we was made t'do."

He looked over at his four sons and gestured with his huge hand.

"C'mon out here now, ye scoundrels. Take off yer hats. Greet the nice lady right proper-like."

Obediently removing their hats, the four sons stepped forward and stood in a line from tallest to shortest. Their faces looked almost identical but their heights and weights were different. They each had their father's strong features and fearsome eyes as well as greasy hair and stubbled faces.

Aidan had never expected Wrath and his sons to be so crude and unrefined, since Abuse and Anger were always dressed in sophisticated clothes and lavish hats. She thought she would faint dead away before the wretched men of Abuse's family.

Starting with the tallest and pointing them out one by one, Wrath introduced his sons.

"This be Rage, me firstborn. Thet thar be Strife, the second born, then Neglect, and down on t'other end thar, thet be the least'un, Murder."

"Hello," Aidan said, her voice shaking, but the sons didn't even nod in response. They just stood before her, their mouths curled into wicked grins, leering openly at her bare neck with hungry expressions. Aidan shivered and pulled at her dress in a vain attempt to cover herself more completely, feeling like a helpless rabbit about to be slaughtered at the hands of these expert hunters.

"You must excuse my appearance," she said nervously. "I have just had a frightful experience and I haven't been able to change clothes yet."

Intense loathing gripped her chest as she stared at them all.

"But then, I suppose you have been with me since I was very young, and I'm sure you know all about what has just happened to me. Indeed, I have no doubt that you were the very cause of it all."

At that, Abuse let out a shrill laugh.

"Oh, have you just now figured that out, Aidan?" she taunted. Then she turned and spoke to her husband and sons, her voice jubilant. "It was rich, simply *rich!* You were still outside in the yard, but I saw the whole thing from beginning to end. Asa did everything perfectly – just as we told him to."

Aghast at her last illuminating statement, Aidan stared at her.

"You should have seen her face when he tore her dress and tried to kiss her! Oh, Strife, how she fought back! But there was no way she could win. It was just pathetic to see her try! Wrath, Rage, I wish you could have seen the way he started beating her in a frenzy – it's too bad you missed it. And Neglect, you would have loved it when she cried so pitifully like a frightened little child from the darkness of the closet. It was just like all those great times we used to have when we convinced Mara to lock her in there!"

Aidan could hardly believe what Abuse was saying. She felt the blood drain from her face.

"But the best part," Abuse went on mercilessly, "the very best part was when our ugly little duckling here went for the knife!"

She raced to the table. Aidan jumped back from her as she grabbed the carving knife, stabbing and slashing at the air with it as though she were fencing. The long flashing blade punctuated her piercing words.

"Oh, how I wish you could have seen it! She was like a scrawny little bird trapped in the snare of the fowler's net, the helpless prey struggling to be free from the hunter's trap. When she saw the knife on the table, she thought she could just cut the net, kill the fowler, and be free as a bird once more."

Abuse laughed with wicked glee.

"Oh, how she wanted to see him die for everything he had done to her! She wanted it more than anything – after I convinced her that it was the only way to save herself!"

"No!" Aidan said, horrified at Abuse's words. "No, it wasn't you – it couldn't be! I never heard you say anything to me. And if I had, I never would have done what you told me to do! Never!"

Laughing delightedly, Abuse whirled around and met Aidan's eyes with a look of triumph.

"Oh, but it was me, Aidan. It was all of us, even though you hadn't seen my husband and sons yet. Believe me, we were right there with you all the time.

You didn't hear us with your ears, but you heard us loud and clear with your heart. We told you to kill Asa and you tried to do it. But you couldn't kill him because it wasn't yet time for him to die. Our work for the Master isn't finished yet, not in his life – or yours."

Her narrowed eyes were flashing as brightly as the metal blade in her hand. She struck a fencer's classic pose and paused as though taking calculated aim before striking.

"I waited, Aidan, I waited until your fingers were on the knife, until you had it right there in your hand. In another second you would have killed him, too – but then I whispered into Asa's ear and told him to look and see what you were doing."

Abuse abruptly screamed with gleeful laughter and tossed the knife, letting it clatter to the floor as she turned back to the others.

"That was when he went into a rage and threw her against the wall and started beating her! That was when he accused her of murder and told her she was cursed and locked her into the closet! Oh, it was *rich*, so *rich!* It was the best part of all!"

They were all laughing now, cruel mocking laughter that made Aidan want to die from humiliation. How she hated Abuse!

Then she noticed that Murder, the one whose arrival she had most feared, was quietly looking at her. He put his hat back on his head, sidled up next to his mother, and bent down to retrieve the carving knife.

The shortest of Abuse's sons, Murder actually looked to be the most powerful. Heavyset with burly shoulders and cruel dark eyes, he had muscular arms and huge fat hands. His grisly countenance featured a short piglike nose that looked as though it had been broken more than once.

He straightened up and for a long moment examined the carving knife. Then he pulled a large hunting knife from a leather sheath on his belt and compared the two. The carving knife was long and narrow next to the hunting knife, which was a vicious-looking dagger with a highly polished blade set into a heavy silver handle.

"I dunno, Ma," he said, shaking his head. "I reckon it might'a' done the job, but t'ain't nearly sharp as mine."

Rage leaned over Murder's shoulder and looked at the two knives.

"T'ain't nobody's knife sharp as yers, Murder," he said admiringly. "Show Aidan yer huntin' knife, why don't ye? I reckon she'll want to use yers next time. It jes' plumb work better. It were made special fer killin.'"

The four brothers laughed loudly at that.

Murder looked hungrily at Aidan. He set the carving knife on the table and his gruesome face broke into the most sinister grin she had ever seen. She trembled helplessly before him, staring at his hunting knife and holding her breath as she wondered what he was about to do.

"C'mere, Aidan," he teased. "Lemme show ye me huntin' knife. It shore be a beauty – the Master give it to me special. I'll let ye use it anytime ye want. I reckon it'll do ye right well next time ye want to kill a man."

Menacingly he stepped closer and Aidan backed away from him, her heart pounding. Then, without warning, he lunged straight at her, thrusting the hunting knife right toward her throat.

Aidan screamed and jumped backwards. Her shaking knees gave out beneath her and she lost her balance, landing heavily in the mess of broken dishes and cold food on the floor. As she tried to break her fall, shards of glass cut deeply into her hands and her dress fell open. She quickly grabbed at the bodice again, leaving blood and a smear of slimy gravy across the torn white collar.

Abuse and her sons roared with laughter. Murder took another step toward her, the knife flashing in his hand. Aidan whimpered helplessly and tried in vain to back away from him, sliding through the mess of food on the floor.

Suddenly Wrath bolted forward and reached out with one of his powerful arms, his face flushed with anger. His huge hand caught Murder's ear and twisted hard.

"Thet be enough now, ye filthy varmint!" he roared. "T'ain't no way to be treatin' a lady and t'ain't the work the Master give us to do here! I oughtta thrash ye a good one, ye cursed wayward! Now put that dang thing away!"

Murder yelped in pain and dropped his knife. "Yes, Pa," he said, his shaking voice suddenly meek and cowardly. Rubbing his ear, he bent down, picked up his hunting knife, and slipped it back into its leather sheath.

"Pardon the boy, ma'am," Wrath said quietly to Aidan. "Like I tell ye, we been huntin' fer the Master and ain't seen no womenfolk fer quite a spell. I reckon he lost his manners in the woods."

"Right along with thet big twelve-point buck he missed t'other day, aye, Pa?" asked Strife. He nudged an elbow into Neglect's side and the two of them snickered.

Wrath turned and stepped toward Strife and Neglect, sweeping his arm quickly across his chest as if he were about to backhand them both a good one. Strife jumped away from him, still laughing, and Neglect immediately thrust his hand in front of his face to ward off the threatened blow. Their actions told Aidan they had felt their father's slaps many times.

But Wrath didn't strike either of them. He stopped short and gave them a warning.

"I ain't seen neither o' ye gittin' many out thar. Now shut yer ugly faces, ye good-fer-nothin' varmints!"

Aidan watched all this in shocked revulsion. How she despised this loathsome family! Having them in her house would be more than she could bear.

As she pulled herself to her feet, shaking uncontrollably from the intensity of her hatred and trauma, she was relieved to hear Gatekeeper's footsteps coming back down the stairs.

"Gatekeeper, come here!" she cried out loudly.

Her butler appeared in the archway. "Yes, Miss?"

"Get all of these vile people out of my house at once," she ordered. "I won't let them stay here another moment. I don't care what the Master has told any of you – I want all of Abuse's family out of my house right now. Find them some other lodging. They'll have to leave."

At this Abuse's family stood back quietly with smug expressions, knowing what Gatekeeper would do.

Shocked at Aidan's reckless demands, his eyes grew huge.

"Oh, no, Miss, I can't do that! Their rooms have already been prepared, and in fact I've just taken their things up and laid them out. You know that as long as the Master has commanded them to stay here with you, they must do so, and I am not allowed to interfere with their work. And there is plenty of room yet in your house for anyone else the Master will choose to send."

Bristling stubbornly, Aidan declared, "No, Gatekeeper, you don't understand. Let me make this very clear. I simply won't have Abuse's family in my house. They are vile and hateful, and I won't have them here. I order you to get them out of here right now!"

She was stunned when Gatekeeper suddenly laughed.

"Miss, you have no authority over me to give such an order. We take our orders from the Master alone. None of us will leave unless he commands it. And why should we?"

He held up the heavy gold chain that he wore around his neck. The key to her front door dangled from it.

"You have given us the key to your heart. We have free reign here. We will never leave until the Master's work in your house is finished."

Aidan looked closely at Gatekeeper. For the very first time she thought she saw a malevolent gleam in his grandfatherly blue eyes which up until now had always smiled so kindly from his pleasant wrinkled face.

None of her guests could be trusted – not a single one of them.

"How long is it going to take, then?" she demanded. "How long will I be forced to endure all of you in my life? Just when will your Master's work in my house be done?"

Abuse laughed.

"You little fool! Don't you understand yet? The Master's work in your house will only be finished at the very moment you die!"

Mocking laughter rippled through the crowd of Abuse's family. Clutching her dress tightly around herself, Aidan backed away from her wretched guests.

"I hate you," she declared vehemently in a rasping voice. "I hate you all! I hate having you in my house and I wish I could kill every last one of you!"

She trembled as she began to lose all control.

"I swear to you with all my life and breath, you won't be with me as long as you think. Somehow, long before the day I die, I will find a way to be free of you all!"

With that, she turned and fled into the kitchen. The raucous sound of Abuse's screaming laughter rose above that of the others and floated after her, but no one followed.

As Aidan came rushing into the kitchen, Drudgery looked up from wiping the table and stared at her in surprise.

"Aidan! What's happened to you?!"

Near hysteria, Aidan backed away as Drudgery began to move toward her.

"Don't touch me! Don't you dare touch me!"

"Aidan," Drudgery said very calmly, "I can see you've had a terrible fright. Tell me what's happened. It's me, Drudgery, your friend – don't you recognize me?"

"Oh, I recognize you, all right," Aidan declared. "I recognize you and all your fellow servants more clearly now than I can bear!"

Her voice filled with bitterness.

"Are you indeed my friend? I trusted you, Drudgery, I trusted you most of all. But when I needed you, you weren't there to help me. I called for you, but you never came! And now you dare to stand there and call yourself my friend?!"

Suddenly something deep within Aidan snapped and she heard herself screaming.

"I have no friends! Don't you understand?! I'm the stranger – the outsider – the orphan nobody ever loved or wanted!"

"Oh no, no," Drudgery declared softly, "that isn't true, Aidan! That isn't true at all."

Her eyes were shining almost hypnotically. She stretched out her hands as though to offer comfort and slowly stepped closer, speaking in a soothing voice.

"You are the Master's most favored one, don't you remember? You are blessed above all other women. It's all written out for you in the stars. He has chosen you for a wonderful purpose – a special destiny. And we have been sent here to help you."

Were the strange points of light in Drudgery's eyes glimmers of wicked delight, as though she were enjoying her mistress' agony – or was that just Aidan's frenzied imagination?

Drudgery came a step closer, her voice low and mesmerizing.

"Let me help you, friend Aidan. I'll draw you a nice hot bath. I'll heat the water just right and take away your torn dress and wash you clean."

"Don't you dare come near me!" Aidan screamed. "Stay away! If you touch me, I swear I'll kill you!"

With that, she whirled and bolted up the back stairs, clutching her torn bloody dress around herself. She stumbled down the hall on shaking legs, ran into her bedroom and slammed the door, latching it securely behind herself.

Chapter Thirty

The Rose In The Fire

Alone in her locked bedroom, Aidan immediately began clawing wildly at her dirty torn dress, as though by tearing it off her body she could somehow shed all the trauma she had endured while wearing it that day. Her cut hands were shaking badly as she vented all of her fury upon it, yanking at it in livid frustration.

This time the sound of ripping fabric was sweet to her ears. Her clothes slid completely off her shoulders and fell into a heap on the floor. In a final fit of rage, she kicked the pile away and savagely stomped on it over and over again.

As she turned to face the full-length oval mirror, she gasped and stared in open-mouthed shock.

She came closer and stood naked before her reflection, barely able to recognize herself. Twisting to the right and then to the left, she examined her bruised and swollen back, her matted and tangled hair, her hands still bloody from broken glass, her arms and legs smeared with sticky cold food and the filth from the closet floor.

But most disturbing of all was the frenzied look on her face.

Her cheeks were flushed bright scarlet against ashen skin. Her huge round eyes were mournful pools of dark tortured pain and unbearable yearning.

She knew she had seen that torment somewhere before, in someone else's eyes, but at that moment she couldn't remember whose.

Aidan turned away and hurried to the washstand in the corner of her room, where she was relieved to see that the porcelain pitcher was full of water and Drudgery had set out towels and washing supplies. She poured cool water into the bowl, then worked a thick lather into a washcloth with a cake of perfumed soap.

Her bruises were tender to the touch and she winced at the sharp sting of the soap in her cuts as she scrubbed herself completely from head to toe, scouring hard to remove all the filth clinging to her body. But even after wringing the cloth out in the water and rinsing herself thoroughly, she still felt unclean. She took up the soap and lathered the cloth and washed herself again and again until the pitcher was empty and the water in the bowl was cloudy with dirty soapsuds and her body smelled as sweet as her rose garden.

But even then she still felt dirty.

She was certain that her soul had somehow been marked with a terrible stain that could never be removed. No amount of soap and water could ever wash away the memory of what Uncle Asa had done to her or the deep shame she felt, as though it had all been her fault.

Shivering, Aidan reached for a towel and dried herself. From the top drawer of the bureau she pulled clean undergarments – her old undergarments, not the new silk ones from Prince Bal'Davarius – and put them on. Then she opened the closet door and began to push through all the fine clothes that Lust and Vanity had brought her, shoving them roughly aside and feeling in the very back for one of her old dresses.

Suddenly she remembered that Lust and Vanity had talked the night before about having Drudgery burn all her old threadbare clothes, and for a terrible moment she panicked. But then her hand closed over one of the dresses and she pulled it out of the closet, as grateful to see it as if it were an old friend.

Patched and worn and comfortable, it was a dress from the time before she had ever met the Dark Prince's servants, a dress that had seen simpler and happier days when her house was not overrun by dreadful guests, a dress she had worn in the summer sunshine while working contentedly in her rose garden.

She slipped it on and buttoned it up, much calmer now, and sighed with relief. Then she brushed out her damp hair and pulled it back beneath a clean scarf.

As Aidan turned around again, she looked down at the heap of shredded fabric on the floor that had been her work uniform. She stared at it for a long moment, stricken by guilt that it was now destroyed. Those dresses had been the loveliest garments she had ever worn before Lust and Vanity had brought her the fine wardrobe from their Master. It was a shame that one had been ruined – especially in such a horrific way.

Impulsively she reached down, scooped up the dress, and crumpled it into a tight ball. Holding it against her chest, she opened the bedroom door and raced down the back stairs.

At the bottom, Aidan peeked into the kitchen very slowly, relieved to see that Drudgery had left and no one else was there. She hurried to the wood-burning cookstove and flung open the door to the firebox, grateful to see there was a nice strong blaze inside. Without hesitation she knelt down and stuffed the ruined dress into the stove, nudging it deep into the flames with an iron poker.

The fire subsided and smoked as the ball of cloth opened up and partially smothered the burning logs. Fabric edges curled and blackened as yellow and orange flames began to rise up around them. Within a moment the dress was fully ablaze.

As the fire gained momentum and brightened, so did Aidan's mood. In a few minutes she would be rid of this terrible reminder of what Uncle Asa had done to her, rid of all the pain she had suffered that afternoon. She poked at the burning cloth again and again with ruthless determination, wanting to be certain that nothing would be left of the dress but ashes. Satisfied at last, she straightened up and moved back a little from the heat, squinting as she peered into the firebox.

Suddenly she saw a distinct shadow of something strange on top of the dress, but she couldn't quite make out what she was seeing. Was it her imagination, or was there really something else there?

All at once a sweet rich fragrance filled the kitchen and she gasped with complete horror.

The tiny white rose from Everestaal!

Aidan froze. She had completely forgotten that it was in the pocket of the dress!

The velvet pouch and the silk square must have already burned away, for she couldn't see them. But now she could clearly see the rose lying there as merciless flames opened and closed around its dainty curling petals like grasping claws.

For one leaden instant Aidan's heart stopped beating and she could hardly breathe for panic. All she could do was stare helplessly at the rose in the fire.

Then she frantically poked at it, trying in vain to push it out of the flames, but the blaze seemed to be growing stronger. She quickly threw the poker aside and even before it clattered against the slate floor she had a shovel in her hand.

But in the second it took her to turn back to the stove, the fire suddenly exploded into a huge inferno. The burning logs cracked and snapped loudly as brilliant tongues of flame white as lightning flared up and leapt out at her – exactly like the fire from the Knight's sword that had burst through the carriage window that morning.

Aidan gasped and jumped away from the stove, suddenly terrified that the whole kitchen was about to go up in flames.

All view of the rose was now completely obliterated – along with any chance of its rescue. She had no choice but to stand far back from the stove, her heart breaking with a sickening wrench more vicious than any beating she had ever suffered.

"No!" she pleaded in a helpless whisper. "Please don't die! You can't die! Please!"

Surely by now the Knight's wonderful gift was nothing more than a smattering of ashes. The tiny creamy white rose edged in crimson, her precious healing rose from Everestaal, was gone forever – burned by her own hand.

To have endured so much agony and so much hope in one devastating day – only to have it end like this!

Chapter Thirty-One

Abuse's Cruelty

What a careless fool she had been! How could she have forgotten about her beloved little rose?

There had to be a way to make something good come out of this tragedy! She would take the remains of the rose to her garden. Surely out of its ashes new life and beauty would arise.

The thought came to her that she had just done what Lady Fairhaven had begged her to do and destroyed the evidence of her treasonous guilt. But somehow knowing this was poor comfort indeed.

The fire died down as abruptly as it had flared up. Steeling herself for what she knew she would find, Aidan knelt down in front of the stove.

But as she peered again into the firebox, her jaw dropped open in utter astonishment. For there, nestled in the ashes of charred fabric, the fire burning in a ring all around it, was the rose!

Aidan blinked, completely bewildered. Surely she must be seeing things! How could it possibly have survived?

Carefully sliding the shovel beneath the rose, she brought it out of the fire. It was perfectly intact, not missing even one petal or leaf. Resting in soft ashes and surrounded by glowing orange embers, the little rose seemed just as pristine as the moment she had first seen it.

Setting the shovel gently onto the slate floor, Aidan gaped at it in wonder. Hesitantly she reached out and tapped at the rose, quickly drawing back her fingers before she realized that it was cool to the touch. She picked it up and cradled it reverently in her palm.

Fully open now, the tiny blossom seemed to sparkle with fresh radiant beauty, as though it had been kissed by sweet morning dew instead of ravaged by a fire. Aidan lifted it to her face and examined it more closely. There wasn't a single smudge of soot anywhere on it or any sign of having been scorched at all. It didn't even smell of smoke. In fact, it seemed much more fragrant than it had been before its fiery ordeal.

Desperate to have answers but knowing none would come, she whispered to it in total awe.

"What *are* you, little rose, that nothing seems to harm you? You've had neither light nor water. You've been wrapped up in silk and closed inside a velvet pouch and pressed beneath a horse's saddle. You've been stuck inside my pocket all day, and I must have even stomped on you upstairs in my room. And now you've been through that awful fire."

She stroked its soft petals.

"Yet nothing crushes you – nothing destroys you. You are something much greater than a healing rose. I don't understand what you are."

As she continued to stare at the rose, Aidan became aware that there was something different about it. She turned it around in her hand and realized that it was larger than it had been before. Then she saw something else and gasped. There was another stem branching out with two tiny leaves and a new bud on it that hadn't been there just a moment before.

The rose was growing before her eyes!

And then she saw the most astounding thing of all. At the end of the stem where it had been cut from its bush, there were tiny white hairs growing.

It was putting forth roots!

Perplexed, Aidan ran her finger very lightly across the delicate root hairs.

"How can this be?" she whispered. "Roses don't grow like this. Once they're cut they live a day or two but then they wither and fade."

She turned the rose over again and again in her hand.

"But you – you just won't die. You just keep living – and the fire only seems to have made you grow!"

Never had Aidan yearned so deeply to have a certain rose growing in her garden as she did at that moment.

Carrying the rose in her hand, she leapt to her feet and hurried out the back door. She snatched her basket of gardening tools from inside the shed and headed for the corner of the house. Her determination to plant the white rose was so intense that she completely forgot to be wary of the Dark Prince's servants. Fortunately, none seemed to be about.

But as she approached the corner of the house, she realized something was very wrong.

She stopped, frozen with shock, staring at the arch that she had long ago planted with climbing roses that were streaked red and yellow. Now all she could see was bare wood.

Her roses were gone!

All that was left of the bushes were two ugly holes in the dirt and some leaves and petals scattered on the ground.

Confused, she passed beneath the bare arbor and walked very slowly toward the second arbor over the wooden gate that led to the front yard. The same variety of red and yellow roses had been growing there as well, but to her alarm that arch too was bare.

"My roses," she whispered, incredulous. "Where are my roses?!"

Aidan suddenly felt like she was in one of Night Terrors' dreams. She reached for the gate, but before her hand touched the latch she heard a familiar shrill voice on the other side. Her heart pounding with dread, she froze again and clasped the white rose protectively against her chest.

"There, Mother, that should do it. That's the last one!"

It was Anger. She heard Abuse snap in reply.

"Well, it's about time! Give that bush to Strife to put in the cart with all the others. You boys, hurry up!"

A drawling voice answered her.

"Ma, tell Murder to stop foolin' around with his huntin' knife and help us chain these dang bushes down tight. He jes' cuttin' all them roses off!"

With a sickening jolt, Aidan suddenly understood what was happening.

Abuse's family was destroying her rose garden!

She yearned to look over the gate, but all she could do was tremble in panic. They were carrying out the evil work their Master had given them to do in her life – and she knew she could do nothing to stop them.

"Murder, put that knife away and get to work!" Abuse snapped. "Wrath, make sure the boys secure all the bushes nice and tight with those chains. We need to hurry!"

Holding her breath and summoning every last ounce of courage she had, Aidan stood on tiptoes and very slowly peeked over the tall wooden gate.

Her entire front yard was now a barren wasteland of freshly dug soil pitted with deep empty holes where her beautiful roses had been thriving since her early childhood. The only thing left of her treasured garden was the flagstone path meandering nakedly between large piles of dirt on its way from the front step to the iron gate.

Abuse's family had even scaled the walls of the cottage and torn down Samuel Teague's latticework trellises that had supported the pale pink rosebushes rambling heavily across the slate roof. Now even those impressive roses, which had been growing since long before Aidan had come to live with Aunt Mara, were gone along with all of her own.

Nauseated and shaking, Aidan quickly ducked back down behind the gate and slumped against the stone wall of the cottage. Her anguish over what was happening to her beloved garden gripped her chest so tightly she could hardly breathe. The violent pain that sliced deeply into her heart was more agonizing than all the fierce blows from Uncle Asa's belt put together.

"Thet's the last'un, Ma," one of Abuse's sons called out. "I reckon they's all chained down now."

Abuse's triumphant laughter rang out with wicked glee.

"Finally! No more nasty thorns! No more buzzing little bees! No more sickening putrid stench! Good riddance to them all, I say! May Aidan's roses be cursed forever!"

Aidan shuddered with agony and gasped for breath. It was all she could do to keep from wailing out loud. She yearned for her condemned roses as though she were a mother forced to watch her own children being slaughtered but completely unable to save them.

Cautiously she peered again over the top of the wooden gate. Abuse was standing across the yard by the stone wall wearing a wide-brimmed straw hat that was exactly like Aidan's gardening hat – except that it was dyed black and tied with a black ribbon.

Outside the iron gate was a huge wooden flatbed cart. Samuel Teague's old latticework trellises had been set upright and nailed to the cart on three sides as supports, leaving the back open for loading. Heaped inside was an immense pile of green branches – all her treasured rosebushes, viciously uprooted and torn to shreds – tightly secured to the trellises with iron chains and padlocks.

Aidan stared in shock at the masses of fading blossoms that now lay so limp and lifeless in that mountain of withered branches.

Had she really grown that many roses?

Were they really all now dying?!

"Depression, now everything depends on you!" Abuse shouted. "Don't mess it up this time! Take Aidan's roses away – and burn them!"

Now Aidan saw that Depression was harnessed to the front of the cart like a work animal. Chains were padlocked around his upper body and his head was secured through a heavy wooden yoke that was made for two and hung down clumsily from his shoulders. The poor man was bent over, barely able to stand beneath the weight of all his burdens. The sight of that skinny weakling trying to pull the overloaded cart was utterly pathetic, even more so than the day he had carried all the baggage for Anger and Abuse into the yard.

Aidan knew without a doubt that Abuse's family had chained Depression to the cart, but she could feel no pity for him whatsoever. She was too overwhelmed by the sight of her roses, her precious roses, now cut into pieces and chained onto the cart like freshly butchered hunter's kill.

She slumped back against the cottage wall again, hating herself for being so wretchedly helpless. This contemptible family had lost no time at all. Just as soon as Wrath and his despicable sons had gotten settled in her house, Abuse had made sure that the work the Master had given them to do was thoroughly completed. Now Depression was going to burn all of her roses and she was powerless to save them. She had been outnumbered and beaten by Abuse's family from long ago.

Her roses were dying, and with them all of her hopes and dreams.

But at that moment, a strong sweet fragrance met her in her worst despair.

Through tears Aidan looked down at the little white rose growing before her eyes right there in her hand. It had gone through a brutal fire – but not only was it still alive, it was thriving. She saw to her amazement that its new bud was fully open and others were forming. Its roots were twice the size they had been just a few moments before. Although she couldn't understand how or why this miracle was happening, she drew great comfort from it.

Suddenly Aidan knew for certain that if she could just plant the rose from Everestaal in her garden, it would quickly grow into a bush that would fill up all the ugly barren spaces left by Abuse and her family.

But she didn't dare go through the gate as long as they were still in the yard. Lord Fairhaven's warning came back to her so strongly she could almost hear his voice behind her.

As long as you possess that rose from our Prince's worst enemy, even if you never go to Everestaal, you are still guilty of high treason – you are guilty right now.

The Dark Prince's servants already suspected that the Knight had given her something. She knew she mustn't let them see the rose. If that happened Aidan was certain they would have her arrested and executed.

Anxiously she looked behind her and then peeked over the gate again, wondering what she should do and wishing her enemies would leave.

Depression began straining with all his might, but the heavy cart wouldn't budge even one inch. The sound of his tortured groans grated against Aidan's ears. Yet Abuse's family just stood back in the yard and watched, taunting him mercilessly and laughing with derision.

"Aw, Depression," Strife cried, "ye're nothin' but a filthy skunk! Ye're as ugly as Aidan's roses and ye stink twice as bad!"

He leapt up onto the back of the cart and started jumping up and down on it. The motion of the bouncing cart yanked the harness chains and jerked Depression cruelly about so that he staggered helplessly back and forth beneath the clumsy wooden yoke.

Suddenly Rage rushed up to Depression and started pounding him with his fists. The poor abused man screamed out in distress, completely unable to defend himself. Rage beat him savagely while Strife howled with hysterical laughter, bouncing the cart still harder and cheering his brother on.

Aidan held her breath, sickened at the scene taking place before her eyes. It brought back all the horror of her own beating at Uncle Asa's hands.

Then Murder pulled out his hunting knife and started toward Depression. The polished blade flashed ominously in the sunlight and Aidan pressed her hand to her lips to keep from crying out at what she feared would happen next.

But at that moment Wrath lost what little patience he had. He grabbed Murder's shoulder and jerked him back, roaring at his two older sons.

"Ye worthless scoundrels! Back off'n that fool afore I give the both o' ye a whuppin' ye'll never fergit! Ye kin have yer fun later, but right now they ain't time! They be work t'do fer the Master!"

As Strife hopped down, the last sudden lurch of the cart caused Depression to completely lose his balance and fall heavily to the ground. Rage kicked him hard, then backed up a step and spit on the poor man.

Laughing scornfully, the two sadistic brothers sauntered back into the barren yard.

Depression's suffering was clearly more than he could bear. He remained bent over on his knees in front of the cart, his thin body convulsed with sobs. His mournful wails rose and fell in loud gasps, yet still his in-laws showed him no compassion.

Wrath abruptly stormed over to Anger and shoved roughly at her shoulder.

"I swear, t'ain't nothin' more disgustin' than a grown man cryin' like a babe! Anyone what'd marry Depression must be as big a fool as he is. Why the Master chose this lazy scum fer yer husband is beyond me, but let me tell ye, girl, what's been done is been done fer keeps."

He shoved her again, pushing her toward the gate.

"Yer the one bound to him as his helpmeet, and right now I reckon this worthless husband o' yers needs a bit o' help pullin' thet thar cart. So git yerself over thar and help him – afore I give ye a whuppin' too!"

Anger scowled furiously at her father and flounced through the gate. As she slid her head into the other side of the yoke next to Depression and grabbed the harness chains, her strident voice railed against him in a venomous rant.

"You pitiful wretch! You can't do anything right, can you? How dare you shame me in front of my family this way! You're nothing but a failure – a total disgrace to the Master! You can't even do the work he's given you to do!"

Depression's miserable countenance was shadowed with dark gloom. He winced at her words as though they were sharp stones being hurled at him, but never uttered a single word in his defense. Wiping the tears from his face with his sleeve, he stumbled to his feet with difficulty.

Anger glared at him. "Now, are you finally ready to do a little work for once?"

He nodded meekly and squared his shoulders with resignation, gathering his strength to try again.

"Well, pull hard this time, you stupid fool, or I swear I'll have my brothers take care of you for good! One – two – three! *Pull!*"

They strained against the harnesses, but barely for an instant. Now that both of them were working together in the yoke, the heavy cart immediately started to roll easily, as though it weighed nothing at all.

Aidan watched helplessly as Anger and Depression took her bound and dying roses away to be burned.

Her stomach was churning with intense rage and her heart ached with longing for her roses. She knew that – unlike the white rose that had gone through the fire – hers could never survive being cut and burned. They would never put forth roots and grow again. They would soon be ashes, and there was nothing she could do to save them or to bring them back.

Her garden – her treasured rose garden that she had nurtured so lovingly and so diligently from the time she was a very small child – was gone forever.

Aidan pressed the little white rose from Everestaal tightly to her breast. Now it was more precious to her than ever.

It was all she had left.

Chapter Thirty-Two

The Black Roses

The voices of Abuse's family floated over the gate to Aidan's ears. The first one she heard was Wrath.

"Wal, Ma, thet's thet. I reckon Anger will make Depression do the job right this time. She ain't got much fer brains, but that gal do have spunk – somethin' her fool husband shore ain't got."

"I heartily agree," Abuse said boastfully, "and I have no doubt that the job will be done thoroughly. In that respect Anger takes after me. I don't let anything stand in my way when there's work to be done for the Master."

She sighed contentedly.

"But I knew from the moment I saw this wretched excuse for a garden that it would take all of us working together to get the job done right, so I waited until you and the boys arrived. I think the Master will be most pleased, don't you?"

"Aye, that he will," Wrath agreed.

"Pa, all this hard work has shore worked me up a appetite," one of their sons said. "Do ye reckon Drudgery might be whuppin' up some victuals?"

"Ye boys kin go in an' see," Wrath replied. "Ye done good – fer once."

Aidan heard the clomping of heavy boots and then the front door opening and closing. Very cautiously she looked over the gate again. Their sons had left but Abuse and Wrath were still lingering behind, admiring their handiwork. She quickly ducked back down before they could see her.

"Wal now, we all done a job we kin be right proud of, I reckon," Wrath declared.

Abuse agreed. "Some of our very best work ever, I'd say. It looks perfect, just perfect! This is my very favorite part of the work the Master gives us to do."

She laughed with cruel delight.

"Oh, I'd give anything to see the ugly duckling's face when she sees her precious little garden now. Her disgusting roses will never grow here again!"

Suddenly a new voice rang out in reply.

"But the Master's will!"

It was Doubt, his voice rising cheerfully over the sounds of horses snorting and the rattling of carriage hitches.

Trembling with fresh dread, Aidan wondered what was about to happen to her garden next. Could she bear any more?

Fearfully she stood on tiptoes again to see what was going on.

Another open wooden cart was pulling up in the street outside the iron gate, this one drawn by what looked like Pride's black horses. In the driver's seat Doubt was pulling on the reins. Discouragement was sitting next to him and their four children were dangling their legs off the back end of the flatbed.

Towering between parents and children in the cart was an immense pile of what seemed to be long dead branches.

Doubt called pleasantly to Abuse and Wrath.

"Hello there! I see you've finished right on time, as usual. We're much obliged to your family for preparing Aidan's garden for us. Now we can get on with the work the Master has given us to do here."

"Aye, we be done," Wrath said. "Ma, let's go in. I reckon I could use a bite o' somethin' meself."

Abuse took one last look around Aidan's ravaged yard and sighed.

"Such a pity! I had so hoped to be here when the ugly little duckling sees it like this. Now, Doubt, you make sure to take excellent care of Aidan's beloved garden!"

Her raucous laughter floated behind her, echoing across the barren yard even after the front door closed behind her and Wrath.

Grateful to see the two of them leave, Aidan kept silent as she watched Doubt's family from behind the wooden gate. Completely absorbed in their work for the Master, they never even glanced her way.

Doubt hopped down from the cart.

"We must get right to work," he said as he helped his wife and children down. "Wrath and Abuse always leave open holes, so we shouldn't have to bother digging new ones. I'm quite sure we'll be able to plant the Master's bushes right where all the old ones were."

"Children, don't forget to wear your heavy gardening gloves," Discouragement said. "Remember, those thorns are razor sharp!"

False Hopes spoke up in her innocent voice.

"Don't worry about me, Mother. The thorns never hurt me. The Master has been teaching me all about the proper way to handle his roses. He says I must learn how to plant and nurture his bushes very carefully. It's a big part of the special work he says I must learn to do."

Discouragement smiled at her.

"I know, dear. Oh! It makes me so proud of you! The Master is giving you very important work."

Doubt issued the assignments for each of his family members to carry out.

"False Hopes and Vain Imaginings, you will unload the cart and bring the bushes into the garden – you can put them along the garden wall over there. Discouragement, you will bring each bush to me and hold it in place while I fill in the holes. Despair and Self-Pity, you will follow us with water and the Master's special fertilizer. All right then, are we ready? Let's get to work!"

Aidan was shocked at the earnest cooperation she saw in Doubt's family as each of them quietly hastened to begin their tasks. It was obvious that they had done this work together many times before.

Shovel in hand, Doubt came through the iron gate first and began looking across the barren yard. Right behind him False Hopes and Vain Imaginings began carrying in what looked like bundles of long thin branches and leaning them up in a neat row against the stone wall. The twins followed, never uttering a single complaint or whine even as they lugged a huge watering can and a sturdy cloth bag through the gate, both of which looked to be extremely heavy. Discouragement followed everyone into the garden, pulling thick leather work gloves firmly over her aristocratic hands.

Doubt walked thoughtfully along the path until he found a freshly dug hole that apparently looked suitable. He gestured to Discouragement, who brought him a bush and held it perfectly straight as he filled the hole with dirt and tamped it down firmly. They finished quickly and went on to repeat the planting process with a second bush and then a third.

Aidan stared in absolute horror at the hideous things they were planting in her garden. They had called them bushes, but they looked nothing like any bushes she had ever seen. Standing straight up at about six feet tall, each one seemed to be a hopelessly tangled mass of spindly grey branches thickly covered with long spiny thorns and bearing not one trace of green foliage.

As far as she could tell, every bush was completely dead.

Her heart broke all over again at the sight of those lifeless grey branches with their wicked thorns. She ached with fresh yearning for her own verdant bushes with their colorful beautifully-shaped roses. Her life would hardly be worth living as long as these repulsive things were in her garden!

As Doubt and Discouragement went on to the fourth bush, the twins quietly stepped up to the first one with the cloth bag and the full watering can. Despair took a small cup and dipped it into the bag, bringing out a black powder which she sprinkled liberally around the base of the freshly planted bush. Then Self-Pity tipped the watering can and carefully drenched the soil around the bush along with the powder.

Immediately the bush began to tremble as though the mountain wind were blowing through it. Aidan watched, stunned, as it unfolded its branches, moving just like a person waking from a long sleep and stretching out their arms.

The twins went on to the next bush and repeated the fertilizing process, then moved on, following their parents around the garden. Strangely, even with thorough soakings, the watering can never ran dry.

Every one of the dead-looking bushes reacted in the same way, moving and spreading out as though they were awakening to new life.

By the time the twins fertilized the fourth one Aidan was shaking from fear, wondering what kind of bushes these were in her garden. Then she looked again at the first one and saw hundreds of large dark buds popping out all over the thorny grey branches. There were still no leaves, but the buds uncurled and opened up before her eyes until the entire bush looked like a plush dark pillar covered with huge blossoms.

The Dark Prince's prized black roses!

So this was what their bushes looked like. Aidan watched in fascination as one by one each of the leafless bushes sprouted masses of reddish-black roses. Within moments her garden was filled with them. Their heavy perfume, as rich and intoxicating as the finest wine, began to permeate the air.

At the sight of all this, to her own surprise, Aidan felt an unexpected surge of relief. They were unusual bushes, to be sure, but the black roses were very beautiful indeed and they covered the ugly branches completely. While she still yearned for her own roses, she found herself thinking perhaps it wouldn't be so bad to have these splendid blooms in her garden. It was much better than bare ugly holes in the dirt, after all.

Suddenly Aidan realized that, ironically, Doubt's family had actually done her a favor. The Master's bushes were so large and the roses so thick and fragrant that she could easily plant the little white rose from Everestaal behind them somewhere, perhaps right in the corner of the stone wall, where it would surely never even be noticed.

Aidan looked down at the rapidly growing bush. She was now holding it tightly in the crook of one arm against her chest, for it was about the size and weight of a large baby. With its many buds and thick leaves and long dangling roots, it would clearly be impossible to hide as she carried it.

Impatiently she looked over the gate again, wishing Doubt's family would hurry up and finish their work.

At last the planting was all done. Doubt straightened up and stepped back to the garden's edge, mopping his brow with a white linen handkerchief.

"Well," he said, "the bushes are taking very nicely, as always. This will be a splendid garden. It looks like the Master's special fertilizer is doing its job."

Despair shook the cloth bag and scattered the last of the dark powder around the base of the very last rosebush.

"Exactly enough as usual, Father," she commented. "The Master always knows just how much fertilizer to send with the bushes."

"They'll do magnificently here," Discouragement said as she pulled off her heavy gardening gloves. "This setting is just excellent for them. Come now, children, let's finish quickly."

Self-Pity watered the last bush, emptying the can.

"Oh, Mother, this is ever so much better," she whined. "I still wish we could just go back to the Master's palace, but at least now it will be bearable here."

Despair's sniveling voice rose up in agreement.

"Self-Pity is right, Mother. Now that the Master's roses are growing here, it will feel so much more like home."

"The Master is very wise indeed," Doubt agreed. "And you children have all done well."

"Darling, drive the cart away while I take the children in to wash up," Discouragement said. "Come along, my dear ones."

With deep satisfaction Doubt took one last look at Aidan's yard.

"This is the finest garden we've planted for the Master yet," he declared.

Aidan watched them go off in different directions. Doubt and his empty cart disappeared from view up the street while Discouragement shepherded her brood through the front door into the cottage.

Welcome silence fell like a shroud over Aidan's violated garden. Her only comfort now was that she was finally alone.

Chapter Thirty-Three

The White Roses

Cradling the white rosebush against her pounding heart with her basket of gardening tools hanging over one arm, Aidan cautiously opened the gate and stepped through it into the yard. She moved slowly and silently along the flagstone path, barely daring to breathe, staring dumbfounded in every direction.

Surely this wasn't really her own front yard. Surely this was some kind of bizarre dream!

But she knew it wasn't a dream. Tall pillars covered with huge dark roses towered like sentinels at attention all around her. The bare cottage and stone garden wall looked naked and ugly.

No, it was all very real. Devastatingly real.

Aidan had never seen the yard without her roses in it. Now all that was left of them was a scattering of wilted flowers and leaves on the dark flagstones.

She bent and picked up a pink rose. It lay limp and lifeless in her hand, as cold and clammy and repulsive as death itself. She shuddered and let it fall back to the ground.

"My garden," she moaned softly. "My beautiful roses!"

Just that morning this garden had been her greatest joy, the only beauty she had in her life. Now her precious roses had been brutally taken from her. Now they were destroyed – and gone forever.

The agony of this loss was more devastating than the physical pain of all the beatings she had ever suffered. In her lifetime she had endured so much and survived through it all – but now she felt all her strength ebbing away. This was a fatal blow and she knew she would never recover from it.

Feeling completely dazed, Aidan walked up to one of the Dark Prince's unusual rosebushes and examined it closely. The massive reddish-black blooms were pressed so tightly against each other that their leafless branches couldn't be seen at all.

Very carefully she pushed her fingers into velvety soft petals and gently pulled a black rose aside to look beneath it. What she saw was astounding – and horrifying.

Completely hidden beneath the flawless beauty of the blossoms, the grey woody branches were thickly covered with viciously sharp spikes. Aidan had seen many different types of rosebushes, but never had she seen thorns like this. Some of them were well over an inch long and some were so tiny they could hardly be seen at all, and the rest were every size in between.

She had not been pricked because she was an experienced rose gardener who knew how to handle the branches. But had she tried to touch one of these roses unaware of the razor-sharp barbs beneath them, she would have been met by a most painful and nasty surprise.

All at once the winelike fragrance permeating the air was so thick and cloying that she felt nauseated. She quickly let go of the black rose and backed away from the bush, trembling as though in the presence of death itself.

And indeed, something deep within Aidan's heart had painfully died. She felt its leaden weight aching terribly within her chest. Wrath and Abuse had wrenched all that was most precious to her from her heart as well as from the earth. In their place Doubt and Discouragement had planted these dark roses whose deceitful beauty was just as treacherous as the thickly barbed branches upon which they grew.

Aidan looked down in bewilderment at the white rose still growing in her hands. In the menacing shadows of the black roses, it seemed to shine with an innocent and pristine beauty. It had no thorns at all and she could already see that it was going to grow into a beautiful verdant bush.

But now the thought came to her that if she planted it here, even hidden behind the other bushes, its dark green foliage and tiny white roses would stand out conspicuously and its rich fragrance would surely make its presence known.

This thought unleashed a chilling wave of fear and despair. Perhaps it would be too dangerous to plant the little rosebush after all. She knew all too clearly that her very life was at stake, for to possess anything from Everestaal was high treason. The gold silk square and the velvet pouch with its incriminating embroidered crest had burned away in the fire, but if the Dark Prince's servants were to find the rose growing in her garden, they would know in an instant that it could only have come from the Knight who had burned the carriage.

Then another heartbreaking thought came to her. This rose had gone through fire and survived, but surely these wicked black roses would choke the life out of it. It was hopeless to think that such a pure and virtuous rose could live surrounded by total deceit and treachery.

As Aidan looked up again at the black roses, she shivered. They loomed around her like merciless soldiers about to close in on her. She vividly imagined being arrested and locked into a tiny dark prison cell to await execution.

At that thought a tear slipped down her face. She stared again at her precious white roses.

"No," she whispered. "No. I can't do it. I just can't."

The awful risk was too great. Aidan was deathly afraid of being hurt again. Hadn't she suffered enough? Indeed she had – much more than anyone should ever have to suffer, even just in that one day, let alone in a lifetime. She knew she could endure no more.

But if she didn't plant the rose in her garden – what was she to do with it?

The remarkable rose seemed to be growing even faster now. No matter where she tried to hide it or how she might try to get rid of it, it would only be a matter of time before her guests found it. And she had already seen that she could not destroy it, not even by fire.

Aidan thought again of the Knight and his kind beautiful eyes that had burned into her soul and filled her with a longing to be close to him. Surely he had risked his own life to bring her his precious gift, although why he had done so was a complete mystery.

She loved this rose as she had loved no other thing in her life. It was truly the only good thing she had left.

Would it indeed die if she did plant it among the black roses? Or would its healing presence bring new life to her devastated garden – and even to her broken heart?

Aidan understood that she would never know unless she actually planted it.

Still she hesitated. Her heart was torn.

"I can't," she moaned again softly, as though the Knight were right there listening to her. "I just can't, don't you see? I'm so afraid. I've been through so much already. I just can't bear any more."

She was weeping in earnest now, tears of agony flowing from the depths of her soul.

"Why did you give me this rose? What does all this mean? Please, *please* – don't ask me to plant it in my garden. They'll find it and kill me. Don't you understand? I'll never get to Everestaal. I'll never be able to find you again. They'll lock me away – and I'll never be free!"

Suddenly a picture of the two stone towers together on the hillside came into her mind. She wondered again why the Knight had built one next to hers. But neither the fortitude of a stone tower nor the power of an oath sworn with all her life and breath could give her the strength to go on.

There was no more fight left in her.

Completely exhausted, Aidan took a deep breath and resolutely brushed away her tears. As terrified as she was, she knew that there was simply nothing else that she could do.

The white rose was growing in her hands. She had no other option.

Let the Dark Prince find it, she thought. *Let him kill me for high treason! What does my life matter now anyway?*

Nothing mattered anymore, nothing at all. Her life was not worth living now that her roses were dead.

In fact, the thought of death was strangely comforting to her, even alluring. Death would release her from bondage and free her from the pain of living that she could no longer bear. She would be free of her wretched lonely existence. Free forever of the unbearable tyranny of the Dark Prince's cruel servants.

Yes. She would plant the white rose and be done with it.

Drawing in all her breath, Aidan made herself as thin as she could. Pressing her back against the stone wall next to the iron gate, she slid carefully around the thorny black roses all the way into the corner. Once she was behind the bushes, she found she couldn't see through them at all and she knew no one could possibly see her. In the corner there was enough space to move around freely.

She knelt down in the dirt and reached into her basket. Stabbing her trowel into the earth like a weapon, she went right to work. The planting only took a moment, for the soil was soft and loose after all her enemies' labors.

Fresh hot tears coursed down Aidan's cheeks as she dug, but she couldn't wipe her face with her dirty hands. Her tears dripped around the base of the rose and soaked into the ground.

With a few final pats of her trowel, she mounded the damp soil over the roots and packed it down firmly. The little rosebush seemed to settle into the earth with a sigh of joy. Its branches immediately stretched out and found the wall, where they began to spread gracefully, climbing in both directions along the corner. She could see more leaves and buds forming right before her eyes.

All at once the sweet fragrance of the tiny white roses enveloped her, rising up so strongly that it drove away the cloying scent of the black roses like the mountain wind pushing clouds across the sky.

But for the first time the healing roses failed to bring peace to Aidan's heart. Strangely she felt no joy at all in planting this, the most precious rosebush she had ever owned.

Her heart was as dead as the garden she had lost.

Not stopping even for a moment to admire her work, she stood up, wiped her hands on her dress, and picked up her basket of tools. Carefully she slid back between the stone wall and the Dark Prince's thorny bushes. Keeping her head down and her eyes on the flagstones so she wouldn't see the black roses, she fled through the wooden gate and out of the yard. Then she ran beneath the two bare arbors and into her shed, where she gently put her gardening tools away.

Chapter Thirty-Four

Stewart's Cruelty

Aidan took a deep breath and stared out of the carriage window at the tall grass swaying back and forth in the mountain wind. Its movements echoed the rhythm of her heart, which had been fluttering with tension ever since she had forced herself to get out of bed that morning.

The carriage jostled and bumped noisily as it made its way up the hill toward the mansion for her lunch appointment with Lady Fairhaven. She was feeling quite sick with dread over everything that had happened the day before, so much so that she had strongly considered sending Gatekeeper to offer her apologies and decline the invitation altogether.

But if living with Aunt Mara had taught her anything, it was that no matter what happened to her, no matter how much pain she was in, no matter how much she just wanted to stay in bed – life had to go on. She had to be strong and keep going and do the next thing that was required of her.

So here she was in the carriage, trying to push away her feelings of impending doom, hoping that her afternoon in the mansion would be enjoyable – but feeling like she really wanted to just turn around and go home.

Looking down at her trembling hands, which still bore the cuts from the broken dishes the day before, Aidan recalled Uncle Asa's cruel promise to return for her after leaving her locked in darkness for two days. Her heart beat faster as she wondered if he would be at the cottage waiting for her when she came home. What would he do when he found out she had escaped? What would she do when he came back?

The thought made Aidan feel sick to her stomach with fear.

As she looked out the window again, she searched the landscape thinking of her frightening encounter with the Knight. To her relief there was no sign of him anywhere. She wondered where he was and if he were still nearby somewhere or if he had returned to Everestaal.

And she wondered again why he had given her the rose.

It had been most dreadful to walk between the black rosebushes that morning on her way to the carriage. As she had passed through the gate, she had looked sideways toward the corner where she had planted the white rose, but she couldn't see it. Her guests never mentioned it, so she was reassured that they hadn't seen it either.

Aidan sighed. So many thoughts were tumbling in her mind, making her stomach churn right along with them. She saw the mansion above them on the hill and began to consider the afternoon ahead of her with Lady Fairhaven.

For perhaps the tenth time that morning she smoothed her navy blue taffeta skirt and the coordinating soft velvet jacket that Prince Bal'Davarius had given her. She was grateful to have such a fine outfit to wear to lunch, but at the same time she felt terribly self-conscious, for she had never set foot inside the mansion dressed in anything but mourning clothes or a servant's work dress.

Suddenly the full force of the noonday sunlight caught the jewels in the necklace at her throat. They glittered with rainbow fires and sent brilliant pinpoints of light scattering across the black velvet curtains like stars in the night sky. Startled, she stared at the lights in awe for a long moment before she realized what was happening.

She touched her beloved diamond necklace and leaned back against the velvet tufting, straightening her back and trying to carry herself like a lady. But beneath her finery her body ached and she couldn't stop trembling or shake that strange sense of foreboding.

Aidan's fingers brushed against the shiny pearl buttons that gleamed from the front of her white silk blouse. She tried once again to convince herself that it was fine to have them there. That it was proper to dress nicely and look lovely for an invitation to have lunch with a noblewoman.

That it was all right to be a friend and not a servant.

In addition to everything else that had happened in the last few days, Aidan knew that a great deal of her present fear had much to do with the way her relationship with Lady Fairhaven was changing. Why should a rich noblewoman want to have a friendship with the likes of her, a poor wretched orphan?

She had been very comfortable and even happy to be a maidservant, but she had absolutely no idea how to be a friend, for no one had ever wanted to be her friend before. And as much as she wanted to have a friend and to make Lady Fairhaven happy, something in her heart was pulling back and strongly resisting this change – but she had no idea why.

The sun suddenly darkened as they rolled through the shade beneath the huge old oak trees. Pride bellowed to the horses and Aidan felt the carriage begin to slow down.

She looked out the window at the mansion looming before them so huge and imposing, and just for an instant she was sure the front door was slightly ajar. But as the carriage came to a full stop she saw that it was indeed closed. Her heart fluttered again with dread as she wondered if she had imagined this.

The horses nickered and swished their tails as Greed leapt down from his rear perch to open the door for her.

"Thank you, Pride and Greed," she said as she stepped into the bright sunlight.

"Good day, Milady," Pride replied, tipping his leather cap as usual. Aidan lifted her skirt and hurried up the steps to the mansion entrance.

When the Fairhavens' stuffy butler opened the heavy front door for her, Aidan greeted him with a smile, mustering all her courage and trying to sound cheerful even as her cheeks were flaming with self-consciousness.

"Good morning, Stewart."

In return Stewart gave her a look as frigid as icy mountain wind and spoke no word of reply. As she stepped across the threshold he stood back and pointedly eyed her finery up and down, his piercing eyes narrow with suspicion. Aidan could tell that this was not just haughtiness. She shrank timidly into herself beneath his scrutiny, for his cold disapproval was obvious as he studied her elegant clothes.

At last he spoke, his voice stiff and formal.

"Lady Fairhaven has informed me that you will no longer be working for us – and that you will be joining her today for the midday meal."

"Yes, that's right," Aidan replied nervously.

The butler sniffed with open contempt and glared at her. He glanced around to make certain they were alone, then bent closer and lowered his voice.

"Tell me then, Aidan, how did all of this come about? Where did you get that carriage and horses? Where did you get those fine clothes – and those jewels?"

She was so shocked at his brusque questions that she didn't know what to say. When she failed to answer right away, Stewart continued, his words betraying his deep resentment.

"You seem to have suddenly acquired wealth and prestige. My Lady tells me you are no longer her maidservant, but are now to be welcomed here anytime as her honored guest. You came to us as poor hired help and then were given the highest position above all of the other women in the mansion!"

Aidan was stunned and speechless at Stewart's accusations – and very afraid of his anger.

"Let me tell you, Aidan, there are a good many loyal and faithful servants here from families who have served in the mansion for generations, all of whom deserve that honor much more than you. And now here you are, all dressed in jewels and silk – meaning to put on airs over the rest of us, no doubt!"

"Why, no, I – I have no such intention," she gasped. "I'm dressed this way to honor Lady Fairhaven. She has invited me for lunch –"

Stewart sniffed arrogantly.

"You don't deserve her invitation to lunch. You don't belong here."

Aidan felt her face burning with shame, for deep inside she knew he was right. Once again she was the outsider, even here, even after all this time.

Then she began to get angry at his condescending insults and snapped at him defensively.

"Lady Fairhaven chose to invite me! What should that matter to you? It certainly isn't any business of yours!"

"But I should say it most certainly is my business!" Stewart declared. "As Lord Fairhaven's valet and chief butler I oversee all of his estate. I am responsible for everything that happens here."

His eyes narrowed again with suspicion and contempt.

"Where did you get that necklace? How is it that you have been riding in that royal carriage? And what were you discussing with my Lord and Lady over tea yesterday? Answer me!"

"That isn't any concern of yours," she declared coldly, hoping he wouldn't notice how afraid she was at his questioning. "You would do well to mind your own business – and to keep your rude comments to yourself!"

Stewart drew in a sharp indignant breath and peered down his nose at her.

"Well," he snorted, "how you have changed! You were such a timid little thing when you first came here. But now that you're no longer a servant for us, here you are, acting as though you think you are mistress over me!"

At that, Aidan bristled with all the fury she had felt toward him for months.

"Perhaps I wouldn't have been so timid if you had been more kind to me! You never once answered my greetings in a friendly way. You're just a pompous old bully, and I've had quite enough of your insults and accusations. Now if you will excuse me, I have an appointment with Lady Fairhaven – and I fear you've made me very late!"

As she began to sweep past him, Stewart's face darkened with rage. He reached out and grabbed her, roughly pulling her back. Aidan cried out loudly in pain as his hand closed tightly around her upper arm where Uncle Asa had bruised her the day before. She cowered before him, suddenly terrified that he too was about to beat her or tear her clothing.

"Let me go!" she shouted.

Her frightened voice resounded across the large interior of the entry hall and echoed against the marble walls and floor. As she struggled to break free of his grasp, he gripped her arm still more firmly and she cried out in pain again.

"How dare you speak to me in such a manner!" he snarled. "My authority in this house is surpassed only by Lord and Lady Fairhaven themselves!"

"Let me go!" Aidan shouted again, trying to pull away from him. "You're hurting me!"

"I won't let you go until you tell me what you were talking about with them in the garden yesterday!"

Aidan was panicking at Stewart's rage. He seemed quite insistent to know about this, but she knew she couldn't reveal what they had discussed.

"I won't!" she cried stubbornly. "I refuse to tell you anything! If everything that goes on in this mansion is truly your business, I should think Lord Fairhaven would have told you himself! Why don't you go ask him?!"

Stewart was just beginning to open his mouth in reply when a deep baritone voice rumbled like thunder across the entry hall.

"And just what is it that you should ask me, Stewart?"

Aidan gasped and twisted around.

Lord Fairhaven was standing at the foot of the grand staircase. It was clear by his smoldering red countenance and flashing eyes that he was livid.

She put her hand to her mouth, a sick leaden feeling in her heart, wondering how much he had seen of their interaction.

Stewart froze, his face completely white. "My Lord," he said meekly.

"Take your hands off of her at once," Lord Fairhaven ordered.

Stewart immediately released his grip and Aidan pulled away from him, rubbing her throbbing arm with a trembling hand.

To her amazement, in his fury Lord Fairhaven spoke to Stewart in a crisp voice that was quiet and controlled.

"I trust that you will be able to give me a full explanation for your completely inexcusable behavior. It is a shame and a dishonor to the Fairhaven name that any servant of mine should treat a guest in my home so disgracefully – in particular a lady."

"I am deeply sorry, my Lord," Stewart declared, bowing low. "I assure you, it shall never happen again."

"You are quite right," Lord Fairhaven agreed. "It most certainly shall never happen again."

He turned to Aidan. His words indicated that he was not angry at her, but she was still terrified by his flushed countenance.

"Aidan, please accept my humble apologies for my butler's appalling behavior."

"My Lord, please, I can explain –"

He quickly cut her off with a wave of his hand and gently but firmly dismissed her.

"Lady Fairhaven is expecting you in the dining room. You mustn't keep her waiting."

"Yes – no – of course, my Lord," Aidan stammered.

She took one last guilty look at Stewart's ashen face. Then, keeping her head down, she picked up her skirt and hurried to the staircase. Never taking his eyes from his butler, Lord Fairhaven said nothing more to her as she passed by him and rushed up the steps.

At the second curve of the staircase, just out of sight from him, she stopped, for her heart was racing so fast she was struggling to catch her breath.

Far below she could hear Lord Fairhaven's resonant voice issuing a firm order.

"Stewart, I shall speak with you at once, privately, in your quarters."

Stewart's groveling reply came in a trembling high tenor.

"Yes, my Lord. At once, my Lord."

Lord Fairhaven's quick heavy footsteps thudded against the marble floor. Aidan could hear the staccato tapping of Stewart's patent leather shoes fading away after him down the first floor hallway.

She didn't know what to think. Part of her was relieved that justice was about to be served for Stewart's cruelty to her, for she had never liked him. But before she could even begin to savor the moment, a huge surge of guilt rose up in her heart that he should have to face Lord Fairhaven's wrath alone for what had happened between them, for she was certain that it was somehow all her fault.

Her impulse was to run after them to convince Lord Fairhaven that all the blame for the incident should be placed upon her, for as much as she disliked Stewart, she was deathly afraid of what he would do to her now that he had gotten into trouble on her account.

Aidan leaned heavily against the carved marble railing, her bruised arm still throbbing where Stewart had grabbed her. As she rubbed her arm and wondered what she should do, the memory of being beaten and molested by Uncle Asa the day before suddenly came back to her in a rush of horror.

For a chilling moment there seemed to be no air to breathe. She clutched the railing, terrified she would faint and fall down the stairs. When she finally managed to catch her breath, her voice came forth in a strangled cry.

At that moment she was startled by another unexpected voice, this one soft and gentle. It came from the second floor landing directly above her.

"Aidan, my dear – are you all right?"

She turned and looked up the stairs. There stood Lady Fairhaven, her hair silvery against a beautiful dark blue dress, her eyes huge with concern.

Relief flooded Aidan's heart. Suddenly the noblewoman's presence reassured her somehow that she would be protected and safe.

"My Lady," she whispered, and quickly climbed the stairs.

As she stepped onto the landing, Lady Fairhaven was watching her carefully.

"Whatever has happened to you, child? Your face – it's white as the mountain snow."

She reached out and took both of Aidan's hands in hers.

"Why, my dear, you're shaking. Your hands are like ice. Tell me what's wrong."

At her kind words and caring gesture, Aidan burst into tears.

"Oh – my Lady – it's all my fault! Everything – all my fault!"

The older woman quickly reached out and gathered Aidan into her arms. Aidan trembled and sobbed against her shoulder for a long moment, clinging to her. Lady Fairhaven held her close, whispering words of comfort and stroking her hair. Her tender voice was soft and soothing.

"Hush now, my child. Come, you must tell me what's happened. Everything will be all right now."

Chapter Thirty-Five

Lunch With Lady Fairhaven

Aidan had walked through the spacious dining room every day on her way to the kitchen for her midday meal. Everything about the elegant room was oversized, for it had been built and furnished long ago as a grand hall for large dinner parties. Its walls rose high above the floor to a pointed dark wood ceiling crisscrossed with heavy beams. At the four corners of the room immense wrought iron candelabras on tall stands each held dozens of tapers that were now fully ablaze.

The grey stone walls were hung with huge woven tapestries which seemed slightly faded with age but still added color to the room. Aidan thought they were beautiful and enjoyed looking at them because they were so detailed that she always found something new to see. Horses and dogs and all kinds of people walked or hunted in landscapes full of various flowers, trees and bushes. A castle on a hill was in the background of several of these scenes.

In Aidan's favorite, a knight on a white horse bent down to hand a rose to an elegant lady in front of a fountain. That scene had always made her think of her beloved fairy tale book about the Princess and her garden, but looking at it now suddenly reminded her of the Knight from Everestaal, and she shivered.

Although the tapestries were there to help prevent drafts, the dining hall still tended to be cold even in summer. A great fire was lit almost every day of the year, as one was roaring now, in the immense stone fireplace. On the wall above its thick wooden mantel two crossed swords were hung beneath a huge decorative bronze shield bearing the Fairhaven coat of arms.

Flanking the fireplace were two pairs of colorful stained glass windows, the feature of the great hall which most fascinated Aidan. The only windows in the room, they were tall and narrow and rose to pointed arches. Each was framed with a glass border of stylized oak leaves and acorns that surrounded scenes of various people and activities – a man and woman planting an oak tree, men building a stone tower, knights on horseback in battle, people tending livestock and fields. The beautiful glass cast colorful points of light across the hall when the sun shone through them, but on a cloudy day they only seemed to accentuate the darkness of the room.

Aidan had often studied the windows while walking to the kitchen. She knew that they depicted events in the lives of Lord Fairhaven's ancestors, but she had no idea who they were or what they were doing.

The room's heavy ornate furniture was made of finely carved and polished dark wood adorned with light colored fabrics and reflective decorations. The long rectangular dining table was surrounded by twenty-four chairs padded with gold brocade upholstery. The tabletop was covered along its full length by white linen and a long shiny blue and gold brocade table runner. The runner held cut crystal vases and several immense silver candelabras, each holding a dozen tall white tapers.

But the only flowers and lit candles that Aidan had ever seen on the table were at its end nearest the kitchen door where Lord and Lady Fairhaven ate their meals each day, his place at the head and hers at his right hand.

Now their places were set as usual along with a third across from Lady Fairhaven's with tableware of white linen napkins, fine silver, cut crystal glasses and light blue porcelain dishes edged with gold. The nearest candelabra was lit and its reflection gleamed from a crystal vase full of colorful roses.

As they walked quickly to the table Lady Fairhaven gestured to an attentive dark-haired servant.

"James, cold water, please."

As he quickly stepped forward, James gestured to other servants who were standing by a sideboard. He gracefully slid Lady Fairhaven's chair out from the table and held it for her as a footman came and held Aidan's chair. Another footman hastened to bring a pitcher and fill their crystal water glasses.

Aidan knew all the servants and her face flamed with embarrassment as she felt their curious eyes on her. She carefully picked up her heavy glass and drank deeply. The water was icy cold and reminded her of the rushing stream where she had built her stone tower.

"Thank you, James," said Lady Fairhaven. "Have the servants leave us alone for a few minutes. I shall ring for you when we are ready for the meal."

"Very good, my Lady," James replied, bowing to her. He signaled to the footmen, who hurried through the kitchen door in front of him. A moment later Aidan and Lady Fairhaven were alone.

"I'm so sorry, my Lady," Aidan said shyly. "I didn't mean to make such a fuss. I'm all right now."

"It's quite all right, my dear," Lady Fairhaven replied sincerely. "Now, please, tell me what's happened to upset you so."

Aidan poured out the whole story of her struggle with Stewart while Lady Fairhaven listened quietly. She was furious to hear about her butler's behavior.

"You've done nothing wrong, Aidan," she said firmly. "You are not at fault here. The way Stewart treated you was disgraceful and completely inexcusable. Imagine a butler greeting a visitor to our home in such a dreadful manner! Whether or not you have been a servant under his authority makes no difference whatsoever. We can't have such a thing going on behind our backs. Stewart must be punished severely."

"What do you think Lord Fairhaven will do to him?" Aidan asked.

"I don't know." Lady Fairhaven shook her head. "When he becomes angry, there is simply no telling what he might do. And very few things make him angrier than a rude servant."

Aidan remembered his flaring temper the day before when she had told him about the Knight attacking her carriage on his property. She still felt guilty about that, and now about the whole incident with Stewart as well.

"I'm frightened by my Lord's anger," she confessed timidly.

"I understand, but it was not directed at you," Lady Fairhaven said. "And I assure you, he would never actually hurt anyone. He is not like that. My husband is a most honorable man."

She paused, then added, "Personally, I should be quite happy if he would discharge Stewart altogether. I have never liked him."

Aidan knew Stewart wasn't popular among the staff, but it surprised her to discover Lady Fairhaven didn't like him either.

"I don't understand," she said. "Hasn't Stewart been your butler for a long time – your loyal servant?"

"Yes, he has," Lady Fairhaven agreed. "In fact, Stewart is one of a very few of our servants whose families have been with the Fairhavens for generations. He grew up here in the mansion and his father was butler and chief of staff before him. Because of his father's seniority in the household, he was groomed from childhood into his present position. He attends Malcolm as his personal valet and oversees the care of the entire mansion and the duties of all our other servants."

"Then – then you couldn't just discharge him," Aidan said. "He'll have nowhere else to go. What would he do?"

Lady Fairhaven gave Aidan a perplexed look.

"Why do you defend him? Stewart's fate isn't your concern."

Aidan looked down, embarrassed. "I'm afraid of him, my Lady. I'm afraid of what he'll do to me now that I've gotten him into so much trouble."

The familiar sapphire eyes were piercing and yet gentle.

"You have no reason to be afraid of Stewart," Lady Fairhaven told her firmly. "And I assure you, you are not the cause of his trouble. You see, there is far more to this situation than you know. Stewart has been thinking himself much too important for quite some time now. I believe that his high position has completely gone to his head, and I find myself trusting him less and less as time goes by. If Lord Fairhaven were to let him go, I would actually be very relieved."

She sighed and picked up her folded napkin, gently shaking it open.

"But right now I don't care to discuss the details of managing an unruly servant. I trust that my husband will see to it that Stewart is reprimanded severely and will take whatever measures he deems necessary. What about you, my child? Are you feeling better now?"

"Yes, much better," Aidan replied, although she still felt very guilty about Stewart.

"Good. Then let's enjoy our meal, shall we?"

Lady Fairhaven picked up a little silver bell that sat at her place. It made a lovely musical sound that brought an immediate response. The doorway that led to the kitchen opened and James came quickly to the table.

Aidan knew James and it seemed to her that he was everything Stewart was not. As the head kitchen steward, he oversaw the preparation and serving of every meal and was excellent at his job. He had been friendly to her from the first day she came to the mansion and she had often heard the other servants speaking highly of him. Although he was exacting and demanded the best from his kitchen staff, he was very kind and laughed frequently. His formal manner to the Fairhavens was always smiling and pleasant, never haughty or stuffy in the least.

Now he bowed slightly to Lady Fairhaven and asked, "Shall I commence with the serving, my Lady, or will you be waiting for my Lord?"

"It would seem that Lord Fairhaven has been detained. You may serve us now, please."

"Very good, my Lady," he replied, and hurried back through the door.

While they waited, Lady Fairhaven smoothed her napkin across her lap. Aidan copied her movements.

"This is all so lovely," she said nervously. "Thank you so much for inviting me. I think this room is very elegant. I have always admired it."

"Why, thank you, Aidan," replied Lady Fairhaven, smiling. "I'm glad you like this room. I suppose it is elegant, but I do wish it were brighter in here. The windows are beautiful but I have always thought this room rather dark and dreary. And so cold and drafty."

"Why is this room so different from the ballroom and the parlor?" asked Aidan. "Those rooms are very bright."

"Well, there are many reasons," Lady Fairhaven told her. "This room faces north and only has these stained glass windows. The ballroom and the parlor have clear windows that face south and let in more light throughout the day. And of course, those rooms are done in white marble and gold leaf and all those glorious pastel colors – so bright and cheerful. I much prefer being in them."

"They are very beautiful," Aidan agreed.

"This room is part of the original house – the very oldest section of the mansion," Lady Fairhaven said.

"I didn't know that."

"Yes, the mansion was begun long ago as a fortified castle during turbulent times when warfare was frequent. That was when the Fairhavens first came into power and began to rule this area. I'm not sure of the exact date, but I know it was about seven hundred years ago."

"Seven hundred years!" Aidan gasped.

Lady Fairhaven smiled at her amazement.

"Oh, yes, our family history stretches back to long, long ago." She gestured to the windows. "Those are scenes from the lives of those who built the original castle – the ancestors who began the Fairhaven family line. Over the centuries there have been all sorts of additions and changes made to this old house."

"I see," Aidan said. "So that is why some rooms are so different from others?"

"Yes, times grew peaceful and styles changed, and fortifications were no longer necessary," Lady Fairhaven said. "The ballroom and the parlor are part of the most recent section of the mansion, which was completed perhaps two hundred years ago. Since then, the only changes made have been minor ones to the interiors of some of the rooms. And the gardens and greenhouse, of course – that was built by Lord Fairhaven's parents."

At that moment James entered followed by two footmen, one of whom was pushing a wooden serving cart that held a large white porcelain tureen. As he lifted the cover, clouds of steam rose from a thick fragrant cream soup. He picked up a silver ladle and served the soup into small bowls while the other footman set out a plate of warm sliced bread. Aidan could easily have made a whole meal just of the delicious soup and bread, but she saved her appetite, knowing more was to come.

Lady Fairhaven motioned to James, who quickly brought a crystal carafe from the sideboard. "Aidan, would you care for some wine?"

"No, thank you," Aidan replied politely. "Just more water, please."

A quick gesture from James summoned the footman who had brought the water pitcher before, and he quickly came and refilled their glasses. James himself poured the wine and waited attentively while Lady Fairhaven tasted it and nodded her approval to him.

When they had finished their soup, the bowls and the serving cart were taken away and a parade of footmen emerged from the kitchen bearing an overwhelming array of dishes filled with steaming savory food. It felt strange indeed to be formally waited on by the other servants Aidan had come to know and she felt very self-conscious.

There was far too much food for the two of them, but she knew that the leftovers would be taken to the servants' hall, where she had eaten with the staff all summer. Lady Fairhaven seemed used to the rich food, even bored by it. She took tiny portions and picked at the things on her plate.

"You look so lovely today," she commented. "Is that one of your new outfits?"

"Thank you. Yes, it is," Aidan replied shyly. "I thought I should dress nicely today."

"That jacket is so becoming on you," Lady Fairhaven told her sincerely. "And I've been admiring your necklace – it's simply fabulous." She leaned forward to get a closer look at it. "Why, it must be worth a fortune."

Aidan felt a surge of pride as she lifted the chain to show off the diamond, which sparkled in the candlelight.

"Thank you, my Lady. My guests tell me that the Prince chose it for me himself from all his treasures."

Lady Fairhaven seemed amazed at this statement. For a long moment she stared quietly at the necklace.

"I do wish we knew what he intends for you," she said softly. "We shall talk more after the servants leave."

Just then clouds moved across the sky outside and brilliant sunlight poured into the dark room through the stained glass windows, sending rainbow colors dancing across the white tablecloth. Polished silver and cut crystal reflected the light as if they had just caught fire.

Aidan thought she had never seen anything so glorious and she stopped eating to stare at the sight. She had never enjoyed a meal so much, formal though it was, and thought it must surely be the most wonderful thing in the world to take meals in this ancient elegant hall every day.

At a moment such as this, with delicious food and pleasant conversation and beautiful colors filling the room, she found it easy to push the traumatic events of the day before far from her thoughts. But she knew Lady Fairhaven wanted to know what had happened after she had left the mansion, and the feelings of dread and impending doom she had fought in the carriage all came flooding back.

James summoned his staff, who came quickly to the table. As they carefully removed the plates and other dishes, another footman pushed the serving cart through the kitchen door for a second time. Aidan was feeling extremely full and was shocked to see more food coming.

Lady Fairhaven noticed her tension and smiled.

"Aidan, have you eaten your fill? Only tea and dessert are left."

"Dessert? Oh," Aidan said, not wanting to offend her. "Yes, that would be lovely. Thank you."

The footman positioned the cart at the end of the table in between the two of them. On the cart was a tall white cake topped with glazed fruit. Lady Fairhaven instructed him to cut two small pieces for them.

As they ate their cake, James came to the table with a gleaming silver tea service. He poured their tea and set their cups before them. Then, bowing slightly and smiling, he said, "I trust that the meal has been to your liking, my Lady, and that the service was satisfactory. May I bring you or Aidan anything else?"

"No thank you, James," Lady Fairhaven replied, smiling back up at him. "Leave us the tea, and that will be all. My highest compliments once again to the kitchen and to your staff. It was a very fine meal indeed, and as usual the service was exemplary."

"Very good, my Lady," James replied, his broad smile conveying his pleasure at her praise. "Thank you very much."

A moment later the kitchen door closed behind him and the two of them were alone again.

Lady Fairhaven held her cup in her hands and inhaled the fragrant steam for a long moment, then placed it back into its saucer without tasting the tea. She looked at Aidan with an anxious expression.

"I was so worried about you all last night," she confessed. "All this business with the attack and the Prince's servants – I've been terribly afraid because of the things we talked about yesterday. I feared that your guests would find that little rose and –" She stopped and shuddered, then took a deep quavering breath. "Is everything – all right?"

It made Aidan feel very uncomfortable to see that she was so worried.

"Oh," she said, "please, you mustn't worry about me, my Lady. Everything is fine."

She looked down into her teacup and sighed.

"Everything is fine," she lied again.

At that moment the sun abruptly disappeared behind clouds and the warm rays of colorful light faded, casting shadows between them across the table and leaving the room dark and cheerless.

Aidan picked up her cup. Even as its steamy warmth floated across her face, there was a coldness creeping into her heart that almost made her shiver. In the space of that shadowy instant, the memories she had so easily pushed from her mind a moment before came rushing back to her – all the traumatic events of the day before.

She yearned to confide in Lady Fairhaven and to trust in this newfound friendship between them. But long ago her fears had constructed protective barricades deep inside her heart that were as strong and fortified as the stone walls around her that had once been part of a castle to defend against enemies. If she were to reveal her private world of suffering, she was certain that her noblewoman friend would despise her.

"Aidan," Lady Fairhaven said sharply, interrupting her momentary reverie. "Everything is *not* fine. I can see it in your face – and in your hands. How did they become cut like that?"

Startled, Aidan looked at her hands with shame and gently set the teacup back into its saucer.

"I broke a dish yesterday and cut myself. It was an accident. I'm all right."

"Those look like very deep cuts."

Lady Fairhaven was quiet a moment, then said sternly, "Aidan, please don't lie to me in the hopes of sparing my feelings."

Aidan stared at her in shock, her heart stricken with guilt.

"I'm sorry," she whispered. "I'm not lying about the cuts – I never meant to lie to you. It's just that – I mean – I just don't want you to worry about me. I'm sorry."

"Oh, my dear, my dear," said Lady Fairhaven sympathetically, "I do understand. But of course I'm worried about you. I'm terribly worried about this whole affair with everything that's happened to you. Now please, you must be honest with me. What did you do with the little white rose? I take it you were able to keep it hidden from those guests of yours."

Aidan took in a deep breath. How could she even begin to explain what had happened to the rose? She would have to reveal everything that Uncle Asa had done to her, including that he had torn her work uniform and she had burned it in her woodstove.

Finally she said, "Yes, I did hide it. They didn't find it."

"Where is it now? Surely it must have wilted," Lady Fairhaven said. "Oh, how I wish you had just burned it!"

The shadows suddenly lifted and glorious colors spilled across the table as the sun burst through the windows again. In that moment Aidan knew what to say.

"Well – yes – actually, I did burn it. In my woodstove."

Lady Fairhaven looked at her in surprise.

"I thought you would never do that. And the pouch and the silk? Did you burn those too?"

"Yes – they were burned too," Aidan said.

Lady Fairhaven looked visibly relieved, as though a crushing weight had just been lifted from her shoulders.

"Oh! This is such good news! I know you loved that rose, but burning it was the right thing to do."

She picked up her teacup and drank.

"Then we have nothing more to worry about. The evidence is destroyed and you can't be arrested. Oh, what a load off my mind! You can't imagine, child."

Aidan was relieved to realize she didn't need to tell Lady Fairhaven the details of how the rose ended up in the woodstove or that she had burned her uniform. She decided to leave the matter at that and not tell her that the rose had miraculously survived the fire and had somehow put forth roots and grown into a small bush.

"Yes, my Lady," she said simply. She picked up her teacup.

"And your guests – was everything all right with them last night?"

A torrent of memories went through Aidan's mind in a momentary rush of scenes. Uncle Asa beating her and locking her in the closet. Abuse's family destroying her garden. Doubt's family planting the Dark Prince's black roses. The little white rose growing in the corner of the stone wall, watered with her bitter tears.

At last she said softly, "Yes, my Lady, everything was fine. I hid the rose and then I burned it and – and then I spent some time in my garden."

"Oh, my dear, I'm so glad," Lady Fairhaven said. "I know how much you love your beautiful garden. It must be such a comfort for you!"

At that moment Lord Fairhaven entered the dining room.

Lady Fairhaven brightened in his presence, as she always seemed to, and greeted him warmly. She lifted her hand to him as Aidan jumped to her feet.

"Hello, my dearest."

"Good afternoon, Eleanora," he replied to her without smiling. "You look lovely today."

He took her hand and quickly touched his lips to it, then turned to Aidan with a slight bow.

"Hello, Aidan. Please, you may be seated. I didn't have a chance earlier to tell you that you also look lovely today. Have you ladies been enjoying your meal together?"

His perfunctory tone did not match his pleasant words. His face was flushed and it was clear that he was still quite upset.

"Oh, yes, my Lord," Aidan replied shyly. "Thank you." She sat back down and nervously smoothed her napkin on her lap.

"It was a lovely meal," Lady Fairhaven said. "Will you be joining us now?"

"I believe I would just like some tea and dessert," he said.

He sat down between them in his chair at the end of the table and shook out his napkin as she rang the little silver bell. Servants hastened to serve him fresh tea and a large slice of cake.

When the three of them were alone again, Lady Fairhaven asked him about what had happened with their butler.

"You needn't worry about Stewart any longer, Eleanora," Lord Fairhaven replied.

His words were curt and Aidan immediately felt strong tension between them. He cut a large forkful of cake with a quick sure stab that made her jump.

"After witnessing what happened this morning, it was clear to me that the problem was much more serious than I had thought, and indeed –" His eyes met his wife's. "– the situation is exactly as you have suspected. We went to his quarters and I confronted him about everything."

He ate the bite of cake and stabbed another.

"Perhaps this will teach me to listen to you more attentively when you tell me of your concerns."

Lady Fairhaven's eyes flashed with a distinct gleam of triumph. Aidan could tell she was very carefully maintaining her composure as she spoke calmly.

"Then you have dismissed him, beloved?"

"Yes," he replied crisply. "I have relieved him of all his responsibilities and told him he is to pack his things. He will be leaving the mansion within the hour."

Aidan gasped. Before she could think, she burst out, "Oh, no – this is all my fault! You can't dismiss him – he's served you all his life!"

Lord Fairhaven stopped eating and turned to her, his face now scarlet. Fire snapped in his bright blue eyes and his voice was tight with careful self-control as he answered her.

"Aidan, I am fully aware of that. But when a servant comes to think altogether too highly of himself, there can be no place in my home for such deplorable behavior. It is my right as master of this illustrious household to do exactly as I see fit with any member of my staff, no matter how long they have served me. So I have dismissed him."

He speared another bite of cake in a gesture that clearly communicated his rage.

"What's done is done, and as I live, I shall not alter my decision!"

Aidan withered in the heat of his rebuke, terrified at his anger and painfully aware that until yesterday she also had been a servant in his household. Did he think she too had come to think altogether too highly of herself?

"I'm sorry, my Lord," she whispered meekly. "I shouldn't have spoken out like that. It was wrong of me. I'm very sorry."

"Please, Malcolm," Lady Fairhaven said. "Aidan feels responsible for what happened and is only concerned about what will become of Stewart."

Lord Fairhaven finished his last bite of cake and put down his silver fork. Speaking quietly but still firmly, he said, "Aidan, you are in no way responsible for what happened this morning. Please do not blame yourself. And please be assured that I am not without mercy. I have not forgotten his family's loyalty or his years of service to me. Rather than press charges, I've ordered the guards to take Stewart to Clearview this afternoon, where he will work in my mill. He'll be paid adequately and will live comfortably in one of my rental houses. But he has been relieved of all his duties in the mansion, and with them his high position. As I live, he'll not set foot on this hill again."

He picked up his cup, which looked tiny in his huge hand. As he drank his tea an uncomfortable silence hung between the three of them. Clouds again passed over the sun outside the windows and all their colors seemed to fade into the dark shadows of the room.

Then Lady Fairhaven spoke up very softly.

"Beloved, does this mean that you will be meeting with your lawyer soon?"

At that Lord Fairhaven's body went rigid as his temper rose to a crescendo. His empty teacup clattered into the saucer and he glared at her.

"Eleanora. I am fully aware of all that I must do," he snapped. "Yes, I have already sent for Martin, and I have no doubt that he is on his way here at this very moment, for he knows he'll be paid handsomely for his services on such short notice. I hope that this now makes you happy, for I know how much you've wanted me to do this for a very long time."

He patted his mouth with his napkin and tossed it onto his plate.

"Now if you will excuse me, I have some important business to attend to. Good afternoon, ladies."

Before Aidan could stand up, he was on his feet. They watched in silence as he stormed angrily out of the room.

He did not kiss his wife's hand.

Chapter Thirty-Six

The Invitation

Lady Fairhaven sighed softly. "You must forgive him, Aidan. I have rarely seen him so angry. But I'm sure he didn't mean to take it out on us."

Aidan was silent, still shaken by Lord Fairhaven's temper.

"Of course, he wasn't angry with you. He was angry with me."

The noblewoman sighed again.

"I've been pushing him to dismiss Stewart for quite some time, and it's annoyed him greatly. Now he's furious to find out I was right all along while he dismissed my concerns. It's deeply hurt his pride."

She picked up the teapot and refilled their cups.

"And of course, he's most angry at Stewart himself – his butler and valet – a servant he has trusted for many years."

"My Lady, I don't understand any of this," Aidan confessed. "But I still feel like it's all my fault."

"No, Aidan, you mustn't feel that way," Lady Fairhaven replied firmly. "Stewart did this to himself. In fact, I am most grateful to you for what happened today. If Malcolm hadn't seen you struggling in the entry with him, I don't think he ever would have let himself admit that Stewart was anything but an excellent butler. But I saw his character much more clearly. He's just a pompous conceited fool."

She hesitated before going on, then added, "He's also a liar and a thief."

Aidan gasped.

"I've had good reason to suspect that Stewart has been stealing from us for some time now. I've mentioned it repeatedly to Malcolm, but because I was never able to prove anything, he refused to believe me and kept defending Stewart. I can't blame him, for they were friends of a sort – and I know only too well how difficult it is for people in our position to find any type of friend here in Hidden. Even a friend like Stewart is better than none at all."

She sighed.

"I'm sure he must feel deeply betrayed right now. He trusted Stewart with everything in the household. But from what he just told me, he has found evidence that our butler has indeed been taking advantage of us."

"So that's what he meant when he said he wouldn't press charges," Aidan said.

Lady Fairhaven nodded. "Under the circumstances, Malcolm is being most generous to him. I'm surprised he trusts him enough now even to keep him on as a common laborer. But for someone like Stewart, such a demotion will be a complete disgrace. To be stripped of his high position and sent off to do physical labor in a mill – and to be banished from the mansion where he and his family have always lived – that will be more than adequate punishment."

"But I still don't understand," Aidan said. "If Lord Fairhaven isn't pressing charges, why is it so urgent for him to meet with his lawyer?"

Lady Fairhaven looked directly into her eyes.

"My husband is compelled to change his will without delay."

Now Aidan was completely confused. "Change his will?"

The sapphire blue eyes were suddenly filled with agony.

"You see, Aidan, because we've never had any children to carry on the Fairhaven name, and because of his high position in our household, Stewart stood to inherit the mansion and all that we have. He was our heir."

Aidan gasped. "Your heir!"

"Yes, our heir – our only heir, by Malcolm's choice. The reason he was so vain was that he knew he would eventually become master of the Fairhaven estate – and a very rich and powerful man."

Her voice became bitter.

"Stewart is the closest thing to a son that Malcolm has ever had – and a wretched excuse for a son, indeed! But you see, that is how things have ended up for us."

Lady Fairhaven's eyes were filling with tears. In the colored light from the windows her face suddenly looked very old and deeply lined, etched with the sad weariness that comes from bearing painful burdens over a long period of time. She looked down into her teacup to hide her tears, but her voice shook with emotion as she continued.

"When we die, the great Fairhaven name and lineage will become a thing of the past. As if that weren't bad enough in itself, you can't imagine how greatly it's pained me to know that an unworthy servant, and a dishonest one at that, would one day take possession of our beloved houses and all of our holdings. That vile arrogant fool! He's not good enough even to be our lowest servant, let alone lord of this house!"

Her hands were trembling with anger and hatred. Aidan was frightened to see her like this. But as she looked up and brushed the tears from her eyes, her face brightened.

"I'm so grateful that he's leaving – you have no idea. Tonight I shall sleep peacefully over this at last. But Malcolm will hold a grudge for a long time. That's the way he is."

Composed and regal once again, she picked up her teacup. Aidan was shaken by her emotional confessions and didn't know what to say. For a long moment the two of them sipped their tea in thoughtful silence.

Then Lady Fairhaven gently placed her cup into its saucer, looked at Aidan's face again, and quietly changed the subject.

"Aidan – I told you that if you didn't feel safe in your cottage you were welcome anytime to come here to the mansion. I should like for you to come right away and live with us – permanently."

Completely caught off guard by this sudden generous invitation, Aidan stared at Lady Fairhaven in surprise.

"I've been thinking," she continued, "that with winter coming on, it will be very difficult for you to go back and forth, and so hard for you to be all alone in your cottage. If you lived here, you would want for nothing – and you would be perfectly safe."

Aidan considered all that she was offering.

To live in the mansion would be like a dream come true. Every day she would be surrounded by beauty and comfort and luxury. She would enjoy sumptuous meals in this elegant room. There would be many books and much time to read them. Perhaps she could even learn to play musical instruments. Best of all, she would have a friend to spend time with throughout the long lonely winter, which was always such a hard season in the mountains.

It was a most tempting invitation.

But – permanently?

She was terrified of Lord Fairhaven's temper and still not sure she could fully trust this new friendship with Lady Fairhaven.

And what would the servants of Prince Bal'Davarius do if she left them to go live in the mansion? Would they try to stop her? What would their Master do?

And what about the white rose? How could she leave it behind? She wondered how it was faring in the corner of her garden. What would happen if her guests discovered it? For all she knew, perhaps they already had.

Aidan very much wanted to accept the invitation, but her fears and doubts were strong. She knew it would not be that simple to just say yes.

"Thank you, my Lady," she said at last. "That is most kind of you. But I – I just don't know."

Lady Fairhaven blinked in surprise.

"Why wouldn't you want to come live in the mansion? Nothing can harm you here. Your guests – even if that little rose has been burned, they are still frightening you. I can see it in your face. Please, my dear, come stay with me. You'll be completely safe here."

Aidan was not at all sure she believed that last statement, for she knew that no matter where she was, she was still guilty of high treason and her life was at stake. Her fears were compelling her to pull back hard and resist Lady Fairhaven's gentle but firm urging to stay.

Yet she really didn't want to go back and live in the cottage either. She could not understand her mixed feelings.

"I don't know, my Lady," she said. "To leave my guests and live here – I don't know what they might do if I just left them. Or what Prince Bal'Davarius will do."

Lady Fairhaven was quiet for a moment. Her disappointment showed in her face, which still looked weary and old in the colored light. Then she smiled, but her eyes were sad. She shook out her napkin and began folding it.

"You are right, of course, and I suppose this is a big decision for you. But the invitation is open to you whenever you should wish to accept it. And I do hope you will."

She sighed and laid her napkin neatly on the table.

"But right now, I suppose I need to talk to my husband and try to calm him down a bit before his lawyer arrives."

She smoothed the napkin thoughtfully with her hands. Then, apparently not about to give up so easily after all, she looked at Aidan again and said, "Why don't you at least stay the afternoon and have supper with us? You could even spend the night to see if you would like it here."

Aidan was feeling very uncomfortable at the noblewoman's insistence.

"Thank you, my Lady," she said as graciously as she could, "but I think I just need to go home for awhile."

Lady Fairhaven looked confused and hurt, and Aidan immediately felt guilty.

"It isn't necessary for you to bring clothes," she persisted. "I have clothes here that I know will fit you. If they don't, I'll have them altered. I have everything here that you could possibly need."

She didn't wait for another answer.

"Stay with me, Aidan," she begged. "Please. We would both be so alone all winter, and you cannot stay another night in your cottage if you're not safe there."

Her eyes and voice betrayed genuine desperation.

"Please, Aidan. Please, say you'll stay here, at least just for tonight. I'm frightened for you. I just need to know you are safe."

Aidan suspected that Lady Fairhaven was quite used to getting her own way, but it was clear that this matter was of utmost importance to her.

It was also clear that she wasn't about to stop pressuring, leaving Aidan backed into a corner without much choice but to accept the invitation.

Finally she smiled shyly and nodded. Perhaps she was just being foolish to refuse such a generous offer. She knew she really wanted to accept it and couldn't understand at all what was making her pull back.

But there was still the matter of the white rose.

"All right, my Lady," she said. "But let me go and fetch some things from the cottage, and then I will come back to stay for tonight."

The light that suddenly flared in Lady Fairhaven's dark eyes was jubilant. Her whole countenance lit up, suddenly filled with fresh energy and renewed youth. Aidan was startled at the unexpected change, for she had never seen her so radiantly happy.

"Wonderful!" she exclaimed. "Oh, I'm so glad, child. I'll make sure everything is ready for you when you return."

She rang the silver bell with vigor and James rushed in from the kitchen.

"Yes, my Lady, have you finished with the tea service?"

"Yes, James, but have one of the others attend to it. Aidan is going home now and I would like you to personally see her to the front door. I must go meet with Lord Fairhaven right away in his library."

As they crossed the room, she tucked her arm firmly through Aidan's and patted her hand. Behind them James summoned the waitstaff with a gesture and then quickly followed them into the hallway.

"Aidan, you have no idea how I've worried. I'm so relieved that you're going to return to stay."

Lady Fairhaven squeezed her arm tightly in the crook of her own. She was excited as a child.

"You'll want for nothing as long as you are living with us. You'll be completely safe here."

Aidan nodded, taken aback at Lady Fairhaven's high spirits – and extremely guilty that she didn't feel anything close to the same way.

But the noblewoman didn't notice her reluctance at all. She talked on enthusiastically about the things they would do together.

"You can help me get the rose garden ready for winter," she said. "And we'll begin music lessons right away."

At the bottom of the grand staircase they paused before parting company. Lady Fairhaven smiled broadly at Aidan, her face beaming with joy.

"I'm so grateful that you've decided to stay. It's been so lonely for me in this big old house – you have no idea. And now I won't spend another sleepless night worrying about your safety."

Aidan was mortified to think that Lady Fairhaven had actually lost sleep over her. She now felt completely confused and miserable, but she forced a smile.

"I'm glad I've decided to stay too," she lied softly.

"Oh, my dear, I do hope so," Lady Fairhaven said, squeezing both her hands. "I'll see you for supper then. You'll come back before dark?"

"Yes, of course."

"Splendid!"

She turned to her steward.

"James, if Aidan's carriage isn't waiting for her, call for mine and accompany her. Instruct Andrew to take her home. The carriage will wait there for her and you will help her as needed. She will be gathering some things and returning here."

"Yes, my Lady," James replied, bowing slightly.

Lady Fairhaven turned her bright smile to Aidan again and embraced her firmly. "Good afternoon to you then, my dear child."

"Yes. Thank you, my Lady."

Aidan turned to cross the entry and James followed two steps behind her. When they reached the front door, she stopped and looked back.

Lady Fairhaven was still standing at the foot of the stairs, watching her silently. Her face was shining, but her eyes had that wistful look that Aidan had seen before.

With a slight bow James pulled open the heavy front door, smiling in his friendly attentive way that Aidan liked, and followed her as she stepped outside. She felt a huge surge of relief when she saw Pride and Greed waiting at the bottom of the steps, for she would have been mortified to go home in Lady Fairhaven's carriage with her servant, no matter how nice he was.

At the sight of her carriage, Aidan saw James freeze and his eyes go wide with shock. She knew he couldn't miss recognizing that it was a royal coach with the Prince's crest on its door. But he kept his feelings to himself, and after a few seconds he turned to her with a gracious smile.

"Is this your carriage, Aidan?"

"Yes, it is," she said.

"Very good," he said pleasantly. "We shall be seeing you for supper, then?"

"Yes," she replied. "Thank you, James."

As Aidan hurried down the steps, Pride tipped his cap to her. "Good afternoon, Milady!" he called. Greed pulled open the door for her and she climbed into the carriage.

"Home, please, and hurry," she instructed as she settled herself onto the seat.

As Greed shut the door, she looked out the window to see James still standing at the top of the steps staring in amazement.

Pride called affectionately to his horses and with a lurch the carriage was on its way down the hill, jostling noisily over the rutted dirt road.

Aidan leaned back against the velvet cushions, face flaming, heart pounding, barely able to breathe for tension. Within the next few minutes she was quite sure the entire mansion staff would know all about her lunch with Lady Fairhaven, her fine clothes and jewels, and her royal carriage. No doubt they were already buzzing over what had happened between her and Stewart – and the fact that Lord Fairhaven had banished him from the mansion in part because of it.

The thought of going back there now filled her with dread, but she had made a promise – a promise to spend one night. But she was sure that Lady Fairhaven had misunderstood and seemed to be expecting her for the entire winter.

Aidan was still mystified about her mixed feelings. Living in the mansion permanently would surely be the best thing that could ever happen to her. She knew she had nothing to gain by leaving there and perhaps everything to lose by going back to the cottage.

The only thing that was drawing her there now was the white rose. She was anxious to know how it was faring in her garden. No matter how dangerous it was, she couldn't leave it behind. There had to be a way to dig it up and take it with her back to the mansion.

Aidan sighed and turned her attention to planning what she would do when she got to the cottage. Knowing that Lady Fairhaven would provide for her every need, she decided she would take with her only the white rosebush and the money she had saved. She would change into one of her remaining two work uniforms and leave behind everything the Dark Prince had given her.

This decision was not an easy one for her to make by any means. It tore Aidan's heart to think of leaving all her beautiful new clothes and jewelry behind. She reached longingly for the diamond necklace at her throat and wistfully caressed its cold sharp stones. Having had a most tantalizing taste of riches, she knew it would be next to impossible now to give them up. But she also knew she couldn't take them with her.

She comforted herself with the thought that all of her needs would be more than met as long as she was living in the luxury of the mansion. No doubt the clothes Lady Fairhaven would provide for her would be every bit as lovely. The safety and security she would find behind the stone walls of the mansion would be worth any sacrifice.

Her biggest problem now, of course, was how she would dig up the white rose and take it with her. The actual gardening work of uprooting the little bush was the least of her worries, since she had done such work many times. But it would be extremely difficult to slip in and out behind the black roses without being seen and without being scratched by those terrible thorns. It would be even more difficult to hide the white rose when she brought it out from behind the other bushes. Most difficult of all would be getting to the mansion in the carriage with the concealed rosebush without raising any suspicions of what she was doing and without letting her guests know why she was going to the mansion at all – or that she had no intentions of ever coming back.

That was when Aidan fully realized the impossibility of her situation.

Because she couldn't go back to the mansion in her carriage. Somehow she would have to dig up the rosebush and carry it with her in her hands as she escaped on foot to the safety of the mansion, all before her absence was even noticed by her many guests.

For if she were truly forsaking everything Prince Bal'Davarius had given her, she would have to leave behind her beautiful royal carriage as well.

Aidan's heart broke. Devastated, she stroked the soft velvet cushions with great sadness. Giving up Pride's royal carriage would be the hardest thing of all.

At that moment they reached the cobblestones of Hidden's main street and the carriage wheels began to clatter roughly. Suddenly Aidan's heart skipped a beat. With everything else happening to her, she had forgotten all about Uncle Asa!

To her relief the street was quiet and he was nowhere in sight.

But all the rest of the way home she shook with fear. How completely foolish it had been to leave the safety of the mansion! As far as Uncle Asa knew, she was still locked in the closet beneath the stairs – and he had said he was coming back for her!

What if he had returned to her cottage while she was gone? What if he were there even now, waiting for her?

Aidan's panic instantly dissolved any remaining doubts over living in the mansion. When Lady Fairhaven had offered her such a kind and generous invitation, she had also unknowingly offered her certain protection from Uncle Asa's terrible abuse.

By the time Aidan reached her gate, her eagerness to return to the safety of the mansion was so strong that she was squirming on the velvet cushion and her heart was pounding in anticipation of what she might find at her cottage.

When at last the carriage rolled to a stop, Aidan waited impatiently as Greed hastened to open the door for her. "Thank you, Greed," she said crisply as she stepped down onto the sidewalk. He bowed slightly and closed the carriage door behind her.

Aidan turned to enter her front gate and took a step forward, bending to brush some dust from her navy blue skirt. As she looked back up, she froze.

Something was different – and very wrong.

Then she gasped in complete shock as she found herself staring at the most bizarre thing she had ever seen in her life.

Chapter Thirty-Seven

Isolation's Chain

All along the top of the stone wall surrounding Aidan's house someone had secured great rings of iron, apparently by drilling or hammering, although the wall itself seemed completely undamaged. Hanging down from the rings in front of the wall was a heavy black iron chain, its links so large her hand would easily have passed through the center of one of them. She took a step closer and saw that the immense chain ran the length of the stone wall and seemed to circle around the corners and presumably all around the cottage. Its two ends were secured together by a huge black iron padlock which hung down inside the iron gate.

Aidan was so stunned at the sight that it took a long moment to find her voice. At last she cried, "What is the meaning of this?! Pride! Greed! What is this chain?"

But Pride and Greed never heard her. Pride was already steering the carriage around the corner of the wall toward the old stable. Greed turned and flashed his malevolent grin at her as he waved from his perch at the rear of the carriage.

"Where is Gatekeeper?" she cried helplessly after him. Then she whirled back to the gate and shouted furiously at the house. "Gatekeeper! Come out here at once!"

Immediately the front door of the cottage opened and two men stepped outside. Gatekeeper was in the lead, hurrying along the walk toward her. The man behind him was a tall muscular stranger.

As they came toward her down the flagstone path, flanked on both sides by rows of tall pillars thickly covered with black roses, Aidan could see that there was nothing timid about this powerful man. She shuddered with revulsion at the thought of another new guest from the Dark Prince.

Her new guest was dressed in the same traditional clothes that Aidan had seen some of the men in Hidden wear when they went mountain climbing. His outfit featured a tan chamois shirt and heavy brown suede breeches with an attached bib and green embroidered suspenders. The breeches were tucked into thick tweedy wool socks that covered his muscular shins to his knees. On his feet he wore tall heavy tan leather boots that laced to well above his ankles. His brown suede alpine hat had a woven red and green ribbon band above its narrow brim and was decorated on one side with a small striped feather.

Around his waist was a leather tool belt that held a small pickaxe, a thick coil of rope, and several other tools attached with clips. As he walked, the tools jangled and the wooden handle of the pickaxe bumped against his hip while sharp metal cleats on the soles of his boots tapped firmly against the pavement stones. Even in those heavy boots he strode leisurely toward the gate with an agility in his confident movements that was surprisingly graceful.

"Good afternoon, Miss," called Gatekeeper cheerfully. "Another new guest has arrived today from the Master."

"I see that, Gatekeeper," she replied with open annoyance. "What is the meaning of this chain?" Turning to her new guest, hoping he would not be able to tell that her knees were quaking with trepidation beneath her skirt, she demanded, "Are you the one responsible for putting this chain upon my wall?"

"Yes, Aidan, it's my chain," the man replied. He smiled without warmth and spoke in a deep gravelly voice. "I fastened the rings to the wall and hung the chain myself while you were gone this afternoon."

Aidan was astounded, for the chain was immense.

"You did all that work today? Alone?"

He shrugged as if such a task were nothing for him.

"The Master gave me orders to hang my chain upon the wall all around your house without delay. Since this was the work he gave me to do here, yes, I did it alone. It wasn't hard at all. I've installed hundreds of such chains over the years."

Aidan softened her voice and addressed this powerful guest more respectfully.

"What is your name, please, sir?"

"I am Isolation."

Aidan's new guest was ruggedly handsome. He had a beardless square jaw with a deeply cleft chin set into a wide craggy face. She guessed that he was perhaps in his fifties because his curly light brown hair beneath the hat was streaked at the temples with golden grey, but he stood so straight and tall and his build was so muscular that she couldn't be sure. It was obvious that, whatever his age, Isolation was no stranger to heavy physical work.

There was something very familiar about his countenance that made her feel uneasy, as if she had somehow seen his face before but couldn't quite place where.

Then Aidan noticed that hanging from the front of his tool belt was a ring of much smaller black chain, which – like the gold chain around Gatekeeper's neck – held a large key, but this one was made of black iron.

"How shall I come into my yard?" she asked. She gestured to the chain at his belt. "Is that the key to this lock?"

He smiled at her as if he were pleased that she had noticed the key, but his furtive dark eyes and intimidating manner gave her the distinct feeling that he was keeping a secret of some kind.

"Yes, this is the key," he said. "I'll unlock it for you now, but once you come inside the gate, I must lock it again behind you. These are my orders from the Master."

Isolation reached for the ring of chain at his belt. As soon as he touched the key it somehow came right off the ring and dropped into his huge strong hand. He stepped up to the gate and had the padlock open before Aidan could blink her eyes. As he removed it, the two ends of the immense iron chain fell heavily away from the gate with a great clanking sound and hung, still swinging, from the iron rings attached to the stone wall.

Gatekeeper came forward and opened the gate for her, but Aidan remained standing where she was, afraid to pass through it and not at all sure what she should do.

"If I come inside and you lock your chain behind me, how will I get out again? Has the Master now commanded that I be imprisoned in my own house?"

Isolation shook his head.

"The Master has no such intention for you, Aidan. You see, my chain is not meant so much to keep you in, but rather to keep others out."

"I don't understand," Aidan said. "If others can't come inside the chain from out here, then it stands to reason that I'll be trapped inside alone."

Isolation made no attempt to deny that statement.

"It's quite simple, really," he said. "My chain has been placed here for your protection. You see, the Master is most concerned for your safety."

"My safety!" exclaimed Aidan in amazement. "And where was your protecting chain yesterday, when I was attacked and beaten in my own home?!"

"That's precisely why I was sent here to install it," Isolation explained patiently. "We are aware of the traumatic events that occurred here yesterday afternoon, and the Master is anxious to keep such a thing from happening again. Now my chain has been secured to your wall. No outsider can enter unless we can be quite certain that no harm will come to you."

He smiled at her again.

"So come right in, Aidan, and enjoy the protection of my beautiful chain. There is nothing to be afraid of. You'll be completely safe here."

Aidan felt a cold shiver course down her spine. Weren't those the exact same words Lady Fairhaven had said to her about staying in the mansion?

It was clear to her that she couldn't trust this new guest any more than she could trust the rest of the Dark Prince's servants. The traumatic events of the day before had actually happened because of them, and she knew that. She suspected that Isolation's forbidding chain would not protect her from any harm at all – indeed, she was quite certain that stepping inside it would actually put her in far greater danger.

Why were all these things happening to her?!

Aidan wished she could figure out what it was about him that seemed so familiar. There was something chilling that seemed to radiate from his secretive dark eyes, a coldness that brought to her mind the night Fear had come to her.

But the feeling in her heart wasn't exactly fear. It was an uneasiness much more vague, an instinctive sense that all was not well. This servant of Prince Bal'Davarius made her want to run away like a deer that knows the hunter is upon her. He made her want to be totally alone, safe with no one around to hurt her.

But the only place of safety she had now was the Fairhaven mansion.

With all her heart she wished now that she had never left there. She wondered if she would be able to get back by nightfall, as she had promised Lady Fairhaven. Indeed, staring at that huge black chain, she wondered if she would be able to go anywhere else ever again.

Now Aidan understood what had made her pull back from the noblewoman's invitation and made her want to go home and just be alone. Isolation had been working to hang his chain all the time she had been with her, and like all his fellow servants, he possessed a strange power over her.

What a fool she had been to leave the mansion to come back here!

Standing her ground outside the gate, she stalled and began to question him in hopes of learning more about this intimidating new guest.

"I know that almost all of you have been with me for a very long time, some since I was in my mother's womb. Tell me, please, how long have you been with me?"

"I have also been with you since before you were born," Isolation told her.

Aidan watched his face carefully as she said, "You've been with me since my mother left her own country, then."

She was hoping to trick him into confirming what she was certain she already knew – that her mother had come from Everestaal. If he became tense or seemed suddenly nervous about divulging too much information, she would know.

But Isolation only smiled at her, perfectly calm and confident.

"Yes, that's right," he answered. "You see, Aidan, I am the governor of this district, or actually, I prefer to think of myself as its prince. I rule over this entire mountain range, from its deepest valleys to its rolling foothills to the snowy tops of its highest peaks. The moment your mother entered into my mountains, she put herself under my firmly established government – and you, her unborn child, as well. I've ruled over you since before your birth, and I'll continue to rule over you for as long as you live here."

Isolation opened his arms wide and swept his hands broadly around his head, indicating that Aidan should look around herself to the snow-covered peaks rising so cold and imposing above the town.

"Yes, these are my mountains, given to me many generations ago to oversee by our wise Master himself. I own every town and village nestled among them – they are all mine to rule. But Hidden is my very special stronghold. It's the most isolated and lonely town in all of Davarius."

Aidan had no doubt of that.

"It must be very difficult for you to travel to all your towns," she said. "They're so far apart – separated by these huge mountains."

She was hoping he would answer with information that would help her leave Hidden.

"It's no trouble for me at all," he told her cheerfully, gesturing to his clothes and to the tools hanging from his belt. "As you can see, I'm well prepared to tackle even the toughest alpine terrain at any time. I know every passage and shortcut throughout my region. Some of them are quite cleverly hidden and very treacherous, but I know right where they are and I use them all frequently. It really takes me very little time or effort to travel throughout my vast domain."

He looked up again with obvious satisfaction at the mountain peaks high above them. Then he turned back to Aidan and gestured toward her front yard.

"Yes indeed, Aidan, I know every inch of my mountains far better than you know your own little rose garden here."

Aidan turned her eyes ruefully to her garden. Behind Gatekeeper and Isolation the Dark Prince's black rosebushes stood perfectly straight and tall like eerie sentinels standing guard. Despite their luxuriant beauty, it pained her to see them in her garden. Her heart ached unbearably for her own beloved roses, now long gone.

"I have no doubt that what you say is true," she told Isolation, her voice hard with resentment, "for I don't know my own little rose garden at all anymore. I don't know my own house anymore. Indeed, I can barely recognize my own heart anymore, since your Master has sent so many of his servants to me."

Just then the front door of the cottage opened. Unloved and Unwanted stepped out and walked down the flagstone path to the gate. As Aidan looked at the sisters, her heart began to race, for she suddenly realized what it was about Isolation that had seemed so familiar. She stared from their faces to his face as she now recognized the same secretive dark eyes, the same stony expressions, the same strong hard features and graceful movements. Now that they were standing next to him the resemblance was unmistakable, despite the fact that he was several inches taller than they were and looked to be at least ten years younger.

As if reading her thoughts, Unloved said, "Hello, Aidan. I see you've met our younger brother."

"Your brother," Aidan replied bitterly. "Of course. I should have known it from the first moment I saw him."

Isolation laughed loudly.

"Enough of this talk. Aidan, come inside now," he urged with a chuckle. "Come in here and I'll lock my chain behind you. Then you'll be safe and thoroughly protected from all harm."

"I believe I'm much safer out here, thank you," Aidan said stubbornly. "Somehow I don't feel I'll be safe at all inside your chain. I think the Master has sent you to trick me. I think you just want to trap me inside there."

Isolation's smile quickly faded and the laughter went out of his eyes.

"Aidan," he said sternly, "my chain was placed here not by my command, but by that of the Master himself. Staying outside it is not an option that is available to you. Have you forgotten that you gave my sister the key to your heart?"

"How can I ever forget that?" she replied angrily. "It was the biggest mistake I ever made. But I only gave it to her because she deceived me. And I know you're only trying to deceive me as well!"

Isolation spoke very firmly, his eyes flashing indignantly. "You must come inside my chain. This is your home. You have nowhere else to go."

Aidan did have somewhere else to go, but the white rose from Everestaal was inside his chain and she couldn't return to the mansion without it. How was she ever going to get to it now?

"Where I go and what I do is my own concern, not yours or the Master's or anyone else's," she replied at last. "I will not come inside your chain!"

At that, Isolation drew in a deep angry breath.

"I am a prince and a ruler over you," he declared. "My authority has been given to me by Prince Bal'Davarius himself, who sent me here to do his work. Do you dare to defy the Master?"

Aidan bristled with fury.

"I will never obey you! I won't be deceived again!"

Isolation's face darkened with rage.

"You little fool! You'll live to regret your insolence!"

At that moment the front door opened and one of her guests stepped out into the yard, followed by another and then another. Aidan watched with alarm as the Dark Prince's servants began to pour forth from her cottage and crowd into the garden.

Suddenly she realized that she was seeing all her guests together for the very first time. There were so many of them that she didn't understand how they could all possibly fit onto the flagstone path, but somehow they did, standing in eerie silence, every eye fixed upon her in an unnerving stare.

At that moment she was startled by a movement next to Unwanted's black wool skirt. She looked down and her gaze met Orphan's huge mournful eyes. For once the timid little boy didn't turn his pale dirty face away from her. He actually stepped out of the folds of the skirt and let go of it so she could see him well for the first time. He stood in front of the two old women, unafraid, hugging his dirty ragged blanket and just staring at her.

For some reason his sudden display of boldness frightened her most of all. She tore her eyes away from him and took a step backward, overcome with unbearable dread as she faced all of her guests.

There was Abuse, uncharacteristically silent for the first time, a triumphant smirk contorting her features below one of her fancy hats. Beside her stood Wrath with his fearsome smoldering eyes glaring from his scarred face. The other loathsome members of their family stood with them. Anger's arms were folded smugly across her ample bosom, her yellow and orange dress shining like flames. Depression's thin shoulders sagged beneath his rumpled grey suit from the weight of all his burdens in life. Rage, Strife and Neglect leered at her with hungry stares like hunters about to pounce on their prey. Murder was holding his huge shiny knife, an evil grin on his piglike face.

Next to them, elegantly dressed in their pastel finery, were Doubt and Discouragement with their spoiled children. Vain Imaginings slumped against his mother's skirt looking sullen and resentful. The twins Despair and Self-Pity pouted and glowered at her accusingly, clearly blaming her for all their misery. False Hopes stood beside her sisters, her countenance completely innocent and slightly confused, as though – like Aidan herself – she was struggling to understand what was going on in the yard around her.

Nearby stood Greed with his arm around his wife Lust, his hand stroking the smooth fabric of her revealing scarlet dress. She leaned against him, her head on his shoulder, and smirked at Aidan with her catlike eyes. Standing next to them, Pride tipped his cap to her, but the look on his face now was hard and condescending. Beside him Vanity, dressed to utter perfection with every last hair properly in place, gazed haughtily down her carefully powdered nose.

Next to them was Drudgery, looking weary and worn and old beyond her years from all the heavy work she had to do. Grief stood next to her, a black handkerchief pressed to her thin lips, frail and ancient and leaning heavily on her twisted wooden cane in mourning.

Finally there was Fear with her cape pulled back behind her shoulders to reveal her silvery blue dress. All of her dark-haired children were clustered around her, more than a hundred of them, with Fear of Death leaning on his homemade wooden crutch behind his siblings near his mother.

It was then that Aidan received the biggest shock of all, for standing right beside Fear with his arm around her was Night Terrors. For the first time she could see her dreaded nighttime enemy clearly in the light with his silken black cape and wicked grin. Was he the father of Fear's children?

By now Aidan's heart was pounding so hard with paralyzing terror and bitter loathing for all her guests that she could hardly catch her breath.

"Why have you all come out to stare at me like this?" she demanded. "Do you think to imprison me there behind Isolation's chain?"

"I order you to come inside here at once, Aidan," Isolation commanded. "I adjure you to obey me in the name of our Sovereign Lord and Master Prince Bal'Davarius!"

Aidan glared back at him with heated defiance. As long as there was strength in her body, nothing would make her comply with his orders.

At that moment she abandoned all hope of taking the white rose with her. Not even her precious healing rose could make her enter the gate to become a prisoner of her hated enemies. She only knew she had to escape from them now, at any cost.

"No!" she declared firmly. "I will not obey you or your cruel Master. Nothing can make me come inside your chain!"

Aidan took a calculated step backwards, tensing her legs to bolt and run in the next instant for the safety of the Fairhaven mansion.

But then she froze. Once again something was very wrong.

All of their faces had changed.

Just as Fear of Being Hurt's face had done in the music room at the mansion, every last one of their faces had suddenly become a perfect mirror image of her own.

At this horrifying sight Aidan gasped for breath, but none would come. There was a tremendous roaring in her ears and she felt suddenly lightheaded.

"No," she moaned, fighting desperately for control. She knew that if she fainted now they would trap her inside Isolation's chain forever.

She struggled hard against the powerful panic that threatened darkly to overcome her. There was no way now to run, for her weakened knees were shaking so violently they were useless to her.

Deep inside she somehow knew that if she could just tear her eyes away from the Dark Prince's servants for one instant, she would be able to run for safety. But her body was completely paralyzed with fear, her eyes locked onto this crowd of deceitful guests who had mysteriously invaded her life to torment and destroy her.

In the garden they stood perfectly still and silent before her in the shadows of the sinister black rosebushes. Over a hundred pairs of her own eyes stared coldly back at her from over a hundred mirror images of her own face.

Aidan felt the world lurch and spin all around her as though the mountains themselves were heaving and swaying. The colors of the afternoon daylight faded to a dim grey fog as the threatening darkness at last overcame her. In the next instant the earth pitched violently and rose up to meet her as her quaking knees gave way.

Moaning softly, utterly helpless before her enemies, Aidan collapsed onto the ground in a dead faint.

Chapter Thirty-Eight

Trapped By Her Enemies

They surrounded her in an instant, swooping down on her like vultures upon carrion. Lost in a twilight world of half-consciousness, Aidan dimly sensed their evil presence and heard their voices all around her. She could hear Isolation giving orders, his voice coming to her as though from very far away.

Suddenly there was darkness all around her, tightening around her arms and legs until she couldn't move. A familiar tingling sensation coursed down the back of her neck. A rushing wind began to blow furiously against her, so forceful that it lifted her right off the ground.

"No," she groaned softly, her voice lost in the tempest. She thrashed about and struggled against the darkness, but it was hard to move. Someone had picked her up and was bringing her into the yard – or perhaps the wind had lifted her and was carrying her. She became aware that she was passing through the threatening shadows of the black rosebushes and heading toward the cottage.

From somewhere far behind her she heard the gate close, followed quickly by the harsh sound of metal clanking against cold metal.

"No," she moaned again. She knew Isolation had locked his chain and she was now trapped helplessly inside it.

Suddenly furious at her captors, Aidan thrashed again, her body finding new strength in her anger. But the darkness tightened more firmly around her and she felt herself moving helplessly through space, propelled by the mighty rushing wind into an unknown fate.

She heard the front door open in front of her and close again behind her as the wind and the darkness carried her up the stairs. Another door opened before her and she went through it.

All at once the tingling wind stopped as the darkness released her and she felt herself falling, falling through a huge expanse of time and space, falling for what seemed an eternity. She screamed out in terror, but no sound came from her mouth.

Then abruptly she landed on something soft.

Aidan opened her eyes and realized they had carried her to her own bed and her head was on her pillows. Panting and shivering, she wondered what her enemies would do to her now.

Faces were hovering over her, but she couldn't be sure if they were really there or if she were dreaming. Murmuring voices came to her as if from afar.

Then Unloved and Unwanted broke through her dreamlike haze into clear focus. Their dark eyes glittered triumphantly and their grins were cruel as their harsh voices came to her.

"You are such a failure, Aidan! No one has ever loved you and no one ever will! But the Master has given us work to do in your house and we have your key. You will be safe here inside our brother's chain. We will help you sustain your life here, for this is the land where you truly belong."

They left her and another face bent over her, shadowed beneath the brim of a colorful hat. Abuse sneered at her in a strident voice filled with contempt.

"You pathetic fool! So you thought you could become a swan and fly far away from here. You'll never be anything but an ugly little duckling!"

Aidan cowered before her but Abuse faded away into the haze as Wrath and his ruthless sons came and stood over her.

"No, not you," she moaned, but her voice was lost beneath the mocking roar of Strife's laughter.

Rage leaned close to her face.

"She ain't dead yit, Pa," he drawled. "She only swooned. Maybe we oughta finish the job."

Rage's face disappeared back into the haze. Now Murder appeared over her, his sinister grin filled with wicked glee, his sour breath hot against her cheek.

"Thet would pleasure me right nice, Pa. Kin I do her in now with me huntin' knife?"

Twisting around but knowing it was impossible to escape, Aidan pleaded, "No! No! Don't hurt me! Oh, please, don't hurt me!"

Then Murder's face was abruptly yanked away and Wrath's voice rumbled threateningly.

"Git yer filthy hands off'n her, ye cursed varmints! T'ain't the work the Master give us t'do here!"

His stubbled face with its fearsome scar came into sharp focus as he bent over the bed and smiled maliciously down at her.

"Master say this one be right special to him – so I reckon we got to take real good care of her."

Aidan writhed helplessly about in her dream world as their faces faded away into the shadows. Somewhere in the distance she could hear wailing and moaning. Grief's lonely cries sent shivers grating up and down her spine.

Who would mourn for her when they killed her?

At that moment a firm contralto voice came to her more clearly than any of the others. Aidan could plainly see the catlike look in Lust's pale eyes as she stood next to the bed.

"Stand aside, everyone, and give poor Aidan some air. Gatekeeper, we need the brandy bottle right away."

She moved aside and Gatekeeper's kind face appeared over Aidan. He lifted her head and held the brandy bottle to her lips.

"Here you are, Miss," he said in his usual pleasant manner. "This will help now."

He tipped the bottle up slightly, just enough so that a small taste of the rich golden liquid dripped onto her tongue.

Aidan propped herself up onto one elbow and swallowed the liquor eagerly. The brandy burned her throat but she welcomed the feeling she knew it would give her. The hazy fog inside her head began to lift a bit just thinking about it. She wanted to drink and drink until delicious warm fire spread through her body and brought its comfort to her.

Craving more, she reached greedily for the bottle with her other hand.

Suddenly Gatekeeper's face was very close to hers, but it was not as she had ever seen it before. It had become twisted and grotesque, dark with an ugly evil grin. His eyes glowed bright red with cruel unearthly fire.

Terrified at the change in him, Aidan gasped and shrank back, but he reached out and grabbed her face roughly with one hand, forcing her mouth open and hurting her. She struggled against him as he lifted the bottle with his other hand and shoved it to her lips.

"So you want more? Then drink, my foolish little Miss! Drink all you can!" he cried, and tipped the bottle up high.

Brandy poured everywhere, searing her tongue and splashing onto her face and dribbling down her chin. Aidan gulped, but not fast enough. Liquor flowed out of the bottle as though it would never stop. She choked and spat and thrashed about as it spilled into her hair and soaked her lovely white silk blouse and navy velvet jacket. Pushing at the bottle and fighting Gatekeeper with all her strength, she was sure he was trying to drown her.

At that moment someone came up behind him and pulled the bottle away.

"That's enough, Gatekeeper," Drudgery said. "The Master will be furious if you hurt her. Do you want him to turn into a lion again? Remember what happened that last time!"

Gatekeeper's twisted face immediately softened again into the gentle grandfatherly one she knew, and then faded away into hazy twilight along with the brandy bottle.

Drudgery sat down on the bed beside Aidan, her face smudged with dirt and her hazel green eyes shining almost hypnotically.

"The Master has chosen my good friend for a very special purpose," she said softly with deep conviction, speaking to Gatekeeper but looking at Aidan's face. "You mustn't harm the Master's chosen one."

She reached out and gently brushed wet strands of hair from Aidan's forehead with her rough calloused hand.

"Everything will be all right now, friend Aidan," she murmured soothingly. "Just lay back and rest. Nothing can hurt you here. You're safe now. Safe in your own bed. Safe behind Isolation's chain. Safe with all of us here to help you sustain your life in this place."

Aidan tried to protest, but there was no fight left in her. Her head sank helplessly into the brandy-soaked pillows. Drudgery pulled at the blankets and tucked them around her.

The last thing she heard as she closed her eyes was Drudgery whispering very softly.

"Yes, Aidan, dear friend, the Master takes very good care of his servants, and he will take good care of you."

Then the world went completely black as she fell into a deep dreamless sleep.

Chapter Thirty-Nine

Encounter With Murder

A soft voice floated gently to Aidan's ears. She heard it but did not respond to it, for her sleep was restful and good and she hated to leave it.

The voice came again, more insistently.

"Aidan, can you hear me? It's Drudgery. I brought your tray. Aidan?"

Reluctantly Aidan opened her eyes. She was in her room, lying in her bed, and Drudgery was bending over her.

"There you are." Drudgery smiled. "I was beginning to worry. You've been sleeping so soundly for the last few hours I haven't been able to wake you up."

Aidan's head was resting on damp pillows. The strong smell of brandy suddenly jolted her to full awareness. She sat up quickly and saw amber-colored stains all over the bedclothes and pillows. Wet silk clung to her skin. Her damp hair hung down in tangled strands reeking of liquor.

Dazed, she stared for a long moment at her clothes and bed. A shudder convulsed through her body as she remembered Gatekeeper's grotesque face bending so cruelly over her, pouring brandy down her throat. If it weren't for the obvious evidence and for the dreadful burning taste that still lingered on her tongue, she would have thought it had all been a horrible dream.

Drudgery gestured to the table by the bedside, where she had placed the silver tray.

"I brought you some tea. Do you think you could drink some?"

Aidan stared suspiciously at her, more angry than afraid.

"No. I don't want any tea. I don't want anything."

Drudgery hesitated, then nodded.

"All right, Aidan. I'll just leave the tray here for you, in case you change your mind."

There was a moment of awkward silence between them. Aidan noticed that the light streaming in through the window was the pale golden color of early evening sun hanging just above the mountains. She studied the light carefully, trying to judge how late it was.

At last she asked, "What happened to me? How did I get here?"

"You fainted outside by the gate. Night Terrors carried you upstairs."

Aidan shivered. So she *had* been trapped inside his evil cape! That explained the sensation of rushing wind lifting her and the dreams that were still so vivid in her mind – if indeed they had been dreams.

"We've tried to revive you, but you wouldn't respond," Drudgery continued. "We've been quite concerned."

Before Aidan could answer, there was a knock at the door followed by a familiar grandfatherly voice. "Drudgery?"

"Come in, Gatekeeper," Drudgery answered. "Aidan's awake now."

The door opened and Gatekeeper walked over to the bed. Aidan's pulse raced as she stared hard at his face. Her butler greeted her with his usual pleasant smile and the same gentle and friendly countenance she had liked the first moment she had met him at her door. His bright blue eyes were round with concern for her.

He clicked his heels together snappily and bowed slightly over the bed. The key to her front door dangled from the heavy gold chain hanging around his neck.

"How do you feel, Miss? You had us quite worried."

Aidan stared at him in complete disbelief.

"Worried? You were worried about me? After the way you forced the brandy bottle down my throat and tried to choke me?!"

Gatekeeper's eyes widened with startled confusion. He turned and looked at Drudgery, then turned back to Aidan.

"I'm afraid I don't understand, Miss. What do you mean?"

"You know perfectly well what I mean," Aidan insisted angrily. She gestured to her wet blouse and the stained pillows. "Look, you spilled the brandy all over the bed. I remember it all clearly. Lust told you to bring the bottle and give me some brandy. You grabbed me and pushed the bottle into my mouth and tipped it up so it came out too fast. You were trying to hurt me – to drown me!"

Still looking completely befuddled, Gatekeeper shook his head.

"Well, yes, Miss, Lust did tell me to give you a drink from the bottle. And yes, I did spill some brandy on the bed. But I'm afraid it was quite unavoidable. You refused to take it. You fought me and pushed it away, and it was hard to keep from spilling it."

Aidan stared at him, shocked to hear him deliberately lie to her.

She remembered clearly that she hadn't fought him at all. She had been eager to take the brandy – until he hurt her. Then she had indeed struggled, but only after the brandy had already spilled.

"Go away," she ordered coldly, trembling with abrupt hatred for him.

He looked startled. "Miss?"

"Get out of my room. Both of you. Take the tray and get out."

Drudgery smiled and spoke soothingly.

"Are you sure, Aidan? It's the Master's best tea –"

"I don't want the Master's best tea. I don't want anything from you. I just want to be alone! Get out and go away and leave me alone!"

Aidan threw herself back down onto the brandy-soaked pillows and turned her back to them.

There was a long silence.

Then Gatekeeper sighed. "Very well, Miss."

She heard him pick up the tray. His tapping footsteps faded through the doorway and down the hall.

"Are you sure you don't want me to stay with you, friend Aidan?" Drudgery asked softly.

"No!" Aidan cried. "I just want you to go away!"

Drudgery sighed. "Very well. I'll come check on you later."

Her weary footsteps crossed the room. A moment later the door closed softly and Aidan was alone.

She was out of bed in an instant, knowing she didn't have a moment to waste. The mountains would very soon cast their cold black shadows across Hidden and it was urgent that she return to the mansion before dark, as she had promised Lady Fairhaven. None of her guests could be trusted and she had to get to a safe refuge as quickly as possible.

As Aidan caught sight of herself in the full-length mirror, she saw that the lovely white silk blouse was soaked with brandy. Her skirt and jacket were also wet, as well as rumpled and dirty from falling outside her gate. It was a shame that such beautiful expensive clothes had been ruined. Prince Bal'Davarius would no doubt be furious when he found out, but she didn't care. She quickly pulled everything off and left the outfit in a heap on the floor.

The diamond necklace glittered coldly at her throat. Aidan fumbled at the clasp with determination until she managed to unfasten it. She laid it carefully on the top of the bureau and gently touched the stones for the last time. Such a beautiful and precious piece of jewelry. It would be so hard to leave it behind.

She went to the washstand and splashed clean water on her face, then took soap and tried to wash the brandy from her body as best she could. After drying off, she put on one of her work uniforms. Her hair was a tangled damp mess and she wiped at it with a wet washcloth but the smell of brandy was still strong. She brushed it out, knowing there wasn't time to fuss with it, and tied a clean scarf around her head.

After a last quick glance in the mirror, Aidan went back to the bed and began pulling at the bedclothes. Hidden beneath the mattress, tied up in an embroidered cloth, was the money she had been saving since spring. She groped with both hands until she found it, then untied it and counted it carefully. Satisfied that all her money was still there, she tied the bundle up again and slipped it into one of the large deep pockets of her dress beneath the apron.

Now she was ready. She had to find a way to escape.

Her heart pounding with tension, Aidan opened the bedroom door and ventured out into the dark hallway. The house was deathly quiet. She wondered suspiciously where all her guests had gone, but at the same time she was grateful to find herself alone. Without making a sound, she rushed down the front stairs.

At the bottom she stopped and looked into the main room. There was a fire burning brightly in the fireplace. She could see the back of a lone figure sitting before it but couldn't make out who it was.

Aidan turned and looked hungrily at the door. She was deathly afraid, but she was determined to be free. Slowly, she took a single step, moving silently from the bottom stair onto the braided rug that covered the wood floor of the entryway.

The person by the fire immediately jumped up and whirled around to face her. A bright silvery flash of metal caught her eye.

Aidan gasped and froze, staring in horror at the razor-sharp blade of a gleaming hunting knife.

"No," she whispered in panic, suddenly finding herself all alone and face to face with the one servant of the Dark Prince she feared the most. "Not you!"

Murder grinned wickedly at her. His tongue darted out of his mouth like a snake's and ran hungrily across his lips. In the flickering firelight his eyes glittered darkly with the menacing look of an experienced hunter closing in on his prey. The huge hunting knife flashed threateningly in his hand as he came toward her, speaking softly in a sinister gravelly voice.

"Ye kept me waitin' a right long time, Aidan. I been settin' here quite a spell fixin' to talk to ye."

Aidan's voice shook as she cowered before him.

"I had no idea you were waiting for me. I – I'm sorry."

He chuckled. "D'ye mean to say if ye'd known I was down here a-waitin' fer ye, ye would'a hurried?"

Murder held his knife with the blade up and came still closer. Aidan cringed, pressing her back against the wall, afraid she would faint dead away at the sight of his vicious-looking weapon.

"What do you mean to do with that?" she demanded in a shaking voice. "Are you going to kill me now?"

"No, ma'am," Murder told her earnestly. "Pa say the Master forbid it. T'ain't the work the Master give me to do in yer house." He examined his knife carefully. "I was jes' polishin' the blade when ye come down. But I reckon I don't need it jes' to talk with ye."

Looking very satisfied with his work, Murder slid the knife into its leather sheath hanging from his belt.

Aidan was relieved to see him put it away, but her heart was still pounding.

"If you don't mean to kill me, then what is the work your Master has given you to do in my house?"

"Wal now, I cain't say exactly what the Master's plans be, but I do know we been together a right long time. I reckon my kin and yers go back quite a spell."

"How long have you been with me?" Aidan asked. "Since my birth? My youth?"

Murder grinned at her and shook his head.

"Naw, a lot longer'n that. More'n two hundred years, I reckon."

She gasped at this news.

"Two hundred years! But – but I haven't even been alive that long. How can this be possible?"

He shrugged.

"I been with yer kin – the kin what come afore ye. I come to ye through yer family line."

"Through my family line?"

"Yes, ma'am, thet be a fact."

"Then – then you must have known my mother."

"No, ma'am," he said firmly, shaking his head. "Don't know yer ma. Now, me brother Neglect, I reckon he knows yer ma's kin right well. If'n ye want to know more about them, ye ought to ask Neglect."

Murder was the only one of her guests who had told her he didn't know her mother. This surprised Aidan greatly.

"If you don't know my mother, then how have you come to me?"

"I know yer pa."

Aidan gasped and stared at him.

"My father? You know my father?"

"Yes, ma'am, I know him right well – Ma and Pa too. It be his kin we come from."

She was struggling to take in all that he was telling her.

"And you and Wrath and Abuse and the others have come to me through him – through the generations of my father's family?"

"Yes, ma'am, thet be the way it happen. We also been close to yer Aunt Mara's kin, fer, oh, I reckon a couple hundred years thar too."

That news didn't surprise Aidan, but she didn't want to discuss Aunt Mara.

"My father – what can you tell me about him? Did he ever know you were there with him?"

"No, ma'am," Murder replied. "He never knew we was there."

His black eyes shone malevolently in a hungry leer that suddenly made Aidan shiver. He chuckled wickedly.

"But I reckon I kin tell ye all about yer pa. He were real smooth-talkin' with the ladies, if'n ye know what I mean. His pa were, too, 'n' that be how he learnt about women. It were easy fer him to git yer ma believin' he loved her. He smooth-talked a lot o' women into believin' that one."

At the thought of what her father had done to her mother, Aidan felt a rush of hatred rise in her heart.

"Where is my father now?" she demanded. "I know you know. Tell me where he is!"

Murder grinned.

"Yes, ma'am, I shorely do know, all right. And I'll be right pleased to tell ye. He be locked away in prison."

Aidan's mouth dropped open in shock.

"Prison! My father – in prison?"

He nodded.

"Yes, ma'am, thet be a fact. And I reckon he ain't never wakin' to the light of a free day agin. He ain't never gittin' out."

Aidan shuddered to think that her father was at that very moment locked inside a tiny cell somewhere. Her deepest fears swept over her, flooding her heart with cold panic.

Would she too end up locked away in a prison cell?

"What – what did he do, that he should be in prison?" she asked.

Murder answered her in a mocking tone. "Wal now, what d'ye think he did? He killed someone! Fact be, he killed two women." He spoke as though he delighted in shocking her. "Yes, ma'am. Yer pa be a cold-blooded murderer."

Aidan was dumbfounded. "He – he killed two women?" Suddenly she could hardly breathe. "No, I can't believe this! You're lying!"

"No, ma'am, I ain't lyin' to ye," Murder insisted. "Both times it were the same. There were a woman he wanted, see, jes' like he wanted yer ma. But this gal weren't so easy to fool, and she refused him. She fought him and he got mad, jes' as mad as kin be. Yer pa, he has a wicked mean temper." He grinned. "So he took a knife – kinda like the one I got but not nearly as fine – and stabbed her."

Aidan gasped, horrified.

Murder went on, reveling in describing the gory details.

"He stabbed her over and over agin til she were good and dead. Then he –"

"Stop, stop! I don't want to hear any more!" Aidan cried. "I can't believe what you're telling me!"

Murder looked indignant at her suggestion that he was lying.

"Wal now, I reckon I should know if he killed somebody, don't ye think?" he insisted. "Happened the same way both times. He killed the first one a long time afore he met yer ma. That time he got away afore anyone found out. But that were how come he always kept movin' on from town to town, travelin' here and there and doin' odd jobs. He were runnin' from the law."

"No," whispered Aidan. How could all this be true?

"But the second time he killed, someone heard the gal scream. They come in and found yer pa, still ragin' in his terrible bad temper. He were holdin' his knife, standin' over the body. Her blood were still warm on his hands."

Aidan shuddered with revulsion at the gruesome image that came into her mind. She was struggling to accept what Murder was telling her. Anger was rising in her heart.

"So he killed the first one before he met my mother – and the second one after he left her."

"Yes, ma'am."

"He was already a murderer – and a fugitive – when I was conceived."

"Yes, ma'am," Murder answered. "I reckon thet be jes' the way it happen. I was with him then – and thet be how I come to be with ye."

Aidan felt nauseated. Her father was far more despicable than she had thought. The emotions that suddenly tore through her heart were so intense that she began to shake uncontrollably with tremendous loathing – and a deep desire for vengeance.

"That wretched, worthless scum!" she raged. "How could anyone do such things? How I hate him! He deserves to be in prison forever! He deserves to die!"

Murder grinned delightedly at her outburst.

"Ye truly feel that way, now, don't ye, Aidan?"

"I hate him," Aidan declared again. "I hope he rots in that prison!"

Completely possessed by violent emotion, she clenched her fists into tight balls as she felt her hatred pulsing within her with a life all its own. Her heart was on fire with the realization that if he were standing before her, she would kill her father with no regrets for what he had done to her mother – and to her.

It was at that moment that she suddenly saw Murder through the eyes of new understanding. He had somehow passed through the years and the generations of her father's family. Murder was her father's only legacy to her.

Somehow Aidan had always known Murder had been there with her, hidden somewhere in the very deepest, most private part of her own heart. It was as though he had been imprisoned in a private room inside her, a secret room that had been closed and locked up so tightly that she herself had been unable to venture inside. She had lived her entire life knowing somehow that Murder was there, but trying to deny it and hoping no one would ever find out.

But he had been in that locked room all along, just waiting to reveal himself to her. And now here he was, standing before her. His moment had come.

Now she had to confront the horrible reality of his presence in her life. She could no longer ignore him and pretend he wasn't there.

For when the servants of the Dark Prince had taken the key to her heart, they had opened that door and set Murder free. Free to do his terrible work in her life – the work his Master had given him to do.

He stood before her, scrutinizing her face with a knowing look in his glittering dark eyes. Suddenly he stepped close and grabbed her tightly by the upper arms. Aidan froze, gasping in terror and pain.

"No!" she whimpered. "Don't hurt me! Oh, please, don't hurt me!"

"Ye'd kill him if ye could," Murder accused in a harsh whisper. "Ain't it true? If he were standin' here right now and ye had a knife in yer hand, ye'd stick him like a pig till he were good and dead. Admit it, Aidan. Ye'd kill him!"

"No!" Aidan cried, shaking her head vehemently and struggling to push him away. She felt a desperate need to deny the truth even in the face of Murder himself. "No! That's a lie!"

He shook her with a vicious jerk, hurting her arms where Uncle Asa had beaten her, and she froze again, whimpering.

"Don't deny it, Aidan. It be the truth, and we both know it. Ye hate yer pa – ye said that yerself. He hurt ye. He left yer ma and broke her heart. It be because of what he done that ye ended up here. He don't even know ye're alive at all and he wouldn't care if he did! Deep down in yer heart ye long to make him pay. Ye said it yerself – worthless scum – he deserve to die!"

"Stop it! Stop it!" Aidan shouted, writhing in desperation to be free of him. Tears were beginning to slip down her cheeks.

But Murder only tightened his grip on her arms and shook her again to drive home his point. His face was right up next to hers and his gaze was savage. She could feel his hot moist breath on her cheek, so disgustingly sour it turned her stomach.

"Jes' like ye tried to kill Asa," he went on relentlessly. "Don't deny it, Aidan! Ye tried to reach the knife fixin' to kill Asa. That were when I walked in yer door, so I know ye did it."

His eyes narrowed into black slits.

"It rose up in yer heart jes' like a hunger. Weren't it like a hunger, Aidan?"

Aidan stared at him in horror. It had been exactly like hunger.

"A hunger," Murder repeated, his voice a grating whisper. "Ye wanted vengeance so bad ye could taste it on yer tongue. Ye were cravin' to spill his blood. Aye. Ye longed to kill Asa. It were jes' like a hunger deep in yer soul."

"No," she whimpered in weak denial. "That's not true!"

Fire was burning in Murder's eyes, a fire so bright it exposed everything in her heart. He jerked her again and she gasped.

"We both know it be true, Aidan! Ye cain't deny it. But now, yer pa and Asa – they ain't the only ones ye wanted to kill. They be others too."

She stared at him, speechless with dread.

"In yer heart ye hungered to kill ever'one in this here town! Ye said it yerself. None of 'em ever tried to be friendly to ye. Ye'd be happy t'see ever' last one of 'em drop dead!"

Aidan knew his accusations were all horribly true, yet still she tried to conceal her iniquity.

"You're lying," she whimpered.

Murder knew she was weakening. His voice rose to a vicious crescendo.

"I ain't lyin' and ye know it! And the one ye hungered to kill most of all were Mara Teague!"

Aidan moaned with shame and covered her face with her hands as her heart was laid bare before her ruthless accuser.

Her secret, her terrible secret, was known.

Murder's rough powerful grip on her arms was excruciating as he shook her mercilessly.

"Admit it, Aidan!" he roared. "Ye rejoiced as she lay there a-wastin' away! Ye could hardly wait fer her to die. Ye wanted more'n anythin' fer her to jes' be quick about it and git it over with. But ever' day she jes' kept hangin' on. Ye watched her linger on and on – fer months – and it were like a torture!"

He dropped his voice again to an accusing whisper.

"And that hunger jes' kept risin' up in yer heart agin and agin. The thought came to ye over and over agin that it wouldn't be wrong to jes' help things along a leetle bit. Ye thought, t'ain't really killin' – it jes' helpin' nature take its course a leetle bit sooner. Ye even thought it'd be a mercy and a help to put her out of her sufferin' – and no one would ever know – she goin' to die soon anyways. Ain't that true, Aidan? Didn't ye think that?"

"No!" Aidan insisted frantically into her hands, hiding her tears. "I never had such thoughts! I never hurt Aunt Mara!"

Murder snarled and jerked her so quickly and roughly that she gasped, taking her trembling hands from her face and staring at him.

"That be a *lie*, Aidan," he whispered fiercely. "I *know* ye had those thoughts. I *know* – 'cause *I* was the one what whispered 'em in yer ear!"

His dark eyes burned into hers and she pressed her back against the wall, cringing from the terrible fury she saw in them.

"*I* was the one what told ye to kill her. And I know ye heard ever' word I said 'cause ye're a cold-blooded murderer – jes' like yer pa!"

"But I didn't kill Aunt Mara!" she sobbed. "It's true, I did hate her – I wanted to make her pay for what she did to me! But I took good care of her. Dr. Caine and I were both with her when she died in her sleep. I never laid a hand on her! I swear I didn't kill her!"

Murder's voice dropped to a grating whisper.

"In yer heart ye did, Aidan. In yer heart ye killed her a thousand times."

He released his grip on her at last and her back slid against the wall as she sank to the floor. She curled herself into a ball and wept bitterly into her hands, her heart crushed beneath the unbearable weight of the worst guilt and shame she had ever known.

Murder was right. Aidan well remembered the winter months she had cared for Aunt Mara as she lay sick in bed. The temptation to kill her had indeed been like a hunger. It had clawed at her heart so many times it became sheer torture to fight it day in and day out.

In the end she had not succumbed to that temptation – but many times she knew she had come dangerously close.

And she would never forget standing at the graveside, suddenly afraid Aunt Mara would rise up from the coffin – that horrific moment when she knew for certain that she would have slammed the lid shut and sent her to her grave, dead or alive.

Yes. Murder had always been there in her heart. She had known it then and she knew it now. And she knew he was there to stay.

"Ye *are* a murderer – jes' like yer pa!" he accused. "Let me hear ye say it, Aidan. Say it!"

"It's true," she moaned. "I *am* a murderer!"

Barely able to breathe, she sobbed a bitter confession into her hands.

"I hated her – with all my heart – and I wanted to kill her – not just once, but a thousand times over! And – and I would kill her right now – for real – if I could! I *am* a murderer – just like my father!"

Satisfied at last, Murder backed a step away from her, his voice calm and triumphant.

"Yes, ma'am, that be a fact," he said. "Ye *are* a murderer. It be in yer heart and soul. But ye kin do better next time, Aidan. I'll be right pleased to help ye whenever ye decide ye want to kill fer real. I helped yer pa do it both times, and I'm here to help ye too."

At that, tears still pouring down her face, Aidan stared up at him. He reached for the leather sheath on his belt and drew out his wicked hunting knife. The polished silver blade flashed brightly as he crouched down and held it right in front of her eyes.

Softly he whispered chilling promises to her.

"I'll help ye kill whenever ye need me, Aidan. Whenever that hunger rise up like a burnin' fire in yer soul, whenever yer cravin' fer revenge git so terrible bad ye kin taste it, I'll be right there with ye. Ye'll know I'm there. Ye'll hear me whisperin' to ye. And I'll help ye kill. Anytime."

Murder straightened up, his cruel burning eyes never leaving hers as he slid his knife back into its sheath.

"It be the work the Master give me to do in yer life. And ye know I cain't leave 'til my work fer the Master be done."

Aidan doubled over with her head in her hands, sobbing in helpless torment. She knew she would never be free of him.

Murder's work in her life would only be finished at the very moment she died.

Chapter Forty

The Way Of Escape

How long Aidan huddled by her front door, bent over and weeping, she never knew. But after some time she looked up and realized Murder had left her and she was alone.

Wiping her tears away, she pulled herself unsteadily to her feet. For a moment she leaned against the wall, breathing deeply and summoning every last ounce of her strength and courage. Her confrontation with Murder had made her all the more desperate to escape these mysterious enemies who had invaded her life and who truly wanted to destroy her.

I swear I will either find a way to go back to the mansion or I will die trying, she thought. *One way or another, tonight I will be free!*

The twilight coming in through the front windows was rapidly fading as the mountain shadows were settling over the valley. Aidan took one last look at the front room, a fleeting glance completely devoid of sentimentality even though she was determined that this would be the last time she ever saw it. She knew she needed to hurry.

Without any further hesitation, she reached for the door, fully expecting that Gatekeeper had locked it. To her surprise the latch moved easily. Isolation must have decided not to keep her from her yard.

She opened the door noiselessly and slipped outside. The sight of what had been her beautiful rose garden was as jarring as the shock of frigid evening air that seized her chest and took her breath away.

Palpable darkness immediately pressed in all around her, pulsing with a suffocating force as it drove the day into night. In the growing chill the cloying scent of the Dark Prince's prized black roses was almost nauseating. Thickly covered with huge blossoms, the menacing bushes towered on either side of the flagstone path like giant warriors about to attack.

Aidan's heart withered at the sight of the eerie pillars that had taken over her garden. Black mountain shadows covered them like a heavy shroud. Somehow it seemed to her that they were drawing strength from the cold and darkness just as her own roses had once thrived in warmth and sunlight.

How could such gorgeous roses seem so deceitfully evil?

Shivering, Aidan stepped onto the flagstones and walked as quickly as she could, keeping her head down to avoid looking at the bushes.

At the end of the path Isolation's ominous chain was hanging across the iron gate. She examined it closely. It was securely padlocked and firmly attached to the wall, and she knew she could neither open it nor remove it. Up close in the twilight it seemed much more intimidating than she remembered.

Suddenly Aidan laughed at herself.

Why, it's just a rusty old chain! How silly! It can't really keep me in here. I can just climb right over the wall!

Aidan laughed again. How could she have been so afraid of a big old chain?!

Her courage renewed, she reached out and tapped the chain gently with two fingertips as she prepared to hoist herself up.

But to her astonishment, intense pain met her hand.

She gasped as she yanked her hand away and stared in shock at tiny red marks left on her fingers. The black iron was colder than frozen metal on a bitter winter's day, icy enough to burn her skin.

Her whole body began to tremble with dread.

This was no ordinary chain, for Isolation was no ordinary person. Like all of the Dark Prince's servants, he was doing the work his Master had given him to do in her life – and he possessed a strong mysterious power over her.

Would she ever be free of her enemies?

It was clearly impossible to go to the mansion now. With a surge of guilt, she remembered the radiant joy on Lady Fairhaven's face at her promise to come back by dark. What would she do when Aidan failed to return? No doubt she was already terribly hurt and insulted, probably even furious by now.

She will never be my friend again, Aidan thought. *She will surely hate me forever!*

Suddenly it occurred to her that perhaps Lady Fairhaven, who had always been so kind to her and who seemed genuinely concerned for her safety, might simply be worried when she didn't come back.

This was followed by a horrifying thought.

What if she came to the cottage to see what had detained her – and found her trapped behind a huge locked chain with no hope of escape?

Aidan was filled with absolute panic at the mere idea that Lady Fairhaven might find out how completely wretched her life really was.

No! she thought. *She must never know! No one can ever know!*

No one should ever know how Abuse and Wrath had destroyed her beautiful rose garden. No one should ever see how Doubt and Discouragement had planted the black roses or how they had watered and fertilized them into full bloom. No one should ever know her private torment, the terrible guilt and shame she lived with night and day.

Above all, no one must ever find out that Murder lived in her heart.

Trapped behind Isolation's chain, Aidan looked up in despair at the blackening sky so high above her rose garden. Pinpoints of starlight were now appearing one by one. She felt herself engulfed in darkness, surrounded by all the ugliness of her life. All hope of light or beauty or freedom was as far out of her reach as the stars so high above – the powerful stars that had ordained her painful destiny from the moment she had been born.

Suddenly she heard a noise from behind the wooden gate leading to the back of the house. She froze, her heart pounding, wondering which of her enemies was about to find her.

What would they do to her when they discovered she was trying to escape?

Frantically she slipped behind the black rosebushes, keeping her back firmly pressed against the garden wall.

Mere inches from her face was a solid barricade of black roses. Her breath swirled in white puffs of vapor against them in the night air. Up so close, their rich perfume was overpowering.

Temptingly soft, the shadowy blossoms silently beguiled her to caress and even embrace them. She knew their velvety petals concealed vicious thorns, yet their strange power was still almost impossible to resist.

Aidan tore herself away and moved against the wall further from the gate. She listened carefully, barely daring to breathe.

There was no sound. The dark garden was deathly still.

Reassured that she was alone and safely hidden, Aidan slid to the ground and curled her body into a ball, wrapping her arms tightly around her legs and resting her head on her knees.

Why is all this happening to me? Why has Prince Bal'Davarius sent his cruel servants to me? What have I done to deserve all this pain and torment in my life?!

In her haste to escape she had left her shawl behind. Now the first killing frost of the season was settling rapidly all around her, piercing through her dress like tiny sharp needles. She could see white ice crystals hardening the damp garden soil and crusting over the black roses. Shivering against the cold stone wall at her back, she held her head in her hands.

Nothing mattered now. She had no more will to live.

All hope was gone.

In the softest of whispers Aidan uttered a desperate plea.

"Let the killing frost come tonight and cover me with ice. Let me die here in this garden I once loved with all my life and breath. My roses are dead. I'm trapped behind chains and I can never be free. I have no more strength to endure my wretched life another day. Aunt Mara was right all along. I am wicked – evil – and I can never be good no matter how hard I try. I deserve to die. Please – just let me die!"

A single tear slipped down her face.

And at that moment, in the midst of the cold and the darkness and the greatest despair she had ever known, a soft sweet fragrance came to her.

Startled, Aidan lifted her head and looked behind the branches of the black rosebushes toward the corner of the stone wall. Her eyes fell upon the most incredible sight she had ever seen.

The white rose from Everestaal!

How could she have forgotten about it?!

She stared in complete awe at the amazing bush that had grown from the Knight's single rose after going through fire in her woodstove. It was now immense, spreading out in both directions from the corner where she had planted it. Verdant branches covered with masses of tiny blossoms and leaves were clinging firmly to the stone wall.

The roses were plainly visible even in the night, for each blossom was glowing softly like a tiny candle flame, just as the first one had when she had been locked in the closet beneath the stairs. They seemed to pulse with life and warmth and beauty. The sight of hundreds of tiny golden lights piercing the frozen darkness of her greatest despair filled her heart with a surge of fresh hope.

Moving carefully against the stone wall to avoid the treacherous black roses, Aidan crawled slowly until she reached the corner. Feeling as though she had found her dearest friend, she knelt before the heavy thornless branches and eagerly opened her arms to embrace them, pressing velvety white petals to her face and breathing deeply of their perfume.

Strength emanated from the tiny healing roses and filled her with joy. All at once peace flooded her heart, washing over her like a rich fragrant balm until tears welled in her eyes and gentle laughter rose from her throat at the same time. For a long time she stroked the soft tiny blossoms and even kissed them.

At last she released the branches to study the way they grew. Most of them were attached to the wall like ivy, spreading leafy vines across the grey stones. But a few of them were growing very strangely and trailing low over the ground. One such tendril had curled itself tightly around the base of a black rosebush and was beginning to spiral upwards through its thorny branches.

Never had she seen a rose that grew like this – or one that grew so quickly.

Aidan began to stand up to get a better look at the upper part of the bush. As she reached out to steady herself, she put her hand through the lower vines onto the stone wall.

Suddenly the most unexpected thing happened.

One of the stones moved!

Startled, she pushed at the stone again. It scraped roughly against the wall around it, but it moved easily.

She knelt back down and pulled leaves and blossoms aside to look more closely. In the dim light from the glowing roses, she could just see that there were small hairlike shoots growing along the vines which had actually dug in between the stones and crumbled the ancient mortar into dust.

For a long uncertain moment she brushed at the dust with her fingers before she fully understood what she was seeing. Then she gave one last push on the loose stone. As it slid right out of the wall, she heard it land with a dull thud on the ground outside, leaving a gaping hole that she could see right through.

She pushed against the stone next to the first. It too landed outside the wall.

Then, barely able to contain her excitement, it was all she could do to keep from shouting out loud. For the second time the white rose from Everestaal was providing the way of escape from her imprisonment!

Aidan glanced around nervously in the frosty darkness, almost expecting that the mysterious Knight who had given her the rose would again appear to her in a vision as he had done when she was locked in the closet. But this was no vision. All she could see were very real masses of peacefully glowing white roses – and a hole in the stone wall.

With all her determination, she started pushing at the stones around the hole. Each one fell out of the wall easily.

Freedom was at hand. Nothing could stop her now!

Within moments Aidan had enlarged the hole until it was just big enough to crawl through. As she pulled the vines aside and knelt down to leave, she looked longingly at the fragrant roses all around her.

The bush was so huge now that she knew it would be impossible to even try digging it up and taking it with her. She also knew that without doubt her enemies would soon find it – which made it even more imperative that she escape to the mansion immediately.

But her heart ached at the thought of leaving it behind. She loved this wondrous rose more than all the others she had lost.

Surely my enemies will destroy it, she thought.

Wistfully Aidan reached out and tenderly stroked one of the soft tiny blossoms, remembering the mysterious Knight who had pursued her to give her this precious gift. She thought again of his kind face and his dark beautiful eyes – and her heart yearned for him too.

Gently she tugged at the little rose. To her surprise, it came right off the vine into her hand. She stared at it in awe.

It looked just like the first rose she had seen in the mansion parlor, so tiny and pristine with dark green leaves on a thornless stem, its creamy petals edged in crimson just beginning to curl away from the bud. Gratefully she kissed it before carefully slipping it into her pocket.

Then, without further hesitation, Aidan bent down, crawled through the hole in the wall, and stumbled awkwardly to freedom.

Brushing garden dirt from her dress and apron, she straightened up and stepped away from the wall. Anxiously she looked around for her enemies, but to her relief she was completely alone.

She had escaped!

Filled with fresh hope that only certain good could possibly be awaiting her now, Aidan took off running through the dark streets of Hidden. She would soon be safe in the refuge of the Fairhaven mansion.

And this time she knew she would never make the mistake of going back.

Epilogue

A Taste of Things to Come in The Rose From The Tower

From *The Renwickes,* Book Two Chapter 16:

The afternoon air was fresh and warm with a pleasant spring breeze as Aidan and the three Renwicke siblings stepped outside. Several attentive footmen helped them climb into a large open carriage that was painted white and elaborately decorated in gold. They settled themselves onto thickly cushioned leather seats with Julian and Cameron facing rear across from Aidan and Maeve.

Julian gave instructions to the coachman, who tapped his crop lightly with a flourish and urged his two chestnut horses forward. Soon they were rolling through the town, chatting amiably as Maeve pointed out the sights to Aidan.

"Clearview is so much bigger than Hidden," Aidan said. "Such a busy place! So many people. And the houses – so large and beautiful."

"I hardly remember Hidden," Maeve said. "We've been there, but the last time was a few years ago. It was a beautiful trip through the mountains. And the mansion – what an interesting place! I loved the stained glass windows."

"So, Aidan," Julian said, "you grew up in Hidden, then."

"Yes," Aidan replied. "This is the first time I've been anywhere else."

"An orphaned infant," he said. "Do you know anything about your father or mother – or how you became an orphan?"

"No, not a thing," Aidan lied.

She had no intentions of telling them that story.

"Did you know the Fairhavens all your life?"

"I only knew of them," Aidan said. "I had never met them before last spring. It was at Aunt Mara's funeral – she was the woman who raised me. A few days after that I began working at the mansion."

"You must have heard Lady Fairhaven play the harp," Maeve said. "I remember that clearly from when we were there. She is a most accomplished musician."

"Yes, she is," Aidan said. "She's teaching me to play the harp now. I'm sure I'll never play anything as well as she does, but I just love learning about music."

"That's wonderful," Maeve said. "I love music too. We all started with piano as children and now I take voice lessons. Perhaps you could play the harp for us sometime."

"Oh, goodness, no," Aidan said with a modest laugh. "I'm just a beginner, really."

They talked about music for the next few minutes until the driver pulled up at their destination.

As they got out of the carriage, Maeve said, "This is Stonebridge Park. My great-grandfather set the land aside for it and now it's a nice public place to walk. It's right on the cliffs and the gardens are quite lovely."

"Oh, I just love gardens!" Aidan said fervently. "I had a rose garden before – well – before moving into the mansion. I love roses more than anything."

"I don't think those are blooming quite yet," Maeve said. "But we have a huge garden at home and there are roses here too. I'll show you sometime. You would love them, I'm sure."

Maeve tucked her arm through Aidan's and they began walking down a stone path. Aidan had never seen a place like Stonebridge Park. Much like the Renwickes' vast estate, it was formally landscaped with tall trees, bushes, small garden areas, benches, and sculptures of stone and bronze. The wide river that ran through Clearview ended in a tall waterfall over the edge of the cliffs.

Before long they passed by a large ornate white gazebo surrounded by a grassy area.

"They give free concerts here in the summer," Maeve told her. "You can bring a picnic lunch and spread out blankets on the grass to listen. It will be so much fun to go together."

"That sounds wonderful," Aidan said.

They walked a bit further and stepped up onto a large grey stone footbridge that spanned the river. Aidan exclaimed with rapture at the sight, as excited as a child, and leaned over the stone railing in fascination to watch the rushing water beneath them.

"This is just beautiful!" she cried in wonder. "I've never been on a bridge like this or seen such a large river!" Then, embarrassed, she quickly added, "You must think me stupid, but all I've ever known is Hidden."

"Oh no, Aidan, I don't think you're stupid at all," Julian said sincerely. "Hidden is very isolated. You just haven't seen much of the world."

Aidan smiled up at him gratefully for his kind reply. He grinned back at her with delight as though her smile was a precious trophy he had just won. She began to relax with her new friends.

And when he politely offered her his arm as they turned to walk on, she didn't hesitate to take it.

Eventually they came to the edge of the cliffs and the waterfall. This was the view Aidan most wanted to see. As they approached the iron railing running along the ledge, she gasped.

Lady Fairhaven had been right. The view took her breath away.

Far below her, the vast plain of Everestaal swept off into the distance, more verdant and wondrous than she could ever have imagined. Green fields and forests stretched for many miles to a hazy blue mountain range far away on the horizon. A strong sweet wind tugged at her skirt. The waterfall nearby rushing over the rocky ledge was deafeningly powerful.

Aidan clutched tightly to the railing as though afraid the wind might blow her away. She stared at the foreign landscape with complete awe, unable to speak for several moments.

When she turned, her gaze met Julian's. He was watching her intently. The serious look in his bright blue eyes frightened her, for she didn't know how to read it.

At that moment Cameron climbed onto the bottom rung of the railing and leaned way over.

"Look right down the cliff, Aidan," he said. "It's fantastic!"

"Cam! Don't do that!" Maeve scolded.

Keeping her feet on the ground, Aidan leaned over cautiously and looked down the cliff at the rocks beneath her and the tiny river far below being fed by the waterfall.

Gasping in fright, she jumped back from the railing.

"Oh my! We're very high up, aren't we?"

"It makes for a great view, doesn't it?" Cameron asked.

"You do know that we're looking into another country, don't you, Aidan?" Maeve asked.

"Yes," Aidan said, turning back to the view of the plain. "The Kingdom of Everestaal. It's beautiful!"

She remembered Lady Fairhaven talking about her desire to follow her heart down out of the mountains. Now she completely understood.

"What an incredible place it must be!" she went on. "Wouldn't it be wonderful to go there?"

"It's forbidden," Cameron warned as he stepped down from the railing. "Be careful of what you say here, Aidan. The Royal Guards could be close by at any time."

Aidan froze.

"Guards? Close by?!"

Suddenly she felt like she couldn't breathe. She hadn't realized the Prince's soldiers could be near.

"Yes, they're everywhere around here," Cameron told her. "They patrol in town all the time because we're right on the border."

In sudden terror Aidan began frantically looking around.

"Aidan – why are you so afraid?" Julian wanted to know. "You've done nothing wrong. They wouldn't arrest you just for saying that."

She looked up at him and then laughed weakly in embarrassment.

"I don't know why I should be so frightened," she said. "It's silly, isn't it?"

But as they rode back to the Renwicke estate in the carriage, she found herself searching the streets for uniformed guards as she fought to hide the panic that was rising up in her chest.

From *Julian*, Book Two Chapter 19:

Julian looked into her eyes. His words were impassioned.

"I must tell you that the first moment I saw you, I just knew you are the one I will love forever. And I am quite certain nothing will ever make me change my mind."

The one I will love forever.

Had he really just said that? Did he love her already?

Julian's words were like summer rain pouring over a parched garden, coaxing withered roses back into bloom. Aidan longed to believe him, to trust in him, but she was still trapped behind the ancient barricades she had long ago constructed around her heart to protect it.

"How could you have known such a thing?" she asked. "There is so much about me you don't know."

"That's why I want to court you. We will get to know each other. There is a lot you don't know about me, either."

He moved closer to her on the couch, eagerly reaching out and grasping both her hands tightly in his.

"Aidan, please," he said fervently. "Please. Give me a chance. Trust me. Don't just assume I will reject you for something you will tell me. You don't know what I will do. Maybe I will just love you all the more for hearing it."

She stared at him. He had said it again.

He loved her!

Unloved and Unwanted were such liars. Perhaps they had lied to her about everything. How could she ever have believed them?

"Open your heart to me," he pleaded. "I promise you, I won't break it."

The barricades were beginning to crumble. She could feel them starting to fall.

Acknowledgments

I think this must be the hardest part of this book to write! Since the original manuscript for what would become *Lies and Deception* was begun over 30 years before publication, there is no way I can thank everyone who has supported me through writing it. I apologize in advance if I've left anyone out.

First and foremost I must thank Richard, my wonderful husband of over 40 years, who has always supported my gifts and talents in so many ways. When God directed me to write full time, he suddenly had to put up with a wife lost in a fantasy world 24/7 ("So what else is new?" he sighs). But he patiently prayed for me, encouraged and cheered me on, held me while I cried, gave tech support, did dishes and laundry, and never lost confidence in me. He even offered helpful (?!) suggestions when I couldn't quite find the right word ("hyperdistribution?" seriously?!). I never could have written *The Rose In The Fire* without his love and support. (Sorry, Sweetie, you're stuck with me!)

Richard and my grown sons, Jared and Rory, patiently listened to me read the manuscripts aloud. The three of them offered so many helpful suggestions that I never would have thought of, in particular giving the male perspective for a story that we all agreed is really written more for women. I have especially appreciated my sons' support and encouragement even though our personal beliefs differ. Their input and viewpoints have been invaluable to me and several times influenced changes to details in the story. I love my geeky family so much! We always have the most interesting (and often hilarious) conversations around here.

Special thanks to my daughter and gym buddy Brianna for adding me to her Spotify account at just about the time I began writing. There were many days when I really needed inspirational and worship music. As I wrote, there was a constant battle raging in my thoughts and emotions, and worship is pure warfare. I'm also grateful for our gym dates. Writing is such a sedentary activity and I found that the gym is a great place to plan out your next chapter while on the weight machines.

Many friends have stood by me, encouraged me, and prayed for me as I worked on the books. In particular I want to thank:

~~ Lisa, my dear friend and fellow former homeschool mom, who was my first beta reader and has been my most faithful supporter all along. From the very beginning she has insisted I need to publish the books, prayed for me, and encouraged me in many other ways. I look forward to many more interesting conversations in our favorite meeting place, the Ithaca Wegmans cafe.

~~ Pat, Val, Barb, and Mary of The Journey Girls (our affectionate name for our former Thursday morning small group as we enjoyed life's journey together). In the spring of 2021 when God began telling me I needed to finish the book I had started thirty years before, I procrastinated, feeling like it was an impossible task. Not long after this, in God's perfect timing, Barb and Val came to the group and shared Karen Wheaton's prophetic message "Do It Now!" and that was what finally sparked me into action.

~~ Special thanks to Pat for letting me read the manuscripts out loud to her and giving helpful input (and for feeding me sandwiches and cookies!).

~~ Andrea, a beautiful sister in Christ and tremendously gifted artist who was willing to stretch herself creatively to make the art for the original book cover. Although I ultimately decided to re-release this book with a new cover, I have been so blessed working with Andrea and am grateful for her friendship and support as well as her willingness to be a beta reader.

~~ Amy, who has been my special cheerleader. I have so appreciated her enthusiasm, encouragement, and prayer support.

~~ Former pastor Dave and his wife Ruth Ann, good friends for many years who have been constant in prayer and caring support for me, especially when I began dealing with treatment for breast cancer just before the first release of this book.

~~ The congregation of the Interlaken Reformed Church, which is a very warm and caring group of people. Their prayers, cards, and encouraging words have meant a lot to me.

~~ I would be remiss if I didn't express my gratitude for the excellent care I have received over the years for various health issues. While it may seem a bit odd to include healthcare providers here, I've shared with most of them about the books and they have generally shown a lot of interest, support, and enthusiasm. Just as I was on the verge of publishing this book I received a surprise diagnosis of breast cancer, which almost derailed my writing completely. Special thanks to my surgeon, Dr. Huynh, who encouraged me to keep going with it. *Lies and Deception* was originally published on my first day of radiation therapy. The cancer was caught early and my prognosis is excellent.

~~ Alessandra Torre and the other organizers of Inkers Con. If I had not enrolled in their New Author Boot Camp in the fall of 2023, I am quite certain that I would still be endlessly editing and tweaking manuscripts in my word processor in total despair, not knowing where to go next. Special thanks to my author besties Bellamina and Loren.

Ironically, some of the people I need to thank may never read this because I have never met them in person, but I must express my gratitude for:

~~ Karen Wheaton and her weekly webcast Front Porch Friends. Her prophetic exhortation in June of 2021 *"Whatever the Lord has told you to do, DO IT NOW! Time is of the essence!"* pierced right through me like the Sword of the Spirit. The very day I heard it, I pulled out my 30-year-old manuscript and in obedience got busy doing what God was calling me to do.

~~ The online ministries of Passion City Church in Atlanta and Passion City Church DC, both of which have greatly blessed me. In particular, their solid biblical teaching on spiritual warfare has validated everything I'm trying to do in my book series. For anyone wanting to learn more about this topic (and I encourage you to do so!), I highly recommend the books *Don't Give the Enemy A Seat at Your Table* by Louie Giglio and *Rest and War: Rhythms of a Well-Fought Life* by Ben Stuart. Each book also has a teaching series.

Finally, I give all praise and glory to the Lord Jesus Christ for His saving grace and deliverance that has brought me to this place in my journey of faith. He has given me the creative gift of writing and the prophetic gifts of words and pictures, and every detail of the story has come from Him. I'm humbled and grateful that He chose to bless me with this assignment, which has brought me closer to Him in so many ways. I've never been very good at finishing things, but the Lord has been fully invested in bringing *Lies and Deception* to publication. I praise Him for His complete faithfulness every step of the way. The other books of *The Rose In The Fire* are all in process and I can't wait to see how He will complete this good work He's begun in me!

Meghan E. McComb
September 2025

About the Author

If you spend any time at all with Meghan McComb, sooner or later she will tell you a story. It might be a tale from her past, an amusing anecdote about her family, or a testimony about something amazing God has done in her life. Words and pictures are her creative and spiritual gifts.

A lifelong daydreamer with an overactive imagination, Meghan has been a writer, artist, and singer for as long as she can remember. She holds a B.A. with Honors in Art History from SUNY Potsdam. What she loved most about her college major was hearing the stories about the artists' lives and works.

In 1983 Meghan married Richard McComb. They have spent almost all their married life near Ithaca in the beautiful Finger Lakes region of upstate New York. For sixteen years she was a stay-at-home mom homeschooling their three now-grown children.

Her romantasy fairy tale series *The Rose In The Fire* paints a vivid picture of spiritual warfare in the life of one young girl. The story grew out of her actual experience of deliverance from fears, depression, nightmares, and other lasting effects caused by her involvement in occult practices as a young teen.

When she is not writing, you will no doubt find Meghan talking out loud to herself as she neglects to water her houseplants, does daily word puzzles with paper and pencil, and brews coffee that will knock your socks off. To learn more about her life, visit her blog at https://theroseinthefire.com or follow her on Goodreads, Instagram, or Facebook. She would love to hear from you and would be most grateful for your review on Amazon.

Printed in Dunstable, United Kingdom

73361436R00201